# The Handbook of Pluralist Economics Education

In 2001 French university students petitioned their economics professors:

> Most of us have chosen to study economics so as to acquire a deep understanding of the economic phenomena with which citizens of today are confronted. But the teaching that is offered, that is to say for the most part neoclassical theory or approaches derived from it, does not generally answer this expectation.

This petition spawned global movements for reforming economics education, with the goal of jettisoning the traditional monist approach of hegemonic intoleration in favour of pluralism – learning from diverse and opposing views across the ideological spectrum and the social sciences.

This book provides a blueprint for those interested in teaching from a pluralist perspective, regardless of ideology. It provides educators, policy makers, and students with helpful suggestions for implementing pluralism into pedagogy, by offering detailed suggestions and guidelines for incorporating pluralist approaches tailored to specific individual courses. *The Handbook for Pluralist Economics Education* specifically provides practical suggestions for professors willing to implement pluralism in the classroom and increases the pedagogical influence of pluralist economics while reducing the hegemony of monism at any level.

All the contributors in this volume were selected for their passionate commitment to reforming economics education. Those interested in this book will include postgraduate students of economics, professional economists, lecturers in political economy and labor studies, university and administration officials concerned with reforming economics education, and social science instructors interested in a multi-disciplinary approach.

**Jack Reardon** is Professor of Economics at Hamline University, Minnesota and is the editor and founder of the *International Journal of Pluralism and Economics Education*.

**Routledge advances in heterodox economics**
Edited by Frederic S. Lee
*University of Missouri-Kansas City*

Over the past two decades, the intellectual agendas of heterodox economists have taken a decidedly pluralist turn. Leading thinkers have begun to move beyond the established paradigms of Austrian, feminist, Institutional-evolutionary, Marxian, Post Keynesian, radical, social, and Sraffian economics – opening up new lines of analysis, criticism, and dialogue among dissenting schools of thought. This cross-fertilization of ideas is creating a new generation of scholarship in which novel combinations of heterodox ideas are being brought to bear on important contemporary and historical problems.

*Routledge Advances in Heterodox Economics* aims to promote this new scholarship by publishing innovative books in heterodox economic theory, policy, philosophy, intellectual history, institutional history, and pedagogy. Syntheses or critical engagement of two or more heterodox traditions are especially encouraged.

1 **Ontology and Economics**
   Tony Lawson and his critics
   *Edited by Edward Fullbrook*

2 **Currencies, Capital Flows and Crises**
   A post Keynesian analysis of exchange rate determination
   *John T. Harvey*

3 **Radical Economics and Labor**
   *Frederic Lee and Jon Bekken*

4 **A History of Heterodox Economics**
   Challenging the mainstream in the twentieth century
   *Frederic Lee*

This series was previously published by The University of Michigan Press and the following books are available (please contact UMP for more information):

**Economics in Real Time**
A theoretical reconstruction
*John McDermott*

**Liberating Economics**
Feminist perspectives on families, work, and globalization
*Drucilla K. Barker and Susan F. Feiner*

**Socialism after Hayek**
*Theodore A. Burczak*

**Future Directions for Heterodox Economics**
*Edited by John T. Harvey and Robert F. Garnett, Jr.*

**Heterodox Macroeconomics**
*Edited by Jonathan P. Goldstein and Michael G. Hillard*

**The Marginal Productivity Theory of Distribution**
A critical history
*John Pullen*

**Informal Work in Developed Nations**
*Edited by Enrico A. Marcelli, Colin C. Williams and Pascale Jossart*

**The Foundations of Non-Equilibrium Economics**
The principle of circular and cumulative causation
*Edited by Sebastian Berger*

**The Handbook of Pluralist Economics Education**
*Edited by Jack Reardon*

# The Handbook of Pluralist Economics Education

Edited by Jack Reardon

LONDON AND NEW YORK

First published 2009
by Routledge
2 Park Square, Milton Park, Abingdon, Oxon OX14 4RN

Simultaneously published in the USA and Canada
by Routledge
270 Madison Ave, New York, NY 10016

*Routledge is an imprint of the Taylor & Francis Group, an informa business*

© 2009 Selection and editorial matter, Jack Reardon; individual chapters, the contributors

Typeset in Times by Wearset Ltd, Boldon, Tyne and Wear
Printed and bound in Great Britain by TJI Digital, Padstow, Cornwall

All rights reserved. No part of this book may be reprinted or reproduced or utilized in any form or by any electronic, mechanical, or other means, now known or hereafter invented, including photocopying and recording, or in any information storage or retrieval system, without permission in writing from the publishers.

*British Library Cataloguing in Publication Data*
A catalogue record for this book is available from the British Library

*Library of Congress Cataloging in Publication Data*
A catalog record for this book has been requested

ISBN10: 0-415-77762-3 (hbk)
ISBN10: 0-203-87258-4 (ebk)

ISBN13: 978-0-415-77762-9 (hbk)
ISBN13: 978-0-203-87258-1 (ebk)

# Contents

| | |
|---|---|
| *List of figures* | ix |
| *List of tables* | x |
| *List of contributors* | xi |
| *Acknowledgments* | xiv |

**PART I**
**The need for pluralism in economics education**    1

1 **Introduction and overview**    3
 JACK REARDON

2 **The meltdown and economics textbooks**    17
 EDWARD FULLBROOK

3 **A revolution from the margin: a student perspective**    24
 NICHOLAS DAN, NICHOLAS HOUPT, SEAN MALLIN, AND FELIPE WITCHGER

4 **Why economics needs pluralism**    32
 BERNARD GUERRIEN AND SOPHIE JALLAIS

5 **History of thought, methodology, and pluralism**    43
 SHEILA DOW

**PART II**
**Reclaiming the principles course**    55

6 **The principles course**    57
 JULIE A. NELSON

7  Teaching economics as if time mattered 69
   I. DAVID WHEAT

## PART III
## Core theory courses 91

8  A pluralist approach to intermediate macroeconomics 93
   IRENE VAN STAVEREN

9  A pluralist approach to microeconomics 120
   STEVE KEEN

10 Mathematics for pluralist economists 150
   STEVE KEEN

## PART IV
## Advanced courses/electives 169

11 Pluralism in labor economics 171
   DELL CHAMPLIN AND BARBARA A. WIENS-TUERS

12 Sustainability economics 181
   PETER SÖDERBAUM

13 International economics 199
   MARIA ALEJANDRA CAPORALE MADI AND
   JOSÉ RICARDO BARBOSA GONÇALVES

14 Money, credit, and finance in political economy: national, regional, and global dimensions 230
   PHILLIP ANTHONY O'HARA

15 Green economics: emerging pedagogy in an emerging discipline 256
   MIRIAM KENNET

## PART V
## Conclusion 265

16 Conclusion 267
   JACK REARDON

   *Author index* 269
   *Subject index* 273

# Figures

| | | |
|---|---|---|
| 7.1 | Price behavior after a demand increase | 75 |
| 7.2 | Price–demand loop, C1 | 76 |
| 7.3 | Price–supply loop, C2 | 78 |
| 7.4 | The RealTime model | 79 |
| 7.5 | Behavior after a demand increase | 82 |
| 7.6 | Behavior after a supply increase | 83 |
| 7.7 | User interface of online version of price–supply–demand model | 84 |
| 8.1 | Adaptation of the macroeconomic flow | 100 |
| 8A.1 | Shape templates | 115 |
| 9.1 | Predictions of the Marshallian model | 122 |
| 9.2 | Simulation results | 123 |
| 9.3 | Convergence of individual outputs | 123 |
| 9.4 | Much higher profits result from the firms' "rule of thumb" | 124 |
| 9.5 | Stigler's proof | 125 |
| 9.6 | The belief that the firm faces a horizontal demand curve | 126 |
| 9.7 | U.S. firm size follows a "scale free" power law distribution | 132 |
| 9.8 | Eiteman's representation of marginal product | 136 |
| 9.9 | No correlation between monopolist's share of output and average price | 139 |
| 9A.1 | Mathcad implementation of a multi-agent simulation | 143 |
| 10.1 | The irrelevance of equilibrium for complex systems | 153 |
| 10.2 | The time path, average and equilibrium of Goodwin's model | 154 |
| 10.3 | Incomes in the simple circuit model | 158 |
| 10.4 | The predator–prey model implemented as a dynamic flowchart | 160 |
| 10.5 | NetLogo multi-agent simulation of predator–prey interactions | 161 |
| 10A.1 | 3D map of the Lorenz position | 164 |
| 11.1 | Approaches to labor market analysis | 173 |
| 12.1 | Decision-making as a matching process or matter of appropriateness | 185 |
| 12.2 | Decision-making in multiple-stage, positional terms | 192 |
| 14.1 | The circuit of money capital | 232 |
| 14.2 | Endogenous–exogenous finance | 234 |
| 14.3 | Interactive game between reserve bank and banks | 235 |
| 14.4 | Kaldorian dynamics of circular and cumulative causation | 243 |

# Tables

| | | |
|---|---|---|
| 7.1 | Default parameter assumptions | 81 |
| 9.1 | Starpower scoring table | 131 |
| 9.2 | The size distribution of U.S. firms | 133 |
| 9.3 | Blinder's summary of his empirical results | 135 |
| 9.4 | Goods in Sippel's experiment | 137 |
| 9.5 | Violations of axioms of revealed preference | 137 |
| 9.6 | Quantity strategy combinations for duopoly | 141 |
| 9.7 | Profit outcomes from quantity strategies | 142 |
| 9.8 | Profit outcomes from varying output at Keen equilibrium | 142 |
| 9.9 | Profit outcomes from varying output at Cournot equilibrium | 143 |
| 10.1 | Account flow dynamics in the simplest Circuitist model | 157 |
| 12.1 | A comparison of traditional and institutional economics | 186 |
| 12.2 | Competing interpretations of markets | 188 |
| 12.3 | Categories of approaches to decision processes and sustainability assessment | 190 |
| 12.4 | Categories of impacts in economic analysis | 191 |
| 13.1 | The international economy, 1900–1987 | 209 |
| 13.2 | Most dynamic global importers, 1991–2000 | 212 |
| 13.3 | Countries that contributed most to global trade growth, 1985–2000 | 212 |
| 13.4 | Evolution of the technological structure of exports in developed countries | 214 |
| 13.5 | Evolution of the technological structure of exports in developing countries | 214 |
| 13.6 | U.S. current account, 1992–1997 | 216 |
| 13.7 | U.S. Net International Investment Position (NIIP), 1991–1997 | 216 |
| 13.8 | Rate of growth of the institutional investors: selected countries, 1980–1990 | 222 |
| 14.1 | Long waves and financial dynamics | 240 |
| 14.2 | Core elements of the taxes-drive-money approach v. orthodoxy | 245 |

# Contributors

**Dell Champlin** is Professor Emerita, Eastern Illinois University. Her research interests include institutional economics, labor, and public policy. She is co-editor, with Janet Knoedler, of the *Institutionalist Tradition in Labor Economics* (2004). She is currently working on a reader on the history of labor economic thought. dpchamplin@hotmail.com

**Nicholas Dan** is entering his senior year at the University of Notre Dame, majoring in Economics and German. He is interested in the history of economic thought and its implications for economic development and policy. He, along with Nicholas Houpt, Sean Mallin, and Felipe Witchger, were lead authors of the University of Notre Dame petition to reform economics education, which led to the Open Education Movement. ndan@nd.edu

**Sheila Dow** is Professor of Economics at the University of Stirling, Scotland, and Director of the Stirling Centre for Economic Methodology. Her research interests include the methodology and history of economics, money and banking and regional finance. She is the author of *Economic Methodology: An Inquiry* (2002). s.c.dow@stir.ac.uk

**Edward Fullbrook** is the founder and editor of the *Real World Economics Review* (formerly the *Post-Autistic Economics Review*) and webmaster of www.paecon.net. He is a research fellow in the School of Economics at the University of the West of England. His most recent book is *Pluralist Economics* (2008).

**José Ricardo Barbosa Gonçalves** is Professor at the State University of Campinas, Brazil. Author of *The Utopy of the Social Order*, his most recent publication is *Financialization, Employability and Their Impacts on Bank Workers' Union Movement in Brazil (1994–2004)*. josericardobg@yahoo.com.br

**Bernard Guerrien** is an associate researcher at SAMOS (Statistique Appliqué et Modélisation Stochastique), affiliated to the Centre d'Economie de la Sorbonne, Paris. Active in economics education he was instrumental in the formation of the Post-Autistic Movement. bernard.guerrien@tele2.fr

**Nicholas Houpt** is a first-year law student at Columbia Law School and attended the University of Notre Dame as an undergraduate. His primary interest is the

xii *Contributors*

environmental crisis, and how to formulate multi-faceted solutions from law, science, and economics. nhoupt@gmail.com

**Sophie Jallais** is Professor at the Université Paris 1 (Panthéon-Sorbonne). Her most recent book, co-authored with Bernard Guerrien, is *Microeconomia. Una perspectiva critica* (2008). sjallais@aol.com

**Steve Keen** is Professor of Economics and Finance at the University of Western Sydney, Australia. He is author of *Debunking Economics* (2001). Keen was one of few economists to predict the global financial crisis, and he maintains an influential blog at www.debtdeflation.com/blogs and an influential website www.debunkingeconomics.com

**Miriam Kennet** is a member of Mansfield College, and the Environmental Change Institute, Oxford University. She is co-founder of the Green Economics Institute, and founder and editor of the *International Journal of Green Economics.* greeneconomicsinstitute@yahoo.com

**Maria Alejandra Caporale Madi** is a Professor at the State University of Campinas, Brazil. Author of *Monetary Policy in Brazil: A Post-Keynesian Interpretation*, her most recent publication is *Corporate Social Responsibility and Market Society: Credit and Banking Inclusion in Brazil.* alejandra_madi@yahoo.com.br

**Sean Mallin** majored in Economics at the University of Notre Dame. He is attending the University of California, Irvine, to pursue a doctorate in Anthropology. His interests lie along and beyond the boundaries of economics, philosophy, anthropology, and cultural studies. He has written several articles on pluralism and economics education. sean.mallin@gmail.com

**Julie A. Nelson** teaches Economics at the University of Massachusetts, Boston. Her most recent books include *Macroeconomics in Context* (2008), co-authored with Neva Goodwin, and Jonathan Harris. She is also co-author with Mark Maier of *Introducing Economics: A Critical Guide for Teachers* (2007). julie.nelson@umb.edu

**Philip Anthony O'Hara** is Professor of Global Political Economy and Governance at Curtin University in Perth, Australia, and is director of its Global Political Economy Research Unit. He is author of *Growth and Development in the Global Political Economy* (Routledge, 2006), and co-author of *Economics: An Introduction to Traditional and Progressive Views* (2008). philohara1@yahoo.com

**Jack Reardon** teaches Economics at Hamline University in Minnesota. He is founder and editor of the *International Journal of Pluralism and Economics Education.* Jreardon02@hamline.edu

**Peter Söderbaum** is Professor of Ecological Economics at Malardalen University, Sweden. His most recent book is *Understanding Sustainability Economics* (2008). peter.soderbaum@mdh.se

**Irene van Staveren** is Associate Professor of Feminist Development Economics, Institute of Social Studies, The Hague, and (part-time) Professor of Economics and Christian Ethics, Radboud University Nijmegen, The Netherlands. She recently co-edited the *Handbook of Economics and Ethics* (Edward Elgar, 2009). staveren@iss.nl

**I. David Wheat** is Associate Professor of System Dynamics, University of Bergen, Norway, and Adjunct Associate Professor of Economics, Virginia Western Community College, U.S.A. He is currently working on a new system dynamics managerial economics text. david.wheat@uib.no

**Barbara A. Wiens-Tuers** is an Assistant Professor of Economics at Penn State Altoona with affiliate status in Labor Studies and Employment Relations. She has published in a broad range of journals. She recently co-authored *Economics: An Introduction to Traditional and Progressive Views* (2007). baw16@psu.edu

**Felipe Witchger** is an Associate, specializing in Climate Change and Clean Energy, at Cambridge Energy Research Associates (Cambridge, Massachusetts). fwitchger@cer.com

# Acknowledgments

All pluralist economists owe a debt of gratitude to Fred Lee, an energetic unifier of the many diverse fields of heterodox economics. Fred is synonymous with the International Confederation of Associations for Pluralism in Economics (ICAPE), founded in 1993, with its guiding principle, "Pluralism and intellectual progress are complements. This is not to say 'anything goes,' but that each tradition of thought ... adds something unique and valuable to economic scholarship."

My debt to Fred, however, runs much deeper. I first met Fred in 2005 at the Western Social Science Association Annual Conference in Albuquerque. In addition to presenting my own paper, "Quantum Physics for Economics," I had the daunting task of discussing Fred's paper, "Teaching Graduate Neoclassical Microeconomics from a Heterodox Perspective," in a panel session on economic education. What novel suggestions and/or criticisms could I, a relative unknown, possibly offer this giant of heterodox education?

Stuck in airport traffic on the way to the conference, I developed the idea for this book as a logical outgrowth of Fred's paper. At least for me, it was a long but productive traffic jam!

Fred's already significant contribution does not stop there, however. After reading my initial proposal for this book, which I presented at the 2007 ICAPE Conference in Salt Lake City, Fred tersely said, "You know, this is not a book proposal." Nevertheless he offered helpful suggestions and was instrumental in landing Routledge as the publisher. Many, many thanks to Fred.

I also thank Yanis Varoufakis, visionary founder of the pluralist Doctoral Program in Economics at the University of Athens, for an invitation to lecture in October 2008. We had a vibrant and interesting discussion on the elements of pluralism, with many provocative questions raised. The discussion frames the contours of Chapter 1 of this volume. In addition, meeting and discussing with his students convinced me firsthand of the benefits of a pluralist education.

I am grateful for the wonderful opportunity to teach at Hamline University, an intellectually flourishing and enriching liberal arts school. I thank Julian Schuster, Dean of the Hamline School of Business, for his novel vision, his support of intellectual growth, and his personal friendship. Special thanks to Amy Zabinski, Petar Mirovic and David McCarthy for helping to put this manuscript together.

Finally, I thank my family – whose love and understanding are immeasurable. I thank my wife Laurie for her love and understanding while I was writing this book. And my delightful children Elizabeth and Patrick – who unfortunately had to learn firsthand the concept of opportunity cost. I hope their generation will have the intellectual resources to learn from each other in order to solve what promises to be a growing set of interconnected problems. It is for my children and their generation that I write this book.

St. Paul, Minnesota<br>
January 26, 2009

# Part I
# The need for pluralism in economics education

# 1 Introduction and overview[1]

## Jack Reardon

In 1620, Frances Bacon urged that "a new beginning has to be made from the lowest foundations, unless one is content to go around in circles for ever, with meager, almost negligible progress" (2000: 31). Buoyed by the scientific optimism of the age, he impugned over-reliance on Aristotolian syllogisms, calling instead for induction, experimentation, and testing hypotheses. "The world," argued Bacon, "must not be contracted to the narrow limits of the understanding (as it has been heretofore) but the understanding must be liberated and expanded to take in the image of the world as it is found to be" (2000: 226).

More than three centuries later, at the start of the new millennium, French university students petitioned their economics professors in the Baconian spirit, as follows:

> Most of us have chosen to study economics so as to acquire a deep understanding of the economic phenomena with which citizens of today are confronted. But the teaching that is offered, that is to say for the most part neoclassical theory or approaches derived from it, does not generally answer this expectation.
>
> ("Open Letter" 2000)

The petition launched the Post-Autistic Economics Movement, whose newsletter, the *Post-Autistic Review*, boasts 10,412 subscribers from over 150 countries.

In 2007, students at the University of Notre Dame posted a similar letter on the internet, in which they stated:

> students deserve an education that explores the full range of ideas.... We oppose a situation in which neoclassical economic theory is taught to the exclusion of other theories ... it is alarming that a student could easily graduate from Notre Dame with a degree in Economics, having never questioned the basic assumptions of or been presented with plausible alternatives to neoclassical economics.[2]

Certainly today's students are just as concerned with grades and graduation as any in the past, but there is a new determination, a new Organon if you will, that is rife. I recently attended a lecture by Howard Kunstler, author of the chilling novel *The World Made by Hand*. After listening to Mr. Kunstler's sobering prognosis, a student asked, "Why do you assume we won't have the determined ability and education to solve these problems that your generation gave to us?" Perhaps a generation ago, this student might have been dismissed as an outlier, but fortunately for us and the planet he is not. He, along with the French and American petition writers, are in the vanguard of a reformation of economics education, a determined movement for a New Organon.

The four Notre Dame students, lead authors of the Notre Dame petition, write in Chapter 3 this volume: "we are a generation with bold ambitions – to end global poverty, to solve the food crisis, to overcome global warming – but are handed an economic framework with stark and limited possibilities." The students, frustrated by the inability of traditional economics courses to discuss contemporary problems, formed their own study groups, meeting once a week.

> Picture this: a dozen or so students huddled around a table half-a-dozen people too small, talking about economics. These gatherings were centered on articles, chosen by the group in advance, to dissect, discuss, and debate. We relished the chance to talk about interesting and relevant topics that could not be done in most of our economics classes. We could engage each problem in a dialogue with traditional economics and political economy. We could question assumptions, interrogate generalities, and ask about the morality of it all. Try doing that in a traditional economics class. We have – it isn't pretty.

Alfred Marshall, in the preface to the eighth edition of his highly influential *Principles of Economics*, wrote that "economic conditions are constantly changing, and each generation looks at its own problems in its own way" (1946 [1920]: v). Today's world is rife with highly visible and interconnected problems, just to name a few, a growing environmental crisis, intractable poverty, a financial crisis – not the first and certainly not the last – and a surge of political instability in the midst of a tectonic global power shift away from the United States and toward Asia.

How can economics education be restructured to solve these problems?

Shearman and Smith (2007), in a sobering analysis of our current environmental predicament, urge revamping university education to train an elite corps to solve global warming, our most pressing problem. Since they blame democracy, with its myopic short-term focus as the preponderant cause, democracy in any form cannot be a solution. However, Shearman and Smith ignore the obvious question: who will train the educators?

While political democracy might be at fault, it is a mistake (an Aristotelian syllogism, if you will) to assume monism is superior in any form to a democracy or, better yet, a pluralism of ideas. The virtue of pluralism is that we can discuss different approaches, within the democratic context of ideas, as legitimate in their own right, whereas monism implies that only ideas compatible with an accepted world view are allowable, while all others are disparaged as without merit. But no single discipline holds the answers to the "problems of our generation"; on the contrary, the authors of this book believe that our problems are complex, requiring a pluralist perspective. Confronted by serious problems, isn't it better to have a panoply of different policies to choose from rather than one, since "in ideas as in nature, variety is the evolutionary fuel. When pluralism and variety disappear, innovation and progress may slow to a halt.... Pluralism is necessary for innovation and scientific advance" (Hodgson 1999: 13, emphasis in original).

But what is pluralism? Unfortunately, it is similar to other multi-faceted concepts like democracy and equality, rich in meaning but lacking a universally accepted definition.³ Indeed, "pluralism means different things to different people" (Vromen 2007: 65). At the same time, a simple definition of pluralism, which efficiently captures its many nuances is: "pluralism recognizes the legitimate existence of alternative ideologies, frameworks and reference."

What is often misunderstood about pluralism, Sheila Dow writes in Chapter 5 of this volume,

> is that, while, on the one hand, pluralism accepts the legitimacy of other approaches on their own terms, pluralism is perfectly consistent with arguing against these terms. In other words, it is important to distinguish the argument that one's own approach is preferable to others in terms of one's own criteria, knowing that no one approach can claim the truth – the essence of pluralism – and arguing against alternatives because they are assumed demonstrably and intrinsically wrong – the essence of monism.

Indeed the antithesis of pluralism is monism. Monist pedagogy, by excluding discussion of alternatives and delegitimizing their existence, is tantamount to proselytization, and unfortunately "students who are proselytized cannot respect alternative views and thus cannot work together to solve problems" (Reardon 1995: 91). While pluralism respects and encourages debate and healthy skepticism, monism does not. Pluralism is consistent with the ideal of a university education, and "is an intrinsic part of intellectual development" (Amaryta Sen quoted in Garnett 2005: 23). Monism is not.

One reason for the definitional confusion of pluralism is its existence on many different levels: ontology – how we understand reality; epistemology – how we construct knowledge about reality; theoretical – how theories of reality are developed; and methodological – how we approach the study of reality. To this I add another level: pedagogical – how we teach knowledge constructed about reality. A common thread uniting these levels is whether one believes the system under study is closed or open. If the former, then all variables affecting the outcome of the system are known. Descriptive and universal laws can be deduced and applied. If the latter, all variables are not known and thus all outcomes cannot be known. The existence of such "radical uncertainty" (Vant 2005: 246) belies the idea that any one viewpoint is the correct one, suggesting the possibility of more than one correct view. Closed systems encourage monism at every level while disparaging alternative views; open systems, however, encourage pluralism.

The purpose of this book is to provide educators, policy makers and students with helpful suggestions for implementing pluralism in pedagogy, by offering detailed suggestions and guidelines for incorporating pluralist approaches tailored to specific individual courses.

It is assumed that heterodox economics readily embraces pluralism while orthodoxy eschews it in favor of monism. But this is a misleading simplification, for heterodox economists "often promote their own ideas and methods as superior to others and do not embrace pluralism" (Holcombe 2008: 52). After all, "disciplines are like tribes, they have a specific culture and specific habits, norms and rules, and they do not easily accept outsiders" (Weehuizen 2007: 165).

At the same time, some argue that orthodoxy has become more pluralist,[4] especially at the methodological level. Diane Coyle ebulliently writes that economics is no longer the monolith it once was: "scholars working on the frontiers of economics have firmly put behind them the inward-looking reductionism which did indeed sometimes characterize the discipline in the past (2007: 3–4). But unfortunately, as Coyle herself laments, "we economists [don't] teach what we preach" (2007: 250). Bowles *et al.* also concur that at least pedagogically mainstream economics is far from pluralist: "unfortunately, the teaching of economics to undergraduates has lagged behind what is widely understood by leading economists. The conventional neoclassical model is taught, often as if it were the only approach in the field" (2005: xvii–xviii).

The purpose of this volume is not to debate whether orthodoxy or heterodoxy is more pluralistic; rather it is to offer suggestions for instructors to incorporate pluralist methods into pedagogy, no matter the ideology.

If pluralism accepts the equal legitimacy of every alternative, can pluralism degenerate into unworkable relativism? What is the limit, if any, for the range and depth of alternative views?

As a former physics major with a keen interest in history and philosophy, who is writing a novel (isn't everyone?), I stand at one end of the spectrum: I view disciplinary boundaries as fluid and amorphous rather than indelibly delineated. I see merit in combining disciplines to form new perspectives. Yet, at the same time, I believe in the efficacy of building a solid foundation in economics to understand society. This touches on the age-old debate of general education versus specialization. From my perspective, however, I welcome the scintillating benefits of fruitful encounters and mixing of different disciplines.

A good example of such a spirit is the book by Arturo Hermann, *Institutional Economics and Psychoanalysis: How Can They Collaborate for a Better Understanding of Individual–Society Dynamics?* (2007). His long title betrays his objective

> institutional theory would benefit from considering psychoanalytic concepts in order to help shed a deeper light on the psychological and more

individual-based side of institutional dynamics; relatedly on the other hand, psychoanalytic theory would benefit in its application to social issues from considering institutional concepts, in order to help clarify the institutional and more collective-based side of psychological dynamics.

(2007: 9)

This is because "the issues of social science [are] so complex and intertwined that co-operation between many disciplines becomes paramount for understanding their dynamics" (Hermann 2007: 9).

To expect educators to be cognizant of every alternative so that every student can master each is a recipe for madness. Instead, pluralism should instill humility and a respectful curiosity about alternative views. Traditional economics has done an enormous disservice to education by pretending that economics is a done deal, with no outstanding areas of disagreement. Let's not be afraid of controversy, debate and disagreement; rather, let's welcome it as a way of moving economics forward.

Once we are convinced of the need for pluralism, the question arises how to teach specific courses within economics from a pluralist perspective. This book provides a blueprint for those interested in teaching from a pluralist perspective, regardless of ideology. *A Handbook for Pluralist Economics Education* offers practical approaches, syllabuses and exercises to stimulate critical thinking about "our world as it is found to be." Specifically, the objectives of this book are: (1) to provide practical suggestions for professors willing to implement pluralism in the classroom; (2) to increase the pedagogical influence of pluralist economics while reducing the hegemony of monism at any level; (3) to increase critical thinking in economics; and (4) to increase student interest in economics.

The primary target for *A Handbook for Pluralist Economics* includes economics professors, professional economists, labor studies teachers, teachers of political economy, university and administration officials concerned with reforming economics education, and social science instructors interested in a multi-disciplinary approach.

The target also includes graduate students. I had the privilege of attending graduate school at the then pluralistic and iconoclastic University of Notre Dame. There I was exposed to different ideologies: Marxism, post-Keynesian economics, feminism, institutionalism, etc. There I read Marx, Keynes, Smith, Marshall, Veblen, and many others. But when I was asked to teach principles of economics for the first time, I, like most graduate students, was on my own. With a high opportunity cost to research available texts and pedagogical techniques, faced with pressure to finish the dissertation, I taught the course as it was taught to me – from a neoclassical monist approach. Graduate students and economics majors face a limited information bias, whose contours are delineated by mainstream ideology. Furthermore, given the high fixed costs of preparing a first course and of landing a tenure-track position, graduate students will likely continue the same pedagogy well into their careers.

This book is also intended for economics majors. I am convinced that students take economics not because they want to master the deductive method and reductionist way of thinking, but because they are curious about their rapidly changing world. Hopefully, this book will enable students to exert pressure from below for the urgently needed reform of economics education.

I initially asked all the contributors to this volume to structure their chapters identically. But in a book on pluralism what was I thinking of? Several authors objected (rightly so) that this is not pluralism. Their legitimate criticism underscored a conundrum that I wrestled with throughout this volume: Can a book offering insights into pluralist pedagogy offer a uniform formulaic recipe? If it can, it is nothing more than monism in disguise. Can a pluralistic approach ever be teleological? If a successful pluralist approach is implemented today, will pluralist teachers of the next generation be better? These are difficult questions without easy answers, which hopefully this book will elucidate.

Each author was selected for his/her enthusiastic contributions to pluralism and economics education. Admittedly, there is a self-selection bias here, but from my perspective the argument for pluralism has been successfully made (Fullbrook 2004; Groenewegen 2007). The purpose of this volume is to move ahead and offer advice for those interested in pluralist pedagogy.

Rather than use the labels "orthodoxy" and "heterodoxy," the former suggesting a smug correctness and the latter a quixotic usurper suffering from perpetual inferiority, this volume will use the terms "traditional" and "political economy" respectively.[5] Julie Nelson in Chapter 6 of this volume suggests that the term "traditional" is bereft of any assumption of correctness. She writes, "calling models traditional, basic, or simple further suggests that, while learning them may be necessary (for whatever reason), [we] will also venture beyond into more up-to-date and/or sophisticated explanations."

Bowles *et al.* make a cogent argument for resuscitating the label political economy:

> we prefer to use [this] older term to describe our approach because one cannot understand contemporary societies very well unless politics, economics, psychology, and the other social science disciplines are all brought together to study the complexities of modern life. Another way of describing the political economy approach, then, is to say that it is interdisciplinary.
>
> (2005: 51)

## Outline of the book

The book contains five parts: The need for pluralism in economics education; Reclaiming the principles course; Core theory courses; Advanced courses/ electives; and Conclusion.

*Introduction and overview* 9

# *I Part I: The need for pluralism in economics education*

Edward Fullbrook opens Chapter 2 with a scathing indictment of the economics profession's failure to predict, understand, and take ownership of the current financial crisis: "Never has a profession betrayed the trust of society so acutely [and] never has one been in such desperate need of fundamental reform." Fullbrook argues that our textbooks and courses instill fundamental misconceptions about how economies work and thus it is incumbent to reform economics education in order to prevent it from facilitating human disasters in the future.

Fullbrook analyzes the bestselling principles textbook by Mankiw, who, as chair of President's Bush's Council of Economic Advisors, was directly involved in the engineering of the current disaster, for clues as to how the economics profession and the public which it educates "becomes so ignorant, misinformed and unobservant of how economies work in the real world." He finds the text guilty of Neoplatonism (holding as self-evident basic truths from which all else is deduced), excessive bullying techniques and emotive appeal, all designed to proselytize rather than to educate, and all anathema to the scientific method. Fullbrook ends his chapter with suggestions to think like a post-crash economist. The important issues he raises in his chapter are further addressed in Part II: Reclaiming the principles course.

After reading the petition from the University of Notre Dame students, I immediately invited the authors to submit a chapter to this volume. I was moved by their visceral and passionate plea for reform of economics education in order to better understand our rapidly changing world.[6] Their argument for pluralism – not to replace one hegemony with another but "to enable a richer and deeper understanding of traditional economics" – constitutes true pluralism. "Learning economics as students normally do," the authors write in Chapter 3, "that is, in a purely instrumental way, is bereft of a rich understanding of the historical evolution of the concepts and their implications."

Bernard Guerrien, lead author of the French petition, and Sophie Jallais argue in Chapter 4 that in order for the seeds of pluralism to germinate, it is necessary to clear away the canonical debris of monist thought, which is unfortunately taught as inevitably true, something to be worshiped rather than critically analyzed. This is an important but often overlooked step in implementing pluralism: it is necessary to clear the deadwood to enable the forest to grow. Guerrien and Jallais demonstrate how, with the heretofore cherished concepts of trade, perfect and imperfect competition, and rationality.

I am pleased that the authors of these two important petitions contributed chapters to this volume. I hope that the two chapters together will connect to students and professors across the globe. At the same time I am dismayed, perplexed, but yet not surprised by the obdurate refusal of traditional economics to reexamine itself and engage in honest self-criticism in order to genuinely reform economics education. This reinforces my belief that the preponderant objective of traditional economics is to proselytize rather than educate.

There is no better indication of this than the willingness of traditional economics to jettison history of thought courses and even to disparage their utility despite their "harbour[ing] an enormous richness in ideas" (Vromen 2007: 80). A central theme of this book and a central precept of pluralism is the importance of history of thought. In Chapter 5 Sheila Dow rounds out Part I with detailed suggestions on how to include history of thought in any course. It is essential to dislodge the canonical and allow the seeds of pluralism to flourish. She writes, "since many students are exposed to the monist approach of traditional economics, the initial hurdle is for them to recognize that other approaches are also economics." History of thought will accomplish this objective and will open the field to a "much wider and richer discourse." Indeed, history of thought "is indispensable in demystifying the notion that things as they are now in economic theory were pre-ordained to become like this" (Vromen 2007: 80).

## *II Part II: Reclaiming the principles course*

The second part of this volume contains two chapters on rescuing the principles course from the ossified tentacles of monism and teaching the course from a pluralist perspective.

For majors, the principles course is the first introduction to economics. As Julie Nelson writes in Chapter 6, "what is taught in principles courses strongly influences student self-selection into (or out of) continued work in economics, and is the first step in the socialization of the next generation of economists." Unique among economics courses, however, the principles course attracts students from a wide variety of intellectual backgrounds and career interests.

The principles instructor plays a key role in shaping the economics discipline over the long run. Nelson poignantly asks:

> who will you inspire to advance in economics – the student concerned about real world economic issues and committed to trying to make the world a better place, or the student primarily attracted by the elegance of models with a special affinity to equation solving and curve shifting? The answer to this question rests in your hands.

Since the definition of economics sets the tone for the whole course, why uncritically accept the scarcity means–ends definition, which unfortunately certified traditional economics as "the science of economizing, maximizing and efficiency devoted to serving business interests while severing ties with other social sciences" (Dowd 2004: 83). This definitional focus turned neoclassical economics inward, precluding it from asking broader and more germane questions, and starkly delineated it from the more humane pursuits of classical economics. One contemporary principles text, for example, begins, "part of teaching economics is teaching economic reasoning. Our discipline is built around deductive logic. Once we teach students a pattern of logic, we want and expect them to apply it to new circumstances" (Case and Fair 2005: xxxi). While deductive logic is an important tool, it is only one among many that students should master, and deductive logic should not be the cornerstone of economic pedagogy. In 22 years of teaching the subject I have yet to meet a student lured into economics by the potential of mastering the deductive method.

Nelson suggests beginning the course with a broader, multi-faceted definition of economics, concomitant with political economy's goal of making the world a better place: "economics is a concern for economic provisioning, or how societies organize themselves to sustain life and enhance its quality." Using this definition will allow discussion directly relevant to today's economic problems such as the survival and quality of life, wealth and income distribution, consumerism, globalization, and environmental problems.

Alfred Marshall wrote in the preface to his eighth edition:

> the main concern of economics is thus with human beings who are impelled, for good and evil, to change and progress. [Thus] the central idea of economics, even when its foundations alone are under discussion, must be that of living force and movement.
> 
> (1946 [1920]: xv)

By strictly focusing on equilibrium in the principles course, traditional economics ignores the passage of time. This, according to David Wheat in Chapter 7, misleads students into thinking that time doesn't matter, nor does the path taken to equilibrium: "students may learn pseudo-dynamic interpretative skills from their textbooks or instructors, but such knowledge can be a dangerous thing if it promotes misunderstanding of economic dynamics and naive expectations about the pace and path of 'long-run' outcomes."

The ignorance of time belies the complexity of the actual economy and the numerous opportunities it affords for action and reaction. The "feedback approach" allows Professor Wheat to demonstrate how endogenous dynamic behavior arises from ordinary events: "the goal is to enable students to see – literally, to observe in a productive manner – both the structure and behavior of dynamic economic systems, thereby improving students' mental models of how particular economies actually work.

## *III Part III: Core theory courses*

This unit contains a chapter for each core course in economics: intermediate macro, intermediate micro and mathematics.

According to Irene van Staveren in Chapter 8 traditional economics suffers from three shortcomings: (1) the assumption that the macroeconomy is simply an aggregation of micro phenomena; (2), the gradual increase in topical complexity, which unfortunately sacrifices realistic feedback effects and the interrelatedness between economic agents; and (3) inclusion of a predictable set of core topics – inflation, growth, business cycles, unemployment, money, interest and trade, etc., while omitting important topics on externalities, disequilibria, risk, instability, the unpaid economy, globalization, and the environment. Staveren suggests restructuring the syllabus to emphasize these critical, omitted and interrelated topics.

Rather than study actual firms, students in traditional microeconomics study hypothetical equilibrium profit and output conditions under different industry structures. Although changes from the existing equilibrium are acknowledged and comparisons between equilibria are made, "it is this *equilibrium* price that we are interested in, not in how the market gets to this equilibrium or how it might change over long periods of time" (Varian 2005: 3, emphasis in original).

The equilibrium emphasis dates from nineteenth-century physics envy where

> the search for the conditions of equilibrium of this and that arose in an era much enamored by science, most especially of Newtonian physics. The method – and much of the focus – of economics developed as though it were studying the very slowly and predictably changing forces of nature instead of the rapid, chaotic and uncertain processes of society.
> 
> (Dowd 2004: 134)

But what firm is interested in equilibrium? Or even in attaining it? Rather

> firms want to break out of the limits set by price competition [by searching for] either monopoly power or breakthroughs, i.e., a new product, new way of recruiting labor, a new technology, or anything innovative that gives one firm an advantage over its rivals.
> 
> (Bowles *et al.* 2005: 262)

Competition is dynamic and not teleological. Thus, viewing the economy as nothing more than a series of equilibria is highly misleading.

Steve Keen's two interrelated chapters, 9 and 10, on microeconomics and mathematics cogently argue that traditional economics uses the wrong math – calculus – to study the wrong problem – optimization under conditions of equilibrium. Keen first critiques then demolishes the traditional theory of the firm, which is built on spurious logic. Once this canonical underbrush has been cleared, Keen offers suggestions for teaching a more dynamic, realistic and evolutionary theory of the firm. In Chapter 10, he offers suggestions for teaching the necessary math – differential equations – to understand the evolution of the firm in today's economy.

Analysis of static equilibrium requires differential calculus, which economic students typically learn, but analysis of the evolution of business and the process of competition requires differential equations and difference equations, which are seldom taught in the economics curriculum. Although understanding calculus is integral to a university education for its illustration of the intellectual capability of the human mind (Berlinski 1995) and for its widespread applicability (launching space satellites, predicting the movement of planets, etc.), calculus has been misappropriated to the study of the behavior of the firm.

## IV Part IV: Advanced courses electives

This unit considers upper division courses taken either as a requirement for a specific field or as an elective. While space does not allow discussion of all possible course offerings, the discussed courses represent a broad and diverse sampling: labor economics, environmental economics, international economics, money and banking, and green economics.

Champlin and Wiens-Tuers in Chapter 11 on labor economics reminds us that until the first half of the twentieth century, labor economics was pluralist, with institutionalists and Marxists actively contributing. Unfortunately, Champlin and Wiens-Tuers note, contemporary labor economics "is not just a course that uses microeconomics; it is microeconomics." Indeed traditional labor economics utilizes neoclassical blocks: utility maximization, supply and demand, isoquants, marginal productivity, equilibrium, and perfect competition. Students exposed only to traditional economics enroll in upper division courses with biased baggage. As one example, since perfect competition is extolled as ideal, any institutional intervention such as the minimum wage or labor unions can only distort otherwise beneficent results.

To reintroduce pluralism, Champlin and Wiens-Tuers suggest structuring the course around key issues of wages, discrimination, labor market structure, and the concept of labor itself, while discussing each from multiple perspectives. This will expose the underlying importance of power in market systems, too often ignored by the focus on equilibrium. Since traditional economics assumes market exchanges are voluntary, "coercive relationships are not in the picture because if everything that matters in an exchange has already been settled by contract, there is nothing for the exercise of power to be about" (Bowles *et al.* 2005: 58).

In the twilight of the carbon era, Peter Söderbaum, in Chapter 12 on environmental economics, notes the contemporary "power game between different actors about how to understand sustainability – business as usual or radical lifestyle changes?" Moving beyond traditional concepts of rational man and profit-maximization firms, Söderbaum discusses the political economic person and the political economic organization – multi-faceted individuals and businesses respectively – while introducing the decision-making tool of position analysis which facilitates dialogue and an interactive learning process, emphasizing active and continuous decision making by all interested parties. This is preferable to cost-benefit analysis, espoused by traditional economics, which relies heavily on the testimony of experts, along with the dubious assumption that all impacts can be monetarized. Söderbaum argues that the nature of pluralism itself is thought-provoking and piques student interest, especially the role of science versus ideology and how environmental decisions should be made.

While it is true that today "commerce and innovation – not plunder and expropriation – have proven to be the greatest engines of wealth creation" (Chua 2007: 326), power underlies the foundation and construction of institutions supporting trade and finance. Power determines how economic development is construed and who benefits from economic growth. Power determines whose interests are recognized and thus who benefits from existing institutions. Thus the crucial question "is not primarily about coercion versus freedom, but about which coercive acts and which interests we defend, so that these interests may thrive" (Vant 2005: 82).

Maria Madi and José Gonçalves in Chapter 13 argue that the historical development of institutions is far more important in understanding international trade than static theories such as comparative advantage and the Hecksher–Ohlin–Samuelson Theorem. Pedagogically, the authors recommend connecting today's events with the history of ideas and the historical evolution of current trade regimes, along with a rich, multi-media exposition to "prevent students from taking refuge in theory and abstraction." A pluralist perspective is more amenable to asking and understanding important questions ignored by traditional economics such as whether trade confers equal benefits, how power affects the terms of trade, how economies develop with uneven resources, etc.

Traditional economics prescribes a one-size-fits-all model for trade, emphasizing the private sector while minimizing the public sector. This of course ignores the "historical fact that the rich countries did not develop on the basis of the policies and institutions that they now recommend to, and often force upon, the developing countries" (Chang 2004: 280).

Development is key, and key to development is the financial sector. History teaches that who controls global finance also controls trade and development. Central to all economies and hence economic pedagogy is the role of money and finance. The political economy perspective of money, credit, and finance is realistic, institutional, historical, and methodologically systemic. Such a perspective is critical to understanding the essence of capitalism and its recurrent financial crises. Phillip O'Hara writes in Chapter 14:

> history matters in political economy; therefore a dynamic view of credit and finance is central to its core theory and policy. Successive institutional changes are embedded into the theory, so knowledge becomes relevant to changes in the real economy. The analysis is historical as different phases of evolution are delineated through time as hysteresis and path dependence impact the economy.

A generation ago green economics was disparaged but, as Thomas Friedman (2007) recently wrote,

> the good news is that after traveling around America this past year, looking at how we use energy and the emerging alternatives, I can report that green really has gone Main Street – thanks to the perfect storm created by 9/11, Hurricane Katrina and the Internet revolution.

Green economics by its very nature is interdisciplinary, juxtaposing two oxymoronic terms, "green" and "economics," which like two particles with the same charge could not be placed together just a generation ago. Ironically, the pendulum is slowly turning, so that traditional economics is ever more at the fringe, while green economics is considered more mainstream, with a palpable and increasing demand emanating from the business community. Nevertheless, green economics is probably the most maligned yet least understood discipline of economics. Green economics casts its pluralist cooperative net far and wide among social and physical sciences to offer a wide range of efficacious and holistic solutions as well as to heed the voices of the disenfranchised of the past, present, and future. Miriam Kennet in Chapter 15 enthusiastically offers fruitful suggestions to incorporate green economics into the economics curriculum.

## Notes

1 The author thanks participants in the Graduate Research Seminar (October 17, 2008) at the University of Athens in Athens, Greece, for stimulating and helpful comments on pluralism.
2 For a full text of the letter please see "Economics at Notre Dame – An Open Letter" (2008) http://openeconomics.blogspot.com/2008/04/economics-at-notre-dame-open-letter.html.
3 See Mearman (2008) for a discussion of the myriad definitions of pluralism and Negru (2009) for a discussion of the emergence of pluralism. For a discussion of the demand for pluralism outside the economics profession see Söderbaum and Kennet in Chapters 12 and 15 below.
4 See especially Holcombe (2008), Davis (2007), and Vromen (2007).
5 On the other hand, orthodoxy's connotation of fundamentalism is, for some, apropos.
6 Although I received both my Masters degree and Ph.D. from the University of Notre Dame, this commonality with the Notre Dame students played no role in asking them to write a chapter.

## References

Bacon, F. (2000) *The New Organon*. Cambridge: Cambridge University Press.
Berlinski, D. (1995) *A Tour of the Calculus*. New York: Vintage.
Bowles, S., Edwards, M., and Roosevelt, F. (2005) *Understanding Capitalism: Competition, Command and Change*. New York: Oxford University Press.
Case, K. and Fair, R. (2005) *Principles of Economics*. Upper Saddle River, NJ: Pearson Prentice.
Chang, H. (2004) "What is Wrong with the Official History of Capitalism?" in E. Fullbrook (ed.) *A Guide to What's Wrong With Economics*. London: Anthem.
Chua, Amy (2007) *Day of Empire – How Hyperpowers Rise to Global Dominance – and Why They Fall*. New York: Doubleday.
Coyle, D. (2007) *The Soulful Science: What Economists Really Do and Why It Matters*. Princeton, NJ: Princeton University Press.
Davis, J. (2006) "The Turn in Neoclassical Economics: Neoclassical Dominance to Mainstream Pluralism," *Journal of Institutional Economics* 2(1): 1–20.
Davis, J. (2007) "Why is Economics Not Yet a Pluralistic Science," *Post-Autistic Economics Review* 43 (15 September): 42–56
Dowd, D. (2004) *Capitalism and Its Economics – A Critical History*. London: Pluto.
Friedman, T. (2007) "The Power of Green," *The New York Times Magazine*. April 15, 2007. www.nytimes.com/2007/04/15/magazine/15green.t.html. Accessed May 2, 2007.

Fullbrook, E. (ed.) (2004) *A Guide to What's Wrong With Economics*. London: Anthem.
Garnett, R.F. (2005) "Sen, McCloskey and the Future of Heterodox Economics," *Post-Autistic Economics Review* 5: 19–31. www.paecon.net?PAEReview/issue35/garnett35.html. Accessed July 1, 2007.
Groenewegen, J. (ed.) (2007) *Teaching Pluralism in Economics*. Northampton, Mass.: Edward Elgar.
Hermann, A. (2007) *Institutional Economics and Psychoanalysis: How Can They Collaborate for a Better Understanding of Individual–Society Dynamics?*. Editrice: Trento, Italy.
Hodgson, G. (1999) *Evolution and Institutions*. Cheltenham, UK: Edward Elgar.
Holcombe, R. (2008) "Pluralism versus Heterodoxy in Economics and the Social Sciences," *Journal of Philosophical Economics* 1: 51–72.
Keen, S. (2001) *Debunking Economics*. Annandale, Australia: Pluto Press.
Lemstra, W. (2007) "A Practitioner's Perspective on Interdisciplinary in Education: the MBT Case" in J. Groenewegen (ed.) *Teaching Pluralism in Economics*. Northampton, Mass.: Edward Elgar.
Marshall, A. (1946) [1920] *Principles of Economics*. 8th edn. London: Macmillan.
Mearman, A. (2008) "Pluralism and Heterodoxy: Introduction to the Special Issue," *Journal of Philosophical Economics* 1: 5–25.
Negru, I. (2009) "The Historical Emergence of Pluralism," *International Journal of Pluralism and Economics Education* 1.
"Open Letter from Economics Students to Professors and Others Responsible for the Teaching of this Discipline" (2000) Translated and available online at www.paecon.net/PAEtexts/a-e-petition.htm.
Reardon, J. (1995) "The Role of Economic Education in Economies of Transition," *Proceedings of the Conference on Economic Education in Transition Economies*. Riga, Latvia: University of Latvia, June 7–10, 1995.
Shearman, D. and Smith, J. (2007).*The Climate Change Challenge and the Failure of Democracy*. Westport, Conn.: Praeger.
Vant, A. (2005) *Institutions and the New Environment*. Cheltenham, UK: Edward Elgar.
Varian, H. (2005) *Intermediate Microeconomics*. 7th edn. New York: Norton.
Vromen, J. (2007) "In Praise of Moderate Plurality" in J. Groenewegen (ed.) *Teaching Pluralism in Economics*, Northampton, Mass.: Edward Elgar.
Weehuizen, Ritka (2007) "Interdisciplinarity and Problem-based Learning in Economics Education: The Case of Infonomics" in J. Groenewegen (ed.) *Teaching Pluralism in Economics*. Northampton, Mass.: Edward Elgar.

# 2 The meltdown and economics textbooks

*Edward Fullbrook*

No discipline has ever experienced systemic failure on the scale that economics has today. Its fall from grace has been two-dimensional. One, economists oversaw, directly and through the prevalence of their ideas, the structuring of the global economy that has now collapsed. Two, except for a few outcasts, economists failed to see, even before the general public saw, the coming of the biggest economic meltdown of all time. Never has a profession betrayed the trust of society so acutely, never has one been in such desperate need of a fundamental remake.

As an epistemological event, the 2008 meltdown of the global financial system ranks with the observation of the 1919 solar eclipse. If professional practice in economics resembled, even in the slightest, that in the natural sciences, then in the wake of today's global disaster economists would be falling over each other to proclaim the falsity of their theories, the inadequacy of their methods, and the urgent need for new ones.

It is now evident to nearly everyone except economists, and increasingly even to many of us, that our collective failure to see the calamity before it occurred and the fact that the system that collapsed had been tailored to fit mainstream teachings, mean that we, the textbooks we use, and the courses that we teach harbour fundamental misconceptions about the way economies, most especially their markets, function. And in economics nothing is more important than teaching, because, as Galbraith senior once observed, economics is primarily a teaching profession. This makes economics pedagogy a natural starting point for an analysis both of how economics went so horribly wrong and of how it might be made less a facilitator of human disaster in the future. Gregory Mankiw's *Principles of Economics*, in all its five versions, has been the dominant basic text internationally for more than a decade. Also its author, as chairman of President Bush's Council of Economic Advisors from 2003 to 2005, was directly involved in the engineering of the disaster. So Mankiw's textbook seems an ideal place to look for clues as to how both the economics profession and the public which it educates became so ignorant, misinformed, and unobservant of how economies work in the real world.

Because we are dealing with a systemic failure, in what follows I am concerned not with specific issues covered by Mankiw's text. Instead I want to consider its general approach to understanding economic phenomena and, no less important, how the author treats the position of trust that he enjoys vis-à-vis the student.

A defining characteristic of traditional or orthodox economics is that it subscribes to a Neoplatonist theory of truth, i.e. it holds its basic tenets or propositions from which it then deduces everything else to be self-evident. This quaint epistemological doctrine was notably enunciated for economists by Lionel Robbins in *An Essay on the Nature and Significance of Economic Science* (1932). He wrote: "the propositions of Economics are on all fours with the proposition of all other sciences. As we have seen, these propositions are deduction from simple assumptions reflecting very elementary facts of general experience" (1932: 104).

And:

> In Economics, as we have seen, the ultimate constituents of our fundamental generalisations are known to us by immediate acquaintance. In the natural sciences they are known only inferentially. There is much less reason to doubt the counterpart in reality of the assumption of individual preferences than that of the assumption of the electron.
>
> (1932: 105)

To a real scientist, of course, economics' Neoplatonism is anathema. For example, the eminent physicist J.P. Bouchaud (2008: 291) recently commented:

> To me, the crucial difference between physical sciences and economics or financial mathematics is rather the relative role of concepts, equations and empirical data. Classical economics [meaning today's mainstream] is built on very strong assumptions that quickly become axioms: the rationality of economic agents, the invisible hand and market efficiency, etc. An economist once told me, to my bewilderment: These concepts are so strong that they supersede any empirical observation.

This doctrine, which alone radically separates economics from the scientific tradition, shapes Mankiw's textbook from cover to cover. As one would expect, it performs heroics at the book's beginning. With a real science, its basic principles, rather than being its beginning, are its highest achievement. But on the second page under the heading "How people make decisions", Mankiw unveils his "four principles of individual decision making". At no point does he allude to how his basic principles were discovered. No names, no dates and no processes of discovery are mentioned. Instead he seeks, by appeal to folksy stories, to persuade the student to accept them on faith. Only a confirmed Neoplatonist or a snake oil salesman would think of beginning an epistemological exercise that way.

A major device which Mankiw and other textbook writers use in persuading the student to accept on faith their principles is to subtly yet forcibly bring emotionality into their presentation. Mainstream or neoclassical economics, especially in the last fifty years, has made a point of raising its flag over snow-white abstract nouns such as "rationality", "choice", "freedom", "equity" and "efficiency", whose meanings change with the wind and which are bottom-heavy with emotion and so float like icebergs through public discussion. Textbook writers like Mankiw use these words of the general culture – and it would be naive to think that they do so accidentally – to emotionalize their presentations and to bully their mostly teenage readers. For example, consider how Mankiw, when presenting his putative four principles of how people make decisions, introduces "efficiency", "equity" and "rationality". Set off in a wide empty margin and opposite where the text says that society faces a trade-off "between efficiency and equity" one finds:

**efficiency**
the property of society getting the most it can from scarce resources

**equity**
the property of distributing economic prosperity fairly among the members of society

At best two students in a hundred will notice that these "definitions" are gems of begging the question: "the most" of what and "fairly" meaning what? Nothing of substance has been broached. What is happening is that the student is being taught to use these words as placeholders, so that gradually and almost imperceptibly they can be filled with neoclassical meaning as the student progresses through the text, lectures, quizzes and exams of the course. All this will be done without a single mention, let alone discussion, of ethical lenses other than Utilitarianism through which one might view economic reality. The students will not even be told that they are being introduced into an ethical system of thought. That could derail the indoctrination process, because students, even nineteen-year-olds, have assorted views on what is fair and have different conceptions of what it means for a society to get the most out of its resources, and some would not knowingly give up their views without a fight.

Mankiw deploys a different tactic, bullying, with his introduction of "rational":

PRINCIPLE #3: Rational People Think at the Margin

(2007: 6)

Mankiw explains that by thinking at the margin he means "by comparing marginal costs and marginal benefits". Why is this bullying? The student, as the author must know, will not read that as meaning "We are going to define 'rational people' as those people who think at the margin." The student will read it not as a definition but as a statement of fact. Most likely the student will not even know that rationality is a normative concept. Nor is the student apt to have any general views to offer in opposition. But what students will have, especially the nineteen-year-olds, is a compelling desire to be regarded both by themselves and by others, most especially by their teacher, as "rational", whatever the word means. I don't mind telling anyone that I don't think at the margin, but the student will rightly fear the consequences of putting him or herself forward as "irrational".

Even if "rationality" is taken in the narrow sense of referring to the adjustment of means to ends, it does not begin to escape its status as a normative concept because different people, depending on the forms of ethics to which they subscribe, will have different notions about what one's ends are or should be. Unfortunately, among economists the obvious needs to be emphasized: *not everyone is a Utilitarian. Not everyone believes that the maximization of individual "utility", whatever that might be, is or should be the goal of human and hence economic life.* "Economists have no right to select one ethics as the 'correct one' for purposes of economic analysis" (Söderbaum, 2004: 162). But they do, and in doing so go about as far away from the scientific as it is possible to go.

If economics textbook authors placed education ahead of indoctrination, the epistemological role of their theory ahead of its ideological one, how might they proceed? Hugh Stretton's *Economics: A New Introduction* shows how it can be done. For example, look at how he introduces "efficiency":

> If you measure efficiency by more than one criterion, you have to decide how much weight to give to each of the criteria. The facts can't do that for you. It takes a value judgment, and that value judgment will be built into your measure of efficiency.
>
> Earlier, you read this: "Common sense says it is efficient to get a given output from the least input." But what does "least input" mean? Does it mean least raw materials? Least work? Least expenditure? You have to decide.
>
> (1999: 48)

A little further on, after addressing non-dogmatically the vexed questions "Efficient at what?" and "Efficient for whom?", Stretton tells the student:

> Most tests of efficiency require some value judgments. They can be made into objective tests by precise specifications: output of *what* per input of *what*. But that merely shifts the conflicts of interest and the necessary value judgments from the conduct of the test to the choice and design of the test.
>
> This principle applies to judgments of many other things besides efficiency.
>
> (1999: 49)

These passages characterize the approach throughout Stretton's book, one which could and should be the approach of every economics textbook: no attempt to mislead, intimidate or bamboozle the student, no dishonesty by omitting known crucial facts, no misusing the educator's position of trust by taking it as an opportunity to indoctrinate, no reluctance to encourage the student to observe from more than one perspective economic issues pivotal to democracies; in short, no inhibitions about trying to educate in the deepest possible sense.

Mankiw continues to present his "Ten principles of economics" in the style of a sales pitch. In the space of a page and a half he invokes "the invisible hand" eleven times and speaks of its "magic" (2007: 9–10). Then having presumably sold without offering evidence his "Ten principles" to the student, Mankiw proceeds to paint "The economist as scientist". He is quite right in assuming that the student will not notice his previous chapter's display of Neoplatonism or know that it is anti-science. Mankiw sets about building in the student's mind an association between economists like himself and real scientists. For this he is only willing to associate himself with the most prestigious of scientists: physicists, biologists and astronomers. He hopes to acquire some of their persona by, in the space of a few pages, repeating over and over a few key words: "physics" four times, "physicist(s)" seven, "biology" five and "biologist" twice. He especially favours combinations like "physics, biology, and economics". But even this is not elite enough for Mankiw's tastes. In the first three paragraphs of this section he mentions Newton and Einstein four times each.

Of course this affectation has a long history in the discipline. It goes back much further than Robbins, and all the way to Walras and Jevons. But perhaps its most humorous example is due to the inventor of the textbook prototype of which Mankiw is now grand master. The science historian Yves Gingras (2007) relates the notorious incident at the award ceremonies for the 1970 Bank of Sweden Prize as follows:

> Paul Samuelson (1970 winner) wrote about his "Nobel coronation" – not his "Bank of Sweden Coronation" – and filled his talk with references to Einstein (4 times) Bohr (2 times) and eight other winners of the (real) physics Nobel prize (not to mention, of course, Newton) plus a few other names as if he were part of this family.

For the last fifty years economics as a profession has shown exceptional talent for self-promotion. Spurred on by self-delusion, it has persuaded the media to call its Bank of Sweden Prize a "Nobel Prize" and in the main has escaped ridicule even when, like Samuelson and Mankiw, it has represented its pursuits and achievements as resembling those of Newton and Einstein. This self-exaltation has in the main enabled its anti-scientific methodology to escape outside notice, with the result that the broader intellectual community has accepted economics' self-assessment. But this was not always the case. Four years after Robbins (1932) published his essay lauding the methods of economics, the American pragmatist philosopher John Dewey favourably reviewed a book by a zoologist and medical statistician condemning them. Dewey (1936), after referring to "the conceptions and methods" of economics as "obscurantist and fatally reactionary", quotes from Lancelot Hogben's *The Retreat from Reason*. It pertains as much to our time, especially to Economics 101 and presidential advisers, as it did back then.

> We can only conclude that economics, as studied in our universities, is the astrology of the Machine Age; it provides the same kind of intellectual relief as chess, in which success depends entirely on knowing the initial definition of moves and processes of checking, casting, etc.... In science the final arbiter is not the self-evidence of the initial statement, nor the facade of flawless logic that conceals it. A scientific law embodies a recipe for doing something, and its final validation rests in the domain of action.
>
> (Hogben, quoted in Dewey 1936: 73)

And the message today from the physicist Bouchaud is much the same.

> Most of all, there is a crucial need to change the mindset of those working in economics and financial engineering. They need to move away from what Richard Feynman called Cargo Cult Science: a science that follows all the apparent precepts and forms of scientific investigation, while still missing something essential. An overly formal and dogmatic education in the economic sciences and financial mathematics are part of the problem. Economic curriculums need to include more natural science. The prerequisites for more stability in the long run are the development of a more pragmatic and realistic representation of what is going on in financial markets, and to focus on data, which should always supersede perfect equations and aesthetic axioms.
>
> (Bouchaud, 2008: 292)

For economics the final arbiter, economic history, has spoken and this time with deafening loudness. Economists in the main may or may not hear, but most of the rest of the educated world has already. Although there is now talk of "intellectual crime" on a scale not seen for several generations, it would be wrong to punish the guilty. But I plead that everyone, students included, do what they can to reform the teaching of economics, especially at its introductory level. If universities continued to use for nuclear engineering a textbook by an engineer who had headed a team managing a nuclear power plant that without external causes exploded creating huge devastation, there would be a public outcry. There should be a similar outcry if Mankiw-type textbooks continue to be foisted on the world's million or so young people who every year in good faith take up the study of economics. Because of human error propagated by a virulent ideology skilfully camouflaged as science, millions of American families are losing their homes, 100 million people in the world stand to lose their jobs and a generation has been deprived of the hope it deserves. We cannot undo that, but we can greatly reduce the chances of it happening again if with all possible speed we bring into use pluralist textbooks that look at real-world economic problems from different points of view, that do not make false claims about economic knowledge, and most importantly, that seek not to indoctrinate but to educate. To these ends I offer the following list.

## Eleven ways to think like a post-crash economist

1. Don't try to pass yourself off as a kissing cousin of natural scientists.
2. Don't speak, except to very small children, of invisible hands and magic.
3. When possible avoid the use of emotive words.
4. Remind yourself every morning that your duty as a teacher is to educate your students, not indoctrinate them.
5. Try to look at economic phenomena from different points of view and teach your students to do the same.
6. Encourage the study of economic phenomena from different points of view.
7. Don't be condescending to your students.
8. Keep your eye on real-world economies rather than imaginary ones.
9. Don't try to hide the troubled but fascinating history and contemporary diversity of economics from your students and the general public.
10. Avoid cranks and try to avoid becoming one yourself.
11. Never try to pass off ideology as objective truth.

## References

Bouchaud, J.P. (2008) "Economics Needs a Scientific Revolution", *Real-World Economics Review*, issue 48, December, p. 291.

Dewey, John (1936) "Rationality in Education", *The Social Frontier*, 3 (December): 71–73.

Gingras, Yves (2007) "Beautiful Mind, Ugly Deception: The Bank of Sweden Prize in Economics Science", in *Real World Economics*, edited by Edward Fullbrook. London: Anthem, pp. 71–76.

Mankiw, Gregory (2007) *Principles of Economics*, 4th edition, Mason, Ohio: Thomson.

Robbins, Lionel (1932) *An Essay on the Nature and Significance of Economic Science*. London: Macmillan.

Söderbaum, Peter (2004) "Economics as Ideology and the Need for Pluralism", *A Guide to What's Wrong with Economics*, edited by Edward Fullbrook. London: Anthem, pp. 158–168.

Stretton, Hugh (1999) *Economics: A New Introduction*. London: Pluto.

# 3 A revolution from the margin
## A student perspective

*Nicholas Dan, Nicholas Houpt, Sean Mallin, and Felipe Witchger*

Economics education is not a zero-sum game; on the contrary, detouring into political economy can only enrich our understanding of traditional economics. Fortunately, some of us learned traditional economics from the ground up. By this we mean that we were allowed to interrogate its assumptions and tease out its implications. This challenged us to seek the limits of every fact or theory and find in them new prospects, new perspectives, and new possibilities. As one of our professors said, "Orthodoxy is one way to tell the economics story. There are many others."

Notre Dame, the storied institution of learning and football, has an even more storied Department of Economics. Long regarded as a refuge for out-of-the-ordinary and not-quite-mainstream economists, the Department prided itself on being different. During the 1970s it built an eclectic Economics Department focusing on labor, development, and public policy programs, with the goal of fostering an intellectual environment encouraging discourse between traditional and political economic approaches. During the 1980s, however, forces inside and outside the department pressured for change. Self-comparison to "peer-institutions" – Harvard, Princeton, MIT, and others – pressured Notre Dame to follow suit. In 2003, after years of internecine struggle, the department split into the Department of Economics and Econometrics and the Department of Economics and Policy Studies. The former focuses on rigorous, mathematical modeling while the latter focuses on socio-economic justice with an openness to competing methodologies. The former gets more money, the graduate program, and all the new hires, while the other gets ... marginalized.

This is the situation we found upon arriving at Notre Dame as undergraduates. None of us began as economics majors; three of us started at the College of Engineering. We were all inspired, however, by our first economics class, which fortuitously happened to be pluralist. We studied traditional economics but only as one of many stories that could be told about the economy. We scrutinized each assumption and imagined how each theory would look with its assumptions turned upside down. Little did we know that this kind of economics education was the exception, not the rule. We soon found out.

But looking back (and around!) we consider ourselves lucky – lucky to have attended a university that still has remnants of a political economy program and, above all, lucky to have been introduced early to the political economy approach. Whether through just a passing mention in an introductory course or a full semester devoted to a political economy course, we were imbued with a questioning ethic – a little nagging voice that asked, "What are the assumptions here?" or "What is being left out?" This microscopic focus is too often ignored in the teaching of traditional economics. Instead of passive acceptance of theory – which is too often dogmatically presented – our first course enabled us to ask, "Is there another way to tell this story?"

Unfortunately, many students are not so lucky. Even at Notre Dame which has a handful of dedicated political economists, most students go four years without any exposure to "alternatives" – and are therefore led to believe that none exist. Students reared in an exclusively traditional environment are presented one economic story as the absolute truth. Fortunately, we were taught differently. Early exposure to political economy enabled us to tease out differences and implications. First encounters with new ideas usually entail a baggage of misunderstandings. We know this as well as anyone. By engaging early and often with political economy, we developed a dynamic understanding of traditional economics and political economy. We know both well enough to use them in our discussions, debates, and analyses.

Giving students a well-rounded education no doubt take time – a scarce resource in college – but, as we stress throughout this chapter, learning political economy enables a richer and deeper understanding of traditional economics. Yes, I know it's counter-intuitive, but learning economics as students normally do – that is, in a purely instrumental way – is bereft of a rich understanding of the historical evolution of the concepts and their implications.

This lack of understanding becomes palpable when friends from other disciplines question concepts and assumptions from traditional economics. It is humbling to find students who have never taken an economics course but display a deeper understanding of the concepts and critiques of traditional economics than most economics majors. How do we reply when our friends from anthropology, history or physics (the holy grail of science!) unleash criticism after criticism of the traditional assumptions if we don't know anything else? They press us with questions about our irrational rationality assumption or our methodological individualism or the lack of – take your pick – culture, ethics, power, exploitation, corruption, psychology, and more, in our economic theorizing. We've experienced it too many times.

It would do economics students a service to, at the very least, introduce them to the basic criticisms of traditional economics to save an embarrassing stutter, "Well ... you see ... supply and demand ... you know ... the invisible hand," in response to every inquisition. Humility is an invaluable asset which is sorely lacking among traditional economists.

In brash defiance of its critics, traditional economics commands reverence from non-economists. It bids all other subjects to bow in obeisance to the queen of the social sciences. Friends from the business school, the "hard" and "soft" sciences, the humanities, and engineering join econ majors to learn traditional economics via Samuelson or Mankiw. These are the world's future doers and thinkers, hoping to forge new and creative ideas, yet learning old and hackneyed economics.

We are a generation with bold ambitions – to end global poverty, to solve the food crisis, to overcome global warming – but are handed an economic framework with stark and limited possibilities. When we try to push the boundaries of the possible, traditional economics stubbornly pushes back. For a discipline so narrow, economics continues to attract a diverse crowd. We fear, however, that students from other disciplines will assume that this superficial and non-critical view of economics is the only way to understand the economy. Some call it disciplinary imperialism. We call it creativity eradication.

So how did we end up in this strange state of economics, where a free market of ideas is crushed under the hegemonic monopoly of traditional economics? Its assumptions are so ingrained in our culture that when students take their first economics course, they may already have accepted the homo economicus model of human nature.

Political economy does not battle traditional economics just in the classroom, but increasingly in our culture as well. Steven Levitt and Stephen J. Dubner's *Freakonomics* (2006), heavily influenced by the Chicago School, has sold over three million copies, simultaneously making economics a "cool" major and introducing a whole new generation of students to the idea that traditional economics can be applied anywhere, everywhere, and to anything.

The four of us came to economics, troubled by a world steeped in poverty and inequality, and suffering resource shortages, religious wars, and global warming. We were told simultaneously that the world is flat, the individual sacred, and the inefficient profane. Instead of investigating intricate problems from sundry angles, students enrolled in a traditional economics course are given a single package of equations and assumptions with the label "non-perishable: good always and everywhere." Out of the arc of economic possibilities, traditional economics claims an infallible truth. Students expecting a more open method of analysis are discouraged – that is the purview of those other social sciences.

When we questioned our Department Chair about informal economies, he retorted that economics doesn't really deal with them. "But they are economies," we insisted, "that by some estimates add up to trillions of dollars a year – totally unaccounted for in GDP! Think of the implications for development policy!" After several seconds of silence, the Chair suggested we look for help outside of the Economics Department.

Students study economics believing it can help solve the pressing issues of today; instead they find an insular and abstract economics lacking its promised practical applicability. Students are corralled around the Thanksgiving table, hoping for a sumptuous spread, only to find ... stuffing ... stuffing ... and more stuffing. What could have been a feast turns out to be a forced-feeding.

Traditional economics courses mass-produce economic doers, not economic thinkers. Our education has become wholly instrumental. Open up any economics textbook and find page after page of polished graphs and mathematical formulas, often highlighted in colorful boxes. It is generally understood that inside those pastel partitions is all we need to know – at least to pass the next exam, or get into graduate school, or devise economic policy. So rather than understand what the model is saying – we memorize, memorize, memorize. Last year, for an exam in advanced macroeconomics, the professor gave us a "study aid" with all the needed formulas. On test day, students arrived with the equations memorized (easily done in ten minutes) and had no problem answering the questions. We imagined our professor beaming with pride that students did so well, especially given the opening exhortation to "teach us how to do economics the way professional economists do." This, unfortunately, is a triumph of efficiency over creativity: a "plug and chug" method that makes reproduction and replication easy at the steep cost of understanding the economy.

Granted, not everyone wants to wrestle with the intricacies of theory; some just want the tools – honed by centuries of great thinkers – to do economics. There is nothing wrong with that. But we see economics education moving decidedly in the direction of imparting purely instrumental knowledge. We see a one-dimensional economics education that stresses the doing but not the thinking. Today, academic economists work long hours in their offices, building models, theorizing, but not peering out their windows at the world. Orthodoxy is a magnificent hammer, but sometimes you need a wrench or a screwdriver.

The confrontation between the visible and invisible hand is nowhere more apparent (or ironic) than on our campuses – ironic because of the ostensible disagreement between what is taught in our economics classes and what students think when they buy consumer goods. A handful of us involved in the living wage campaign at Notre Dame are also economics majors. We look past the simplistic argument that wage distortions will cause market inefficiency to questions of justice. College is and should be an opportunity for a cosmopolitan education. Many embrace this chance, adopting broader world-views and expanded moral sensibilities. But in the traditional economics classroom, these ideals and opinions are to be left at the door.

Last year, we asked faculty and administrators, "Why is history of economic thought not required for the major while econometrics is? Why can't the ideas of political economy be introduced in our introductory courses? And why are there fewer and fewer political economy courses offered at the upper levels?" The unambiguous response was that those theories are just not practical; they don't get students into top-tier graduate school or help in the business world. Above all, they said, there just isn't the demand.

Is this true? Are students here and elsewhere really indifferent to alternative ideas? This year at Notre Dame, classes in Marxian economic theory, political economy, consumption and happiness, and history of economic thought filled up completely. Marxian economic theory even had a waiting list. Our peers at Harvard, UC Berkeley, MIT, and elsewhere are also demanding courses beyond traditional economics. We've met students interested in economic policy and development, and, more importantly, in alternatives to traditional economics. It is not a lack of interest, but rather a lack of opportunity that conditions the mass production of traditional economists. It is simple supply-and-demand; except here, supply is artificially separated from demand.

The rigorous, analytic thinking encouraged in traditional courses is laudable; yet at the same time it is important that economists understand the complicated details of real-world problems. Analytical thinking is a double-edged sword: it helps only if we know how to use it. If not, it will be indiscriminately applied to every problem. This narrowness isn't desirable; it's deadly.

We believe the situation can change; in fact we believe it already is changing. The four of us found each other through a shared desire for a more pluralistic economics education. We soon found like-minded others from inside and outside the major. We supplemented our traditional economics training with an out-of-class discussion group. Imagine a dozen or so students who could be more "efficiently" spending their time on homework or studying, huddled around a table that is half-a-dozen people too small, talking about economics. These gatherings were centered on articles chosen by the group in advance to be dissected, discussed, and debated. We relished the chance to talk about interesting and relevant topics in ways were not possible in most of our economics classes. We could engage each problem in a dialogue with orthodoxy and its many alternatives. Here, we could question assumptions, interrogate generalities, and ask about the morality of it all. Try doing that in a traditional economics class. We have – it isn't pretty.

After a year, we happily report the discussion group is still going strong. While this was highly satisfying to us, we realized we could not be indifferent to the larger issue of the lack of pluralism in economics education. The loss for our fellow students is too great, and the stakes – in terms of poverty, policy, international development, and other crucial issues – are too high. We went beyond our discussion group. We reached out to other students and wrote letters to the faculty and administration voicing our discontent. In May of 2007, the four of us wrote an Open Letter to the Notre Dame community expressing our dissatisfaction with the economics situation we had inherited. In addition to the letter, we started an online petition addressing our concerns. Within days we had several hundred signatures and an incredible outpouring of support. This was encouraging, yet we were cognizant of the insurmountable barrier posed by the dominance of traditional economics in the classroom. In order to make real progress, we had to bridge the gap between our extracurricular discussion group and in-class education. Our idea was to create a class – led by students – to allow for an expansive study of a specific economic issue. Several of us got together and wrote a syllabus and got approval from the university to teach a one credit seminar in the spring of 2009. The topic is "Alternatives to the firm," which differs from the standard economics course by incorporating articles, documentaries, and guest lectures to promote in-depth discussion and debate. Instead of coming into each class insisting, "This is how you should think about this topic," we ask, "How should we think about this – and how can we think differently?"

Through these student-run classes and discussion groups, we are reclaiming our education. This alternative education will enable us to interrogate the prepackaged training of today's orthodoxy. When we find our education lacking, when we have questions that go unanswered, we will learn elsewhere.

We readily admit that eschewing the neoclassical classroom is only a short-run reaction to the problem, not a long-run solution. We don't pretend to have a single, quick-fix solution – that would be very unpluralistic of us. But we have several observations and recommendations on how to change economics for the better. How can economics be taught so that it is both challenging and engaging? How do we connect its historical development with contemporary applications? And how can we learn economics that is "real" while acknowledging the barriers? These are indeed colossal tasks.

Our education is monopolized by orthodoxy. This is as true at Notre Dame as it is for our friends at Harvard and MIT. As undergraduates, students learn orthodoxy without unpacking its real-life implications, or connecting the theory with reality. This poverty of alternatives is the first obstacle we confront. In addition, there is a palpable political reality: because of orthodoxy's despotic position in academia, the range of what an economics major can "safely" study is unfortunately very slim. If we want to be "real economists" we are warned against taking classes from those "faux economists" who don't subscribe to the orthodox paradigm. We are told that if we want to get into a "real" graduate program, we had better not take that class in Marxian economics. We should load up on math classes or, better yet, major in mathematics. The hegemony of orthodoxy powerfully forms and shapes economics education.

One solution is to learn traditional economics better. Yes, we want orthodox theory, but in dialogue with alternatives. We want to study economics from the infinite perspectives in which it is lived. Theory viewed this way becomes a human product rather than a divine law. By denaturalizing traditional theory, students are empowered to think differently. If we are to implement a more pluralist and open economics education, a reevaluation of standard teaching practices is in order. Orthodoxy is often taught dogmatically and badly at that. But heterodoxy can be taught badly too. We do not expect a Dead Poets Society education in every class but, let's face it, there are ways that economics can be taught more pluralistically and more informatively.

A suggested solution is to construct classes based on "case studies." We care about development, the environment, the financial crisis, labor rights, and other issues. These problems are global in nature and global in consequences, requiring fundamental new approaches in analysis, understanding, and teaching. As students, we do not expect an elixir; and even if we did, we don't expect professors – traditional or political economists – to have the answers. We want to dive into these issues with all their problems and implications. We want to think differently. We want to grab an idea, turn it upside down, twist it, and see something new.

In a course on environmental economics, for example, rather than a traditional professor pontificating, "This is the proper and only lens through which to view the environment," we would leave it more open. Instead of only giving answers, we would ask questions – "How should we value and use our resources?" and "What are the different methods of treating externalities?"

Philosophy, political science, law, and the sciences could be juxtaposed to foment a lively discussion. These disciplines can provide critical perspectives – if engaged on an equal footing.

Unfortunately, the benefits of a case studies approach might be lost on upper-division students with no prior introduction to or knowledge of alternative theories. Thus, it is important to adopt a pluralist perspective from the start. Learning in this way does not produce a class of radicals or Marxists. Students should be taught that traditional economics provides an incomplete grasp of a whole arc of economic possibilities. Rather than being handed a finished theoretical product, students should be enabled to question all of the assumptions of orthodoxy. Introductory courses should juxtapose alternative theories to offer a vivid comparison of the strengths and weaknesses of each.

In a sea of economic chaos, where do we cast the net? People give and take, buy and sell, share, hoard, and steal. Laws exist but are not always followed, borders are constructed but not always respected; a world of economic activity flows outside of our textbooks, each with its own story. While the global economy continues to expand, our definition of what is "economics" remains anchored to orthodoxy. Sure, we can drown in our pluralism, but to solve the pressing problems of our time we need to reframe the way we think and do economics. A more inclusive definition of economics is in order. A plural world needs a plural economics.

While traditional economics education has been incredibly efficient at mass-producing economists, the future calls for a more dynamic economics education. A new breed of economist is on the horizon. Students today are throwing off the shackles of orthodoxy in search of a broader, more worldly economics. The future of the dismal science remains unclear, but there are many reasons to be optimistic.

An unfinished story lies before us – what will the next chapter bring? There is no doubt that many contemporary crises – social, political, and environmental – will be catalysts for change in the near future. Milton Friedman (1982: ix) famously said

> only a crisis – actual or perceived – produces real change. When that crisis occurs, however, actions will depend on available and accessible ideas. That, I believe, is our basic function: to develop alternatives to existing policies, to keep them alive and available until the politically impossible becomes politically inevitable.

His words were spoken with different intentions from ours, but there is (in the spirit of pluralism!) something we can learn from him.

Opportunity lies in the lap of our current problems. The time is ripe for new ideas to be developed, put forward, and taken seriously. The position of political economy at the margin may now be its most valuable asset; a view from the edge allows one to see different possibilities. With a renewed confidence, we can write new stories.

## References

Friedman, M. (1982) *Capitalism and Freedom*, Chicago: University of Chicago Press.
Witchger, Felipe, Mallin, Sean, Hoapt, Nicholas, and Dan, Nickolas (2008) "Economics at Notre Dame: An Open Letter," *Open Economics* ND, 14 April. http://openeconomics.blogspot.com/

# 4 Why economics needs pluralism

*Bernard Guerrien and Sophie Jallais*

Traditional economics is no doubt hegemonic and imperialistic, extending its reach to all aspects of social life – marriage, crime, education, art, health, history, geography – while at the same time impugning other social sciences for lacking a formalistic model. And while ostensibly convincing to the point of intimidation, the simplistic, hegemonic, and monist approach is highly misleading if one can peer through the veneer. Economic imperialism is the antithesis of pluralism and as such is inconsistent with the objectives of this book. If we want economics to be relevant (it must be!) and if we want our students to understand how the economy works, then economics needs other social sciences. Economics must become pluralist and not imperialistically monist. To understand how we must first understand why.

Traditional economics purports not to explain or understand reality, but rather to make it possible, via an appropriate set of assumptions, to demonstrate the compatibility of individual decisions, i.e. the mathematical existence of equilibrium. But traditional economics fails even at this fundamental objective. This chapter discusses individualist fallacies which reveal the need for other methodological foundations, especially a theory which accounts for institutions. Moreover, we show that traditional economic theory is often nothing more than a list of conditions for the existence of an equilibrium that could never be achieved *even if those conditions were all fulfilled*. Why look for such conditions, if this research does not help to make predictions or to prescribe economic policy? Don't we need economic theories that help to understand the economic world or to whisper in the ears of princes?

## A specious individualism

In his Nobel Lecture, Gary Becker (1992) argued that traditional economics assumes that individuals maximize utility as they conceive it, whether they are selfish, altruistic, loyal, spiteful, or masochistic; while at the same time actions are constrained by income, time, imperfect memory and calculating capacities, limited resources, and limited opportunities available in the economy. The individual is the point of departure – institutions and society come after. This typifies methodological individualism. Markets – explicit or implicit – are ubiquitous and the utility-maximizing rational individual is assumed to explain many phenomena. The simplest form of social organization (for example often given by traditional theorists in an exchange economy is individuals – consumers or households)[1] is represented by a preference relation (their tastes) and an endowment in goods and property rights. The only "institutional assumption" is that trades are voluntary.

If consumers' tastes or endowments differ, then the basis for mutually advantageous exchange exists. Self-interested individuals will bargain for the most favorable rate of exchange. Nothing more can be said about the outcome of their bargains. To set the scene, David Kreps asks his readers to

> imagine consumers wandering around a large market square with different kinds of food in their bags; when two of them meet, they examine what each has to offer, to see if they can arrange a mutually agreeable trade. To be precise, we might imagine that at every chance meeting of this sort, the two flip a coin and depending on the outcome, one is allowed to propose an exchange, which the other may either accept or reject. The rule is that you can't eat until you leave the market square, so consumers wait until they are satisfied with what they possess.
>
> (Kreps 1995: 196)

Even this very simple "market square" economy, however, must introduce simple rules such as "flip a coin" and "nobody can leave before the end of the process," which preexist individual choices – contrary to precepts of methodological individualism. Kreps admits, however, that the exploration of this economy – a rough sketch of what we call "market economies" – is "in relative infancy." We can be sure that it will never grow up.

In fact, central to the pedagogy of traditional economics is the imagining and conjuring of models with rules and simple institutions to avoid bilateral relations and indeterminate bargaining. Recognition that actual markets are comprised of institutions which evolve over time differentiates political economy from traditional economics, along with respectful learning from other social sciences. The annexation of institutions into traditional economics exemplifies its monist imperialism. Rather than study history, psychology, and other social sciences from a pluralist perspective to gain understanding of the relationship between individuals and institutions, institutions are recognized primarily for constricting the range of individual maximizing behavior (Vant 2005).[2] Traditional economics ignores how the exercise of power can enable economic actors to shape institutions to their benefit.

## Perfect competition

No better example of monist imperialism exists than perfect competition. Pedagogically, it is the ideal benchmark representing the frictionless market. Given numerous buyers and sellers, each too small to influence prices, it is assumed that all individuals, households, and firms within the world of perfect competition are price takers. Traditional economics assumes rationality, yet a rational student would ask who sets the price and why everyone is content to accept it. Why don't economic actors jostle to obtain the best price, which from their perspective is indeterminate beforehand. After all, isn't this how prices are determined in the real world? Perhaps, but not in the model of perfect competition. Here the market determines the price, and this is greatly preferable to its being set by government or institutions, since it is "democratically" set by opposing forces. But isn't the market composed of individuals and businesses? These questions, often asked by rational students, are parried by traditional economics with the simple but misleading dictum that the market sets the price. How can this be? Is the market a person? But isn't the market comprised of persons?

An honest yet self-defeating attempt to avoid circular reasoning assumes that all agents "take" prices and that "someone" sets prices, either a secrétaire du marché (Walras), a market or fictitious agent (Arrow and Debreu), or an auctioneer. The latter is highly misleading since in real auctions, agents are "price makers" and not price takers. For our purposes we use the name "Center" to designate the "price setter" within the model of perfect competition. The appropriateness of this label will become clear.

Perfect competition assumes that the Center first adds agents' quantities at given prices, then compares them. The market not only sets prices, but it also adds! That's the height of absurdity. As prices are randomly "shouted," there is no rationale for assuming the equality of total supply and total demand. A new assumption therefore has to be added: the Center changes prices according to the interaction of supply and demand. Prices increase when total demand is greater than total supply and prices decrease when total supply is greater than demand. The Center continues the process until total demand equals total supply, when prices reach their "equilibrium value."

## About the law of supply and demand

Traditional textbooks do not discuss price adjustment in the general case; rather they restrict themselves to partial equilibrium, with supply and demand intersecting at equilibrium. This idea is so ingrained that we forget it is true only if agents are price takers with a Center who sets prices and adds quantities across individuals. Textbooks explain the importance of equilibrium as a resting point from a process of increasing or decreasing prices.[3] But, as game theorists argue, such a process is incompatible with competitive equilibrium, which presupposes price-taking agents (Bénicourt and Guerrien 2008). If trades are out of equilibrium, then equilibrium depends on the path taken to reach it. This "path dependency" underscores the indeterminacy that the extravagant assumptions of the perfect competition model try to avoid. Traditional economics is cognizant of path dependency (Coyle 2007) although it is conveniently forgotten when textbooks are written. Mathematical economists unsuccessfully tried to prove, half a century ago, that in the "pure" case – when price variations depend on differences between total supply and demand – prices converge (as fast as possible) to their equilibrium value. They reached the opposite conclusion: in general, processes following the "law of supply and demand" never stop (they are cyclical or chaotic). This disturbing result[4] is a consequence of the Sonnenschein–Mantel–Debreu theorem (Mas-Colell *et al.* 1995).

The preferred traditional model for pedagogy at the introductory level, the supply–demand cross diagram, is relevant only for centralized economies with the Center somehow miraculously setting equilibrium prices. In all other cases, equilibrium is path dependent and, consequently, indeterminate. Only ideology can explain the importance of this diagram – and, more generally, the model of perfect competition.

## Perfect competition and ideology

Perfect competition in traditional economics has nothing to do with the commonly held view of competition as a survival struggle between persons, ideas, and institutions. The model assumes that agents ignore each other, paying attention only to prices set by the Center. According to the assumptions of the model, they are not allowed to change prices or even trade with each other.[5] As it becomes "perfect," competition vanishes! But why is such a system with an obtrusive Center more efficient than a system where people spend time and energy finding and bargaining with partners, based on their predilection to truck, barter, and trade?

Even though

> virtually all economists recognize that the competitive model is not a perfect representation of actual economies ... most economists still use it as a convenient benchmark ... while the basic competitive model may not provide a *perfect* description of some markets, economists recognize that it may provide a good description – with its predictions matching actual outcomes well, though not perfectly. In fact most economists believe that the basic competitive model gives us tremendous insights into a wide range of economics issues, and for that reason, it is the foundation on which economists build.
>
> (Stiglitz and Walsh 2006: 27–28, italics in original)

Why? Ideology! Introductory textbooks discuss the assumptions of perfect competition without mentioning that the Center must set prices and add quantities across individuals. To abandon perfect competition is painful for ideological reasons but also for psychological ones. Without it, traditional economics is stripped of a "great model," and theory is reduced to models whose "results" are very sensitive to the (arbitrary) choice by the modeler of their parameters.

## About imperfect competition

Only one assumption separates the models of imperfect competition and perfect competition: in the former, economic firms are not price takers. But to avoid the indetermination of the bargaining outcome, centralization is still assumed.[6] With at least one price maker, however, the existence of equilibrium is impugned. Models of imperfect competition are therefore restricted to partial equilibrium. The demand function is given and price maker firms are supposed to know it. Each firm must then anticipate the other firms' choices and make conjectures about the reaction of the rest of the economy to its own choices. Different assumptions of firms' beliefs about "the rules of the game" generate different models. For example, in the Cournot, Stackelberg, and Bowley models firms do not set prices; they decide how much to produce, with the Center determining the price equalizing total supply and total demand. On the other hand, in the Bertrand model as well as the monopolistic competition models, firms set prices.

What is the purpose of such models? Let's examine the most popular model of imperfect competition: the Cournot duopoly. Here, firms compute their reaction curves, given their conjectures about competitors' reactions. Since one doesn't know the other's choice, the probability of reaching equilibrium quantities is practically nil. Equilibrium thus is not a prediction of the theory. The situation is even more striking with the Bertrand model, where the only prediction is that firms never propose the equilibrium price. The reason is obvious: at equilibrium price, profit equals average cost.[7] A rational firm will propose a price greater than equilibrium in order to earn a positive profit. If a price is randomly chosen so that the firm proposing the lowest price gets a positive profit, and the other a zero profit (as in equilibrium), the firms' expected profits are positive. However, this is not equilibrium.

To justify equilibrium as a prediction of the theory, orthodoxy suggests a "resting point" of a sequence of decisions. For example, in the Cournot model, Firm A makes a random offer; and Firm B, after observing this offer, determines an offer from its own reaction curve. Firm A reacts to this offer with a new offer, and so on, until equilibrium is reached. But, as in the "tâtonnement" case, firms' behavior is inconsistent since they do not incorporate information of the process itself (Bénicourt and Guerrien 2008). If they do, and change conjectures about the other's reaction, reaction curves – and hence equilibrium – will move. Equilibrium is then path dependent and cannot be determined from the model's parameters.[8] D. Carlton, after surveying industrial economists' knowledge about market clearing, wrote, "the evidence on price behavior is sufficiently inconsistent with the simple theories of market clearing that industrial economists should be led to explore other paradigms" (Carlton 1989: 943). Indeed, Carlton typically uses game theoretic models, which, however, are quite similar to models of imperfect competition. But what can we expect from game theory?

## About game theory

Unlike perfect competition, game theory does not have a basic model. It is often introduced through stories – the Prisoners' Dilemma, the battle of the sexes, the ultimatum or the "chicken" game – that have some relation to real-life problems, while also, being presented as branch of mathematics. Its prestige derives from its mathematical origin and its associated rigor. Assumptions about players' information and strategies (choices that they are allowed to make) and rules of the game (institutions and payoffs) must be defined in detailed.[9]

Game theorists are circumspect about solutions. They prefer the term "concepts of solutions" – that is, conditions that players' choices must accommodate – and this which in turn reflects what the modeler expects to find. A less restrictive concept of solution than rationality is "rationalizability," where players are rational, believe that everyone is rational, believe that everyone believes that everyone is rational, etc.[10]

If a game has a unique rationalizable outcome, it can be considered a prediction of the theory. One reason for the popularity of the Prisoners' Dilemma is that both players have a dominant strategy, so that the profile of strategies is the unique "solution" compatible with rationalizability. It may be a good prediction about players' choices, but the crux of the "dilemma" is that it is not efficient (Pareto optimal): the dilemma becomes more acute as the game is repeated.[11] Unique solutions are the exception rather than the rule for games with rationalizability. In general, when dominated strategies are eliminated, many issues remain. Assuming players are rational, and that rationality is common knowledge, does not restrict the set of solutions of a game, except in very special cases. A more restrictive concept of solution, the Nash equilibrium, occurs when each rational player correctly anticipates other players' choices – an ad hoc condition. When a solution is obvious for every player – as in the Prisoners' Dilemma – it is a Nash equilibrium. But the reciprocal is not true: in general, a Nash equilibrium is not an obvious solution (prediction) of a model. In fact, the Nash equilibrium is considered a stable social convention which "emerges" from habits or as a "focal point" that is "culturally determined" (Mas-Colell *et al.* 1995: 248–249). The Nash equilibrium is therefore a pluralistic concept!

According to David Kreps,

> in the great majority of the applications of non-cooperative game theory to economics, the mode of analysis is equilibrium analysis. And in many of those analyses, the analyst identifies a Nash equilibrium (and sometimes more than one) and proclaims it as "the solution." I wish to stress that this practice is sloppy at best, and probably a good deal worse.[12]
>
> (Kreps 1995: 405)

Game theory does not resolve concrete problems or make predictions about player choices. It focuses on the complexity of the decision interactions of persons conscious of being in interaction. As the renowned game theorist Ariel Rubinstein explains,

> game theory is a fascinating and abstract discussion that is closer to philosophy than to the economics pages of the newspaper. It has no direct applications, and if it has any "practical utility" (which I doubt), then it is in the winding and inscrutable way that our minds absorb ideas and use them when the time comes for real action. And this too must be proved.[13]
>
> (Rubinstein 2000)

## About asymmetry of information

Beginning in the 1990s, the idea of asymmetric information became fashionable among microeconomists. Its popularity increased after Ackerlof, Selten, and Stiglitz won the Nobel Prize in 2001. Asymmetric information typifies "discoveries" by traditional economists of something obvious to others – to anyone who has ever traded or signed a contract on the basis of unequal or incomplete information about the other. Insurance companies, banks, employers, and governments are aware of problems inherent in asymmetry of information, "moral hazard," and "adverse selection."[14] What, then, is the contribution of today's orthodox microeconomists, especially the Nobel Prize winners? They have mathematically proved that asymmetry of information is a source of inefficiency – sometimes preventing the attainment of equilibrium. But so what? Mathematics is not needed for this proof; common sense is sufficient.

Stiglitz insists that incorporating asymmetric information changes the general theoretical analysis as well as policy recommendations. But this can be accomplished through words: one doesn't need to read Stiglitz's academic papers, full of mathematics, to understand his argument. In fact, the more striking aspect of asymmetric information models is their *normative* flavor. Typically, there is a "principal" and an "agent," the former trying to implement a "mechanism design" so that the latter's choices are efficient (that is, Pareto optimal). Nothing new under the sun here. Insurance companies have implemented various inducements to limit "opportunist behavior" by their employees or their customers. Mathematical models of "mechanism designs" are of little help, for many reasons. First, beliefs about the others' characteristics (for example, risk aversion) and behavior play an important role in the models. They take the form, however, of ad hoc probability distributions, difficult to understand (especially for workers and managers whose behavior they are supposed to describe!). Second, they have a logical flaw: institutions are necessary to enforce contracts.[15] Agents can corrupt guardians watching their behavior; thus, guardians are needed to watch over guardians; but as they, too, can be corrupted, somebody must watch over them and so on. A lot of energy is devoted to finding solutions to this problem. Third, the relation between principal and agent is *bilateral*, and not with the market; thus, it cannot avoid the (eternal) problem of sharing the gains of trade.

## The fallacy of reservation prices

A principal and agent will contract voluntarily if this is mutually advantageous. If so, there is a gain from trade, and each tries to get the bigger part of the cake – or all the cake, if possible! Now, the size of the cake – the total gain from trade – depends on the contract between them. A contract is inefficient if another contract exists in which principal and agent can earn more. Agents in the traditional model are interested not in the size of the cake, but only in their personal gains. The principal (or the agent) prefers an inefficient contract to an efficient one, if she earns more with the former than with the latter.

Traditional economists are irresistibly attracted by efficient outcomes, probably because of their conviction that "markets" eliminate inefficient outcomes. It is a question of faith.[16] Some economists, however, advocate efficient outcomes for normative reasons. With an infinite number of efficient outcomes, the problem is choosing among them. One possibility is that principal and agent agree to divide the total gains from trade equally. This is dismissed by traditional economists as ad hoc. They prefer competition to eliminate indetermination. With a contract between the firm and its employees, competition from other workers decreases the wage until the reservation wage is attained. All gains from trade then accrue to the firm; and thanks to competition, there is one determined solution or prediction.

Practically all microeconomics textbooks (advanced or not) assume that "competition" pushes the principal or agent to its reservation wage.[17] But this "solution" is nonsensical: there is no reason to trade if you do not earn more than if you refuse to do so. A rational person agrees to work for a firm if she can obtain at least the same satisfaction without working. When traditional economists are asked, they typically respond, "Well, it is reasonable to suppose that the principal gives a 'little part' of the total gain to the agent, so that he accepts to work for him." Behind this "commonsense" assertion there is a fallacy, as the "little part" is undefined. Principal and agent will bargain and nothing is resolved.

David Kreps argues that a solution consisting of the principal "sweetening the contract just a bit, so the agent isn't indifferent" to it is not valid because "there is no optimal amount of sweetness" (Kreps 1995: 599). He concludes:

> The only way we get equilibrium is to assume that ties are broken in a fashion that favors the principal. This is a "problem" with the style of analysis we use that you should learn to live with, because it is pervasive in the literature.
>
> (1995: 599)

Why must we learn to live with a problem which does not have a satisfactory solution, even if it is pervasive in the literature? We can only conclude that "literature" – i.e. theory – is a dead-end.

## Conclusion

Traditional economics assumes fictitious agents making decisions in fictitious worlds. Special attention is paid to equilibrium, even though it is not a prediction of the theory. Rationality is not an adequate basis for correct expectations. Irrelevant or non-realistic assumptions – i.e. markets represented by a centralized system – do not lead to predictions that can be tested. The "as if" argument, often advanced as justification for more questionable axioms, leads us nowhere.

The raison d'être of these fictitious entities is not to describe or explain reality; it is to demonstrate the mathematical existence of equilibrium. Unfortunately, as this chapter has demonstrated, equilibrium cannot be interpreted as a prediction of the model. Traditional economics is neither predictive nor prescriptive. In order to understand our world, economics needs other theories.

To understand something about our world, we have to jettison methodological individualism. A starting point is John Stuart Mill's "states of society,"[18] and observation of how they resolve questions of production, trade, and distribution. Economists' specific task is to examine the consequences of agents' desire for wealth in different contexts and institutional arrangements. They can even try to explain why individuals' decisions tend to reproduce the state of society during long historical periods. Help from other social sciences such as history, sociology, and psychology is essential.

Since decisions are often made on the basis of elementary calculations, it is not relevant to use complicated mathematics to explain – or predict –actual choices. Moreover, in a world where uncertainty is very important, habits and routines may be a reasonable way of acting. In spite of appearances, traditional economics has little to suggest about real-life economic problems. Better help is generally obtained using introspection, observation of facts, and common sense. Only a pluralistic approach can improve our knowledge on economic relations, which cannot be isolated from the social network in which they are embedded.

## Notes

1 The fact that traditional theoreticians feel the need to speak of households – a holistic concept – underscores the limits of methodological individualism.
2 This differentiates the "old" or "classical" institutionalism of Veblen and Commons from the New Institutionalism.
3 For example, Mankiw writes in his *Principles of Economics*: "Suppose that price is higher than equilibrium price.... Sellers will try to increase their sales by lowering the price of the good. Prices lower until equilibrium price is reached" (2007: 75).
4 For more details, see Kirman (1989) and www.sss.ias.edu/publications/papers/econ-paper73.pdf.
5 When equilibrium prices are found, the model assumes a "clearing house" (Walras's *maison de compensation*) where everyone delivers their goods supplied and leaves with their goods demanded. Costly, long, and indeterminate search for trading partners is then avoided.
6 Bargaining can happen with a monopolist seller and a monopsonist buyer, with an indeterminate outcome.

7 Bertrand assumes, as does Cournot, constant average cost and that each firm can satisfy market demand when price equals average cost. If a firm's production capacity is limited, or if average cost increases with quantity, then equilibrium does not exist, as Edgeworth proved a long time ago.
8 Path dependency occurs when rational agents observe what happens during the process and consequently change their beliefs.
9 See, for example, www.autisme-economie.org/article106.html?lang=en.
10 A less restrictive concept of solution is "*nth* order rationality": the chain of beliefs stops at the *nth* step. Game theorists usually suppose that *n* is infinite. They say then that rationality is "common knowledge."
11 Repeated Prisoners' Dilemma and Rosenthal's centipede game (Kreps 1990) give striking examples that rational behavior does not lead to collective rational issues.
12 Kreps admits in a footnote that he, too, adopts sloppy practice: without Nash equilibria as benchmarks, developments full of mathematics about games solutions are no more justified.
13 For more details, see http://arielrubinstein.tau.ac.il/articles/PDE.html.
14 Moral hazard for an insurance company lies in the possibility that people are less cautious once they are insured. Adverse selection reflects the tendency that the people more exposed to a risk are more likely to insure themselves against it than people less exposed to it.
15 The 2007 Nobel Prize was awarded to Leonid Hurwicz, David Maskin, and Roger Myerson for their work on mechanism designs. See the Hurwicz Nobel Lecture, "Who Will Guard the Guardians?," www.econ.umn.edu/working papers/hurwicz_guardians.pdf; and the Myerson Nobel Lecture, http://home.uchicago.edu/~rmyerson/research/hurwicz.pdf.
16 Pertaining to the contract curve in the Edgeworth diagram, rational individuals will agree at some point because there are no more mutually advantageous opportunities.
17 In his *Microeconomic Theory* (1994), Varian considers the symmetric case, where competition pushes firms to their reservation price where profit equals zero. There is only one solution, where workers receive all the gain from trade.
18 Defined as

> a simultaneous state of all the greater social facts or phenomena, such as the degree of knowledge and intellectual and moral culture existing in the community, and on every class of it; the state of industry, of wealth and its distribution; the habitual occupations of the community; their division into classes, and the relation of those classes to one another; the common beliefs which they entertain on all the subjects most important to mankind; ... their form of government, and the more important of their laws and customs.
>
> (Mill 2008: book VI, chapter 10, §2)

# References

Becker, G. (1992) "The Economic Way of Looking at Behavior," http://nobelprize.org/nobel_prizes/economics/laureates/1992/becker-lecture.html. Accessed July 17, 2007.
Bénicourt, E. and Guerrien, B. (2008) "Is There Anything Worth Keeping in Microeconomics?," *Review of Radical Political Economics*, 40: 317–323.
Carlton, D. (1989) "The Theory and the Facts of How Markets Clear: Is Industrial Organization Valuable for Understanding Microeconomics?," in R. Schmalensee and R. Willig (eds) *Handbook of Industrial Organization.* Amsterdam: North Holland Press.
Coyle, D. (2007) *The Soulful Science: What Economists Really Do And Why It Matters. Princeton*, NJ: Princeton University Press.

Kirman, A. (1989) "The Intrinsic Limits of Modern Economic Theory: The Emperor Has No Clothes," *Economic Journal*, 99: 126–139.

Kreps, D. (1990) *Game Theory and Economic Modeling*. Cambridge, UK: Cambridge University Press.

—— (1995) *A Course in Microeconomic Theory*. Princeton, NJ: Princeton University Press.

Mankiw, G. (2007) *Principles of Economics*, 4th edn. New York: McGraw Hill.

Mas-Colell, A., Whinston, M., and Green, J. (1995) *Microeconomic Theory*. Oxford, UK: Oxford University Press.

Mill, J.S. (2008) *A System of Logic*. Online version, http://oll.libertyfund.org/index.php?option=com_staticxt&staticfile=show.php%3Ftitle=246&Itemid=2. Accessed July 1, 2008.

Rubinstein, Ariel (2000) "Garbage Disposal and the Nuclear Arms Race," http://arielrubinstein.tau.ac.il/articles/PDE.html. Accessed September 15, 2008.

Samuelson, P.A. and Nordhaus, W. (2007) *Economics*, 17th edn. New York: McGraw Hill.

Stiglitz, J. and Walsh, C. (2006) *Economics*, 4th edn. New York: Norton.

Vant, A. (2005) *Institutions and the Environment*. Cheltenham, UK: Edward Elgar.

Varian, H. (1994) *Microeconomic Theory*, 3rd edn. New York: Norton.

—— (2005) *Intermediate Microeconomics*, 7th edn. New York: Norton.

# 5 History of thought, methodology, and pluralism

*Sheila Dow*

A pluralist approach to teaching economics should address the peculiar challenge posed by the hegemony of traditional economics. An asymmetry exists between traditional economics and other economic approaches since the former presents itself as the sole arbiter of what is and is not economics. Rather than being pluralist (advocating a range of approaches), it has traditionally been monist (advocating only one general approach). Thus, while other disciplines within economics are pluralist in that they acknowledge the traditional approach and their relation to it, traditional economics recognizes no such need.

What is often misunderstood about pluralism is that while, on the one hand, it means accepting that other approaches may be legitimate on their own terms, it is perfectly compatible with arguing against these terms. That is, an important distinction exists between arguing that one's own approach is preferable to others in terms of one's own criteria, knowing that no one approach can lay claim to truth (pluralism), and arguing against alternatives because they are thought to be demonstrably wrong (monism). But given that monism in effect purports to define the discipline, there is an important difference between arguing, as a pluralist, that another approach is not (by one's own terms) good economics, and arguing, as a monist, that another approach (by one's own terms) is not even economics.

Since many students are exposed to the monist approach of traditional economics, the initial hurdle is for them to recognize that other approaches are also economics. The second hurdle, which logically follows, is to recognize that any argument in economics is contestable, and contestable on a range of grounds. Thus, students themselves may reasonably have differences of opinion with what they read and with what they are taught. Once these pedagogical hurdles are overcome, the field is open for a much wider and richer discourse.

The purpose of this chapter is to explore how teaching the history of thought and methodology can help students overcome these hurdles, thus enabling them to form a richer discourse. It will be argued that history and methodology are usefully taught as specialist subjects specifically to address the hurdles posed by the traditional mindset which many students inherit. However, once these hurdles are overcome, history of thought and methodology are most effective when integrated into the teaching of the content of economic theory. We begin with methodology, to clarify what is meant by pluralism.

## The methodology of economics

Like most terminology, the word "methodology" depends on the approach to knowledge we employ. Again, the most important distinction is between the monist and pluralist approaches. The traditional approach assumes that the method of economics is mathematical (Allen 2000), combining analyses from deductive logic with axioms of rational individual behavior. The advantage of this method is that arguments are equally commensurate for easy comparison and checking of logic and that the conclusions of the analysis can be tested empirically against the facts. This is the methodology of logical positivism (Caldwell 1982). Methodology, then, is only concerned with the particular mathematical techniques used in theory and in econometric testing: a purely technical subject.

Nevertheless, this method poses wider methodological questions, and particularly as applied economics gains vis-à-vis pure, deductivist economics. As Diane Coyle boasts, traditional economics "is more empirical than ever, drawing on much wider ranges of evidence than in the past (surveys, experiments etc.), facilitated by cheap computer power while moving away from explicit ... optimizing models" (Coyle 2007: 240). Indeed, "traditional economists are even challenging rationality axioms, as in experimental economics' (Coyle 2007: 124–125).

Traditional economics is departing in important ways from the principles of logical positivism, but without establishing alternative methodological principles. What we are seeing, therefore, as discussed in Chapter 1 of this volume, is what some identify as growing pluralism within mainstream economics (Vromen 2007, Davis 2008), but without methodological discussion (Dow 2007).

Once we open up the question of how best "to do" economics, then we enter the field of methodology proper, venturing beyond questions of technique to questions of philosophy of knowledge, i.e. epistemology: given the subject matter of the economy, what is the best way to construct knowledge? The role of mathematical formalism is opened up for scrutiny, but so are many other aspects of knowledge often taken for granted, such as the very essence of "facts." Thus, there is scope for understanding the nature of the economy differently, and analyzing it in terms of different theories. What might be a fact to one individual may be questionable to another. For example, a new classical economist assumes all unemployment voluntary, since all agents are rational, while a Keynesian economist assumes unemployment is generally involuntary. If mathematical argument is open to question (as the sole vehicle for argument) and if we do not have an uncontested set of facts independent of theory, then serious methodological questions are posed as to how we do economics.

The more we explore methodological questions, the more important becomes the scope for variety, or plurality. Plurality may indeed be inevitable. If there is no one shared understanding of the nature of reality (ontology), never mind how best to build knowledge about it, then inevitably there is going to be variety of opinion. Pluralism goes further in arguing that this variety is to be welcomed and supported. In order to explore why, we need to clarify some basic issues of pluralism.

Pluralism applies at a range of levels, which are sometimes confused in the literature.[1] These levels are: understanding of reality (ontology), theory of knowledge (epistemology), approach to the practice of economics (methodology), and theory. At the ontological level, a distinction is drawn between understanding the economy as an open or closed system. If the latter, then behavior is law-like and at least in principle it is possible to identify these laws. This is the presumption of traditional economics, which seeks confirmation for theory in empirical evidence of event regularities. Deviations from law-like behavior are assumed reactions to "shocks"; and since these events are assumed random – a strong knowledge presumption – these shocks are part of the closed system.

For many economists, the economy is understood to evolve, subject to forces which evolve; thus there is no intrinsic closure (Lawson 1997). As a reminder, it only takes one condition for closure not to be met for the system to be open (Chick and Dow 2005). If the economy is an open system (or even if it is a closed system, but our cognitive limitations preclude such knowledge) consequences exist for how we build knowledge. An open system evolves, and evolves in a variety of ways and in a variety of contexts (otherwise it would be possible to establish laws of evolution and we would be back to a closed system). Thus, with an open system we expect a variety of understandings of the nature of reality, and therefore a variety of approaches to building knowledge about it. Even if we all start with a general open-system understanding of reality, we very quickly develop different approaches to building knowledge about it. The general theory of knowledge therefore supports pluralism at the level of methodology. Once we move away from closed systems, there is no longer any demonstrably superior methodology.

Thomas Kuhn's (1970a, 1970b) concept of paradigm is useful here. Kuhn's study of the history of astronomy demonstrated that knowledge develops within communities which have shared understandings of reality, a shared approach to knowledge, and thus shared meanings of terms, techniques, and theories. Knowledge progresses, but only by the criteria of a particular paradigm. Purveyors of the paradigm argue for the relative merits of their approach to knowledge, and communicate it by teaching from textbooks full of exemplars; in this way, through persuasion, paradigms grow in strength. Debate may exist with other paradigms, and indeed knowledge may progress as a result of this interchange (again by the criteria of a particular paradigm). But there is no basis for authoritative adjudication between paradigms.

Knowledge builds within the dominant paradigm, parrying challenges to its understanding of reality and ignoring contrary evidence, until it becomes untenable. A revolutionary episode then installs an alternative paradigm, with its own understanding of reality, meaning of terms, techniques, and theories. But once again, no independent set of criteria exists to compare the two paradigms (because the subject matter is open and so cannot generate one best way of establishing truth). The paradigms are not directly comparable, although some scope for communication may exist. The paradigms are not completely incommensurate; nor are they completely commensurate.[2] Thus, it is best to allow a range of paradigms with a plurality of alternatives. As in biology, species survivability increases with an increase in plurality: given environmental change, the current strain declines and another more suited to the new environment will emerge.

Given a variety of opinion, a range of paradigms allows knowledge to develop in parallel according to different approaches. This range of paradigms is, however, bound to be limited. Knowledge progresses within communities. So if meanings differ between paradigms, than individualistic paradigms inevitably fail through communication failure. Pluralism is sometimes misunderstood as "anything goes" – a "pure" form of pluralism. But if indeed any economist could claim anything as fact and any theory tenable, that is the end of knowledge. Rather, in order to be workable, pluralism must be structured around a limited number of approaches (Dow 2004a). This is not a matter of signing up to manifestos, just a matter of practically functioning within the society of economics. Economists, in addition to choosing how to do economics, must decide which conferences to attend, which journals to subscribe to, etc., according to whose approach is closest to one's own and therefore where communication is likely to be most productive. Categories (as in paradigms) are a helpful shorthand, but the reality rarely involves strict boundaries. Indeed, many great economists are great because they creatively intermix ideas from more than one paradigm.

This is how pluralism is most commonly understood at the epistemological and methodological levels: accepting that an open-system subject matter can be understood in a variety of ways, and thus it is beneficial to have a range of approaches to building knowledge. This is toleration beyond the level of common academic courtesy and ethics, compelling though such considerations are (McCloskey 1994, Screpanti 1997). It follows from the nature of the subject matter that there is no universal best way of establishing knowledge, so that it is better to allow a range of flourishing approaches in order to have more reliable knowledge overall.

However, this is not a prescription for economists to follow more than one approach to knowledge. That way madness lies – it is incoherent to simultaneously sustain competing understandings of reality and meanings of terms. Any synthesizing of different approaches to knowledge, to be coherent, must be a new approach to knowledge (Groenewegen 2007).

Pluralism is often discussed at other levels, notably the levels of method and of theory. If pluralism is denied at the methodological level, a presumption exists that there is one best way of approaching knowledge. This best way might consist of a range of methods, yielding a range of theories, as in traditional economics. But a monist position at the methodological level presumes the subject matter yields laws to account for human behavior, which implies a mathematical method is sufficient, and in principle one theory should emerge to represent these laws. This thinking is implicit in traditional economics, implying one best model to represent reality. The growing plurality which some have identified in the methods and theories of traditional economics is incongruent with the underlying monist methodological approach – it doesn't make sense. Indeed some economists pursuing different methods and theories have the explicit goal of bringing them within the traditional deductivist framework.[3]

If a pluralist approach is taken to methodology, because of the nature of the subject matter, then pluralism in terms of methods and theories within one particular approach among the range which structured pluralism engenders makes sense. If the complexity of the subject matter supports a range of approaches, then it should not be surprising to find that these approaches do not rely on one particular method.

Keynes (1921) provides some guidance. When we aim to establish reasoned grounds for belief under uncertainty, we construct arguments from a range of evidence, conventional judgment, and intuition; in other words, we attach greater weight to an argument when supported by more relevant evidence. Thus if an argument is supported by a range of methods, i.e. conceptual, mathematical, historical, etc., and also by a range of types of evidence (data series, survey evidence, experimental evidence, discussions with experts, etc.), we attach high weight to it. Inevitably, with a range of methods, but more generally with an open-systems approach to knowledge, different theories will exist as partial contributions to knowledge. If there is no expectation of establishing knowledge about the economy in the form of one complete best model, then knowledge is constructed by a range of partial models and theories, explaining some aspect of reality. Furthermore, these models and theories are treated as provisional, recognizing that the evolution of the economy over time, and differences between economies over space, may require adaptations.

How do we compare and discuss different theories derived from different methods? If an advantage of the mathematical method is making all theories commensurate, then how do we handle the consequences of a plurality of methods and theories? Clearly there is some incommensurability, but is it absolute or a matter of degree? This question has particular significance when theoretical differences between traditional and political economics are considered. Is communication possible across methodological divides? Communication is hampered by such basic factors as differences in meaning attached to terms; not to mention monist mainstream logic excluding anything not fitting its methodological approach as not economics.[4] Clearly communication difficulties are of a different order than those between different pluralist approaches.

I believe, however, some communication is possible. The subject matter is the same, and overlaps of meaning exist. Further, the unofficial discourse of orthodox economists differs from the monist official discourse (McCloskey 1983). Indeed much of the plurality of modern orthodoxy, however incongruent with its methodological approach, is an attempt to develop theory more reflective of reality. Further, as both Marshall and Keynes argued, vagueness of language beneficially allows communication where differences of meaning and understanding exist (Coates 1996, Davis 1999). Open systems thinking means an absence of watertight boundaries and therefore some scope for communication.

## History of economic thought

Studying the history of economic thought is an ideal way to understand pluralism. The first issue to address is methodological pluralism. If we accept that only one best approach to economics exists, then the history of thought is teleological; in other words, the one approach is gradually perfected as knowledge about law-like behavior approaches the truth. From that perspective, the only rationale for studying the history of thought is antiquarian, since everything of value is already embedded in modern economics. As Klaes (2003: 497) observes, "more than four decades ago, Paul Samuelson ... noted with contempt that it was those economists who were not sufficiently competent to follow the mathematical revolution of postwar economics who were seeking shelter in the history of economic thought."

However, if economic systems evolve over time, differences exist between economic systems in different parts of the world. Since historically different methods have been employed to develop different types of theories, a rich plurality exists in the history of thought which can yield a multitude of ideas for today. History of thought opens our eyes to a range of possibilities. And indeed, since monism is a relatively recent phenomenon in economics, dating from the mid-twentieth century (Morgan and Rutherford 1998), history of thought yields a rich harvest of plurality without necessarily considering the divide between traditional economics and political economy which monism has created and perpetuated. Indeed, pertaining to the academic courtesy argument for pluralism, studying the history of thought discourages any presumption that modern economics is inevitably superior; rather, it increases respect for the past along with greater modesty for the present.

Pedagogically, it is incumbent to get students over the hurdle of presuming that economic thought necessarily progresses, and that textbook accounts are as close to the truth as economists are able to achieve. Certainly traditional economics involves some attention to differences between theories, but the tenor of such discussion usually follows lines of right and wrong, truth and falsity.[5] The monism of traditional economics has the unfortunate side-effect of classifying differences – if recognized at all – as ideological (by implication separate from economics). History of thought, however, provides a less dualistic way of understanding theoretical and methodological differences.

In my experience, an effective method of enabling students to surmount the hurdle of history of thought from the traditional perspective (if that is all they know) is the following exercise. Invite them to choose a passage from any economics text which has attracted their attention (something they agree or disagree with, find particularly elegant, topical, etc.), then explain to the class why they chose it. Just inviting students to express an opinion about a text is an eye-opener for many. I usually do this about a week into lectures, by which time we have already started discussing a historical text – inevitably students find something attractive in the text. For those who choose contemporary texts, just expressing an opinion about them other than one identical to the author helps them understand that they don't have to take what is written at face value, and that there is scope for differing opinions about texts. Here, the class can play a vital role. My experience has been that, until this exercise, students generally don't know what to expect from the history of thought. But afterwards they engage with increasing enthusiasm, reporting how it enables a better understanding of the literature in their other courses.

Debate exists pertaining how to approach the history of thought (Weintraub 2002). Again the approach to knowledge is significant. If one accepts the argument that knowledge inevitably progresses, history of thought is an account of that progress. But different approaches exist. One is to study history in order to identify "wrong turnings," which can provide historical authority for alternative approaches to modern economics. Political economists have been criticized for using history of thought in this way. In particular, studying history of thought from the perspective of a modern agenda (of either progress or wrong turnings) distorts interpretation.

Another approach is that of the historian Quentin Skinner (1969, 1988), which explicitly recognizes that meaning is not independent of context and intention, so that deliberate effort is required to escape from modern preconceptions. This approach focuses on the context in which the texts were written and the intentions of the author, as well as the author's paradigm. This enables understanding of paradigmatic difference away from the heat of debate in modern economics.

For some methodologists there has been a movement so far away from the rule-setting stance of traditional methodology that all that is deemed possible is description of ideas and context. This movement, called science studies, extends beyond the boundaries of economics. It too, of course, cannot deny that the narrators of history must themselves have some paradigmatic stance. Since this is inevitable, it is necessary to honestly reveal to the reader what that stance is (Davis and Klaes 2003). The outcome is a range of narratives with no overriding narrative. But even Weintraub (1999) in presenting such an approach cannot avoid some overriding narrative.

And, in fact, much can be learned by approaching the history of thought with the purpose of illuminating particular methodological issues. Here we are concerned with issues surrounding pluralism, and history of thought can aid our understanding of pluralism. In particular, we can identify the origins of pluralism with the origins of modern economics, particularly in the Scottish Enlightenment. Both David Hume and Adam Smith understood the nature of the social world as too complex to allow human understanding of the underlying causal mechanisms (this was Hume's problem of induction). In particular, reason is not an adequate basis for knowledge in itself; knowledge must start with sentiment, belief, and experience before reason can draw out provisional principles which might be acceptable explanations. Knowledge ultimately is founded on (social) psychology: it requires motivation to build knowledge in the first place (to set the mind at rest), it requires aesthetic appeal, and needs to connect in some way to existing knowledge in order to persuade others to accept it.

Since knowledge is social (involving persuasion), there is no question of an individualistic pure pluralism rather than structured pluralism. The aim is to develop principles which accord with experience; but since that experience changes and differs across contexts, principles, and theories are only provisional. They represent an attempt to explain real causal mechanisms, while recognizing that no one set of principles can claim the truth. This is the pluralist approach to knowledge. Furthermore, it follows that different methods are employed, and that a range of theories may emerge, so it is also an approach involving pluralism at the level of method and theory.

Indeed it is hard to study history of economic thought without also considering methodology. If we are to understand the context and intentions of the author, we also need to understand both the author's methodological approach and the alternative approaches which the author addresses.

## Integrating history of thought and methodology into other teaching

In order to understand modern economics we need to understand how it evolved, both its historical underpinnings and its methodological approach. Ideally, history of thought and methodology should be integral to economics teaching. This too was a characteristic of the Scottish tradition (evident in Scottish universities until a few decades ago). If no best account of economic knowledge exists, then it is important to provide a flavor of the range of accounts, and to be able to discuss them, which in turn requires awareness of methodological difference with all that entails (difference of meaning, understanding of reality, etc.).

A natural way of communicating this is to focus on debate, which expresses differences in relation to some issue (preferably, as in the emergence of economics in the teaching of moral philosophy in the eighteenth century, some topical policy issue with which students can engage). Indeed the virtue of teaching through controversies is one of the central themes of the Post-Autistic Economics movement.

It is important for students to understand how policy-making interacts with both academic theorizing and institutional design. Karl Niebyl (1946) provides an illuminating discussion of monetary policy. Drawing on history of thought and methodology material, academic ideas become embedded in institutional design, which establishes constraints on monetary policy-making, based on ideas reflecting the power structure of the society. But real conditions may change so that existing ideas and institutions are no longer appropriate, causing problems which in turn require that they be reassessed and revised, and so the evolutionary cycle continues.

Thus, for example, Chick (1993) argues that attempting to control the quantity of money might have been reasonable in the early days of banking, when this policy first emerged, but not today. Nevertheless, the design of such institutions as the European Central Bank and the Monetary Policy Committee of the

Bank of England reflects this eighteenth-century view about monetary control and the independence of money and prices from real variables. Monetary policy for many central banks is now focused on inflation targets, which make sense only if central banks have the capacity to control inflation. We are now seeing the problems emerging from the inappropriateness of this framework; yet monetary policy, constrained by this framework, is having real effects, on output and employment.[6]

Policy-makers are more cognizant than academic economists of the difficulties of putting theory into practice. It is interesting that monetary policy-makers themselves are broaching the question of pluralism, with considerable discussion about the uncertainty of which model to use. An open-system reality requires an open system of knowledge to address uncertainty. The Bank of England (1999) has even made an explicit argument for pluralism, by which it means drawing on a range of models. It is most unusual for a central bank to publicly reflect on its approach to models, beyond the normal discussion of modeling itself.

This requires some methodological awareness in order to analyze their thinking, as well as historical awareness in order to understand how the current institutional environment came about. Historical awareness of the growing power of traditional economics also enables understanding of why, in spite of actual and professed espousal of pluralism in terms of theory and method, there is no corresponding pluralism at the methodological level (Downward and Mearman, 2008).

## Conclusion

Issues raised by teaching monetary policy provide just one example of how history of thought and methodology are integral to a pluralist pedagogy. The science studies approach to teaching economics offers a gamut of theories and approaches for students to choose among. All practicing economists must choose an approach and be able to defend that choice. But economics teaching also means enabling students to make that choice. Economics teachers inevitably have their own preferences for an approach to economics, and it is incumbent on them to be intellectually honest with students so they can understand the context and intentions of their teachers. But this requires an understanding of the methodological and historical concepts and issues involved, which means that there needs to be explicit discussion of the historical origins and methodological approaches of the different theories being taught. This should all the part and parcel of pluralist teaching.

## Notes

1 See Mearman (2008) for helpful clarification.
2 See Rossini *et al.* (1999) for further discussion.
3 See, for example, Kahneman (2003) and Hong and Stein (2007) regarding experimental economics.

4 Consider the following passage from Coyle:
> We in the profession count [Paul] Krugman as a bona fide economist. By contrast many of us spurn Galbraith because he wasn't a modeler ... so we modelers can read *The Affluent Society* and even agree with it, without finding it persuasive ... economics isn't defined by its subject matter but by its way of thinking.
>
> (2007: 231–232)

5 The rhetoric literature discusses how this is achieved; see for example Klamer (1995).
6 See Chick (2008) for an application of her historical approach to theorizing about banking and monetary policy in the current environment.

# References

Allen, B. (2000) "The Future of Microeconomic Theory," *Journal of Economic Perspectives* 14: 143–150.
Bank of England (1999) *Economic Models at the Bank of England*. London: Bank of England.
Caldwell, B.J. (1982) *Beyond Positivism: Economic Methodology in the Twentieth Century*. London: Allen & Unwin.
Chick, V. (1993) "The Evolution of the Banking System and the Theory of Monetary Policy," in S. Frowen (ed.), *Monetary Theory and Monetary Policy: New Tracks for the 1990s*. London: Macmillan.
——. (2008) "Could the Crisis at Northern Rock Have Been Predicted? An Evolutionary Approach," *Contributions to Political Economy* 27: 115–124.
Chick, V. and Dow, S.C. (2005) "The Meaning of Open Systems," *Journal of Economic Methodology* 12: 363–381.
Coates, J. (1996) *The Claims of Common Sense: Moore, Wittgenstein, Keynes and the Social Sciences*. Cambridge, UK: Cambridge University Press.
Coyle, D. (2007) *The Soulful Science: What Economists Really Do And Why It Matters*. Princeton, NJ: Princeton University Press.
Davis, J.B. (1999) "Common Sense: A Middle Way Between Formalism and Post-Structuralism?," *Cambridge Journal of Economics* 23: 503–515.
——. (2008) "Heterodox Economics, the Fragmentation of the Mainstream, and Embedded Individual Analysis," in J.T. Harvey and R.F. Garnett (eds), *Future Directions for Heterodox Economics*. Ann Arbor: University of Michigan Press.
Davis, J.B. and Klaes, M. (2003) "Reflexivity: Curse or Cure?," *Journal of Economic Methodology* 10: 329–352.
Dow, S.C. (2004a) "Structured Pluralism," *Journal of Economic Methodology* 11: 275–290.
——. (2004b) "Uncertainty and Monetary Policy," *Oxford Economic Papers* 56: 539–561.
——. (2007) "Variety of Methodological Approaches in Economics," *Journal of Economic Surveys* 21: 447–419.
Downward, P. and Mearman, A. (2008) "Decision-Making at the Bank of England: A Critical Appraisal," *Oxford Economic Papers* 60: 385–409.
Fullbrook, E. (ed.) (2003) *The Crisis in Economics: The Post-Autistic Economics Movement: The First 600 Days*. London: Routledge.
Groenewegen, J. (ed.) (2007) *Teaching Pluralism in Economics*. Cheltenham, UK: Edward Elgar.

Hong, H. and Stein, J.C. (2007) "Disagreement and the Stock Market," *Journal of Economic Perspectives* 21: 109–128.
Kahneman, D. (2003) "Maps of Bounded Rationality: Psychology for Behavioral Economics," *American Economic Review* 93: 1449–1475.
Keynes, J.M. ([1921] 1973) *A Treatise on Probability. Collected Writings, Volume VIII*. London: Macmillan for the Royal Economic Society.
Klaes, M. (2003) "Historiography," in W. S. Samuels, Jeff, E. Biddle, and John B. Davis (eds), *A Companion to the History of Economic Thought*. Oxford: Blackwell.
Klamer, A. (1995) "The Conception of Modernism in Economics: Samuelson, Keynes and Harrod," in S.C. Dow and J. Hillard (eds), *Keynes, Knowledge and Uncertainty*. Cheltenham, UK: Edward Elgar.
Kuhn, T.S. (1970a) *The Structure of Scientific Revolutions*, 2nd edn. Chicago: University of Chicago.
——. (1970b) "Reflections on My Critics," in I. Lakatos and A. Musgrave (eds), *Criticism and the Growth of Knowledge*, Cambridge, UK: Cambridge University Press.
Lawson, T. (1997) *Economics and Reality*. London: Routledge.
McCloskey, D.N. (1983) "The Rhetoric of Economics," *Journal of Economic Literature* 21: 434–461.
——. (1994) *Knowledge and Persuasion in Economics*. Cambridge: Cambridge University.
Mearman, A. (2008) "Pluralism and Heterodoxy: Introduction to the Special Issue," *Journal of Philosophical Economics* 1: 5–25.
Morgan, M.S. and Rutherford, M. (eds) (1998) "From Interwar Pluralism to Postwar Neoclassicism," *History of Political Economy* (Annual Supplement) 30.
Niebyl, K. (1946) *Studies in the Classical Theories of Money*. New York: Columbia University Press.
Rossini, R., Sandri, G., and Scazzieri, R. (eds) (1999) *Incommensurability and Translation*. Aldershot, UK: Elgar.
Screpanti, E. (1997) "Afterword," in A. Salanti and E. Screpanti (eds), *Pluralism in Economics*. Cheltenham, UK: Edward Elgar.
Skinner, Q. (1969) "Meaning and Understanding in the History of Ideas," *History an Theory* 8: 3–53.
——. (1988) "A Reply to My Critics," in James Tully (ed.), *Meaning and Context; Quentin Skinner and His Critics*. Oxford: Oxford University Press.
Smith, Adam ([1795] 1980) "The History of Astronomy," in W.L.D Wightman (ed.), *Essays on Philosophical Subjects*. Oxford: Oxford University Press.
Vromen, J. (2007) "In Praise of Moderate Plurality," in J. Groenewegen (ed.), *Teaching Pluralism in Economics*, Northampton, Mass.: Edward Elgar.
Weintraub, E.R. (1999) "How Should We Write the History of Twentieth-Century Economics?," *Oxford Review of Economic Policy* 15: 139–152.
——. (2002) "Will Economics Ever Have a Past Again?," *History of Political Economy* Annual Supplement 34: 1–14.

# Part II
# Reclaiming the principles course

# 6 The principles course

*Julie A. Nelson*

Economists of many stripes are dissatisfied with the usual content and pedagogy of principles courses. Many traditional economists complain about the cut-and-dried, uninspiring, outdated, and/or increasingly one-sided neoliberal approach characteristic of much introductory teaching. Developments in game theory and behavioral economics, as well as policy controversies, are neglected in most introductory textbooks. Economists more skeptical about the value of traditional economics are of course are even more frustrated. Institutional, radical, feminist, ecological, socio-economic, Austrian, post-Keynesian, green, and critical realist economists, as well as instructors who want to draw from a number of schools and/or interdisciplinary insights, find the standard curriculum stifling. Whatever extension and/or alternative to traditional economics an instructor favors, at best most standard textbooks mention it in an easily skipped feature box or footnote, if at all.

This chapter critically examines challenges faced by the instructor in teaching a principles course that embraces alternative approaches, as well as possible responses to these challenges. The chapter concludes with a guide to materials including textbooks of an alternative or hybrid nature, materials that can be used to supplement a standard textbook, and background readings for instructor use.

## Standard course(s)

In standard principles of economics courses, students are expected to master a narrow set of concepts without raising any questions about the history, limitations, or ethical implications of what they learn. Whether in microeconomics or macroeconomics, or a combined course, they are indoctrinated into a narrow view about what is economics. In microeconomics, students are taught that economics is about scarcity, choice, and markets. They spend long hours learning "how economists think," which is equated with learning how to manipulate the static, individualistic models of traditional economics. They learn that rational actors make decisions by comparing marginal-this to marginal-that; that the central problem for producers is deciding how many widgets to make under conditions of decreasing returns; that perfectly competitive and efficient markets form a relevant default scenario; that non-market phenomena such as unpaid labor and environmental degradation are not part of the core subject matter of economics; and that government "interferes" in economic life instead of being a necessary part of it.

In macroeconomics, students are taught that economics is about Gross Domestic Product, unemployment, and inflation. Increasingly, macro textbooks downplay Keynesian business cycle concerns, focusing instead on classical microfoundations, simplistic models of GDP growth, the (purported) benefits of free trade, small governments, and conservative monetary policies. Market equilibrium and full employment are taken as the (long-run) default scenario. New Keynesian models of market "imperfections" may be presented as justification for a limited range of short-run activist government policies.

The basic question asked in the standard course is, "How can we explain issue X in terms of our given set of (traditional) methodological tools?" – not "How can we best explain the economic world we live in?" Introductory economics courses are still predominantly taught in a chalk-and-talk format with emphasis on abstract logical concepts. Standard courses do not capture students' interest, do not encourage them to develop their critical thinking skills, and do not equip them to understand real-world economic developments.

## Considerations in the principles course

Instructors who want to improve their principles courses, however, face challenges. For one thing, it is rare that an instructor can choose to start with a blank slate. Some are told by their department exactly what their course should cover, and perhaps even what textbook they should use. Many, even with more choice, feel obligated to prepare students for later intermediate courses that will be taught from the traditional perspective – even though relatively few principles students go on to study more economics. Other instructors feel it is incumbent to teach the traditional approach (even if not only that approach) because it is the lingua franca of contemporary economic discussions. Even though the instructor may feel that one or more alternative paradigms is vastly preferable to the traditional one, he or she will probably still need to present some aspects of orthodox microeconomics and new classical and new Keynesian macroeconomics. Many hope that with time this situation will change; but this is the situation currently facing most instructors.

Another issue is that instructors of principles classes – in contrast to more advanced classes discussed later in this book – have to pay special attention to the more limited level of cognitive development and more diverse interests of their students. If the students fall largely in the young adult age range typical for early university studies, it cannot be assumed that they are ready for sophisticated readings and high-level critical thinking. Some students will enter the course as concrete learners, wanting "just the facts" about the economy. Some will be mastering abstract logic and reason – a learning stage congruent with the simplistic mathematical modeling of the standard curriculum. For many students, however, one course may be all they take in economics. Even among economics majors, many may be pre-MBA students with little interest in social science, much less in intellectual history. While the instructor of a more advanced class may have more freedom in course design, the principles teacher is more constrained both in the content that can be incorporated and in the level of resource materials.

## Three main approaches

The instructor who wants to go beyond standard orthodox teaching, then, has to carefully consider curriculum demands and student receptivity. In general, the alternative principles courses tried over the years can be classified into three main approaches:

1   Single alternative: economic principles are presented from the point of view of a single heterodox school.
2   Competing paradigms: orthodox and one or more heterodox approaches are explicitly compared and contrasted, within the context of a discussion of philosophies and the history of economic thought.
3   Broader questions and bigger toolbox: economics is defined so as to encompass a broad set of concerns, and methods of analysis are drawn from many schools.

The single alternative approach – e.g. teaching an "institutionalist principles of economics" or "principles of political economy" class while skipping the usual orthodoxy – might be most appealing for an instructor who strongly identifies with a particular heterodox school. But the compelling need discussed earlier to include traditional materials means this luxury is rarely afforded. While political economy materials designed for introductory classrooms exist (e.g. Hahnel 2002; Bober 2001; Bowles *et al.* 2005), institutions that offer a distinctly heterodox introductory course generally treat it as a supplement to, rather than as a replacement for, a more orthodox introductory course.

The competing paradigms approach has been adopted more widely in recent decades, and as a result, a number of helpful resources exist. One common way of constructing such a course is to adopt a standard textbook and supplement it with either a set of instructor-selected readings or a published volume of readings that reflect views from one or more non-traditional paradigms.[1] Another suggestion is to adopt a textbook explicitly built on a competing paradigms framework, such as Riddell *et al.* (2008), with or without further supplements. A third approach is to teach from a largely standard textbook but encourage discussion from the viewpoints of competing paradigms (Colander 2008).

Certainly, the competing paradigms approach has been used successfully at many colleges and universities, and it has been recommended by a number of writers (e.g. Knoedler and Underwood 2003; Mearman 2007). But a competing paradigms approach may not be ideal for a particular instructor's situation, for a number of reasons. Some principles students, given their likely interests and stage of cognitive development, may find the competing paradigms approach more frustrating than enlightening. If they are anxious to learn how contemporary economies work they might be turned off by an approach heavy on the history of economic thought or alternative modeling techniques. If the course is highly critical of traditional economics, it might foment student resistance as they ask, "Why do we have to learn this if it's all wrong!" Or students may adopt a disengaged, unhelpful "everybody has a right to their own opinion" attitude. The same students may, in a learning environment that develops their critical thinking skills over time, become more able to deal with diverse theories. But the beginning of a principles course, when economics is new and unfamiliar, may not be the right time to emphasize disputes in economic thought.

From the instructor's point of view, it is also problematic that existing readers and textbooks with a competing paradigms approach tend to focus on a narrow range of alternatives, which the user may or may not find adequate. A number of alternative principles materials were originally developed during the 1970s and 1980s, when the prevailing style was to argue that one's own particular heterodox paradigm (in most cases, radical or Marxian) was superior to – and should serve as the sole replacement of – orthodox economics.

In recent decades, movements towards a more pluralistic, mutually tolerant and open approach to teaching and research have gained ground – at least among political economists, if not from orthodoxy as well (e.g., Fullbrook, 2003; Garnett 2005; Groenewegen 2007). While some materials based on a competing paradigm approach have been expanded in recent decades to include other concerns (e.g., environmental or feminist), there remains a basic distinction between a paradigmatic framework that focuses on argumentation between (or among) different schools, and a pluralist one that, while not being uncritical or seeking a false unity, involves a less adversarial effort to examine reality from diverse perspectives. This may be as much a matter of tone, presentation, and ordering of topics as the specific course content. Is the student primarily being exposed to in-house professional debates or to real-world economic phenomena and ways in which such phenomena might be understood?

The broader questions and bigger toolbox approach is more congruent with a pluralist, rather than paradigmatic, approach to economic research and teaching, and may be more appropriate for the learning stage of the typical introductory economics student. Rather than beginning with a philosophical or history-of-thought introduction to various perspectives, such an approach starts with interesting and engaging questions, and then proceeds to draw from a variety of perspectives to help students think about the issues. The course, ideally, focuses primarily on preparing students for citizenship rather than for intermediate theory courses, while giving them a taste of lively, investigative social science processes.

The remainder of this chapter will describe some ways in which this can be done.[2] Taking a broader questions and bigger toolbox approach in the classroom may enrich teaching, whether or not particular print resources are used.

## Broader questions

A good way to reframe the principles course is to think of economics as defined by the concern of economic provisioning, or how societies organize themselves to sustain life and enhance its quality. Such a definition is much broader than definitions of economics that focus on individual rational decision-making, markets, or GDP growth. Such a definition, or one similar to it, will be familiar to many economists from institutionalist and socio-economic backgrounds, and is wide enough to encompass concerns from other perspectives as well.

Because it does not focus on individual rational choice, this approach can encompass social and economic institutions, real human psychology, and the actual unfolding of historical events. Because it is broader than a concern just with markets, it is inclusive of government and community activities, as well as the economic contribution of unpaid household labor. Because it points directly to questions of survival and the quality of life, it invites questions about whether current patterns of wealth and income distribution, consumerist attitudes, and the use and abuse of the natural environment serve valuable ends.

To operationalize this broader definition of economics, it helps to add a fourth economic activity to the usual list of three – production, distribution, and consumption. Call it resource maintenance and define it as "the management of natural, manufactured, human, and social resources in such a way that their productivity is sustained" (Goodwin *et al.* 2008). This gives priority concern to the social and environmental contexts of economic life that are too easily (and often) neglected in traditional economics. In addition, it is helpful to widen the domain of the traditional subject heading of distribution. While in a standard course distribution focuses mostly on market exchange, adding an explicit discussion of distribution such as one-way transfer opens up a wider set of issues, from the spoils of war, to the care of dependent children, to the effect of inherited wealth on the distribution of economic power.

Yet, because the broader definition of economics in terms of survival and flourishing is also inclusive of questions of financial incentives, human intention, choice, markets, efficiency, and the aggregate level of economic activity, it does not preclude discussion of more conventional topics as well. An instructor is then spared the awkwardness of arguing that the traditional concerns that they are required to teach are wrong. Instead, the instructor may point out that they are too limited – and then segue into more interesting and relevant topics.

People in industrialized countries, for example, consume more every year, contributing to massive degradation of the natural environment, but they are not on average getting happier (Layard 2005). This is an interesting – and highly relevant – puzzle that a principles course could explore. Depending on instructor interest, one could also discuss provocative questions about trends in income inequality, the role of corporations in social and economic life, the meaning of development, quality of life in the workplace, how technological change happens, the effects of globalization, and other issues that affect students' – and everyone's – lives. Of course, the instructor cannot incorporate every crucial issue and question, hence the need to be selective. But by introducing interesting topics for readings and discussion the instructor can move beyond the dry chalk-and-talk of traditional courses.

Defining economics around issues of sustaining life and enhancing its quality, involves, of course, an ethical judgment that this is an appropriate goal. Principles students – as well as intellectually honest economic thinkers of all stripes – are unlikely to challenge such a value judgment. It is natural to want intellectual endeavors, like other endeavors, to serve useful ends. It is, however, the false aura of objectivity, promoted in positivist expositions of traditional economics, which introductory students perceive as contorted, dishonest, and unrealistic. Because they are not yet indoctrinated into the strange beliefs of traditional economics, new students are usually more willing than advanced and "sophisticated" economics students to venture beyond the standard narrow focus on self-interested behavior and efficiency.[3] This is to the advantage of the principles-level instructor.

## A bigger toolbox: beyond the standard models

A very powerful rhetorical move, when one wants to teach a pluralistic microeconomics course, is simply to put a name to the core mainstream models of producer, consumer, and market behavior. If these are labeled as belonging to the "orthodox model," or "basic neoclassical model," or "simple mechanical model," the material's implicit claim to abstract, appearing-out-of-nowhere generality is immediately put into perspective. Putting a name on mainstream models suggests that alternatives are possible. Calling models "traditional," "basic," or "simple" further suggests that, while learning them may be necessary (for whatever reason), the course will also venture beyond into more up-to-date and/or sophisticated explanations.[4]

A second powerful move is to spend time discussing the assumptions of the traditional model. What is assumed about human behavior, about technology, about institutions, and the different social and economic forces acting in the world? What are some real-world phenomena that the models might plausibly explain? And, conversely, what phenomena might require different models?

As an example, in explaining the traditional production model in my micro principles text, we present data on the effect of fertilizer applications to a field of corn (Goodwin *et al.* 2008). This is a scientifically documented case illustrating diminishing returns and increasing marginal costs. Yet it can be made fairly obvious to students that diminishing returns constitute only one aspect of the problem. Students, savvy with computer software and web-based music, understand that the biggest issue facing the producer is not the marginal cost of production (which is virtually zero). The instructor can segue into alternative institutional approaches to thinking about production and pricing, including network externalities, that move beyond the traditional treatment. The example of fertilizer application can also lead into a broader discussion of how the market price of a good does not fully reflect the environmental externalities caused by its use, along with the centrality of an oil-based agriculture system and what this means for global commodities.

Again, with a bigger toolbox approach, the instructor need not show that traditional tools and concepts are wrong, but rather, by describing their highly restrictive assumptions, the instructor can enable students to understand the limited range of the models. And then, perfectly reasonably, one can segue on to explanations that cover other cases. One can, by a similar strategy, present a number of pluralistic approaches. The instructor can discuss self-interested rational choice behavior and habit-driven behavior, behavior influenced by advertising, and behavior based in social solidarity or influenced by social norms. The instructor can discuss market forces as well as entrenched prejudice against women and minorities in labor markets or the political lobbying force of large monopolistic corporations. And the instructor might explain the notion of a stable market equilibrium and explore the fundamentally unpredictable dynamics of innovation or the psychology of speculative bubbles. Students can appreciate the possible gains from global trade and the simultaneous downsides of free trade. In a pluralistic approach, as opposed to a competing paradigms approach, it is not necessary to give students the impression that they are expected to take sides.

Turning to macroeconomics, a tradition already exists for teaching in a historical context. Standard introductory textbooks generally give some background about the Great Depression, while explicitly discussing classical, Keynesian, and monetarist schools. But here again, more openness can be gained by, for example, naming the standard method of macroeconomic national income accounting as "traditional," describing its assumptions, and then expanding into a discussion of the value of unpaid work and methods of social and environmental accounting. Similarly, the classical–Keynesian synthesis, combining a model of short-run economic fluctuations with a vertical long-run aggregate supply curve, can be labeled as a particular approach, rather than treated as perfectly general and the apex of macroeconomic knowledge. Keynes' own thought (and that of many post-Keynesians) can be used to venture beyond the underlying assumption of long-run stability, and the importance of uncertainty, time, and evolutionary dynamics can be added to the students' toolbox.

Students can be shown that macroeconomics is itself an evolving field, and encouraged to think about new challenges.[5] For example, while the problems of the Great Depression led to Keynes' innovations in macroeconomics, and the supply shocks in the 1970s to greater attention to supply issues, societies are now confronted with pressing challenges of global climate change, resource depletion and other environmental issues, as well as persistent global inequalities. Existing macroeconomic theories are inadequate to these challenges. How will macroeconomics, and particularly macroeconomic treatments of growth and development, respond? Such a question moves the course beyond cut-and-dried models into the realm of a lively and relevant search for knowledge.

## A bigger toolbox: beyond the standard methods

Besides expanding the range of approaches presented, there is also the question of methods or styles of analysis. Traditional economists consider the uniting force in economics of a set of techniques to be even stronger than that of a common subject matter or model. In a conventional principles course, students are taught that "doing economics" is largely a matter of manipulating equations and shifting curves. Some political economists agree that economics is defined by mathematical modeling techniques, and only disagree about the particulars. An improved principles course, from such a point of view, might just contain more or different algebraic and graphical models.

Other non-traditional views, however, consider this a very limited perspective, based on an inadequate understanding of the nature of scientific investigation, and perhaps tainted by gender-related biases against methods that may appear to be relatively soft or imprecise (Ferber and Nelson 1993). Based on a broader view of social science practice, while mathematical representations may be precise and elegant, they often fail miserably on the criteria of richness and relevance. In a principles course in particular, where students often have minimal mathematical training and are just being exposed to the world of social science, it seems particularly shameful to focus on deductive methods and mathematical modeling techniques when much can be learned by other means.

Economics principles students – and unfortunately, too many advanced graduate students and faculty – are often woefully ignorant about rudimentary economic geography, economic history, institutions, human behavior, environmental science, and current events. They are also sometimes sadly lacking in expository writing skills. A principles course is a perfect place to start to remedy these deficiencies, through reading and writing assignments that help students gain the breadth of knowledge that understanding economic issues demands, and the skills necessary for effective communication. Such exercises may, of course, be disparaged by methodological hard-liners as "only verbal" or "only descriptive" – or as "not economics" if they involve interdisciplinary reading. But, as well as being useful in themselves, they are also, of course, an essential precursor to any satisfactory – rich, relevant, and connected to the real world – analytic research.

Skills in empirical exploration, whether accomplished through accessing web-available data, in computer labs, or gathering and analyzing data through surveys or experimental methods, provide another useful set of tools for students. While such work is often relegated to a separate course for majors, the result is that principles students get a dry introductory course with little insight into what economists actually do, and perhaps what they themselves might do in future studies or employment. Such exercises need not involve sophisticated statistical techniques; straightforward percentage calculations, simple charts or tables, and basic analysis of qualitative data can often yield considerable insight into economic phenomena.[6] Experiential learning, such as through service learning projects (McGoldrick and Ziegert 2002), is another way of connecting students' theoretical learning with their interests and with real-world problems.

## Conclusion

Instructors seeking to improve their principles course may contemplate teaching an alternative economic paradigm or a set of competing paradigms. This chapter, however, establishes a rationale for a course focusing on broader questions of human well-being rather than on disputes in economic thought, and which adopts a more tolerant and synthetic, rather than adversarial, approach to teaching models and methods.

We would do well to remember that, in addition to educating the citizenry at large, the principles instructor plays a key role in shaping the economics discipline over the long run: what is taught in the introductory course strongly influences student self-selection into (or out of) continued work in economics, and is the first step in socialization of the next generation of economists. Who will you inspire to advance in economics – the student concerned about real-world economic issues and committed to trying to make the world a better place, or the student primarily attracted by the elegance of models who has a special affinity to equation solving and curve shifting? The answer to this question rests in your hands.

## Notes

1. See for example, readers by Carson *et al.* (2005) and Fireside *et al.* (2008, 2006).
2. I must disclose working on various materials that embody the approach I describe, including stand-alone textbooks (Goodwin *et al.* 2008a, 2008b), supplementary materials (Goodwin *et al.*, various), and a guide for teachers at the secondary level (Maier and Nelson 2007). I have, however, no direct financial interest in promoting the materials produced in my collaborative work. All royalties from these go to the Global Development and Environment Institute at Tufts University.
3. For some evidence of this, see Frank *et al.* (1993).
4. If students later take a standardized economics exam, such as the Advanced Placement or Graduate Record Exam in the United States, which is thoroughly mainstream, they are instructed to mentally add the phrase "In the simple mechanical model," to the beginning of each question.
5. One of my favorite moments in teaching was when a student came up to me, with an expression of great discovery on his face, and said, "You know, Professor Nelson, macroeconomics keeps *changing!*"
6. Too often I find that even intermediate or advanced students do not fully understand for example, the difference between the percentage of nurses who are women and the percentage of women who are nurses, or the difference between a *percent* change and a percentage *point* change. While perhaps this problem is more common in the U.S. than elsewhere, I find the idea of sending someone who cannot handle such basic interpretations out into the world with economics credentials to be frightening.
7. Despite attempting to include materials appropriate for a variety of approaches to alternative principles teaching, this list is very incomplete and, due to the author's own limitations, confined to mostly English-language – and predominately U.S.-centric – resources. Listing is for information only, and does not constitute endorsement. Despite the strenuous attempts of many to develop materials for teaching political economy views, such textbook and reader offerings remain considerably more limited than for traditional courses. As a result, factors such as the difficulty level of the writing and analysis, specific national orientation, and the availability of supplements such as test

banks may still create obstacles to course adoption, even if an instructor approves much of the content of a particular resource. Because of the current narrower demand for alternative materials, materials sometimes become outdated or go out of print, and are rarely available in translations.

## Brief annotated bibliography of classroom materials[7]

Bober, Stanley (2001) *Alternative Principles of Economics* (New York: M.E. Sharpe). This book is designed to supplement a standard text. While, according to the publisher, it aims to "provide a complete introduction to Post-Keynesian and other alternative theories of economics," the emphasis is clearly on only the first alternative. Considerable mathematics and graphical analysis are used to lay out post-Keynesian theories of mark-up pricing, economic growth, and the like.

Bowles, Samuel, Edwards, Richard, and Roosevelt, Frank (2005) *Understanding Capitalism* 3rd edn, Oxford University Press. This micro-macro textbook is written from a Marxist-influenced political economy point of view. The book emphasizes capital/labor issues, inequality, and economic change, presenting detailed models of profit rates and labor extraction. It includes discussions of the history of economic thought, ecology, race, and gender, and many applications of real-world issues.

Carson, Robert B., Thomas, Wade L., and Hecht, Jason (2005) *Economic Issues Today: Alternative Approaches*, 8th edn, New York: M.E. Sharpe. This book is designed to supplement a standard text, and is available as separate micro and macro volumes. Each chapter focuses on a selected economic issue, such as the size of the federal deficit or U.S. income inequality, on which "Conservative, Liberal, and Radical" perspectives, as formulated by the authors, are presented. An introduction discusses the philosophical and intellectual history of the perspectives covered.

Cohn, Steven Mark (2007) *Reintroducing Macroeconomics: A Critical Approach*. New York: M.E. Sharpe. This book is described as a "companion volume for students in introductory economics courses." It introduces principles of radical, institutional, feminist, post-Keynesian, ecological, and social economics, in a format that parallels a standard textbook. One might note that covering both a standard textbook and this material in one semester may be, in many cases, quite ambitious.

Colander, David (2008) *Economics*, 7th edn, New York: McGraw-Hill. This textbook is available in combined or separate micro and macro volumes. While largely standard in content, beginning with the sixth edition the book has included, according to the publisher,

> special end-of-chapter questions [which] present an opportunity to discuss and analyze the material from the wide range of differing schools of thought in Economics – feminist, Marxist, Austrian, public choice theory, etc. For those instructors who prefer a more mainstream approach, the Questions from Alternate Perspectives may easily be skipped.

Fireside, Daniel, Miller, John, Snyder, Bryan, and the D&S Collective (eds.) (2008) *Real World Macro*, 25th edn. Somerville, Mass.: Dollars and Sense. This book of supplementary readings, according to the publisher, "along with covering the basics … includes a chapter on major controversies in macroeconomics, such as the legacy of Keynesianism in the United States and the basics of Marxist economic theory."

Fireside, Daniel, Rao, Smriti, Snyder, Bryan, and the D&S Collective (eds.) (2008) *Real World Micro*, 15th edn. Somerville, Mass.: Dollars and Sense. This book of supplementary readings, according to the publisher, "rubs neoclassical theory up against reality, in which disparities of wealth, power, and organization shape the economy, and benefit some groups at others' expense."

GDAE (various years) *Teaching Modules on Social and Environmental Issues in Economics*. Medford, Mass.: Global Development and Environment Institute. Reflecting GDAE's "contextual" approach, these free, downloadable materials written by various GDAE-affiliated researchers are designed for use as supplements to standard textbooks. Each module includes a student reading (typically 20–40 pages), references, and discussion questions. Currently thirteen modules are available, including titles such as "Consumption and the Consumer Society" and "Environmental Justice: Income, Race, and Health" (www.gdae.org).

Goodwin, Neva, Nelson, Julie A., Ackerman, Frank and Weisskopf, Thomas (2008a) *Microeconomics in Context*, 2nd edn. New York: M.E. Sharpe. This textbook includes standard issues and models but goes beyond them to incorporate social and environmental concerns and additional approaches throughout. In the final chapter, the assumptions underlying free market ideology are examined in detail and alternative schools of thought are briefly described. (Translations of earlier versions are available in Italian, Vietnamese, and Russian. See www.gdae.org.)

Goodwin, Neva, Nelson, Julie A., and Harris, Jonathan (2008b) *Macroeconomics in Context*. New York: M.E. Sharpe. This textbook includes standard topics and approaches, but also gives serious attention to issues including ecological sustainability, non-marketed production, the quality of life, and income distribution. Economies are treated as evolving, with the model of long-run full employment equilibrium treated as only one among several theories.

Hahnel, Robin (2002) *The ABCs of Political Economy: A Modern Approach*. London: Pluto. This "introduction to modern political economy," according to the publisher, "teaches the reader the essential tools necessary to understand economic issues today from a modern perspective, searching for ways to replace the economics of competition and greed with the economics of equitable co-operation" by drawing on "the work of Marx, Keynes, Veblen, Kalecki and other great political economists."

Pluta, Joseph E. (2007) *The Market: Mainstream and Evolutionary Views*. Dubuque, Iowa: Kendall Hunt Publishing. Billed as a "principles of microeconomics book," this book also includes a "history of economic ideas from ancient times to the present"; discussion of the ideas of Thorstein Veblen, Wesley Mitchell, and other institutionalist economists; and explanation of evolutionary concepts such as circular causation and the "instinct of workmanship."

Riddell, Tom, Shackelford, Jean, Stamos, Steve, and Schneider, Geoffrey (2008) *Economics: A Tool for Critically Understanding Society*, 8th edn. Lexington, Mass.: Addison-Wesley. This one-semester introductory textbook features, according to its publisher, "a heterodox approach" and a "strong historical perspective."

Sherman, Howard J., Hunt, E.K., Nesiba, Reynold F., O'Hara, Phillip A., and Wiens-Tuers, Barbara A. (2008) *Economics: An Introduction to Traditional and Progressive Views*, 7th edn. New York: M.E. Sharpe. The intention of this textbook is to introduce students to both standard material and progressive critique. It includes coverage of historical figures such as Veblen and Marx.

Stretton, Hugh (1999) *Economics: A New Introduction*. New South Wales University Press, Ltd. for Australia; Pluto Press elsewhere. According to the publisher, this book

> employs a pragmatic mix of old and new methods to examine the role of values and theoretical beliefs in economic life and in economists' understanding of it ... In focusing on ... abuses of affluence the text draws on institutional, Keynesian,

> green and feminist theories, whilst emphasizing all approaches to understanding economic life.
>
> While this book is a rich source of ideas, potential users should be forewarned that, with sixty chapters spanning 864 pages, students may consider it to be less than user-friendly.

Teller-Elsberg, Jonathan, Heintz, James, and Folbre, Nancy (2006) *Field Guide to the U.S. Economy*. (New York: New Press). Written in a lively format with cartoons and graphs on every page, this supplement, according to the publisher, "brings key economic issues to life, reflecting the collective wit and wisdom of the many progressive economists affiliated with the Center for Popular Economics." It includes discussion of

> workers, women, people of color, government spending, welfare, education, health, the environment, macroeconomics, and the global economy, as well as brand-new material on the war in Iraq, the Department of Homeland Security, the prison-industrial complex, foreign aid, the environment, and pharmaceutical companies.

## References

Aerni, A.L. and McGoldrick, K. (eds.) (1999) *Valuing Us All: Feminist Pedagogy in Economics*. Ann Arbor: University of Michigan Press.

Aslanbeigui, N. and Naples, M.I. (1996) *Rethinking Economic Principles: Critical Essays on Introductory Texts*. Chicago: Irwin.

Ferber, M.A. and Nelson, J.A. (1993) *Beyond Economic Man: Feminist Theory and Economics*. Chicago: University of Chicago Press.

Frank, R., Gilovich, T., and Regan, D.T. (1993) "Does Studying Economics Inhibit Cooperation?," *Journal of Economic Perspectives* 7: 159–71.

Fullbrook, E. (ed.) (2003) *The Crisis in Economics: The Post-Autistic Economics Movement: The First 600 Days*. London: Routledge.

Garnett, R.F., Jr. (2005) "Whither Heterodoxy?," *Post-Autistic Economics Review* 34: 2021. www.paecon.net/heterodoxeconomics/Garnett34.htm. Accessed April 1, 2007.

Groenewegen, J. (ed.) (2007) *Teaching Pluralism in Economics*. Cheltenham, UK: Edward Elgar.

Knoedler, J.T. and Underwood, D.A. (2003) "Teaching the Principles of Economics: A Proposal for a Multi-Paradigmatic Approach," *Journal of Economic Issues* 37: 697–725.

Layard, R. (2005) *Happiness*. London: Penguin.

McGoldrick, K. and Ziegert, A.L. (eds.) (2002) *Putting the Invisible Hand to Work: Concepts and Models for Service Learning in Economics*. Ann Arbor: University of Michigan Press.

Maier, M.H. and Nelson, J.A. (2007) *Introducing Economics: A Critical Guide for Teachers*. Armonk, NY: M.E. Sharpe.

Mearman, A. (2007) "Teaching Heterodox Economics Concepts," *Economics Network: "The Handbook for Economics Lecturers."* www.economicsnetwork.ac.uk/handbook/heterodox/.

# 7 Teaching economics as if time mattered*

*I. David Wheat*

High on the list of priorities of the 2001 "Kansas City Proposal" for fundamental reform in economics is "consideration of history" (Pringle and Leclaire 2003). Elaborating, the KC Proposal emphasizes that:

> Economic reality is dynamic rather than static – and as economists we must investigate how and why things change over time and space. Realistic economic inquiry should focus on process rather than simply on ends.

This chapter is about teaching dynamics, and the focus is on delay processes that cause disequilibrium behavior in economic systems. To introduce and illustrate the method, we use a simple price–supply–demand model that does not presume higher-order math skills and, therefore, is accessible to a wide range of undergraduates. The method relies on simple feedback diagrams to illustrate the structure of economic systems and user-friendly software to simulate their dynamic behavior. Using the model in conjunction with a standard price–supply–demand graph underscores the implicit ahistorical feature of static, equilibrium models.

We begin by highlighting some of the problems associated with ahistorical approaches to economic analysis and instruction. That is followed by a brief description of the *feedback method* of teaching economic dynamics, and what we expect it to accomplish. The third section demonstrates the method and enables the reader to form some impressions of its pedagogical potential. The final section includes suggestions for engaging students with the simulation model via its interactive learning environment.

## Time matters

Keen's (2001) critique of orthodox "rapid transition" policy guidance provided to economic planners in post-Soviet Russia constitutes a headline example of why time matters when teaching and learning economics. He argues that the policy of rapid privatization of state assets was disproportionately beneficial to those who were institutionally capable of exploiting the hasty change: "the old Party apparatchiks and organized crime." Moreover, he attributes the policy guidance to a "simplistic belief in the ability of market economies to rapidly achieve equilibrium" and reliance on "equilibrium models that presumed the system could rapidly move to a new equilibrium once disturbed." He concludes that "a time-based analysis" would have generated "gradual transition" policy guidance that anticipated delays in equipping Soviet-era factories with modern technology and new management styles, delays in developing market-based distribution systems, and delays in changing both laws and cultural norms in ways that facilitate private exchange and consumer protection – all of which take "substantial time to put in place."

Perhaps part of the problem is the exporting of advice containing temporal implications that might be misinterpreted. Hayden's (2005) comments on *Seven Cultures of Capitalism* (Hampden-Turner and Trompenaars 1993) indicate that corporate planning and production reflect "temporal views" that vary among different cultures having their own brands of capitalism. Not only does time matter, it matters differently in different cultures.

Failure to foresee the U.S.-bred financial epidemic that infected world economies in 2008 illustrates another weakness of timeless economic analysis – inadequate attention to a festering ailment because its systemic emergence is far removed in time (and space) from the initial infection. Monetary policy is famously challenged by "long and variable lags" (Friedman 1960); that much is well known. Unfortunately, disequilibrium models that take lags seriously are less well known and not likely to be found in the orthodox economic policy toolkit.

Examples need not be limited to macro policy issues. Market price–supply–demand graphs are static by design. Thus, undergraduate microeconomics students are hard pressed to see that time matters in orthodox theories of producer and consumer behavior.

Yet even Marshall (1946) observed that implicit "demand and supply schedules do not in practice remain unchanged for a long time together, but are constantly being changed; and every change in them alters the equilibrium amount and the equilibrium price" (1946: 346–347). While in disequilibrium "constantly," price and quantity are behaving in ways that are beyond the explanatory scope of the static model.

Of course, the static graph was never intended to display dynamics, either the fluctuations implicit in Marshall's mental model or the more common pseudo-dynamic chalkboard demonstrations of "movement" of one curve that disturbs an initial equilibrium and "leads" to another. Indeed, the very notion of a static graph that changes over time is an oxymoron, and criticizing a static model for not being dynamic is disingenuous. Instead, we should provide incentives to develop and use models that *can* represent economic dynamics in ways that are accessible to a broad spectrum of students.

One refuge of the static modeler is the *long run*, notwithstanding the irony of depending on the passage of time to dismiss the significance of time. "To assert the existence of a long-run equilibrium when its attainment requires an infinite length of time is to imply ... either that time does not matter or that one has no explanation" (Boland 2005: 6). Boland's words are reminiscent of Keynes' (1923) criticism that economists are useless if they can only say the ocean will be flat again after the storm has past.

A second refuge is both a solution and a curse. Economic models that rely on higher-order mathematics can display endogenous dynamics. Of course, the structural validity of such models – and all models – is a case-by-case question. More to the point is that mathematically complex models are not accessible to a wide range of students, particularly undergraduates who may take only an introductory principles course. Students could observe the behavior of such models, but few would have the intellectual capacity to study – much less understand – the structure that produces the behavior.

It would be useful to have a way to teach economic dynamics to a diverse group of students whose math skills are as varied as their social, cultural, and genetic attributes. In the next section, we discuss such an approach and indicate what we expect from it. We call it the *feedback method* of teaching economics (Wheat 2007).

## The feedback method

The feedback approach to teaching economics emphasizes how endogenous dynamic behavior arises from the feedback structure in economic systems. The goal is to enable students to see – literally, to observe in a productive manner – both the structure and the behavior of dynamic economic systems, thereby improving students' mental models of how particular economies actually work. The development of the feedback method was prompted by documented weaknesses in economics education that relies on traditional graphical approaches (e.g., Cohn *et al.* 2001;, Colander 1995), and the methodology was inspired by J. Forrester (1961), Mass (1975, 1980), N. Forrester (1982), Richardson (1991), and Radzicki (1988, 1993, 2003), among others.

The boundary of the economic system under study could be wide (e.g., an open macroeconomy) or narrow (e.g. an inventory management process within a firm). Intuitive diagramming techniques are used to draw a simplified representation (i.e., a model) of the system, with the aim of highlighting and explaining key functional relationships between elements in the diagram. Each relationship in the pictorial model has a one-to-one correspondence to an equation in a computer version of the model developed with user-friendly simulation software. Those equations remain below the surface in introductory undergraduate courses, but are easily accessed if instructors want their students to study the engine under the hood.

If the prospect of looking at an equation – much less writing one – produces sweaty palms or glazed eyes, rest assured that skills in addition, subtraction, multiplication, and division are almost always sufficient. The software even makes it easy to "write" nonlinear equations by using a simple drawing tool to represent the shape of the effect of one variable on another (e.g. concave, convex, s-shaped, upward or downward sloping). Without a doubt, all economists – including those who are most resentful of traditional economics becoming a mathematical sandbox – have the requisite skills to use the software as a modeling tool. More important than math is a clear understanding of the structural hypothesis of economic behavior that is implicit in each equation, and that is true for instructors who create the models and students who study them.[1]

It is even possible to get some of the benefits of the feedback method with mere "chalk-and-talk" application of the diagramming techniques, without using the simulation software. Engaging students in conversations about both proximate and distant cause-and-effect relationships (e.g. "What causes prices to change?") is facilitated by the diagrams, which encourage clear expression of hypotheses. As hypotheses emerge (e.g. "An increase in demand causes prices to rise"), discussion ensues and leads to more questions (e.g. "What causes demand to change?") and more hypotheses (e.g. "Demand increases after prices fall"). As this simple example illustrates, the separate hypotheses can be combined to illustrate the concept of feedback: demand has a positive effect on price, and price has a negative effect on quantity demanded.

When this discussion eventually leads to the discovery of the first feedback loop, there is a good chance that an alert student will raise the "circular reasoning" objection: "How, logically, can X cause Y and Y cause X?" When such a question implies *simultaneous* two-way causality, the fallacy of circular reasoning is exposed. However, when allowance is made for the passage of time, the logical objection evaporates. Tinbergen (1939) was perhaps the first macroeconomist to explicitly acknowledge that mutual causation takes time, and that circularity is not a logical fallacy when viewed over time. Feeling compelled to justify an observed two-way causal relationship between profits and investment, he wrote:

> Taking the fall in general investment from 1929 to 1930 – which contributed considerably ... to the fall in profits in 1930 – we find ... that profits one-half year before were the chief explanatory series. Here we meet a very important feature. It would seem as if this were a circular reasoning: profits fell because investment fell, and investment fell because profits fell. This is, however, an inexact statement. Profits in period t fell because investment in period t fell, but the latter fell because of a fall in profits in period $t-1/2$; and owing to this time lag there is no danger of circular reasoning.
>
> (1939: 127)

In other words, time matters not only in the economic process but also in the understanding of that process.

The diagramming part of the feedback method can help students discover basic structure but it cannot demonstrate that structure's behavior. The students can see the model, understand individual relationships to a high degree, and visualize the feedback loop, but they cannot watch it behave – without some help. All instructors using this approach quickly learn to illustrate and explain ("chalk and talk") the behavior that emerges from simple structures (e.g. one-loop models that cause exponential growth, goal-seeking behavior, or oscillations, and perhaps a nonlinear two-loop model that produces s-shaped growth). However, even experienced instructors cannot visualize – and, therefore, cannot anticipate – the net effect of multiple feedback loops. That is why the second part of the feedback method is so important.

Converting the pictorial model into a computerized simulation model enables visualization of the behavior that emerges from structure.[2] In addition, there are methods for analyzing which parts of the structure are responsible for particularly noticeable features of the behavior pattern generated during the simulation run. At a minimum, the simulation results can confirm (or reject!) an instructor's prior explanation of how a simple structure works and what behavior to expect. For more complex structures, the simulation permits observing the change over time of key variables and provides students with vicarious economic experiences that might take a lifetime to observe first-hand. Perhaps most important of all from a pedagogical perspective, the software enables students to conduct simulation experiments – with alternative parameter assumptions or with certain feedback loops cut – and to observe how behavior changes when structure changes. Assignments can be designed to engage students in interpreting how behavior emerges over time from certain interacting pieces of the structure.

For several years, the feedback method has been the central organizing framework in my distance learning course for macroeconomics students at Virginia Western Community College in the U.S. It has also been used with system dynamics graduate students in an economic development planning course at the University of Bergen in Norway. And it has been demonstrated in guest lectures elsewhere in Europe and in South America. In these courses, students use *MacroLab*, an interactive learning environment with an underlying system dynamics model of the U.S. economy.[3] They vicariously build and interpret the model while simulating its behavior each step of the way. The feedback approach has also been adapted and used with microeconomics students.

Anecdotal evidence suggests that most students respond favorably to instruction that gives them an opportunity to experience economic dynamics through simulation. Most seem to like what they call "the loops approach" to learning economic structure. The interactive learning environment heightens interest as they observe changes in both historical and simulated data that correspond to media headlines they see on a daily basis. Controlling the simulator also gives the students a feel for scientific experimentation, and it reinforces the message first encountered in the diagrams; namely, that each functional relationship in a theory – each link in a model – is really a hypothesis that can and should be tested in many different ways. From the beginning to the end of the course, the evolution of the quality of students' explanations of how a simple structure contributes to observed behavior convinces me that real learning of economic dynamics is taking place, albeit at a simple introductory level.

Formal assessment is necessary, however, to build confidence that the feedback method is worth the effort required for instructors to add something new to their instructional toolbox. In addition, formal assessment helps to identify strengths and weaknesses and, thereby, ways to improve this approach. Assessment of a full course presents many practical challenges that have yet to be overcome. However, four controlled experiments have been conducted to test whether some of the techniques used in the feedback method are appealing to students and are effective as instructional tools. The experiments were conducted with 288 student volunteers (in sample sizes ranging from 37 to 177) in community colleges in Virginia and high schools in Oregon and Massachusetts. The results (Wheat 2007) provided statistically significant evidence that students prefer the feedback approach over traditional methods that rely on equations or static graphs, and also that the feedback approach enhances understanding of macroeconomic concepts laden with dynamics (e.g. GDP and business cycles).

As a working hypothesis, the feedback method has been gaining support. Additional experimentation is needed to accumulate even more evidence but, at this stage, the feedback method appears to be a promising alternative to traditional methods of economics instruction. That is particularly important when a primary goal is to impart a sense of dynamics to a diverse group of undergraduates who may be mathematically unprepared for traditional analysis of economic dynamics. The next section gives the reader a glimpse of this approach in a familiar microeconomics context: market price, supply, and demand.

## A demonstration

The simple model described here comes in two flavors – RealTime and NoTime. They differ only in their assumptions about the influence of time delays on producer and consumer decision-making. To set the stage for explaining the different behavior patterns generated by each version, Figure 7.1 compares the price response when RealTime and NoTime were subjected to the same exogenous increase in demand ("rightward shift of the demand curve") in a simulation experiment. The long-run price in Figure 7.1 is the same for both, but the transition patterns over time are quite different. The variations in price behavior reflect the relative influence of time delays in the two versions of the model.

The behavior of NoTime shows it to be a trivial dynamic model. Its quick transition between equilibria is similar to the implicit "behavior" of a static price–supply–demand graph and reflects assumptions that production, consumption, and pricing decisions respond instantaneously to causal influences. These features, however, make NoTime behavior a useful benchmark against which to compare the performance of RealTime, a model that takes time seriously.

Of course, this simulation experiment begs the question of whether it is good practice to develop a dynamic model that merely incorporates supply and demand curves (i.e., the schedules behind them) as if they actually exist. When modeling a complex dynamic problem in real-world markets, it is obviously better to seek empirical evidence of what influences production, consumption, and price decision-making.[4] In the present context, however, the challenge is how to move away from misleading pseudo-dynamic interpretations of static price–supply–demand graphs and towards a model that is dynamic yet still

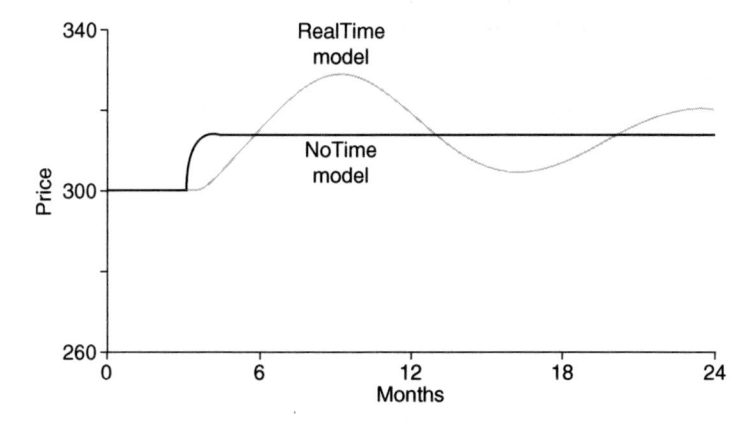

*Figure 7.1* Price behavior after a demand increase.

accessible to undergraduates. We believe the credibility of the approach presented in this chapter is enhanced by a demonstration that, *even when the long-term result is the same as predicted by a static model*, the behavior along the transition path depends on the length of time delays in a dynamic model. We leave for another day the issue of a thousand-and-one disturbances – some systemic and some random – that preclude attainment of equilibrium in real economies.[5]

We use feedback loop diagrams to present the simple price–supply–demand model.[6] To facilitate introduction of the model, we examine its price–demand and price–supply structures separately in Figures 7.2 and 7.3. Then we combine them in Figure 7.4.

*Price–demand loop*

Loop C1 in Figure 7.2 represents our hypothesis about the mutual dependence of price and demand. The clock icons denote delays expected during information processing, decision-making, and action-taking along the loops. The delay processes are discussed later in this section.

The loop is merely the result of connecting a series of paired relationships, each of which constitutes a separate hypothesis or definition. To "read" the hypotheses in sequence, pick any variable along the loop and follow its link to the next variable, in this case moving in a counterclockwise direction.[7] Let's begin with price. We expect that an increase in price would put downward pressure on quantity demanded. After a rise in price, quantity demanded would be lower than it otherwise would be; hence the minus sign on the cause-and-effect arrow running from price to quantity demanded. Conversely, a decrease in price would cause quantity demanded to be higher than it otherwise would be.

The next link along loop C1 is merely a definition: since quantity demanded is the denominator in a supply–demand ratio, an increase in quantity demanded

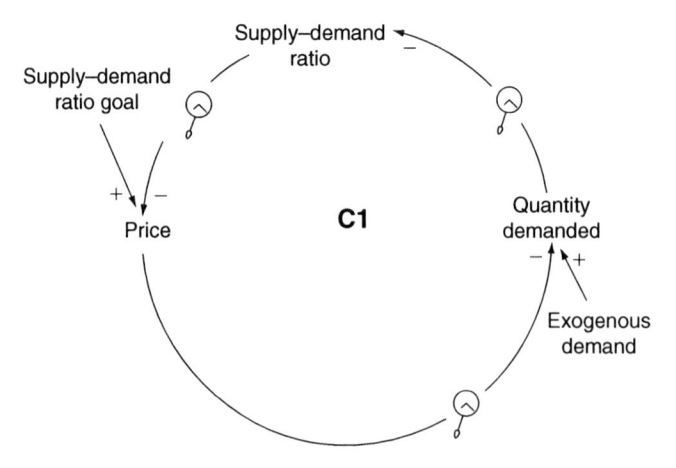

*Figure 7.2* Price–demand loop, C1.

would reduce the numerical value of the ratio (and conversely). The remaining link along C1 represents the expectation that an increase in the supply–demand ratio will put downward pressure on price (and conversely). Since we assume producers aim to match supply with demand, the supply–demand ratio goal is assumed to be 1.0. Thus, price would fall when the supply–demand ratio exceeded the goal of 1.0 (and conversely). In addition to the endogenous relationships between price and quantity demanded, there is also an exogenous demand influence on loop C1. Exogenous demand represents the effect of factors *other than price* on quantity demanded. In the language of price–supply–demand graphs, a change in exogenous demand corresponds to a shift in the demand curve. In loop C1, an increase in exogenous demand reflects a rightward shift in the demand curve, while a decrease implies a leftward shift in the curve.

C1 is a *negative* feedback loop – also called a *counteracting, balancing,* or *goal-seeking* loop. Loop polarity can be deduced by counting the number of negative links along a loop. A negative loop always has an odd number of negative links (Sterman 2000), and C1 contains three.

To confirm the loop polarity intuitively, we can use a thought experiment informally called the walk-around method. Start with a presumed change in any loop variable; e.g. suppose quantity demanded increases. Then "walk around" the loop in the direction of the arrows, note the induced impact on each variable along the way, and identify the eventual feedback effect on the loop variable that initiated the movement. If the starting-point variable (quantity demanded, in this example) receives feedback pressure to *decrease* after its initial *increase*, the loop has a counteracting effect – an indication of a negative loop such as C1. On the other hand, if the feedback loop causes quantity demanded to rise even more, the loop has a reinforcing impact, which signals the "snowball effect" of a positive feedback loop.

Summarizing with loop C1, suppose there is an exogenous increase in demand, causing an initial increase in quantity demanded. That would lead to a decrease in the supply–demand ratio, upward pressure on price, and a feedback effect that would reduce quantity demanded. We start with an increase in quantity demanded, but after one trip around the loop there is downward pressure on quantity demanded.

The thought experiment supports what the mathematical logic of the link polarity method had deduced: C1 is a negative feedback loop. As such, it is goal-seeking. It tends to counteract conditions that depart from the systemic goal to which it adheres. Its function is to eliminate discrepancies between a system's goal and the current condition of the system. Unlike nature's goals in biological systems, the goals in social systems are not preordained or necessarily natural. In social feedback systems, a systemic goal is an institutional construct – one of the rules of the game – that reflects the cultural and historical setting of the system. In this case, we assume the goal is equality between quantities demanded and supplied, the same goal as assumed in a static supply–demand analysis. In the thought experiment, therefore, the systemic goal was a supply–demand ratio goal of 1.0, and the loop would continue to push price upward until quantity demanded fell sufficiently to bring the actual supply–demand ratio in line with its goal. As we saw in Figure 7.1, however, convergence of a counteracting loop toward its goal may be either a smooth process or an oscillatory process. The latter results when quantity demanded falls more than necessary, causing the supply–demand ratio to shoot past its goal, only later to approach it from the other direction.

*Price–supply loop*

Figure 7.3 displays the price–supply loop, C2. It has the same generic structure as loop C1 but, of course, the details concern supply instead of demand. First, there is a positive link running from price to quantity supplied; as price increases, the quantity supplied is hypothesized to be higher than it otherwise would be (and conversely). Next, since quantity supplied is the numerator in the supply–demand ratio, that link is positive. Closing the loop, a rise in the supply–demand ratio causes price to fall, and conversely. In addition to these endogenous relationships, there is a link representing the effect of exogenous changes in supply.

Loop C2 contains an odd number of negative links; thus, it is also a negative feedback loop. The deduced negative polarity of the loop is supported by a thought experiment that assumes an initial increase in quantity supplied due to exogenous factors. That would raise the supply–demand ratio above the goal of 1.0 and put downward pressure on price. When price fell, subsequent quantity supplied would be lower than it would be otherwise. Thus, loop C2 counteracts departures from its systemic goal.

*Time delays*

The feedback loops acknowledge the role of real time in the structure of economic systems, albeit a simple system in this case. Each loop contains three clock icons denoting process delays occurring along the loop.

78  I.D. Wheat

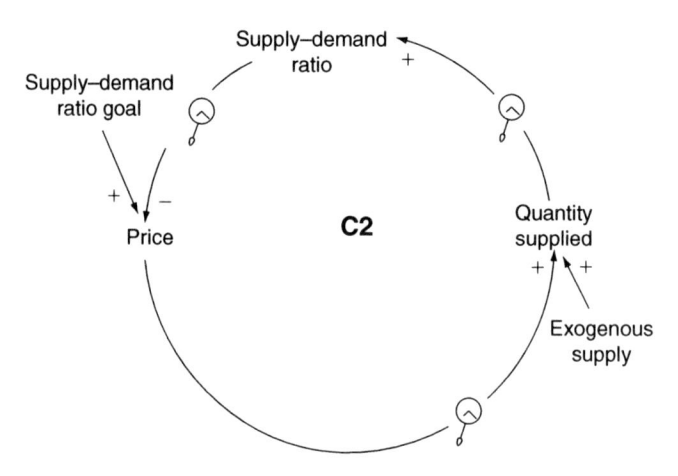

*Figure 7.3* Price–supply loop, C2.

Common to both loops is a delay between changes in the supply–demand ratio and changes in price. The time required for studying the production and sales data and for the market-focused decision-making process is part of the pre-price change delay. The pre-price change delay requires time to collect and analyze information about production and sales ("quantities supplied and demanded"), decide what to do, and then carry out the decision. Adjusting prices involves serious and uncertain risks because of the immediate impact on sales and revenue and the longer-term effects on customer loyalty and market share. Such decisions take time.

Moreover, after a pricing decision is made – even in a single firm – implementing that decision requires an additional flurry of activity that could take days or run into weeks. When decision analysis and price administration occur within an entire industry that is responding to changes in market supply and demand, the total delay can be conceptualized in terms of an average time and a distribution around that average, since some firms are aggressive and others are conservative in their pricing policies. In our model, the delay formulation allows for such a distribution of price change activity around an average adjustment time.

Post-price change delays are also likely. In Figure 7.2, there is a delay between a change in price and a change in quantity demanded. Some consumers would react immediately to a price change. Others would take longer to observe and respond to a new price and change their spending habits. Here, "respond" means moving along the demand curve, and the length of the delay means the average time for that movement by all consumers in the market. Figure 7.3 indicates that a change in quantity supplied would also lag behind a change in price. Gearing up production in response to higher prices or cutting back production when prices are falling could take several months, depending on labor market conditions, institutional arrangements, and norms surrounding overtime and temporary layoffs or the hiring and firing of workers. Even more time would be

*Teaching economics as if time mattered* 79

required to evaluate favorable price signals and respond with capacity-enhancing capital investments.

## *The complete model*

The feedback loop structure in Figure 7.4 combines the separate loops from Figures 7.2 and 7.3 and represents the complete price–supply–demand model with delays. The model reflects our premise that price, supply, and demand are *mutually dependent over time*, and that a distinction between so-called independent and dependent variables is meaningless in a dynamic context.[8]

The model in Figure 7.4 is the RealTime model. To envision the NoTime model, imagine Figure 7.4 without the clock icons. There would be no delays along the loops. When simulating the NoTime model, the delay times are reduced to one day. Thus, NoTime is merely an extreme case of RealTime. The two versions have identical structures but rely on different parameter assumptions about how quickly those structures operate, with NoTime assuming virtually instantaneous adjustments.

## *How to read the model*

To illustrate how to "read" the structure of the two feedback loops in the model and infer dynamic behavior, we will contrast it with the pseudo-dynamic interpretation of the price–supply–demand graph. When simulated under the same assumptions about the location and shape of the supply and demand curves (and the rightward shock to the latter), the behavior of the Figure 7.4 model would eventually reach the same stable outcome under most reasonable assumptions about time delays. As we learned from the price behavior in Figure 7.1, however, we should expect the pattern of convergence to be different when time delays play a role in the functioning of the system.

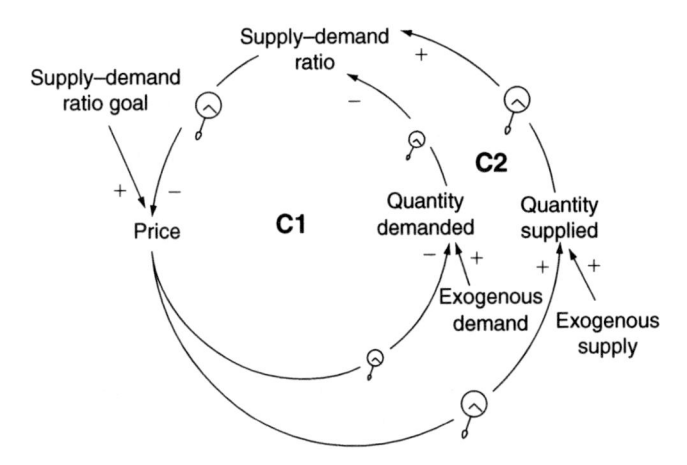

*Figure 7.4* The RealTime model.

After the demand curve shift (represented in Figure 7.4 by an assumed increase in exogenous demand), quantities demanded in loop C1 would rise, pushing the supply–demand ratio below 1.0, and putting upward pressure on prices. After the price increase, quantity supplied would also rise, *ceteris paribus*, as suggested by the positive link in loop C2. Thus, one effect of rising prices would be to encourage more production. Meanwhile, as the negative link in loop C1 suggests, a price increase tends to push consumption down. Thus, rising prices would discourage additional consumption, and quantity demanded would fall back from its post-shift peak. So far, the analysis resembles the standard interpretation of the price–supply–demand graph.

Now, however, we will see where the feedback loop version of a price–supply–demand model parts company with a static graph. In the feedback diagram of Figure 7.4, the initial impact of a changing price on quantities demanded and supplied is not the end of the story. The quantities are not just pushed continuously in the "right direction" until stability is achieved. Instead, information about the changing quantities feeds back to change price again. Depending on which effect – quantities demanded or supplied – is quicker and stronger, price will either rise further or fall, and the process will continue around the loop until the systemic goal is reached. All three variables are mutually dependent over time.

In Figure 7.4, one could imagine the possibility that, after the initial shock and one walk around the loop, the first *feedback* effects on price from loop C2 (downward price pressure from supply) and loop C1 (upward price pressure from demand) would be of equal strength and would arrive simultaneously. In that case, the supply–demand ratio and price would immediately stabilize, a sign that equality of quantities supplied and demanded had been restored on the first trip around the loop. Students will not find that scenario realistically appealing, and neither did Marshall (1920), who described the effects of exogenous shifts in demand and supply in terms of "a pendulum [that] oscillates about its lowest point" (1946: 345).

Some degree of oscillatory behavior should be expected from the model in Figure 7.4. Oscillations could result from recurring unequal opposing forces at the common point of feedback, or different arrival times of those opposing forces, or both. Perhaps less obvious is the potential for each negative feedback loop acting alone to produce oscillations due to delays along its single loop; that behavior can also be demonstrated with simulation experiments.[9]

### *Behavior of the model*

Simulating the model requires using some numerical values for the time delays conceptualized above, and Table 7.1 lists the default parameter assumptions for both versions of the model. The model's interface is designed as an interactive learning environment that permits parameter assumptions to be modified by the person using it. The model is freely accessible online, and any reader wondering about its sensitivity to a particular parameter assumption may run it under different assumptions about the length of the delays, ranging from one day to a trillion years! It is the one-day assumption for each delay that is used to simulate the behavior of the NoTime version of the model.[10] The RealTime Model assumes that delay processes require much more time than the virtually instantaneous adjustments by the NoTime model.

The default parameter assumptions in Table 7.1 are only illustrative. For the RealTime model, we assume a three-month average delay in the price adjustment process resulting from changing supply and demand conditions. That assumption stems from the average delay in Blinder's survey (1997), but of course he would caution that the lengths of delays would vary according to the product. And it should be remembered that the delay formulation provides for a distribution around the average to reflect the range of adjustment times that one might expect across an industry.

There are three other parameter assumptions along the loops. Two are reflected in the supply and demand schedules used to determine quantities supplied and demanded, given a price. The default schedules reflect a constant elasticity equal to 1.0 and –1.0 for quantities supplied and demanded, respectively, with elasticity measured from the initial equilibrium values, producing straight-line "curves." The default assumptions are easily modified in the user interface so the model can also be tested under various elastic and inelastic conditions.

An estimate is also required for the parameter representing the sensitivity of price to changes in the supply–demand ratio. A simple linear proportional response is assumed by default, so that a supply–demand ratio that is perceived to be 10 percent higher than 1.0 will cause a 10 percent reduction in price. However, alternative effects on price – including nonlinear effects – are easily formulated in the user interface.

With the parameter assumptions, it is possible to simulate the models and compare their behavior. To illustrate, Figure 7.5 displays the results of an exogenous rightward shift in *demand*. The shock registers first on quantity demanded (top graph in Figure 7.5). The NoTime model stabilizes almost immediately at a new price and quantity of about $314 per widget and 629 widgets per month, the same result obtained by a price–supply–demand graph having the same slopes as those in the models. More to the point, the sequential effects on quantity demanded, price (middle graph), and quantity supplied (bottom graph) are imperceptible. For NoTime, time does not matter.

*Table 7.1* Default parameter assumptions

| Parameter | Default values | |
| --- | --- | --- |
| | *NoTime* | *RealTime* |
| Quantity demanded adjustment time | 1 day | 3 months |
| Quantity supplied adjustment time | 1 day | 3 months |
| Supply–demand perception adjustment time | 1 day | 1 month |
| Price adjustment time | 1 day | 3 months |

82   I.D. Wheat

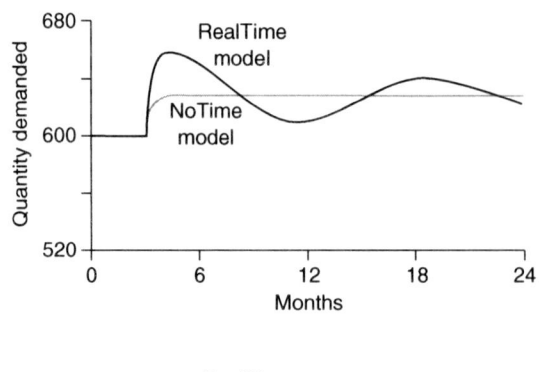

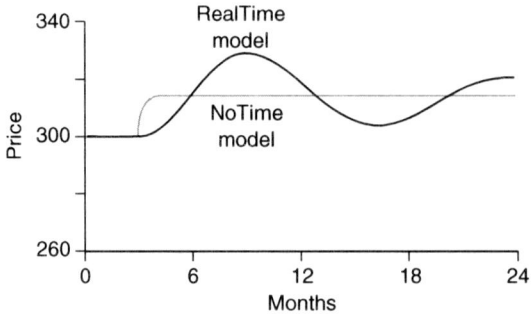

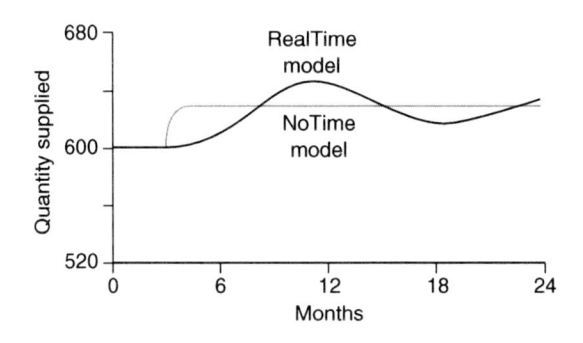

*Figure 7.5* Behavior after a demand increase.

The behavior of the RealTime model is strikingly different. In particular, note the cascading effect from top to bottom in Figure 7.5. Quantity demanded peaks soon after the exogenous shock, but prices continue rising for another six months. Quantity supplied peaks about nine months after the initial demand shock and about three months after the price peak. Moreover, all three variables overshoot and undershoot their eventual equilibrium levels before stabilizing, due to the delays in the negative feedback loops.

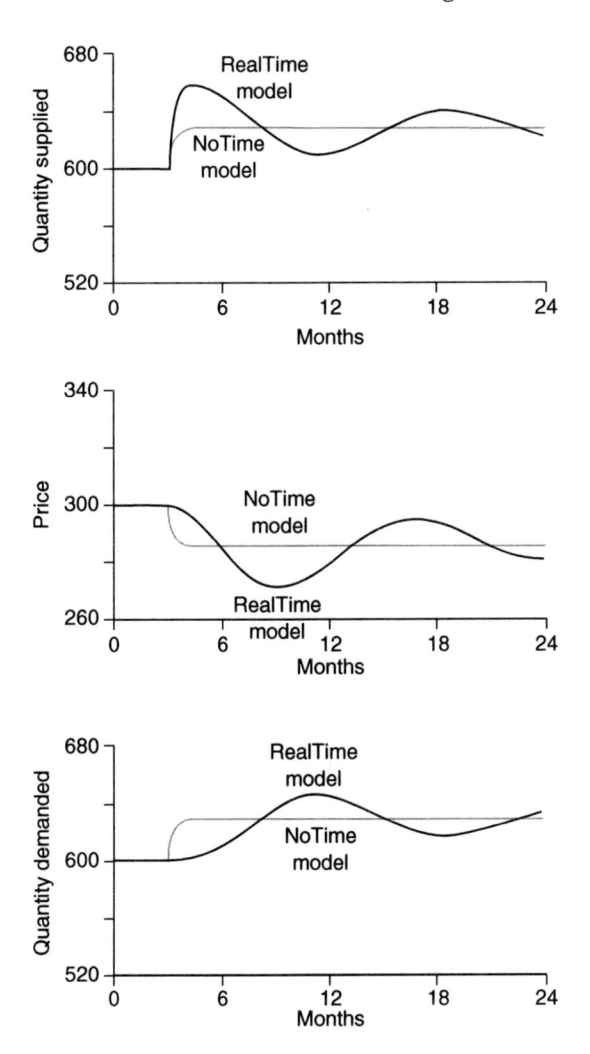

*Figure 7.6* Behavior after a supply increase.

Figure 7.6 displays the simulation results of an exogenous increase in *supply*. The shock registers initially on quantity supplied (top graph in Figure 7.6), and is transmitted next to price (middle graph), and then to quantity demanded (bottom graph). The difference between the behavior of the NoTime and RealTime models is obvious. Again, the lagged effects in the RealTime model are unmistakable. While quantity supplied peaks soon after the initial shock, the price trough occurs about six months later. Quantity demanded peaks about nine months after the initial supply shock and about three months after the price trough.

## Some pedagogical possibilities

A version of the simulation model that users can run online without special software has been posted on the Internet.[11] The user interface for that version is displayed in Figure 7.7, which shows the results of two simulations following an exogenous demand shock. Curves 1 and 2 display the behavior of the NoTime and RealTime models, respectively. (Note that the current parameter settings for the second simulation run are the default settings for the RealTime model in Table 7.1.)

In addition to the graph page for price, there are pages for quantity demanded and quantity supplied, and turning pages is as simple as clicking the turned-up corner. The other controls are also designed for easy manipulation. The "run" button on the graph page activates the simulation. Above the graph, at left, are on/off switches that activate exogenous shocks to the model. Two types of shocks are currently available: the supply and demand curves can be shifted, and it also possible to cause a sudden change in price. Step-by-step instructions are provided on another screen.

Above the graph on the right is a data entry table that permits changing assumptions about adjustment times – parameters affecting the length of delays in the model. To the left of the graph, users can modify the shapes of the supply and demand curves, as well as the sensitivity of price to changes in the supply–demand ratio.

At the top left are two navigation buttons that can reveal the structure of the model that is producing the behavior displayed in the graph. Clicking the "loops"

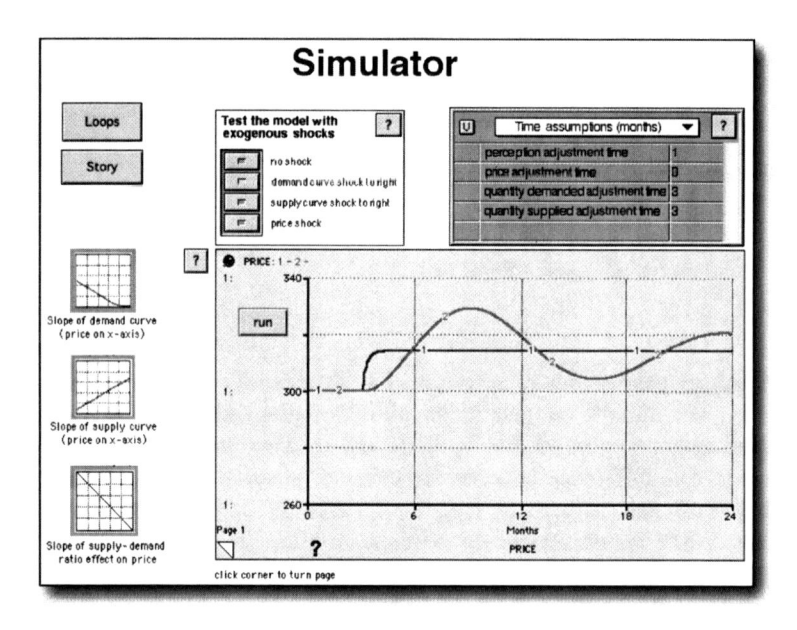

*Figure 7.7* User interface of online version of price–supply–demand model.

button opens a picture of the feedback loop diagram in Figure 7.4. Clicking the "story" button reveals an annotated explanation of the stock-and-flow structure of the model. The structure of the model is revealed in steps, as in a slide show, with the logic of the relationships between variables explained in non-technical terms at each step.

During a classroom lecture, an instructor could demonstrate the model's behavior under alternative assumptions. In a computer lab, students could run their own simulation experiments. Ways of using the model as a teaching tool will be as diverse as instructors' imaginations.

For example, instructors may wish to emphasize the limitations of the price–supply–demand graph, thus providing a teachable moment to clarify appropriate and inappropriate use of static models. In a principles course, that could go hand in hand with providing a reality check for students who might otherwise naively think that equilibrium conditions can be achieved soon after a policy initiative such as a trade agreement, a monetary policy action, etc. In an upper-level course, the learning objective could extend to a broader theoretical discussion of static and dynamic models and the criteria for choosing between them when modeling specific problems, as well as dynamically illustrating the distinction between endogenous and exogenous effects on quantities supplied and demanded. The topic could shift to political issues raised by oscillatory transition paths of policy effects, at least in departments where multidisciplinary conversations flourish (in contrast to those dominated by perspectives that look only toward "long-run" outcomes).

At the other end of the ambition spectrum, some instructors may see simulation modeling as a learning tool with great potential for engaging students in fruitful discussions about economic dynamics, even before the students acquire the higher-level mathematics training that is usually considered a prerequisite for such discussions. For that ambitious vision, this model would be only the beginning. Additional simple models could have a variety of learning objectives associated with understanding economic behavior in terms of feedback structure that operates over time. Moreover, it would encourage learning how markets work by testing textbook hypotheses in simulation models instead of accepting conventional economic wisdom (or, possibly, rejecting economic mantra altogether).

Notwithstanding the need for goals to guide instructional design, serendipity enlivens a lecture. What the students learn is often surprising and earns *ex post* credence as a worthy instructional objective. While it would be presumptuous to suggest a specific lecture plan, we offer a brief outline of an approach that instructors might find useful. Adopt or adapt as you see fit.[12]

- Define the model's "widget" as a particular consumer product, and work with a price–supply–demand graph having the same curves used in the model. Shift the demand curve to the right so that, at the original equilibrium price of $300 per widget, the quantity demanded would rise from 600 to 660 widgets/month. Students should estimate the new equilibrium price

($314 per widget) and quantity (629 widgets per month) by inspecting the graph or by solving the simultaneous linear equations.
- Encourage a discussion about the possible length of time and shape of the transition path for each variable. Remind students of the intended purpose and limitations of static graphs, notwithstanding the tendency of some textbooks and instructors to use static graphs as a basis for pseudo-dynamic representations of transition between equilibria.
- Give students access to the model and have them simulate the effects of various exogenous shocks. The default parameter values are set for the NoTime model, so students will see quick adjustments to equilibrium. Explain the adjustment time concepts, and how the NoTime assumptions approximate the instantaneous adjustment of a static price–supply–demand graph. If students experiment with different parameter settings, they will see that increasing the length of the delays causes the model to behave quite differently from the NoTime behavior. Then engage in a discussion of each delay process. Get an average classroom estimate for each parameter and run the model with those settings. Eventually, try RealTime's default settings in Table 7.1.
- Next, the students should study the structure that is producing the behavior – the loop diagram and the model's "story" – and try to envision the model's behavior, given the delays along the loops.
- Encourage further experimentation via adjustments to the slopes of the quantity curves and also by using a nonlinear effect of the supply–demand ratio on price.

This simple model is merely an illustrative example of stock-and-flow simulation models that can be used to teach economic dynamics. At the other extreme in terms of complexity is *MacroLab*, discussed earlier. Even that 500-equation open economy model of the U.S. economy is accessible to undergraduates because it is structured in sectors that can be studied and simulated separately, and insightful discussion arises from consideration of connections between domestic sectors and also with the rest-of-the-world sector.[13]

## Conclusion

Admittedly, there is one clear benefit from using a static price–supply–demand graph: it provides students with a simple method of inferring the long-run directional impact on price and quantity when there is an exogenous shift in supply or demand. But that entails a high cost since students have no intuitive way to gauge the time needed for equilibrium conditions to prevail. In fact, there is usually no consideration of the temporal issue. Moreover, the route between the shores of equilibria, while always relevant to policy considerations, is impossible to infer from a static graph. Students may learn pseudo-dynamic interpretative skills from their textbooks or instructors, but such knowledge can be a dangerous thing if it promotes misunderstanding of economic dynamics and naive expectations about the pace and path of "long-run" outcomes.

Teaching economics as if time mattered    87

The simulation model presented here is a tool to encourage investigation of how markets change over time. It focuses on processes that influence dynamics rather than presuming end results. Realistic adjustment times in the delay processes are empirical challenges, but estimating those parameters precisely is less important pedagogically than discussing and understanding the processes to which those parameters apply. Indeed, simply seeing the iconic clocks on the feedback diagram or seeing the behavioral response to longer delays causes attention to focus on the real-world meaning of such processes. After changes in supply and demand conditions are perceived by producers, what causes delays in price decision-making and implementation? What factors influence delays in the consumer response to price changes? What institutional and cultural norms, in addition to market conditions, influence the delays inherent in the producer response to price changes? Answering such questions requires finding out how people actually behave over time.

## Notes

\*  I appreciate the helpful advice received from University of Bergen colleagues Erling Moxnes and Tone Ektvedt. They discovered errors and omissions and made suggestions that improved the clarity of the paper. Any remaining mistakes or obscurity are my responsibility.
1  Very quickly, motivated students will be building their own models. The software is that friendly. A free demonstration version of *STELLA* is available at www.iseesystems.com/.
2  It may appear to students that the development sequence is pictorial model first and computer model second. In practice, it is an iterative process, with different modelers having equally compelling reasons for beginning with one or the other.
3  Documentation of *MacroLab* is available at https://bora.uib.no/handle/1956/2239. Readers interested in receiving a demonstration copy of the model should contact the author at david.wheat@uib.no.
4  Noticeably absent from this chapter's model are endogenous inventory management effects on production as well as the endogenous effects on production arising from awareness that sales have changed. Neither is part of the static price–supply–demand analytic framework, which we are transforming here into a dynamic process. The next logical step would be to assess the shortcomings of such a transformed model (and, by implication, the shortcomings of the static model from which it evolved) and make further improvements. Also, the resource adequacy assumption can be relaxed in more realistic versions of this model. A common feature of system dynamics inventory models is formulation for inventory rationing in case of threatened stock-outs, in which case sales would be lower than quantity demanded. Adding such realism to the model is easy but not justified by our present purpose, given the distraction of unnecessary diagram details.
5  Even in this simple model, some combinations of time delay assumptions and particular slopes of supply and demand curves can produce divergent behavior, in which case equilibrium would not be achieved.
6  Feedback loops can be drawn by hand or with graphics software. Here, they were drawn with tools in the system dynamics software package called *Vensim*, a product of Ventana Systems (www.vensim.com/). The online model's stock-and-flow structure was drawn with tools in another system dynamics software package called *STELLA* (www.iseesystems.com/). *STELLA* was also used to formulate and simulate

the model. Demo copies of both software packages are available at their respective websites.
7 The chain of cause-and-effect relationships in loop C1 is displayed in a counterclockwise direction, but that has no substantive significance. It could just as easily be displayed as clockwise movement. Later, we explain that C1 is an example of a *negative* feedback loop, sometimes called a *counteracting* feedback loop. The polarity of the loop has nothing to do with the direction of the arrows around the loop, and no meaning should be attached to the similarity of the terms "counterclockwise" and "counteracting." It is a counteracting loop because it contains an odd number of negative links and not because the arrows are displayed in a counterclockwise direction. Moreover, the direction of the arrows was not selected in order to convey any information about the polarity of the loop.
8 The larger size of loop C2 has no significance. If the two loops had been drawn the same size, one would be superimposed on top of the other, making it difficult to distinguish between them in the diagram.
9 A single negative loop with significant delays is sufficient for generating oscillations. See Sterman (2000).
10 Even the trillion-year adjustment time assumption can be useful. Such an assumption approximates a situation in which an adjustment *never* occurs. When implemented during a simulation run, such an extreme assumption effectively "cuts" the feedback loop along which the infinitely-long delay occurs. Cutting loops is a useful diagnostic technique for isolating the source of particular types of dynamic behavior in a model, such as oscillations, exponential growth or decay, or s-shaped growth.
11 The current URL is http://forio.com/broadcast/netsim/netsims/DavidWheat/delay-spsdonline/index.html. If, at a future date, that link is broken, interested readers should contact the author for information about accessing the model, either online or as a free runtime version that could be downloaded to a personal computer. Also, from time to time, there may be updates to the online version of the model, and it may differ somewhat from the description provided in this chapter.
12 Readers interested in establishing a dialogue on using this model or other models with students are encouraged to contact the author at david.wheat@uib.no.
13 Professor Martin Schaffernicht's Chilean undergraduates at the University of Talca have been engaged in such exercises, discussed in Schaffernicht (2008).

## References

Blinder, A. (1997) "On Sticky Prices: Academic Theories Meet the Real World," in N. G. Mankiw (ed.) *Monetary Policy*. Chicago: University of Chicago Press.
Boland, L. A. (2005) "Economics in Time vs. Time in Economics: Building Models so that Time Matters," *History of Economic Ideas* 13: 121–132.
Cohn, E., Cohn, S., Balch, D. C., and Bradley, J. (2001) "Do Graphs Promote Learning in Principles of Economics?," *Journal of Economic Education* 32: 299–310.
Colander, D. C. (1995) "The Stories We Tell: A Reconsideration of AS/AD Analysis," *The Journal of Economic Perspectives*, 9: 169–188.
Forrester, J. W. (1961) *Industrial Dynamics*. Cambridge, Mass.: Wright-Allen Press.
Forrester, N. B. (1982) "A Dynamic Synthesis of Basic Macroeconomic Theory: Implications for Stabilization Policy Analysis," Unpublished Ph.D. dissertation, Massachusetts Institute of Technology, Cambridge, Mass.
Friedman, M. (1960) *A Program for Monetary Stability*. New York: Fordham University Press.
Hampden-Turner, C. and Trompenaars, A. (1993) *Seven Cultures of Capitalism*. New York: Doubleday.

Hayden, F. G. (2005) *Policymaking for a Good Society: The Social Fabric Matrix Approach to Policy Analysis.* New York: Springer.
Keen, S. (2001) "The Russian Defeat of Economic Orthodoxy," *Post-Autistic Economics Review* 10, www.paecon.net/PAEReview/index.htm, accessed September 15, 2008.
Keynes, J. M. (1923) *A Tract on Monetary Reform.* London: Macmillan.
Marshall, A. (1946) *Principles of Economics* (8th edn). London: Macmillan.
Mass, N. J. (1975) *Economic Cycles: An Analysis of Underlying Causes.* Cambridge, Mass.: Wright-Allen Press.
—— (1980) "Stock and Flow Variables and the Dynamics of Supply and Demand," in J. Randers (ed.) *Elements of the System Dynamics Method.* (pp. 95–112). Cambridge, Mass.: MIT Press.
Pringle, D. and Leclaire, J. (2003) "The Kansas City Proposal," in E. Fullbrook (ed.) *The Crisis in Economics: The Post-Autistic Economics Movement: The First 600 Days.* London: Routledge.
Radzicki, M. (1988) "Institutional Dynamics: An Extension of the Institutionalist Approach to Socio-Economic Analysis," *Journal of Economic Issues* 22: 633–665.
—— (1993) "A System Dynamics Approach to Macroeconomics," Guest lecture at the Department of Information Science, University of Bergen.
—— (2003) "Mr. Hamilton, Mr. Forrester, and a Foundation for Evolutionary Economics," *Journal of Economic Issues* 37: 133–173.
Richardson, G. P. (1991) *Feedback Thought in Social Science and Systems Theory.* Waltham, Mass.: Pegasus Communications.
Schaffernicht, M. (2008) "Hacia el uso de los bucles de retroalimentación en el diseño instruccional – el caso de MacroLab," Proceedings of the Sixth Latin American System Dynamics Conference, Santiago, Chile, October 2008.
Sterman, J. D. (2000) *Business Dynamics: Systems Thinking and Modeling for a Complex World.* Boston: McGraw-Hill.
Tinbergen, J. (1939) *Statistical Testing of Business Cycle Theories: I – A Method and its Application to Investment Activity; II – Business Cycles in the United States of America.* New York: Agathon Press.
Wheat, I. D., Jr. (2007) "The Feedback Method of Teaching Macroeconomics: Is It Effective?," *System Dynamics Review* 23: 391–413.

# Part III
# Core theory courses

# 8 A pluralist approach to intermediate macroeconomics

*Irene van Staveren*

Whereas there is some diversity in the supply of macroeconomics textbooks, there is nonetheless a core of traditional macroeconomics covered by each – methodology, pedagogy, and topical coverage. I will briefly review these commonalities without necessarily doing justice to the treatment they receive in the textbooks.

The macroeconomic methodology employed in traditional textbooks assumes the macroeconomy is merely an aggregation of micro phenomena. For example, aggregate investment is the aggregation of individual investment decisions, without consideration for the interactions between investors through mechanisms such as cumulative change in risk perception, which may lead to herd behavior. Or, as another example, the simple aggregation assumption leads to summing individual consumer expenditures, as the major component of GDP, without acknowledging that some expenditures are undertaken to ameliorate reduced well-being, such as cleaning up environmental damage caused by economic growth. A third example of the misplaced aggregation assumption is that unemployment is the aggregate outcome of individual decisions to supply labor at the current wage rate, and hence a reflection of the extent to which members of the labor force are willing to work for the going wage. By accounting for the level of aggregate demand, the political economy approach argues that unemployment may be a macro phenomenon resulting from low aggregate demand, which can occur even when individuals are willing to work for lower wages than the market wage.

As a consequence of the aggregation assumption, traditional macroeconomics insists on the representative agent. This is a microeconomic actor with given preferences, who maximizes his utility given a budget constraint. Using the representative agent enables macroeconomic relationships to be construed as if they were individual decisions – indeed as aggregations of individual choices. Moreover, the assumption that the macroeconomy results from aggregation of individual decisions by representative agents (the 'median voter') does not necessitate a role for the state other than as guardian of property rights and as the second-best solution to market failure.

The second common feature of traditional textbooks is pedagogy in which a simple closed macroeconomy is first introduced to students, then gradually a more complex, open economy with financial markets, the labor market, and trade, with fixed and then floating exchange rates. This step-by-step approach is reflected in the macroeconomic flow diagram: the first version contains only households, firms, and the state, whereas the later version also includes the foreign sector. The strength of this approach is, of course, the gradual increase in complexity; but unfortunately at a price which economists such as Smith, Marx, and Keynes considered too high. The gradual increase falsely implies that the macroeconomy is an extension of micro analysis of markets: adding up demand and supply and including the international level through trade, international capital flows, and exchange rates. The danger is that feedback effects, positive and negative externalities, and cumulative causation are not only left out of the analysis, but are very difficult to incorporate once this picture of aggregation has been fixed into the minds of the students. Interrelatedness between markets, externalities, disequilibria, instability, and business cycles are indeed complex macroeconomic phenomena, but treating them as isolated occurrences, or as inconsequential side-effects of macroeconomic processes, strips much of the realism from macroeconomics teaching.

The third common feature is the core set of topics found in the majority of macroeconomics textbooks, such as inflation, growth, business cycles, unemployment, money and interest, and trade; with a concomitant exclusion of poverty, the relationship between efficiency and equity, globalization, instability, the unpaid economy, and the environment. In most textbooks, these topics get some attention, but do not have a chapter of their own. Each deserves attention through a more realistic and holistic teaching of macroeconomics; that is, macroeconomics for understanding the basics of the real economy.

This chapter on teaching political economy macroeconomics is a modest attempt to provide some basic elements for the teaching of a more realistic macroeconomics. Because of its subject matter, it will rely more on post-Keynesian economics than on other traditions within political economy, although ample attention will be devoted to institutions, social structures, and relations including gender, and the unpaid economy which features so prominently in feminist economics. It will try, within the limits of just one chapter, to address all three gaps referred to above, providing alternative suggestions.

The next section will form the core of the chapter, briefly discussing ten interrelated topics crucial to macroeconomics in the political economy literature and integral to any pluralist macro course. The following section will provide suggestions for pedagogical tools, and the last section will suggest a course outline.

## Macroeconomics for the real economy

Not all ten topics need to be covered to the same extent. This will depend on course length, the level of the course – this chapter pitches an intermediate level – and student background and interests. Nor should each topic be treated in the same sequence and categorization. But all ten should be part of a genuine pluralist macroeconomics course, as either core topics or important dimensions in the treatment of other topics.

## Topics for pluralist macroeconomics

### *Macroeconomic measurement*

Whereas traditional textbooks introduce Gross Domestic Product as the major measure for the macroeconomy, several alternatives have been developed over the past few decades. These should not be confused with refinements of the GDP measure, such as correcting for purchasing power differences (including *The Economist*'s 'Hamburger Index') or the one following the UN guidelines for the System of National Accounts, allowing estimation of part of agricultural subsistence production (also sometimes referred to as family labor). The alternative macroeconomic measures go beyond these, and start with a thorough critique of GDP as the measure for national well-being. This critique of the standard GDP can be summarized as follows:

- It ignores well-being decreases, such as air pollution which increases the incidence of asthma.
- It ignores environmental damage that directly decreases human well-being and also damage that does not (directly) affect humans, such as a decrease in biodiversity or long-run global warming.
- It ignores unpaid production contributing to well-being, which tends to be much bigger than the estimations allowed for family labor in the adapted national accounts.

The best-known alternative measure of national well-being was developed by Amaryta Sen in cooperation with the United Nations Development Program (UNDP). Known as the *Human Development Index* (HDI), it is published annually in UNDP's Human Development Reports. The HDI is a composite index, consisting of three objective dimensions of well-being: purchasing power, education, and health. Whereas purchasing power is measured as GDP per capita, the standard measure of well-being, education is measured as a combination of a country's performance on literacy and school enrollment, and health is proxied by life expectancy. The index is a number between 0 and 1, and the *Human Development Reports* publish results for almost every country in the world.

The HDI is not without its critics, however. First, in terms of GDP per capita, the richer countries dominate the top of the list. Second, comparisons over time are unreliable: the index has been constructed for comparison of countries in the same year, and is less suitable for comparisons over time. Third, although HDI is broader than the money metric of GDP, its extension is limited to education and health, thereby ignoring other dimensions of human development, such as fundamental freedoms as well as social dimensions of poverty. As a response, the *Human Development Reports* now include a broader index, the Human Poverty Index, which, however, is unable to fully address the above-mentioned criticisms. Finally, the HDI ignores disparities within countries, in particular between sexes, ethnic groups, and regions.

This last criticism has generated two responses. One, development of national-level *Human Development Reports*, with disaggregated HDIs per region, often reflects urban/rural differences as well as ethnic differences; sometimes explicit measures for ethnic groups are included. Second, the Gender-related Human Development Index (GDI) and the Gender Empowerment Index (GEM) are now also calculated. The GDI incorporates gender disparities as 'punishments' for a country's HDI level: the higher the disparity, the lower the GDI score relative to the HDI score. GEM is a complementary measure consisting of the share of women in decision-making positions, such as the female presence in parliament, in management, and the professions.[1]

An alternative to GDP per capita is the National Index of Happiness used by the Government of Bhutan. The Index contains three elements, which unfortunately are not completely quantifiable: first, derived from Buddhism, human well-being – both spiritual and material, – with emphasis on health and education; second, environmental preservation, measured as extent of protected (forest) areas; and third, self-reliance, in particular in food, and independence from foreign loans.

Another macroeconomic indicator relies on subjective happiness data, constructed from questionnaires on which respondents indicate their subjective happiness in answer to a wide variety of questions. Such measures are currently being developed by economists such as Frey and Stutzer (2002) in response to the so-called Easterlin Paradox whereby above a certain level of income, happiness does not improve with higher levels of GDP per capita.

Other well-being measures focus on the environmental dimensions of economic development, which may be limited to impacts on human well-being or may encompass intrinsic environmental value, so that changes in the stock of nature will affect the measure of well-being or, more generally, development. For example, in the Genuine Progress Indicator (GPI), developed by environmental economist Herman Daly, environmental damage is subtracted from GDP whereas unpaid production is added.

Finally, feminist economists have developed several measures of well-being deriving from unpaid production, largely performed by women. Estimations of the economic value of unpaid work vary widely, but an oft-cited measure[2] is 70 percent of GDP. At the 1995 UN Women's Conference, countries agreed to support construction of satellite accounts for unpaid production in the system of national accounts.[3] The money value of unpaid production is the opportunity cost of the work time involved, which can be valued by one of three different proxies: the average wage rate per level of education of the person carrying out the unpaid work; the wage rate per unpaid work task, independent of the level of education of the unpaid worker; and three, the market price of the final good produced in unpaid work time.

Measures of women's unpaid work are often used complementary to GDP, although recent research suggests that a strict distinction between the paid and unpaid economy does not exist, and thus it is advised not to add two measures of well-being – paid and unpaid – to generate total well-being. Instead, caring is better understood as a fundamental human activity contributing to well-being through personal relationships, the value of which cannot be captured with money-based measures for the time involved. Often, time is not the defining characteristic of a caring activity, and hence the opportunity cost is not the best proxy. The contextual basis of caring, however, makes it very difficult to measure on a macro basis; thus studies measuring the economic value of caring remain largely micro-based.

*Social structure and institutions*

Every economy is embedded in a larger social framework, with its social structures and institutions. Structures are social regularities, such as segmentation between groups of people; institutions are social rules underlying such regularities, which may have moral content and may be different for different groups, such as gender norms. These structures and institutions influence macroeconomic processes, by constraining and enabling; thus they can be recognized as 'structures of constraint' (e.g. discrimination) but also as 'enabling' (e.g. collective action). At the same time, structures and institutions are also influenced by macroeconomic trends, policies, and processes. In institutional economics, this relationship between the social and the economic is understood in terms of co-evolution and the middle way between over-determination (by dominant structures) and under-determination (by entirely autonomous agents).

This recognition is crucial for macroeconomics to help elucidate why the macro level is not simply an aggregation of the micro, since it is mediated by structures and institutions, often through the meso level of the economy, where interactions between agents often lead to externalities, cumulative causation, collective action, power, and other types of feedbacks.

A central characteristic of social structures and institutions is that they are enduring, existing over time, not generally changing from one day to another, whereas their development takes time. It is this relatively stable social and institutional setting that influences the basic macroeconomic features of an economy and partly explains differences between stages of economic development. The Industrial Revolution, for example, and the fall of the Berlin Wall are major institutional changes that explain stages in economic development. But differences between economies at the same period of time can also partly be attributed to different institutional set-ups of the macroeconomies. This can be illustrated by inequality between major groups, such as landowners and landless farmers, or by the extent of trust between ethnic groups and classes.

Whereas inequality tends to constrain economic interaction, and hence the efficiency of allocation in markets (leading to high transaction costs, segmentation, and exclusion), trust can reduce transaction costs when social structures do not express high inequality. Such an enabling effect of social structures (relative equality) and institutions (trusting norms) is recognized as a beneficial role of social capital for the macroeconomy: the more social capital, the better the economy's aggregate efficiency. Studies measuring the macroeconomic impact of trust, and other moral, cultural and social norms, suggest they are helpful in explaining the relative economic success of some countries (such as the Scandinavian countries). At the same time, however, macro-level social capital studies have been criticized for their sweeping generalizations across cultures, simplistic measures of norms (for example in the World Values Studies), and lack of attention to mediating mechanisms between social and economic variables. What is clear, though, is that social structure and institutions matter for the macroeconomic performance of countries over time and vis-à-vis each other, as they provide the social context in which economic variables are embedded.

There are various ways to incorporate this into macroeconomic pedagogy, especially by using a comparative perspective, either over time – necessitating a long-run perspective, linking macroeconomic changes to institutional changes – or cross-country, where differences in social structures and institutions are highlighted. For simplicity, major categories of social differentiation are political, social, cultural, and moral.

Two caveats must be stressed, however. First, the role of macroeconomic policies should be distinguished from the long-run and resilient influence of social structures and institutions; at the same time, it should be understood that policies may strengthen or undermine certain structures and institutions. Second, not only within but also between countries, social relations involving structures and institutions may affect macroeconomic performance, either constraining (e.g. colonialism, debt burdens, decreasing terms of trade for regions such as sub-Saharan Africa) or enabling (e.g. control of a scarce resource such as oil, or membership of a strong trade bloc such as the EU).

## *Pluralist agency*

The macroeconomy has no micro foundations. Instead, behavioral economics, economic psychology, socio-economics, and game theory emphasize that economic agents are pluralist, driven by a variety of motivations, from self-interest to fairness and from power-seeking to love. They do not maximize most of the time; instead they rely on intuition and emotions. Sometimes they obey social norms and sometimes just follow others. And their behavior is interdependent at the micro level – i.e. strategic behavior in experimental economics – as well as at the macro level – i.e. herd behavior in financial markets and the rat race for diplomas as investment in human resources. This interdependence of behavior makes macroeconomic behavior more than the sum of micro behavior, and different from the aggregate of a representative agent.

In other words, what distinguishes a real-world economic agent from the representative agent of traditional textbooks is that she is a social being, which is expressed positively – through other-regarding behavior – and negatively – through power-seeking behavior; and neutrally – through the following of certain non-moral norms, habits, and routines. Macroeconomic phenomena are not merely aggregations of individual behavior but very often include important interaction effects. Two well-known examples are briefly discussed here: herd behavior in financial markets and the social norms allocating unpaid work to women in households.

Herd behavior was first recognized by Keynes in his analysis of the 1929 financial crises. With the increased openness of financial markets, this phenomenon is more visible globally. In today's crisis, it is the collective, though uncoordinated, behavior of investors leading to a cumulative response to weak stock market values, an overvalued exchange rate, and various asset bubbles, such as real estate markets. The sudden run on bank deposits, sell-off of stocks and termination of loans by foreign and domestic investors led to a spiral of asset sales and falling asset prices, which in turn resulted in bankruptcies, currency devaluations, and unemployment, reducing GDP levels.

The 1997 Asian herd behavior was led by large investors at commercial banks and (pension) funds, followed by small-scale asset owners and deposit holders, and triggered emergency policies by central banks – on the advice of the IMF – raising interest rates or blocking deposits (as in Argentina). Various political economy analyses conclude that the larger investors reduced their losses by lobbying the governments concerned for emergency packages (often backed by the IMF). This in fact resulted in bail-outs for the (foreign) commercial investors, leaving local small-scale investors, deposit holders, small- and medium-scale enterprises, and workers with the full burden of the losses. In fact, these crises are sad examples of how agency effects via rent-seeking, market power, corruption, and risk-shifting may result in moral hazard with significant macroeconomic impact.

The second example of macro behavior that cannot easily be reduced to the aggregation of micro behavior is not unrelated to the first, as it involves a response at the household level to the risks of financial instability and the felt impacts of the crisis on households' resources: the increase in women's unpaid work. This can be explained by the interaction of individual agency motivated by caring attitudes, social norms about the gender division of labor, and the disadvantaged position of women in markets, which together sustain a vicious circle of high unpaid work for women, a relatively inelastic female labor supply, and the buffer function of unpaid production in households helping to substitute part of income losses during crises and downturns of the business cycle. In fact, women's increase in unpaid production, replacing consumer goods with homemade food, medicine, and clothing, as well reduced or more expensive public services such as health care, transport services, drinking water, and energy, tends to cushion the livelihoods of households; but at the same time may keep aggregate demand relatively low, which may prevent economic recovery. This negative macroeconomic effect of prudent micro-level strategies is similar to the well-known savings paradox.

Thus, economic agents have pluralist motives which are not necessarily self-centered, and which may result in uncoordinated collective, cumulative, or interactive behavior, with significant macroeconomic effects. This is why some attention to agency, although a microeconomic topic, should not be left out of pluralist macro teaching.

### Uncertainty and risk

Whereas traditional economics assumes either perfect information or risk with known outcomes, political economy recognizes a more fundamental understanding of imperfect information: uncertainty, which implies not only the impossibility of assigning probabilities to possible future events, but also that the number and types of possible future events are unknown and that the understanding of time in economic analysis is irreversible. Consequently, the economy is not a closed system moved by external shocks, but an open system generating irreversible changes into an open, unknown future.

This view allows for exogenous changes, but is not limited to them. Whereas traditional economics explains high growth and episodes of crisis by technological development, population growth, war, or political shifts, political economy emphasizes endogenous change. This view emphasizes the interrelatedness of economic variables, for example through feedback effects between investment, production, employment, purchasing power, and aggregate demand, while recognizing the role of social variables such as power, institutions, and inequality. Another implication of uncertainty in the economy, besides endogenous change, is that agents pursue risk-mitigating strategies, which may have important macroeconomic effects. Such effects may be expressed in savings, investments, labor supply, export diversification, import restrictions, and price controls, as well as in other variables, such as supply and demand for unpaid work.

The open systems approach to economics implies that the economy is both embedded in a wider system which influences the economy and in turn is influenced by it. This leads to the adaptation of the macroeconomic flow shown in Figure 8.1.

Figure 8.1 suggests a more complex view of the economy than orthodox economics. Two relations will be highlighted, via uncertainty. First is the interrelatedness of the environment and the economy. The environment partly functions as a resource, an often unpriced input into the economic process, even though clean air and water obviously have a value and are becoming increasingly scarce. The environment also enables the economy to develop, however. By providing the preconditions for the economy, nature circumscribes its limits, which, when

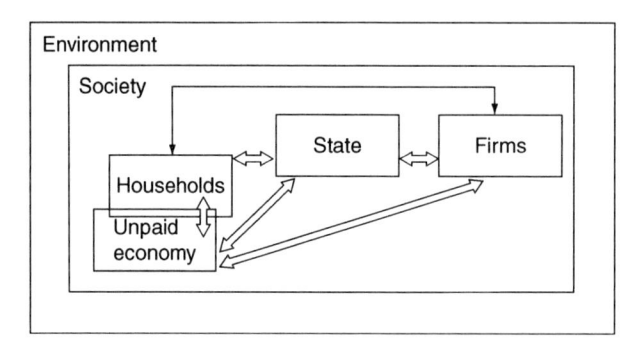

*Figure 8.1* Adaptation of the macroeconomic flow.

crossed, may generate not only environmental damage but also negative feedbacks, visible in stock depletions (oil and fish, for example), in erosion, in decreasing agricultural productivity, and in global warming, the long-run effects of which are yet unknown.

Within its boundaries, systems tend to be self-adjusting: i.e., an out-of-balance situation can be corrected within the system, either automatically, for example through market forces, or with the help of anti-cyclical fiscal policies. But when a system moves beyond its borders, it will develop uncontrollably (and unpredictably), moving faster away from 'equilibrium' into chaos (the 'butterfly effect'). Chaos theory has been applied to interactions between the environment and the economy but also to chaotic but purely economic phenomena, such as financial markets.

The second illustration builds on an earlier example of the role of the unpaid economy. This part of the economy, supported by power relations, is not unrelated to the rest of the economy. The unpaid economy functions as a buffer during crises, and hence is part of households' risk-mitigating strategies. It functions as a substitute for commodities, and hence as a form of non-monetary savings; as an alternative form of employment – next to paid work and leisure time; and as a source for reinforcing and transmitting social norms between generations. In this last function, as the source of social cohesion and social norms such as trust, the unpaid economy also generates caring motivations in (future) economic agents and other motivations that are other-regarding, in which agents engage in economic behavior outside the unpaid economy. Economic agents are human agents and carry the beliefs, norms, commitments, and emotions they have in one domain of life with them to other domains, such as consumer behavior, investment behavior, and contributing to government revenues.

The role of uncertainty and risk-mitigating strategies of households and firms, and societal and environmental feedbacks should not be underestimated at the macro level. Unfortunately such impacts are difficult to measure but, nevertheless, indirect indicators suggest their significance. Opportunity costs of unpaid work time, loss of foreign direct investment due to political and social instability, and, of course, the impacts of financial crises cannot be omitted from macroeconomic analysis as exogenous phenomena to be absorbed and quickly overtaken by a new stable equilibrium. There may very well be no path leading back to equilibrium, and hence uncertainty may have very serious real effects.

## *Unemployment and poverty*

Poverty and unemployment are closely related and therefore may best be discussed under the same heading. At the same time, it should be emphasized that the majority of the world's poor are working poor, either working for low wages in the formal economy (sometimes combining two jobs), or underemployed in the informal economy. So although poverty is not necessarily caused by unemployment, it is often closely related to various types of non-regular employment: work for very low wages, at low labor standards, with flexible contracts or no contracts at all, or underemployed as family labor (often in agriculture) or self-employed (often in the urban informal economy in the developing world), or working unpaid because of pressing caring needs in the household in combination with asymmetric norms assigning this work to women.

Traditional economics assumes poverty to be a consequence of low growth of GDP per capita (either due to low GDP growth or high population growth or both), whereas political economy emphasizes other dimensions of poverty such as lack of entitlements for certain groups, resulting in structural inequalities, too open international financial markets, and unregulated globalization. Consequently, policy advice for poverty reduction differs substantially between the two traditions. GDP growth (and fertility control) is favored by traditional economics, assuming a trickle-down process within countries and a convergence of growth rates between countries. Internationally, this policy view is expressed by the World Bank, the US Treasury, and the IMF, also referred to as the 'Washington Consensus.' This consensus consists of a basic policy package of trade liberalization, domestic market deregulation, privatization, reduction in government expenditures, and labor market flexibilization, as well as institutional changes favoring an under-defined notion of 'good governance.'

In the political economy approach, it is not growth per se, but pro-poor growth generating a sufficient number of jobs that is central to poverty reduction. Moreover, political economy also emphasizes redistribution and (national and international) regulation supporting job-intensive growth with a high poverty reduction elasticity. This implies growth that increases the ratio of wage earnings over capital earnings, stimulation of labor-intensive sectors, and a redistribution of resources (such as land) in order to crowd in production and productivity by the poor. The political economy approach involves similar policies to those followed by the OECD countries in the 1960s and 1970s, as well as policies still pursued with success – and against the liking of the Washington-based institutions – by countries such as China and Chile.

For unemployment, a similar divergence of views exists. According to traditional economics, the major reason for excess supply in the labor market is wage rigidity, caused either by minimum wage legislation or by institutional factors underlying 'sticky wages' such as trade unions and the insider-outsider phenomenon in labor markets. The policy advice is abolition or reduction of minimum wage laws, and reduction in the power of trade unions. Alternatively, political economy emphasizes lack of aggregate demand as the underlying cause of unemployment.

Moreover, in a globalized economy, aggregate demand may be weakened by cost competition decreasing real wages, reduced government expenditures following tax reductions in order to attract Foreign Direct Investment (FDI), and an increased import bill due to currency devaluation, or loss of competitive advantage in crucial sectors of the economy such as food. Therefore, unemployment is not merely a labor market phenomenon caused by high wages, but the result of a multitude of macro (and micro) economic processes, reinforcing feedback effects between aggregate demand, investment, and labor demand.

For both poverty and unemployment, global data suggest some groups are more disadvantaged than others. Unemployment rates are highest for women, immigrants, and youth; the majority of the global poor are women and children, often belonging to ethnic minorities or migrant groups. This suggests that structural inequalities interact with the above-mentioned macroeconomic feedbacks to cause poverty and unemployment: some groups are more likely to be unemployed or poor than other groups. Consequently an increase in aggregate demand, for example via a more successful export strategy, does not necessarily improve the position of the poor and unemployed. It may further increase income inequality if the export success is based on competition on low labor costs, as in some South Asian export industries employing a majority of women. Thus, complementary policies are necessary at the micro and at the meso level, in order to extend economic development. The trickle-down mechanism of growth is very unreliable, slow, and sometimes non-existent. Complementary policies vary from investment in the education and health care of disadvantaged groups to anti-discrimination policies in labor, land, and credit markets; and investing through public goods in the productivity of the unpaid economy (for example by providing better access to drinking water and energy). Teaching about unemployment and poverty, therefore, should include: the macroeconomy with its level of aggregate demand; formal and informal labor markets; and the role of public goods to crowd in production and productivity of the poor.

*Underdevelopment and instability*

While unemployment and poverty are the most pressing macroeconomic problems, underdevelopment and macroeconomic instability are closely related. The gap between rich and poor countries has increased during the past four decades, along with the incidence of debt, exchange rate, and fiscal crises. While absolute poverty levels have decreased in most regions of the world, relative poverty has increased, both in relatively well-growing economies and in stagnating economies. Given the multiple causes of poverty, the major macroeconomic problem is not lack of growth, but underdevelopment. In some political economy perspectives, the roots of underdevelopment lie in history, in particular in colonization, which has made developing economies dependent upon unequal trade with former colonizers while at the same time the structure of their economies makes it very difficult to break free. The lock-in consists of a traditional trade pattern with decreasing terms of trade, an infrastructure supporting monoculture rather than a diversified agricultural sector, lack of industrialization keeping value added low, underinvestment in health care and education, and political instability, constraining innovation and capital inflows (sometimes even leading to net capital outflows). Other political economy approaches emphasize current power imbalances between the developed and the developing world, through high foreign debts, protection of EU and US agricultural markets, dumping of subsidized overproduction, and the increased bargaining power of footloose Western multinationals over labor in developing countries. Underdevelopment, thus, goes beyond lack of growth, while the growth convergence theory has been challenged by political economists, suggesting that global laissez-faire will not solve the problem of underdevelopment.

Instability, in particular financial instability, is one of the few macroeconomic issues recently understood by traditional economics as important. This has led to a shared view that unregulated financial markets can cause more harm than good because of the instability inherent in the large volume of capital flows in today's financial markets, which exceed by more than 100-fold the value of international trade in goods and services. Without a global central bank, a single world currency, and a system of global taxation (such as a Tobin Tax on currency transactions), financial markets are the largest and most liberalized markets today.

Although theoretically, national institutions such as central banks and international institutions such as the IMF could stabilize these markets, in reality maneuverability has become constricted. This is partly due to the sheer volume of trade in money and financial assets, and partly due to the risk of diversion of financial transactions away from regulated markets to off-shore financial centers. Financial markets exemplify markets where moral hazard (due to expected bailouts), free riding (through off-shore banking), and herd behavior (following any random trigger) can significantly affect the economy, with possible GDP setbacks for several years. The subsequent cumulative effects on employment and interest rates may suppress aggregate demand for a period of time, while regional 'contamination' may make it difficult to recover in a situation in which export partners suffer from the same conditions.

Instability, then, may become another factor in the dynamics keeping developing countries behind developed economies, the latter being better able to protect themselves from financial instability through a more regulated banking system and the more transparent role of their state institutions, and because these economies offer fewer opportunities for rent-seeking to foreign investors.

### *Endogenous growth and increasing returns*

In political economy, economic growth – as well as stagnation – is endogenous rather than exogenous. Business cycles are generated within the economy, whereas growth is caused as much by endogenous factors as by autonomous trends such as technological advancement and improved education. Whereas in Marxist-related strands of economics, growth is largely determined by the particular distribution of the surplus (too much of either capital or labor will dampen growth through a wage-profit squeeze or high unemployment); in institutional economics, growth largely depends on conducive institutions generating a path-dependent growth trajectory. Such institutions in turn create a stable context for innovations and intra-firm and inter-firm learning to take place, and reduced risks and uncertainties for investments in new, potential growth sectors. In the post-Keynesian tradition, growth is generated by a virtuous circle of low unemployment and high aggregate demand, boosting investor's optimism, and leading to innovation and market expansion.

Whether growth is further supported by increasing returns is of particular interest to post-Keynesian economists. The economy is not necessarily bound by constant returns to scale, as assumed by orthodoxy, but may very well exhibit increasing returns. In traditional economics literature on increasing returns, the source is mostly attributed to human resources: a better-educated workforce is likely to be increasingly productive through on-the-job learning, team work, intra-sectoral mobility of specialized workers, and other learning spillovers. In the political economy literature, other aspects are emphasized such as efficiency wages increasing productivity, and reductions in structural inequalities, such as land reform.

A simple endogenous growth model is the 'AK model', in which growth is assumed to be caused by the combination of capital (K) with a particular level of human resources (A): $Y = f(A, K)$. This model, however, treats A as a constant and cannot explain increasing returns. Increasing returns models have a Schumpeterian character, and include human resources because of its various interactive and cumulative effects. This, in turn, shifts attention to the meso level of the economy, with concepts such as learning-by-doing, collective learning, and R&D spillovers.

Such models recognize explicitly technological development – and its endogeneity – for capital, and of human resources (HR) for labor (L), as influencing labor productivity beyond the impact of capital and technology on labor productivity: $Y = f(A, K, HR, L)$.

Furthermore, such models recognize the importance of distribution. This is no longer assumed to have a negative impact – this is the outcome of Paretian welfare economics in which efficiency and equity are constructed as trade-offs. Under certain conditions, redistribution may be conducive to growth. Marxist approaches emphasize the distribution of factor incomes: a higher share of wages versus profits is likely to increase aggregate demand (through a higher propensity to consume from wages than from profit incomes), hence stimulating growth through higher consumer demand. Other approaches emphasize the distribution of resources such as land, likely to boost marginal returns of agriculture in economies with high inequality in land ownership, and the gender distribution of wages, likely to generate extra product competitiveness in international markets through low cost prices, as well as extra profits through a lower ratio of profits over wages, enabling the purchase of new technology.

### *Globalization*

Globalization is not exclusively a macroeconomic issue. It is highly interdisciplinary and studied in international relations, political economy, development studies, and many other fields. Several interdisciplinary books on globalization (DeMartino 2000, Rodrik 1997) contain useful chapters for a political economy course. Of course, globalization is a container concept which, when studied more closely, includes many of the topics already discussed above. At the same time it is worthwhile to devote some attention to globalization for three reasons. First, it is a hot item, with many heated debates about global labor standards, the impact of China on world trade, the current demand for a new international financial architecture, and the shifting of power to the emerging countries of China, India, Brazil, and South Africa; not to mention, the increasing empirical support impugning longtime accepted theories such as the Stolper–Samuelson theorem on factor prices, the convergence hypothesis, and absolute versus relative comparative advantages. These debates, not limited to academia and international policy forums, are also conducted in newspapers, sometimes even leading to a mobilization of crowds by NGOs and demonstrations of critics and anti-globalists at international policy meetings. So students will be familiar with parts of the debates, which will help to connect them with macroeconomic teaching.

Second, although globalization is assumed to be new, the world has experienced earlier phases of globalization, from colonial times onwards, peaking at the end of the nineteenth century. Hence, a focus on globalization will help disentangle myths, particularly those in the popular press, for example on the relative extent of globalization (80 percent of EU trade is between member states), and the distorted view that all production factors have become globalized, when in fact globalization is largely limited to capital (world migration has been more extensive, with much more liberal migration policies, in earlier times, in particular at the beginning of the twentieth century). But there is an important qualitative difference today compared to earlier bouts of globalization: the introduction of global value chains. Decreasing transport costs and technological advances in communication have enabled a global division of labor – mainly between Northern skilled/high-wage labor and Southern unskilled/low-wage labor in the production processes. An important share of global trade today consists of intermediate products.

And third, treating globalization as an issue of its own enables the instructor to demonstrate the tenets of macro political economy vis-à-vis traditional macroeconomics: market interconnectedness, feedback effects, cumulative causation, path dependence, power, and the need for markets to be balanced by state regulation (and the lack of a global state to do so).

For teaching purposes, globalization may be distinguished in three, interconnected, parts: (1) global trade in goods and services, including property rights; (2) short-term and long-term global financial flows; and (3) globalized production systems/global value chains, including the role of multinationals.

Globalization may be linked to development. The major question from a development perspective is, of course, whether globalization will enable or constrain developing countries in attaining higher levels of development and reduced poverty. This debate has many dimensions and strong advocates on either side, and may be expressed pedagogically by distinguishing the low road and high road to development. The low road emphasizes globalization in order to attract FDI, offering low wages, cheap labor standards, and tax holidays to MNCs, and minimizing trade unions; whereas the high road challenges the race to the bottom by competing on the basis of productivity. This entails a deliberate and more coordinated strategy of strong investment in human resources, technological upgrading, developing own global value chains, in combination with policy measures to control the inflow of short-term capital and, possibly, limit the importation of goods that would otherwise destroy infant industries. The low-road/high-road pedagogical approach may be illustrated with empirical case studies on the Asian tiger economies, including the more recent examples of countries that managed the shift from a low to a high road development trajectory, such as Malaysia.

*Money, finance, and volatility*

Political economy emphasizes money's role in social relations, especially debt relations. Money is not simply a unit of account – the numéraire in the Walrasian economy – or a provider of individual utility like other commodities, as in orthodox microeconomics, where money is assumed redundant and its real-world existence cannot be adequately explained. Political economists argue that money is real, not neutral, affecting and being affected by the real economy; hence, money is assumed endogenous, created through the demand for loans. In addition, money is related not so much to monetary policy but more to credit and fiscal policy, specifically through the state's multiple roles as lender-of-last resort and tax collector.

Political economists emphasize the varied and inherently social roles of money. One such role is as generalized purchasing power, rather than as a commodity in itself. This entails the functions of means of exchange, hoarding, and payment, underscoring money's role as a source of social, political, and economic power. Moreover, all forms of money – coins, checks, plastic cards, and book balances – entail a promise to pay, which, again, implies a social relation. This underscores the importance of trust in a monetized economy, in particular with fiat money. Money relies on important social values, without which monetary systems would have high transaction costs and require a much stronger role for the central bank. This recognition links back to micro themes such as rationality and agency and accommodates attention to recent themes such as the role of trust in the economy or local exchange systems with local moneys.

When money is understood as a social relation evolving from promise, trust, and resulting debt relations, the focus can be shifted to credit and finance. Indeed, some political economists argue that money is credit and that the two cannot be separated. A macroeconomic view of finance necessarily includes an international perspective, as most financial markets today are very open, dominated by short-term speculative capital flows. Whereas traditional economics explains financial flows by interest rates and differences in rates of investment return, adjusted for differences in perceived risks, political economists (especially post-Keynesians) argue that investment is not driven by a cost-benefit analysis of expected returns on investment; rather, investment is largely exogenous, determined by the so-called 'animal spirits' of investors. In turn, these individual motivations are highly influenced by social factors, easily leading to herd behavior when asset values or relative prices (of currencies for example) transcend certain psychological boundaries. This may further increase volatility in financial markets and eventually lead to booms and bursts, with attendant real impacts. Institutional economists suggest a much stricter international monitoring system with early warning indicators for a country's debt burden and for currency over- or under-valuation, as well as for bank solvency rates.

Apart from more structural reforms proposed for the international financial architecture, less complex but potentially more difficult to implement policy measures have been proposed. One is a global currency which, given the long gestation of the European Monetary Union, is not likely to be feasible, at least in the near future. Another reform debated for several decades is the Tobin Tax – a small tax on international capital flows to discourage speculation and help generate a global fund to support developing countries.

### *Macroeconomic policy*

Obviously, each topic discussed above deserves its own discussion of policy. This sub-section, therefore, will not review particular macroeconomic policies, such as monetary or trade policy, but rather provide suggestions for how the role of the state and other policy-making institutions, especially at the international level, can be incorporated in macro pedagogy. This implies a meta-level view of macroeconomic policies, concerned with the relationship between the state, market, and civil society. Traditional economics tends to ignore civil society while emphasizing market expansion vis-à-vis state contraction. Consequently the macroeconomic role of the state is understood as twofold: creating conditions for markets through liberalization policies and (temporarily) regulating markets only when they exhibit high instability, such as long-term trade imbalances or structurally high unemployment rates.

Each of the constituent policies of the Washington Consensus has been criticized by political economists. Monetary policy may do more harm than good when interest rates skyrocket with small- and medium-scale businesses unable to repay loans. Fiscal restraint not only has severe social consequences, contributing to greater inequality, but may also lead to under-investment in human resources, in particular through lack of support for poor parents to send or keep their children in school, and the levying of user fees for public heath care services as well as the privatization of health care. Privatization can often lead to asset ripping by foreign companies, often abetted by local rent-seeking elites, rather than to the crowding-in of productive investments. Domestic market liberalization does not necessarily reduce prices and improve quality, as shown in developed countries by railways and the taxis for example, and in developing countries by drinking water. Trade liberalization is impugned because of increases in income inequality that accompany even the most successful cases such as China and Ireland. At the same time, shifting resources toward exports – either through currency devaluations or subsidized inputs for export agriculture or institutional changes – may negatively affect other markets. This risk has been recognized particularly in Africa where men's plots with cash crops have expanded at the cost of women's plots for food production. Finally, labor market flexibilization in an era of globalization has helped to retain labor cost competitiveness but at the cost of informalization, deteriorating labor standards and pressure on wages, which may in the end negatively affect purchasing power and hence aggregate demand.

Political macroeconomics is varied and is not simply a unified response to the failure of the Washington Consensus. The common denominator is less emphasis on market liberalization and more state responsibility in shaping and regulating markets. Examples of policies with a stronger role of the state are employment programs, controls on the inflows of foreign capital, infant industry protection, fiscal policies which favor a reasonable deficit rather than a balanced budget, and monetary policies which target not single-digit inflation rates but rates that remain below a context-specific critical limit (presumably around 20 percent). At a more strategic level, political macroeconomics stimulates regional trade agreements, such as Mercosur in South America, rather than the more unequal ones under the aegis of the WTO or individual rich nations, such as the proposed Free Trade Area of the Americas.

Political macroeconomics supports proposals for a new international financial architecture emanating from developing countries – which have suffered most from financial crises – such as regional alternatives to the IMF, like an Asian monetary fund. In addition, it supports international solutions to problems extending beyond the national level, such as the Tobin Tax, a world currency, regulated trade, reform of the World Bank and IMF (including the voting system biased in favor of rich countries), and more liberalized global labor markets (reducing the immigration barriers in Europe, the US, and other OECD nations).

Finally, a small section of the political economics literature emphasizes the importance of the unpaid economy, civil society, or the care economy at the macro level. Macroeconomic policies affect not only the role of the state and the extent and efficiency of markets, but also the size and effectiveness of the unpaid economy. Whereas some policies are likely to dump costs on this economy – increasing unpaid labor time and reducing non-monetary dimensions of well-being, other policies may support the effectiveness of this economy, through investments in labor-saving technology, improving the productivity of unpaid work, and enabling collective action among weaker groups in the economy such as small-scale entrepreneurs, giving them access to credit and other resources as well as new markets. The objective of macroeconomic policy is to achieve balance between the three domains of market, state, and the unpaid economy in order to increase well-being.

## Teaching tools

Teaching economics in an engaged way, making it as realistic as possible, and enabling collective learning, is much more difficult for macroeconomics than for microeconomics. Role playing, experimental game theory, or case studies with local data collection are very hard to apply to the study of the macroeconomy.

But this should not discourage movement away from 'chalk and talk,' as techniques exist to make macroeconomics more real and engaging for students. Two such techniques that I have found useful are a role play on macroeconomic policy and the world trade game.

---

**1 Role play on macroeconomic policy**

Class size: 15–55 students. Equipment: access to the university library; access to the internet with a maximum density of 4 students per computer, and a printer. The lecturer plays the role of judge, a small group is the jury, and two larger groups constitute two parties, each defending a particular macroeconomic policy and its policy efficacy.

Possible policy objectives:

- poverty reduction;
- reduction in unemployment;
- increased economic growth;
- less instability.

Duration of the game: 3.5–6.5 hours:

- 15 minutes' instruction, including websites and reports (available in the university library) as relevant sources;
- two–four hours' group work for the two parties preparing their statements, and for the jury to get background information on the topic:
- one hour (two hours) for the role play, including a fifteen-minute break for the jury to prepare the verdict:
- ten minutes for group A;
- ten minutes for group B;
- 20 minutes' discussion between A and B.

If desirable, another round

- 15 minutes' break for the jury;
- ten minutes' verdict (favoring A or B) with arguments;
- ten minutes' wrap by the judge.

Possible cases:

- World Bank versus development NGOs (Oxfam, Women's Environment and Development Organization, etc.) on economic reform and/or Poverty Reduction Strategy Papers (PRSPs);
- government of country X in debt crisis versus IMF on stabilization measures and assistance package;
- African farmers versus US or EU farmers on agricultural trade policy;
- WTO versus country X or group of countries on a particular trade policy;
- incoherence between development objectives (gender equality, poverty reduction, millennium development goals) and Washington Consensus policies.

Suggested websites and reports for the info sheet:

- IMF: www.imf.org;
- World Bank: www.worldbank.org;
- Joe Stiglitz on IMF: www.thenewrepublic.com/041700/stiglitz041700.html;
- WTO: www.wto.org;
- NGO sites: www.tradeobservatory.org, www.wtoaction.org, www.oxfam.org, www.oneworldaction.org, www.igtn.org;
- UNDP's *Human Development Reports*;
- World Bank's *World Development Report*;
- UNCTAD's annual trade reports;
- countries' PRSPs (on World Bank website);
- ILO's database of labor statistics Laborsta (on www.ilo.org).

## 2 The world trade game[4]

This game uses very basic equipment, with only one staff member for up to 240 students; all the necessary instructions can be given within two minutes. Students are divided into teams, each of which acts as a separate 'country,' sharing a table, with between two and ten students in each team. There are five or six countries (tables) in a game. A game can be played with 10–60 students. More than one game can be played simultaneously, if the room is big enough, but there must be no interaction between games. Countries compete against each other to 'manufacture' paper shapes (circles, triangles, rectangles, etc.) and sell them to an international commodity market trader at posted prices, which vary with supply and demand. The objective for each country is to make as much money as possible. There are three types of country in a game:

- two rich industrialized countries;
- one or two middle-income countries;
- two low-income countries.

Students are not told this; they find out as they play the game. Only one lecturer is required as game leader, but one additional person is required to act as a 'commodity trader' in each game. It is also useful to have one or two 'observers' for each game. These too can be students. The game takes 45–90 minutes to play. This is followed by scoring, reporting by students, and adjudication by the lecturer, who will probably want to draw various economic lessons from the game. This all lasts a further 20–45 minutes.

*Preparation*

- Prepare an envelope of resources for each country (A).
- Put up posters on the wall showing the shapes, their measurements, and their initial values (normally two per game). These posters are enlarged (e.g. from A4 to A3), so that students cannot simply trace out the shapes (see Appendix 1).
- Prepare an envelope for the commodity trader (normally one per game) (B) (see Appendix 2).
- Prepare an envelope of resources for yourself as game leader (C).

## A: Envelopes of materials for countries

Each team (country) is given an envelope of materials at the start of the game. You will need to fill each envelope with the appropriate materials in advance and label the envelope. The following envelopes are required for each game.

*Rich countries: A1, A2*
- two pairs of scissors
- two rulers
- one compass
- one set square (the exact size of the large triangular shape)
- one protractor (the exact size of the semi-circular shape)
- two pencils
- one sheet of A4 paper
- six £100 notes (or €100 or $100).

*Middle-income countries: B1, B2*
- two pencils
- one ruler
- ten sheets of A4 paper
- three £100 notes (or €100 or $100)

*Low-income countries: C1, C2*
- two pencils
- four sheets of A4 paper
- two £100 notes (or €100 or $100)

## B: Envelope of materials for international commodity market trader (one per game)

The trader is given an envelope with money and a template of the shapes, so that he/she can check whether the shapes are the right size. The template also gives the opening prices for the shapes. The envelope contains:

- template of shapes with their prices
- banknotes: 30 @ £50, 60 @ £100, 20 @ £500, 40 @ £1000
- pencil and rubber for marking changes to the prices of shapes
- large envelope for keeping completed shapes 'secure.'

## C: Envelope or box of materials for game(s) leader
- whistle
- six small colored sticky shapes per game
- ten sheets of A4 paper per game
- pencil sharpener
- rubber.

## Instructions

Tell the students to leave all bags and any equipment (e.g. paper or pens) at the front and then to sit around the clusters of tables. Distribute the envelopes to each of the countries. The game requires minimal but clear instructions before the students open their envelopes. The dynamic of the game requires there to be no preamble explaining the purpose of the game and certainly no summary from the lecturer explaining what the game is supposed to illustrate. It is important for the students to work out what they should do. See Appendix 2.

*The game*

At the beginning of the game there will be lots of confusion and students will have many questions, such as 'Where can I get scissors?'; 'Why have we only got paper?'; 'Can we buy things off other countries?'; 'Can we combine with other countries?'; 'Can we have a loan?' Resist all temptation to answer these questions. Just repeat what you said at the beginning. After a minute or two they should begin moving around the room and trading, but the initiative should come from them, not you. The rich countries (A1 and A2) will probably begin making shapes, as they have all the materials and equipment that they need, but they will soon run out of raw materials and will probably try to buy some paper from other groups.

*Role of observers*

Use the observers to report back. This is necessary for the debriefing session. For example, get them to find out what is happening to the scissors – the one crucial implement that has to be used for all shapes and is possessed initially by only two countries. Do the rich countries form a scissors cartel? Do they sell one pair to another country? Or do they hire them out? Observers should watch how groups negotiate the prices of paper and other materials. They should note the formation and operation of any alliances and deals and any cheating that takes place. Observers should also report to you any malpractice, such as stealing other countries' paper, implements, or shapes. It is your decision whether you should ignore the problem, thereby encouraging countries to do their own policing, or whether you should impose a punishment, such as suspending them from making shapes for five minutes, confiscating certain materials or fining them.

*Role of commodity trader*

The trader must be careful in measuring the shapes and reject any that have not been cut out. Alternatively, if they have been torn carefully against a ruler, or are only slightly too large or small, a reduced price could be given. You could leave this to the trader to decide, or you could agree on a policy in advance. The trader must keep a close eye on the money to prevent students stealing it, preferably keeping it out of their reach. Shapes that have been sold should be put into an envelope or box, again out of reach of students.

Traders should not normally give loans, unless you want to build this in as a feature of the game, in which case you should decide in advance what interest rate to charge – probably a high rate, such as 50 percent. If loans are allowed, the trader should keep a record. In such cases, it might be a good idea to allocate an assistant to the trader. It is easiest for loans not to be repaid, but at the end of the game, when money is totaled, the trader will simply announce how much has to be deducted (outstanding loan plus interest) from each team.

*Role of game leader*

You will need to keep in regular contact with the trader. Find out which shapes are sold in large quantities (probably the triangles and rectangles) and which are hardly sold (probably the circles and the protractor-sized semi-circles). Then blow the whistle and announce that, owing to the forces of demand and supply, the prices of certain shapes have changed. You can choose how much to change prices, but a dramatic change stimulates more interest and provides a stronger focus for later discussion. For example, during the debriefing session, it is easier to refer to the importance of price elasticity of demand and price elasticity of supply when price changes have been dramatic. For similar reasons, it is better to change prices very infrequently. The price of particular shapes will also affect the value of particular tools. If circles go up in price, this will affect the demand for compasses. This relationship can be identified later in the debriefing.

*Elaboration*

Extra dimensions can be introduced into the game. For example, you could increase the stock of capital by selling a further pair of scissors by auction. This will need to be done early in the game and you will need to announce your intention five or ten minutes beforehand. Although the poor countries would dearly like to buy a pair, one of the rich countries is more likely to be successful at the auction. It might then hire out the scissors to a poor country.

As the game progresses, paper will rapidly run out. Trade in paper is likely to take place, with the price of paper rising to meet its value in terms of the shapes that can be made from it. The game can be prolonged by introducing more paper (simulating the discovery of new raw materials).

*End of the game and debriefing*

The students should be given a five-minute warning of the game ending, which should generate a flurry of activity as they rush to make shapes with their remaining paper and bring those shapes to the commodity trader. When the game ends, the game leader should ask all the students to return to their countries and to answer three questions:

1   What are the similarities and differences between the results from different groups?
2   How does the game simulate the real world and in what ways is it unrealistic?
3   How can the ways the students have analyzed their experience in the game be compared with the insights derived from economic ideas and the evidence from economics?

# Appendix 1: shape templates (to be enlarged to A3)

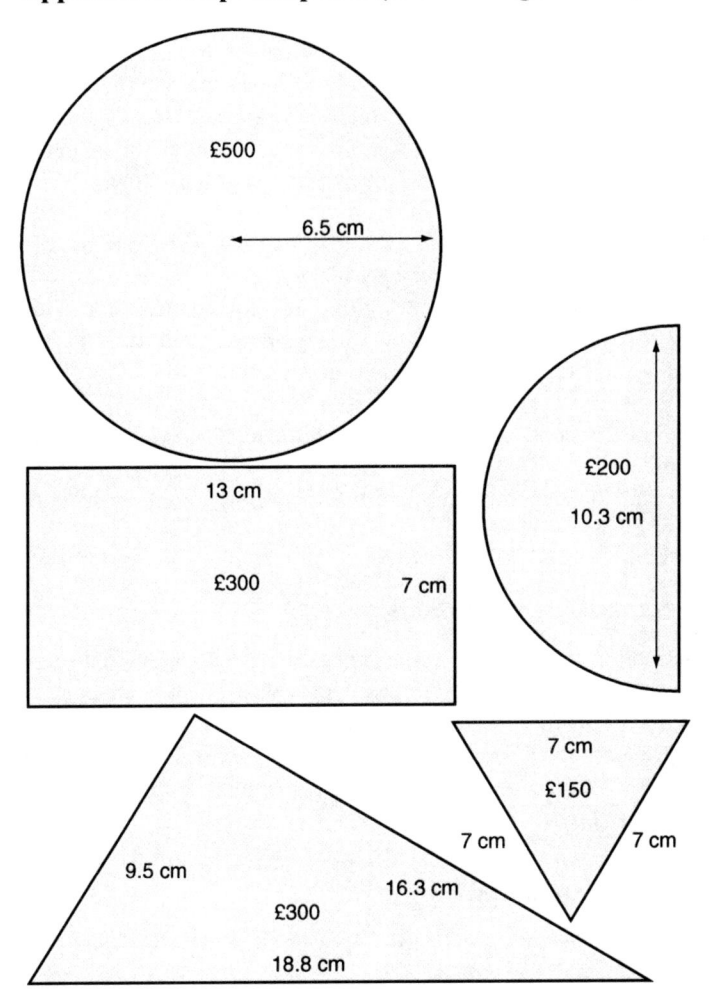

*(Circle labelled £500, radius 6.5 cm)*

*(Rectangle labelled £300, 13 cm × 7 cm)*

*(Semicircle labelled £200, diameter 10.3 cm)*

*(Large triangle labelled £300, sides 9.5 cm, 16.3 cm, 18.8 cm)*

*(Small triangle labelled £150, sides 7 cm, 7 cm, 7 cm)*

# Appendix 2: instructions for starting the game

As students come into the room, the game leader should do the following:

- Tell the students to leave all bags and any equipment (e.g. paper or pens) at the front and then to sit themselves around the clusters of tables.
- Distribute the envelopes to each of the countries.
- Give the following instructions about the game:

Each of the groups is a team and represents a country. The objective for each country is to make as much money for itself as possible by using the materials in the envelope. No other materials can be used. Use the materials to manufacture paper shapes. You can choose to make any of the shapes shown on the diagrams on the wall.

All shapes must be cut with clean sharp edges using scissors and must be of the exact size specified on the diagrams. The shapes can then be sold in batches to the trader, who will check them for accuracy and exchange them for cash. Inaccurate shapes will be rejected. You can manufacture as many shapes as you like – the more you make, the richer you will become.

You must not cut up your envelope!

[If applicable] You can move around the rom, but must not cross into the neighboring world(s), who are playing a parallel game.

If you hear me whistle [demonstrate], you must immediately stop what you are doing and pay attention. If there is any dispute, I will settle it. My word is final! No physical force is to be used in the game.

- Give no further instructions. It is important for the students to work out what they should do.
- Announce the start of manufacturing and tell them how long they have to play the game.

## Appendix 3: course outline suggestions

Below is a course outline for 15 two-hour sessions, along with suggested readings according to the ten major areas discussed previously in this chapter. A shorter course may combine these into ten sessions. For a more intensive course, extra sessions may be scheduled for tutorials or working groups, in addition to a written exam, one or two essays on one of the topics, including a case study of a country of the student's choice.

### Session 1. Macroeconomic measures

Daly, Herman (1996) *The Economic of Sustainable Development*. Boston: Beacon Press.
UNDP (various years) *The Human Development Report*. Oxford: Oxford University Press.

### Session 2. Social structures of power and inequality

Folbre, Nancy (1994) *Who Pays for the Kids? Gender and the Structures of Constraint*. London: Routledge.
Shorrocks, Anthony and van der Hoeven, Rolph (2004) *Growth, Inequality and Poverty. Prospects for Pro-Poor Economic Development*. Oxford: Oxford University Press.

### Session 3. Institutions

Bortis, Heinrich (1997) *Institutions, Behaviour and Economic Theory. A Contribution to Classical–Keynesian Political Economy*. Cambridge: Cambridge University Press.
Rodrik, Dani (ed.) (2003) *In Search of Prosperity. Analytical Narratives on Economic Growth*. Princeton, NJ: Princeton University Press.

## Session 4. Pluralist agency

Dow, Sheila (1996) *The Methodology of Macroeconomic Thought. A Conceptual Analysis of Schools of Thought in Economics.* Cheltenham, UK: Edward Elgar.
Holt, Richard and Pressman, Steven (eds.) (2001) *A New Guide to Post Keynesian Economics.* London: Routledge.

## Session 5. The unpaid economy

INSTRAW (1995) *Measurement and Valuation of Unpaid Contribution: Accounting Through Time and Output.* Santo Domingo: INSTRAW.
Picchio, Antonella (ed.) (2003) *Unpaid Work and the Economy. A Gender Analysis of the Standards of Living.* London: Routledge.

## Session 6. Unemployment

Geest, Willem and van der Hoeven, Rolph (1999) *Adjustment, Employment and Missing Institutions in Africa.* Geneva: ILO.
Trevithick, James (1992) *Involuntary Unemployment. Macroeconomics from a Keynesian Perspective.* New York: Harvester Wheatsheaf.

## Session 7. Poverty

Cornia, Giovanni Andrea (2006) *Pro-Poor Macroeconomics: Potential and Limitations.* New York: Palgrave Macmillan.
Mody, Ashoka and Pattillo, Catherine (2006) *Macroeconomic Policies and Poverty Reduction.* London: Routledge.

## Session 8. Endogenous growth

Aghion, Philippe and Howitt, Peter (1999) *Endogenous Growth Theory.* Cambridge, Mass.: MIT Press.
Jones, Charles (2002) *Introduction to Economic Growth.* Second Edition. New York: Norton.
Salvadori, Neri (2003) *Old and New Growth Theories. An Assessment.* Cheltenham, UK: Edward Elgar.

## Session 9. Increasing returns

Aghion, Philippe and Howitt, Peter (1999) *Endogenous Growth Theory.* Cambridge Mass.: MIT Press.
Arthur, Brian (ed.) (1994) *Increasing Returns and Path Dependence in the Economy.* Ann Arbor: University of Michigan Press.

## Session 10. Globalization

DeMartino, George (2000) *Global Economy, Global Justice. Theoretical Objections and Policy Alternatives to Neoliberalism.* London: Routledge.

Harris, Jonathan and Goodwin, Neva (eds.) (2003) *New Thinking in Macroeconomics. Social, Institutional and Environmental Perspectives*. Cheltenham, UK: Edward Elgar.

Rodrik, Dani (1997) *Has Globalization Gone Too Far?* Washington D.C.: Institution for International Economics.

### Session 11. Trade, global value chains, and MNCs

Gereffi, Gary and Korzeniewicz, Miguel (1994) *Commodity Chains and Global Capitalism*. Westport, Conn: Praeger.

Toye, John (ed.) (2003) *Trade and Development. Directions for the 21st Century*. Cheltenham, UK: Edward Elgar.

### Session 12. Money

Davidson, Paul (2002) *Financial Markets, Money and the Real World*. Cheltenham, UK: Edward Elgar.

Lavoie, Marc (1992) *Foundations of Post-Keynesian Economic Analysis*. Cheltenham, UK: Edward Elgar.

Lecq, S.G. van der (2000) *Money, Coordination and Prices*. Cheltenham, UK: Edward Elgar.

### Session 13. Financial markets and instability

Davidson, Paul (2002) *Financial Markets, Money and the Real World*. Cheltenham, UK: Edward Elgar.

Michie, Jonathan and Smith, John Grieve (eds.) (1999) *Global Instability. The Political Economy of World Economic Governance*. London: Routledge.

### Session 14. Macroeconomic policy: challenging the Washington Consensus

Chang, Hao-Joon (2002) *Kicking Away the Ladder: Development Strategy in Historical Perspective*. London: Anthem.

Ellerman, David (2005) *Helping People Help Themselves. From the World Bank to an Alternative Philosophy of Development Assistance*. Ann Arbor: University of Michigan Press

Nelson, Julie (2008) *Macroeconomics in Context*. New York: Houghton Mifflin.

### Session 15. Macroeconomic policy: the role of the state and civil society

Bromley, Simon, Mackintosh, Maureen, Brown, William, and Wuyts, Marc (2004) *Making the International: Economic Interdependence and Political Order*. London/Milton Keynes: Pluto Press/Open University Press.

Bello, Walden (2004) *Deglobalization. Ideas for a New World Economy*. London: Zed.

Setterfield, Mark (ed.) (2002) *The Economics of Demand-led Growth. Challenging the Supply-Side Vision of the Long Run*. Cheltenham, UK: Edward Elgar.

## Notes

1. A problem with the GDI, like the HDI, is its strong correlation with a country's GDP, so that countries with relatively high gender equality but low GDP levels rank lower than countries with higher GDP levels but less equality. Responding to this weakness, Dijkstra and Hanmer (2000) proposed replacing absolute levels of human development indicators with female/male differences for each indicator. So the level of GDP per capita is replaced by the female income share, and similarly, for education and health, gender differences are measured, rather than absolute levels. This gives a surprisingly new ranking of countries, with former communist states such as Poland and Latvia doing very well and Arab countries performing poorly; but rich countries with low female labor force participation, such as the Netherlands, also dropped in the list in favor of poor countries with high female labor force participation, such as Vietnam, and hence smaller income disparities between men and women.
2. See UNDP (1995, 2003).
3. In particular, recommendation 165 (g) urges governments

   > to measure and better understand the type, extent and distribution of unremunerated work, particularly work in caring for dependents and unremunerated work done for family farms or businesses ... for possible reflection in accounts that may be produced separately from, but consistent with, core national accounts.
   >
   > (UNDP 1995)

4. The game was adapted from Action Aid by John Sloman in 2002 (© 2005, University of Bristol). For more details, see www.economicsnetwork.ac.uk/showcase/sloman_game.htm.

## References

DeMartino, G. (2000) *Global Economy, Global Justice. Theoretical Objections and Policy Alternatives to Neoliberalism*. London: Routledge.

Dijkstra, A.G. and Hanmer, L.C. (2000) 'Measuring Socio-economic Gender Equality: Towards an Alternative for UNDP's GDI,' *Feminist Economics* 6(2): 41–75.

Frey, B.S. and Stutzer, A. (2002) *Happiness and Economics: How the Economy and Institutions Affect Wellbeing*. Princeton, NJ: Princeton University Press.

Ingham, G. (2005) *Concepts of Money. Interdisciplinary Perspectives From Economics, Sociology and Political Science*. Cheltenham: Edward Elgar.

Keen, S. (2001) Debunking Economics. *The Naked Emperor of the Social Sciences*. Annandale, Australia: Pluto.

Kitson, M. and Michie, J. (2000) *The Political Economy of Competitiveness. Essays on Employment, Public Policy and Corporate Performance*. London: Routledge.

Minsky, H. 'The Financial Instability Hypothesis: An Interpretation of Keynes and an Alternative to Standard Theory,' *Nebraska Journal of Economics and Business* 16: 5–16.

Rodrik, D. (1997) *Has Globalization Gone Too Far?* Washington D.C.: Institution for International Economics.

UNDP (1995) *Human Development Report 1995*. Oxford: Oxford University Press.

UNDP (2003) *Human Development Report 2003*. Oxford: Oxford University Press.

Veenhoven, R. (2008) *World Database of Happiness, Distributional Findings in Nations* Rotterdam, Netherlands: Erasmus University. Available at: www.worlddatabaseofhappiness.eur.nl.

# 9 A pluralist approach to microeconomics

*Steve Keen*

A great strength of traditional economics is the absence of a well-developed, coherent alternative. The pressure to teach *something* often results in orthodox microeconomics ruling the roost. However, political economists should not be afraid to teach approaches which, in apparent contrast to the logically complete traditional economics of the firm, are inchoate and do not answer every question. A new approach is never born complete but evolves, and the process of teaching an alternative from an incomplete starting point can lead to its development over time.

However, an essential first is to demonstrate to students that the ostensibly well-developed and coherent traditional model is in fact an empty shell. That is difficult in a principles course, since the increase in business majors and the relegation of economics to a service role has dumbed down the content so much that critiquing it is problematic: it is hard to critique something that is itself so nebulous.

The potential for a critique arises at the intermediate level, where the mathematical treatment is first encountered. Many political economists eschew mathematics, often because it is seen as part of why traditional economics is so flawed. Ironically, however, it is precisely when traditional economics is presented mathematically that it is most vulnerable – especially at the level of intermediate microeconomics, where the foundations are still essentially Marshallian – because the mathematics itself is fallacious.

I begin my teaching of heterodox microeconomics by recapping traditional microeconomics, and then demonstrating that the following two key aspects of the theory are mathematically false.

1   Under the assumptions of the traditional model, a competitive market populated by profit-maximizing firms will produce a higher output than a monopoly, and at a lower price (Keen 2004; Keen and Standish 2006).
2   The market demand curve derived from a set of utility-maximizing consumers is necessarily downward sloping (Gorman 1953; Shafer and Sonnenschein 1982).

Once these two assertions are demonstrated to be fallacies, the task of convincing students that a different approach should be considered – even if it is incomplete – is much easier.

## Testing Marshall

I begin my course with a computer simulation that demonstrates the falsity of the first proposition, and effectively turns Friedman's methodological defense of orthodoxy on its head (Friedman 1953). Friedman argued that while expert billiard players did not know "the complicated mathematical formulas that would give the optimum directions of travel ... unless in some way or other they were capable of reaching essentially the same result, they would not in fact be expert billiard players" (1953: 21). By analogy, he argued that the same could be said of firms: while they did not do calculus to set their output levels, unless they behaved

> as if ... they knew the relevant cost and demand functions, calculated marginal cost and marginal revenue ... and pushed each line of action to the point at which the relevant marginal cost and marginal revenue were equal ... it seems unlikely that they would remain in business for long. Let the apparent immediate determinant of business behavior be anything at all – habitual reaction, random chance, or whatnot. Whenever this determinant happens to lead to behavior consistent with rational and informed maximization of returns, the business will prosper ... whenever it does not, the business will tend to lose resources.
>
> (1953: 21–22)

I put Friedman to the test in class, using a multi-agent model of a market. This model uses standard market demand and aggregate marginal cost curves, with equations and parameter values as shown in Equation (9.1).

$$P(Q) = a - b \cdot Q$$

$$MC(Q) = c + d \cdot Q$$

$$MR(Q) = a - 2 \cdot b \cdot Q$$

$$TC(Q) = c \cdot Q + \frac{1}{2} \cdot d \cdot Q^2 + k$$

where $a = 800$; $b = 10^{-8}$; $c = 100$; $d = 10^{-8}$; $k = 10^6$ (9.1)

These parameter values generate a model market with realistic output levels so that a simulated comparison can be made between a single monopoly producer and a competitive industry with, say, 10,000 firms.[1] Neoclassical theory then makes the following predictions for the output levels of a monopoly and competitive industry respectively:

$$\text{Monopoly } M_Q = \frac{a-c}{2b+d} = 2.333 \cdot 10^{10}$$

$$\text{Perfect Competition } PC_Q = \frac{a-c}{b+d} = 3.5 \cdot 10^{10} \quad (9.2)$$

122   S. Keen

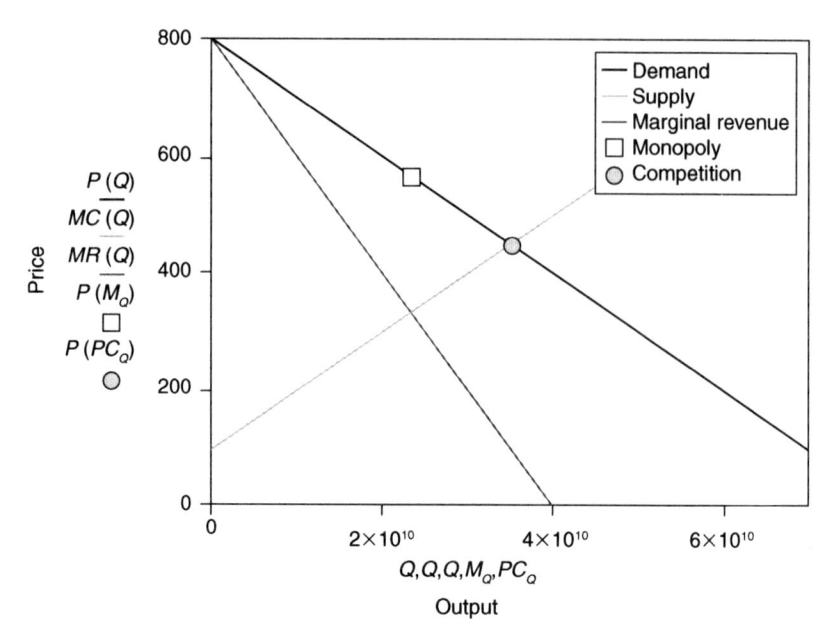

*Figure 9.1* Predictions of the Marshallian model.

The model and its predictions are shown in Figure 9.1.

As Friedman notes, actual firms do not do calculus, but follow other procedures which, *if the orthodox model is correct*, must nonetheless correspond to them behaving as if they were setting marginal cost equal to marginal revenue. My model tests this by populating this artificial market with agents who follow the simplest possible rule of thumb for profit maximization: choose an output level, and then change it by a fixed amount (either positive or negative). If profit increases, keep moving in the same direction; if profit decreases, move in the opposite direction by the same amount. I then run the model with a single firm, and also 10,000 firms, and check the results. The results[2] of two typical runs are shown in Figure 9.2.

The theory's prediction for the monopoly level of output is correct, but the prediction for the competitive industry is clearly wrong: rather than producing where supply equals demand, the competitive industry produces much the same level as the monopoly. "Oh dear, something has gone terribly wrong": these instrumental profit-maximizers *don't* do what neoclassical theory predicts! The individual firms all follow very different strategies (see Appendix A), which are extremely complex despite the simple nature of the behavioral algorithm (see Figure 9.3).

The firms also achieve much higher profits from their simple rule of thumb than orthodox theory predicts (see Figure 9.4). They are clearly better at making profits than orthodoxy is at predicting the profit-maximizing output level. This simulation thus sets the scene for a comprehensive demolition of the Marshallian

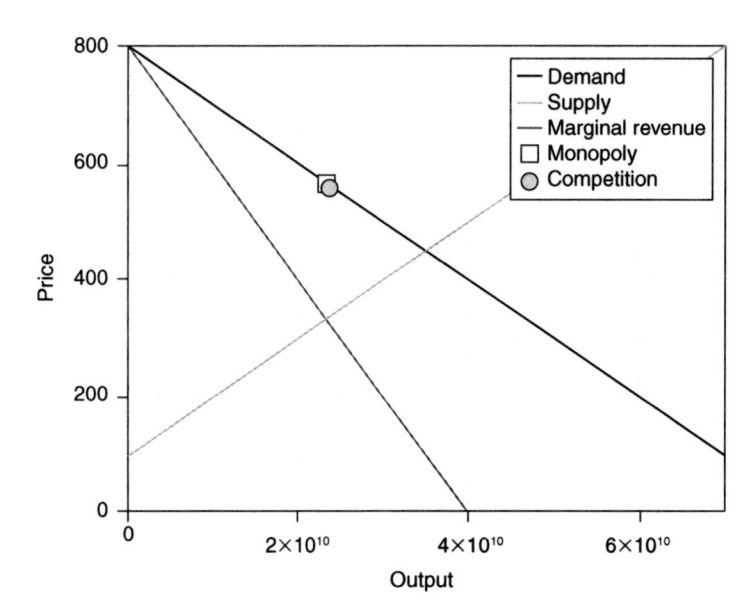

*Figure 9.2* Simulation results.

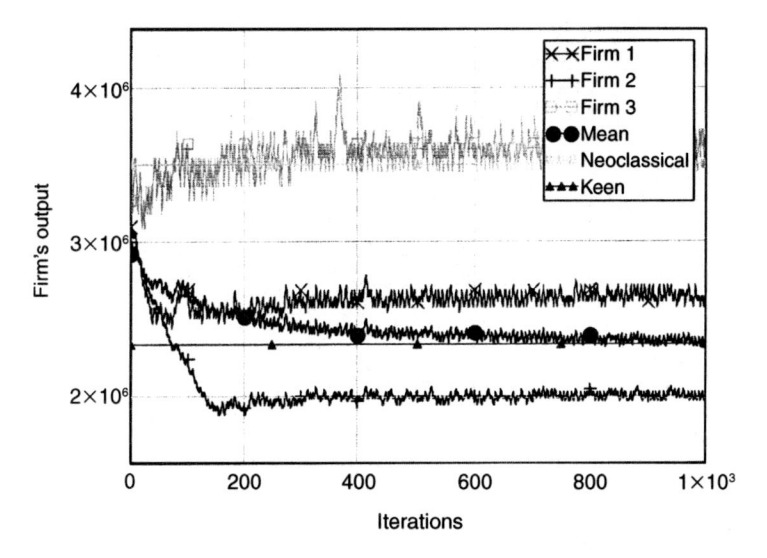

*Figure 9.3* Convergence of individual outputs (three randomly chosen firms and average outcome).

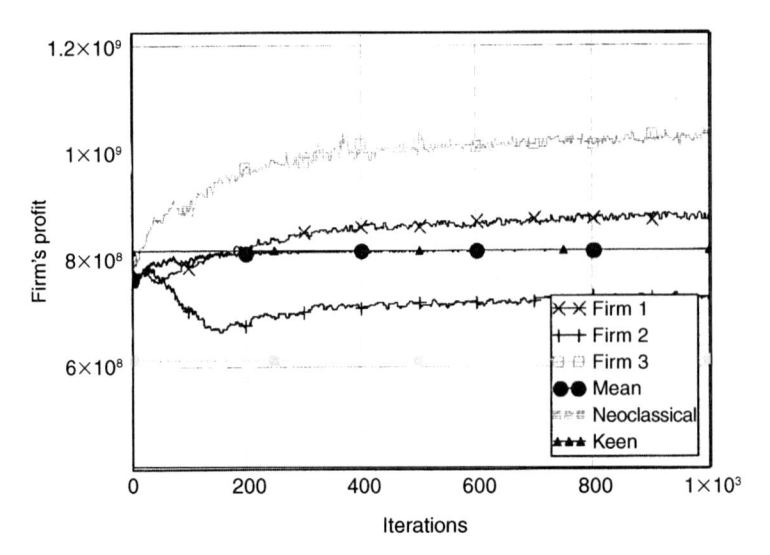

*Figure 9.4* Much higher profits result from the firms' "rule of thumb" (three randomly chosen firms and average outcome).

model. The first step in this process is proving that a key proposition of the neoclassical model, that competitive firms face a horizontal demand curve, is mathematically false under the Marshallian assumption of atomism.

## Refuting Marshall

This result was first proven in 1957 by, of all people, George Stigler (1957: footnote 31), as shown in Figure 9.5.

$$\frac{dp}{dq_i} = \frac{dp}{dQ}$$

Stigler's logic simply applied the assumption of atomism which characterizes the Marshallian model of competition[3] – that competitive firms neither know of, nor react strategically to, the output decisions of other firms. Given that assumption, if the $i^{th}$ firm changes its output by an amount $dq_i$, other firms in the industry don't react – and therefore industry output $Q$ changes by the same amount, so that $\frac{dQ}{dq_i} = 1$. Given this result, the conclusion that the slope of the demand curve perceived by the competitive firm $\frac{dp}{dq_i}$ is precisely the same as the slope of the market demand curve $\frac{dp}{dQ}$ is derived by simply applying the chain rule:

$$\frac{dp}{dq_i} = \frac{dp}{dQ} \cdot \frac{dQ}{dq_i} = \frac{dp}{dQ} \qquad (9.3)$$

This in turn means that the demand curve perceived by the individual firm is *not* horizontal, and that marginal revenue for the competitive firm is less than price:

> ### THE JOURNAL OF
> ### POLITICAL ECONOMY
>
> Volume LXV    FEBRUARY 1957    Number 1
>
> PERFECT COMPETITION, HISTORICALLY CONTEMPLATED
> GEORGE J. STIGLER
>
> [31] Let one seller dispose of $q_i$, the other sellers each disposing of $q$. Then the seller's marginal revenue is
>
> $$\frac{d(pq_i)}{dq_i} = p + q_i \frac{dp}{dQ} \frac{dQ}{dq_i},$$
>
> where $Q$ is total sales, and $dQ/dq_i = 1$. Letting $Q = nq_i = nq$, and writing $E$ for
>
> $$\frac{dQ}{dp}\frac{p}{Q},$$
>
> we obtain the expression in the text.

Figure 9.5 Stigler's proof.

$$\begin{aligned}
MR_i &= \frac{d}{dq_i}(P \cdot q_i) \\
&= P \cdot \frac{d}{dq_i} q_i + q_i \cdot \frac{d}{dq_i} P \\
&= P + q_i \cdot \frac{d}{dQ} P < P
\end{aligned} \qquad (9.4)$$

Though the mathematics of this result is straightforward, the fallacy of the horizontal demand curve is so strongly ingrained[4] that I find I have to provide a multi-pronged attack on the commonly held defenses of this fallacy. Multiple counters to defenses of it in the light of this result. The three most common defenses are:[5]

1. The equation $\left(\frac{dp}{dq_i} = 0\right)$ is just an assumption.
2. The omniscient consumer argument, that if a firm charges above the market price, it will have no customers, while if it charges below the market price, it will face the entire industry demand curve (see, for example, Varian 2006: 6, Figure 22.1).
3. That competitive firms behave as if they face a horizontal demand curve, or that they are too small to perceive the negative slope of the demand curve they face.[6]

The first proposition appears to be an application of Friedman's dictum that a theory cannot be tested by the "realism" of its "assumptions" (Friedman 1953: 23), but in fact it is a mathematical fallacy. It asserts that it is valid to have a model in which mathematically incompatible assumptions play an essential role. Assuming a negatively sloped market demand curve $\frac{d}{dQ}P < 0$, and atomism (so that $\frac{\partial}{\partial q_i}q_j = 0$), then it follows that $\frac{d}{dq_i}P = \frac{d}{dQ}P < 0$, as Stigler showed.

The second contradicts the assumption of price-taking behavior, which is also an essential aspect of the model of competitive behavior: competitive firms do not set price, but produce a quantity and then accept whatever price the market demand curve throws back at them. Once a single firm has changed its output, then all firms will receive the new market price, and *there is no seller charging a lower price to whom the consumers can turn*.

The third argument is a possibility, but only if firms behave *irrationally*. *If* the demand curve for the market is negatively sloped, *and* atomism applies, *then* the demand curve for the individual firm is negatively sloped: to believe otherwise is to behave irrationally[7] (see Figure 9.6). The too-small-to-perceive slope argument is also contradicted by the computer simulation shown above: even with 10,000 firms in the artificial market, the aggregate result contradicts the outcome that would apply if this defense were valid.

Once students have accepted the mathematical truth that $\frac{d}{dq_i}P = \frac{d}{dQ}P$ under the assumption of atomism, we proceed to the coup de grace for the Marshallian model: the neoclassical mantra that profits are maximized by equating marginal cost to marginal revenue is false in a multi-firm industry. The easiest proof for intermediate micro students[8] is the following: assume that all competitive firms follow the advice of neoclassical theory and set their marginal revenue equal to their marginal cost. Then for an *n*-firm industry, the sum of this across all firms will also be zero:

$$\sum_{i=1}^{n}(MR_i(q_i) - MC_i(q_i)) = 0 \tag{9.5}$$

This can be expanded to the following, using the crucial result that $\frac{d}{dq_i}P = \frac{d}{dQ}P$:

$$\sum_{i=1}^{n}\left(P(Q) + q_i \cdot \frac{d}{dQ}P(Q)\right) - \sum_{i=1}^{n}MC_i(q_i) = 0 \tag{9.6}$$

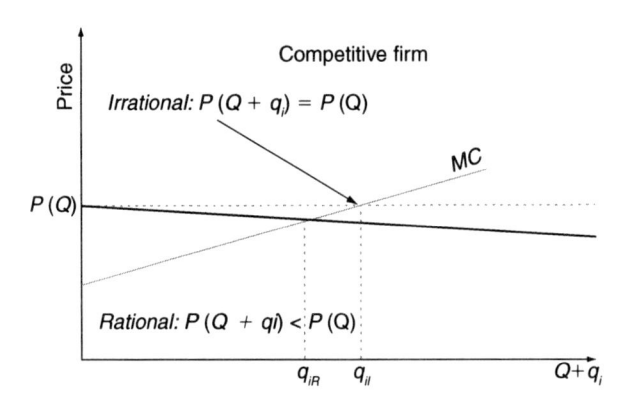

Figure 9.6 The belief that the firm faces a horizontal demand curve.

Expanding the summation over $n$ firms from equation (9.6) yields $n$ copies of $P$ from the first term, $Q \cdot \frac{d}{dQ}P$ from the second, and $n$ copies of marginal cost ($MC(Q)$) from the third[9] so that:

$$n \cdot P(Q) + Q \cdot \frac{d}{dQ}P(Q) - n \cdot MC(Q) = 0; \text{ or } (n-1) \cdot P(Q) + MR(Q) - n \cdot MC(Q) = 0 \tag{9.7}$$

It is then possible to rearrange equation (9.7) to yield this expression in terms of industry-level marginal revenue, marginal cost, and price:

$$MR(Q) - MC(Q) = -(n-1)(P(Q) - MC(Q)) \tag{9.8}$$

This result demonstrates the aggregation fallacy in the neoclassical so-called profit-maximizing formula: if each firm sets its output so that its marginal revenue equals marginal cost at the level of the individual firm, market output will *exceed* the point at which marginal revenue equals marginal cost. As a result, some of the output produced will be produced at a loss – and therefore each individual firm is producing part of its output at a loss if it produces where marginal revenue equals marginal cost. The actual profit-maximizing rule in terms of marginal revenue and marginal cost can be derived by equating equations (9.5) and (9.7):

$$\sum_{i=1}^{n}(MR_i(q_i) - MC_i(q_i)) = (n-1) \cdot P(Q) + MR(Q) - n \cdot MC(Q) \tag{9.9}$$

and then rearranging terms to leave market-level $MR(Q)$ and $MC(Q)$ on one side:

$$\sum_{i=1}^{n}(MR_i(q_i) - MC_i(q_i)) - (n-1) \cdot (P(Q) - MC(Q)) = MR(Q) - MC(Q) \tag{9.10}$$

then bring terms inside the summation and equate market-level marginal revenue and marginal cost to find the aggregate profit maximum:

$$\sum_{i=1}^{n}\left(MR_i(q_i) - MC_i(q_i) - \frac{n-1}{n} \cdot (P(Q) - MC(Q))\right) = 0; \text{ so that}$$

For profit maximization set $MR_i(q_i) - MC_i(q_i) = \frac{n-1}{n} \cdot (P(Q) - MC(Q))$ (9.11)

The actual profit-maximizing rule – the one the instrumental profit maximizers in the multi-agent simulation were clearly following – is thus not to equate marginal cost and marginal revenue, but to make the gap between them equal to $(n-1)/n$ times the gap between price and marginal cost.

The final step in establishing the hollowness of the Marshallian model of competition is to demonstrate that, if a competitive industry produces the same amount as a monopoly when their cost structures happen to coincide[10] then on Marshallian grounds a monopoly should be preferred to a competitive industry if its costs are lower, since it will produce a larger amount at a lower price. In the real world, economies of scale normally mean that a monopoly has lower marginal costs than the smaller firms of hypothetical competitive industry, further strengthening the neoclassical case in favor of monopolies over competitive industries!

So much for the neoclassical model of supply. Turning to the model of demand, we find that it is equally flawed.

## The shape of the market demand curve

The derivation of an individual demand curve from a set of indifference curves and a budget constraint is straightforward. However, the process of summing individual demand curves to derive a market demand curve is a non-trivial problem because, in the traditional model of a market economy, consumer incomes are determined by prices and quantities set in markets. Changing relative prices therefore changes incomes – something that is ignored when an individual's demand curve is derived, but which can't be ignored when aggregating to derive the market demand curve in a single market.

Over half a century ago, Gorman proved that the only condition under which a market demand curve necessarily had the same characteristics as an individual demand curve is "that an extra unit of purchasing power should be spent in the same way no matter to whom it is given" (Gorman 1953: 64) – in other words, that the distribution *and scale* of income have no effect on consumption. This in turn requires (a) that all Engels curves are straight lines (homothetic preferences); and (b) that all consumers have parallel Engels curves. Without these restrictions, then *a market demand curve can have any shape at all.*[11] This result – now known as the Sonnenschein–Mantel–Debreu (SMD) conditions after their rediscovery by these researchers in the 1970s – is clearly and emphatically articulated in the authoritative *Handbook of Mathematical Economics*:

> First, when preferences are homothetic and the distribution of income (value of wealth) is independent of prices, then the market demand function (market excess demand function) has all the properties of a consumer demand function.... Second, with general (in particular non-homothetic) preferences, even if the distribution of income is fixed, market demand functions need not satisfy in any way the classical restrictions which characterize consumer demand functions.... The utility hypothesis tells us nothing about market demand unless it is augmented by additional requirements.
> 
> (Shafer and Sonnenschein 1982: 671–672)

In contrast, the treatment of this same issue in Varian's *Intermediate Microeconomics* borders on mendacity. In his discussion of individual demand he spends several pages discussing homothetic preferences before concluding that they aren't very realistic (Varian 2006: 102). Later, in his chapter on market demand, he notes the dilemma that the aggregate demand (for a market) will generally depend on prices and the *distribution* of incomes, but continues:

*A pluralist approach to microeconomics* 129

> However, it is sometimes convenient to think of the aggregate demand as the demand of some representative consumer who has an income that is just the sum of all individual incomes. The conditions under which this can be done are rather restrictive, and a complete discussion of this issue is beyond the scope of this book.
>
> (Varian 2006: 267)

Students are thus left with the impression that realistic individual Engels curves are compatible with well-behaved market demand curves – an impression intensified by Varian's chapter summary that begins: "The market demand curve is simply [*sic!*] the sum of the individual demand curves" (Varian 2006: 281).

In reality, the SMD conditions are the transformation problem of neoclassical economics: the two conditions can only strictly apply in a one-consumer *and one-commodity* world, since in a multi-agent world changing prices will change the distribution of income, while in a multi-commodity world increasing income will alter relative demand, which in turn will change the distribution of income.

An intellectually honest response to these results is,

> If we are to progress further we may well be forced to theorise in terms of groups who have collectively coherent behaviour. Thus demand and expenditure functions if they are to be set against reality must be defined at some reasonably high level of aggregation. The idea that we should start at the level of the isolated individual is one which we may well have to abandon.
>
> (Kirman 1989: 138)

The SMD conditions thus validate the focus of the classical economists on class-based analysis: while it is nonsensical to aggregate all consumers into a representative agent and all products into a representative commodity, there is some validity in treating different classes as having coherent tastes, and consuming uniform commodities. Distribution of income within a class can then be ignored – but distribution *between* classes cannot. Nor can the distribution of income be reduced to a market process, because the dilemma of market demand curves having any shape at all undermines the proposition that the return to a factor of production is its marginal product.

## From an empty shell to emergent properties

It would be possible to continue with other flaws in traditional microeconomics[12] but I prefer to use the SMD conditions to segue into a crucial, but hard to understand, insight from complexity theory: the concept of emergent properties – that a complex system will have properties that can't be understood simply by understanding the isolated properties of the entities that compose it. The SMD conditions show that an economy consisting of perfectly well-behaved neoclassical agents will *not* behave like a scaled-up individual consumer at the market level, because the relations between consumers – the distribution of income – dominate the isolated behavior of each individual at the aggregate level of a market. The fact that a market demand curve derived from aggregating downward-sloping individual demand curves can have any shape at all is thus a classic emergent property.

This draws a line in the sand between micro and macro – the phenomenon of emergent properties in a complex system means that there is a limit to reductionism, whereas the neoclassical research program is essentially reductionist. Neoclassical economics effectively demolished Keynesian macroeconomics in the 1960–1970s, arguing that it did not have good microfoundations – with the explicit proposition that an economy populated by neoclassical-defined agents could not demonstrate the macro-phenomena of involuntary unemployment, a key tenet in the Keynesian perspective. In fact, an economy populated by neoclassically defined agents can't even generate the essential neoclassical parable of a downward-sloping market demand curve. It can thus be said that neoclassical microeconomics doesn't have good microfoundations either!

The SMD conditions enable the instructor to preface a pluralist approach to microeconomics with the caveat that there is a legitimate divide between microeconomics and macroeconomics: macroeconomics cannot be reduced to additive microeconomics.

## A political economy alternative

The ultimate reason why a pluralist approach to microeconomics should supplant a monist one is that realism should be the guiding principle of economic analysis – and traditional neoclassical microeconomics is both internally flawed and unrealistic. The starting point of pluralist microeconomics therefore should be the facts: the actual data on industry structure, and the behavior of firms and consumers. That alone will distinguish a pluralist course from a neoclassical one – by way of illustration, there is not one single table of empirical data in Varian (2006).

However, I prefer to take an interlude, after critiquing neoclassicism, with a market simulation known as Starpower. Not only does it put the many functions of a market and self-interested exchange in context, it also enlivens a topic that neoclassical pedagogy has made mind-numbingly dull, and forces students to engage directly and personally with each other, very early on during a semester.

## Starpower

This is a multi-person trading game that works best with between fifteen and twenty participants, but can work with as few as twelve and as many as thirty. I introduce it after a free-ranging discussion of the merits and drawbacks of the market system, where comments by students normally provide a fertile basis for debriefing after the game – and a reasonable measure of the extent to which it affects their opinions. I have played this game over 500 times, and every time it has caused a dramatic shift in initial perceptions of a market economy.

I describe it as a trading game. Its objective is to amass 1200 points, and it is over once three players have reached that level. Each player takes five poker chips from one of three boxes – which commence with identical distributions of five colors of chips – and then calculate their initial point score on the basis of Table 9.1.

The value of different combinations of chips produces opportunities for trade: for example, while two green chips are worth only 20 points, three are worth 60. A player with two green chips will gain from trading a red or white in return for an extra green. Trading must be on a one-for-one basis, and players are required to shake hands while they trade. They also can't reveal their hand to anyone else, and can only trade by saying what they will give in return for what they want – a red for a green, for example. If they can't reach agreement, then the traders are forced to remain holding hands until the end of the trading session – which lasts about two minutes.

After the first round, players are ranked by score, divided into three groups – Squares, Circles, and Triangles – and required to wear corresponding badges. The chips are then collected from each group and returned to a box *which then belongs to that group for the remainder of the game* – which of course simulates the inheritance of wealth (and of poverty). Two further two rounds ensue, and after each round students are moved between groups if their scores warrant it – and of course, they take their chips with them. Before round 4, it is announced that the Squares have been doing so well that they can make the rules for the next round.

As you can imagine, pandemonium can ensue: the top group can make any rule changes they like – so long as they reach a consensus – and normally they make rules that favour them (as well as often removing technicalities like having to shake hands to trade). The game then continues, ending normally with three of the Squares winning (though in the 1970s it would often end in revolution!), after which the students are debriefed.

Obvious questions arise – such as whether the game was fair, whether it was realistic, and so on. Important major points involve the role of inheritance and chance, the relatively minor role of trading in enhancing wealth, and the three tendencies that invoke inequality – inheritance, mobility between groups, and the trading table itself that necessarily encourages the top group to accumulate

*Table 9.1* Starpower scoring table

| Colours | Number of chips | | | | |
|---|---|---|---|---|---|
| | 1 | 2 | 3 | 4 | 5 |
| Yellow | 60 | 120 | 180 | 240 | 300 |
| Blue | 40 | 70 | 130 | 170 | 220 |
| Red | 30 | 50 | 100 | 160 | 180 |
| White | 20 | 40 | 90 | 120 | 160 |
| Green | 10 | 20 | 60 | 80 | 130 |

132  S. Keen

high-value chips and the lowest group to accumulate low-value ones. As well as provoking discussion about how good a model of capitalism Starpower itself is, it also helps emphasize the point that models, even heterodox ones, are models and not the real thing. The closest we will get to that comes from surveys and empirical data.

## Just the facts, ma'am

There is fortunately a wealth of empirical data on firms available from the U.S. Census Bureau (2008) (www.census.gov/csd/susb/susb.htm) and the U.S. Small Business Administration Office of Advocacy (2008). The latest available aggregate dataset is shown in Table 9.2.

The first two columns in the secondary table at the bottom of Table 9.2 are graphed on a log-log scale in Figure 9.7: U.S. firm size follows a "scale free" power law distribution, which emphasizes the irrelevance of the neoclassical model of the firm: there is no ideal firm size. Instead, the distribution of firm sizes in the real world follows what physicists have dubbed a Power Law. Graphically, this results in a straight line plot between the number of firms of a given size and that size when both are plotted in logs.[13] Intuitively, this means there is no average, representative, or ideal firm size – the distribution of firm sizes is instead scale free. The actual process of competition has resulted in a distribution from many very small firms to many very large, so that just as there is no representative-sized animal in biology, there is no representative-sized firm in economics.

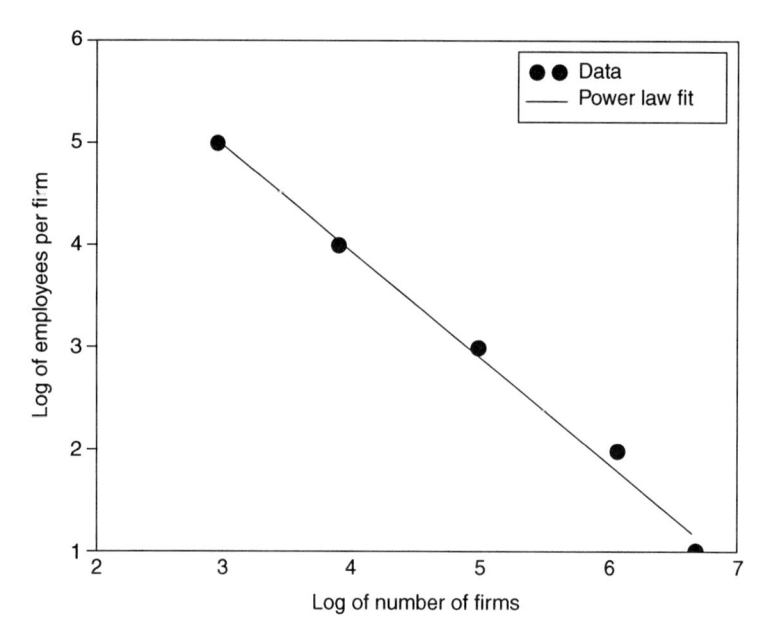

*Figure 9.7* U.S. firm size follows a "scale free" power law distribution (2005).

*Table 9.2* The size distribution of U.S. firms

*Employer firms, establishments, employment, and annual payroll small firm size classes, 2005*

| Employment size of firm | Firms | Establishments | Employment | Annual payroll ($1,000) |
|---|---|---|---|---|
| Total | 5,983,546 | 7,499,702 | 116,317,003 | 4,482,722,481 |
| 0–3 | 823,832 | 824,952 | 0 | 42,182,002 |
| 1–4 | 2,854,047 | 2,859,095 | 5,936,859 | 177,827,102 |
| 5–9 | 1,050,062 | 1,062,907 | 6,898,859 | 206,178,084 |
| 10–14 | 415,989 | 432,470 | 4,865,539 | 153,325,562 |
| 15–19 | 213,957 | 229,727 | 3,588,315 | 116,091,356 |
| 20–24 | 131,514 | 147,060 | 2,870,060 | 94,111,977 |
| 25–29 | 88,097 | 101,840 | 2,365,072 | 78,099,071 |
| 30–34 | 63,260 | 76,225 | 2,016,475 | 67,807,561 |
| 35–39 | 47,373 | 50,241 | 1,746,960 | 59,433,250 |
| 40–44 | 36,656 | 48,154 | 1,535,517 | 52,703,860 |
| 45–49 | 29,143 | 39,773 | 1,366,993 | 47,040,730 |
| 50–74 | 84.607 | 130,095 | 5,095,569 | 178,105,960 |
| 75–99 | 40,247 | 75,994 | 3,447,703 | 123,150,994 |
| 100–149 | 38,694 | 93,959 | 4,673,931 | 169,007,646 |
| 150–199 | 18,538 | 61,697 | 3,189,340 | 115,639,275 |
| 200–299 | 17,383 | 82,949 | 4,208,878 | 153,071,046 |
| 300–399 | 7,999 | 52,447 | 2,756,388 | 103,080,535 |
| 400–499 | 4,671 | 40,947 | 2,082,503 | 75,725,730 |
| 500–749 | 5,823 | 67,664 | 3,539,488 | 135,650,216 |
| 750–999 | 2,878 | 43,464 | 2,478,859 | 95,138,017 |
| 1,000–1,499 | 2,845 | 56,614 | 3,456,833 | 139,104,676 |
| 1,500–2,499 | 2,314 | 75,406 | 4,435,321 | 185,189,876 |
| 2,500–4,999 | 1,787 | 111,752 | 6,199,781 | 276,630,183 |
| 5,000–9,999 | 918 | 123,808 | 6,438,639 | 297,593,815 |
| 10,000+ | 912 | 600,462 | 31,123,497 | 1,340,823,957 |
| Max employees | Firms | Establishments | Employment | Payroll |
| 10 | 4,727,941 | 4,746,954 | 12,835,342 | 426,187,188 |
| 100 | 1,159,843 | 1,341,579 | 28,898,203 | 969,870,321 |
| 1,000 | 95,986 | 443,127 | 22,929,387 | 847,322,465 |
| 10,000 | 7,864 | 367,580 | 20,530,574 | 898,518,550 |
| 100,000 | 912 | 600,462 | 31,123,497 | 1,340,623,957 |

These data confirm Marshall's assertion: "the Mecca of the economist lies in economic biology rather than in economic dynamics" (Marshall 1920: 19), because this kind of distribution manifests itself in systems subject to evolutionary competition. Of course, Marshall did not develop this apt analogy – that was done by Schumpeter, to whom I turn after considering two further pieces of empirical research which confirm that neoclassical micro is a dead-end.

## The law of constant marginal product

It is not commonly appreciated that Friedman's methodology paper was intended to derail empirically researched actual firm behavior, but evidence abounds throughout:

> The lengthy discussion on marginal analysis in the *American Economic Review* some years ago ... neglect[s] what seems to me clearly the main issue – the conformity to experience of the implications of the marginal analysis – and concentrate[s] on the largely irrelevant question whether businessmen do or do not in fact reach their decisions by consulting ... marginal cost and marginal revenue.
>
> (Friedman 1953: 15)

> The billiard player, if asked how he decides where to hit the ball, may say that he just figures it out but then also rubs a rabbit's foot just to make sure; and the businessman may well say that he prices at average cost, with of course some minor deviations when the market makes it necessary. The one statement is about as helpful as the other, and neither is a relevant test of the associated hypothesis.
>
> (Friedman 1953: 22)

> The evidence cited to support this assertion is generally taken either from the answers given by businessmen to questions about the factors affecting their decisions – a procedure for testing economic theories that is about on a par with testing theories of longevity by asking octogenarians how they account for their long life.
>
> (Friedman 1953: 31)

In one sense, Friedman's critique is reasonable: what businessmen *say* they do and what the market forces them to do may be very different.[14] Just as asked octogenarians to account for their longevity will give spurious reasons, but nonetheless reliable data on, amongst other things, whether they drink a bottle of scotch a day, asking businessmen about their businesses yields important data – *including how many face rising marginal cost*. These data, to cite Alan Blinder, yield overwhelmingly bad news for economic theory in that apparently only 11 percent of GDP is produced under conditions of rising marginal cost (Blinder *et al.* 1998: 102).

Blinder's survey was merely the last in a long line of empirical work that contradicted an essential *structural* assumption in the traditional model: if firms do not *in fact* face rising marginal cost, then the model of perfect competition can't function. The best survey of this long, ignored tradition of work is in Lee (1998), but Blinder's survey is the most recent, and has impeccable professional standing and empirical methods.[15] The key empirical findings are summarized in Table 9.3, and it describes a world that is very different than the traditional model.

*Table 9.3* Blinder's summary of his empirical results

| | |
|---|---|
| Summary of selected factual results | |
| Price policy | |
| Median number of price changes in a year | 1.4 |
| Mean lag before adjusting price months following: | |
|     Demand increase | 2.9 |
|     Demand decrease | 2.9 |
|     Cost increase | 2.8 |
|     Cost decrease | 3.3 |
| Percent of firms which: | |
|     Report annual price reviews | 45 |
|     Change price all at once | 74 |
|     Change prices in small steps | 16 |
|     Have nontrivial costs of adjusting prices of which related primarily to: | |
|         The frequency of price changes | 14 |
|         The size of price changes | 14 |
| Sales | |
|     Estimated percent of GDP sold under contracts which fix prices | 28 |
|     Percent of firms which report implicit contracts | 65 |
|     Percent of sales which are made to: | |
|         Consumers | 21 |
|         Businesses | 70 |
|         Other (principally government) | 9 |
|         Regular customers | 85 |
|     Percent of firms whose sales are | |
|         Relatively sensitive to the state of the economy | 43 |
|         Relatively insensitive to the state of the economy | 39 |
| Costs | |
|     Percent of firms which can estimate costs at least moderately well | 87 |
|     Mean percentage of costs which are fixed | |
|     Percentage of firms for which marginal costs are: | |
|         Increasing | 11 |
|         Constant | 48 |
|         Decreasing | 41 |

Source: Blinder *et al.* (1998, p. 106).

The first is that most firms are price-setters, and prices are normally set for extended periods (and are not generally subject to discounting); price-taking is an interesting phenomenon in agricultural and some commodity markets, but not the modus operandi. Second, sales to other businesses dominate demand: commodities are produced, as Sraffa (1960) emphasized, by commodities in an input-output system, and the net product sold to final consumers and government is only a fraction of total product (a phenomenon which helps explain the overall stability and infrequency of changes to prices). Third, sales are not anonymous but generally repeat sales to a network of customers – on average, 85 percent of sales are to existing customers.

Finally, if there is any law of product in the real world, it is the law of constant marginal product, in contrast to the law of diminishing marginal product of

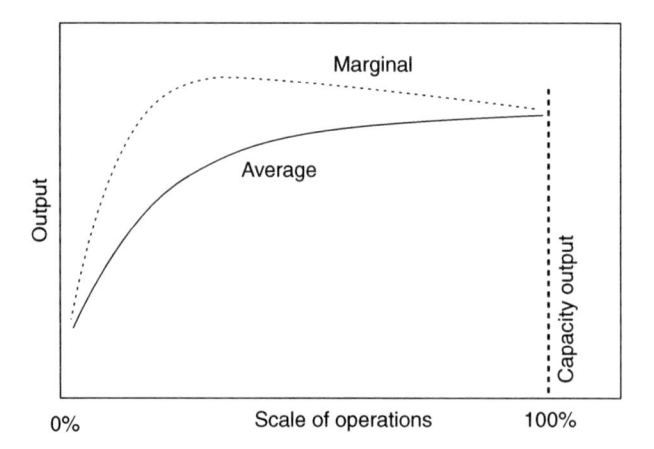

*Figure 9.8* Eiteman's representation of marginal product.

orthodox fantasy (Varian 2006: 329). The fantasy arises from the parable of one factor being held constant by a producer while the other is varied.[16] The reality results from a business being designed by engineers

> so as to cause the variable factor to be used most efficiently when the plant is operated close to capacity. Under such conditions an average variable cost curve declines steadily until the point of capacity output is reached. A marginal curve derived from such an average cost curve lies below the average curve at all scales of operation short of peak production.
>
> (Eiteman 1947: 913)

This now almost ancient literature on firm costs that Friedman actively dissuaded economists from considering remains the best basis on which to teach the actual cost structure and decision-making processes of firms, and Fred Lee's *Post Keynesian Price Theory* (1998) gives an excellent survey.

## Dimensionality, habit, and rationality

The developing field of behavioral economics provides a good foundation for discussing actual consumer behavior and its departure from the traditional vision of rationality, but I prefer to commence any discussion of consumer behavior with the results of an experiment that confirmed the irrationality of the traditional vision of irrationality – Sippel's test of Samuelson's model of revealed preference (Sippel 1997). This experiment was in fact an unsuccessful attempt to apply the theory, but the very careful manner in which it was done, and its failure examined by Sippel, makes it possible to reverse the economic definition of rationality – from an emphasis upon considering all alternatives, to limiting choice in a manner that makes decision-making in finite time possible.

*Table 9.4* Goods in Sippel's experiment

| Goods | Description | Range |
|---|---|---|
| Videoclips | Watching videoclips with rock and pop music | 30–60 min |
| Computer game | Playing Super Blast (in Exp1) or Pinball (in Exp2) | 27.5–60 min |
| Magazines | Reading a selection of German newspapers and magazines | 30–60 min |
| Coca-Cola | Cold soft drink | 400–2,000 g |
| Orange juice | Cold drink | 750–2,000 g |
| Coffee | Prepared when demanded | 600–2,000 g |
| Haribo | Popular German brand of candy, licorice, etc. | 600–2,000 g |
| Snacks | Pretzels, peanuts, etc. | 600–2,000 g |

*Table 9.5* Violations of axioms of revealed preference in Sippel's experiment

| | Consistent subjects (%) | Inconsistent subjects (%) | With ... violations | | | | | | |
|---|---|---|---|---|---|---|---|---|---|
| | | | 1–2 | 3–4 | 5–6 | 7–8 | 9–10 | 11–20 | >20 |
| Exp1 | | | | | | | | | |
| SARP | 1 (8.3) | 11 (91.7) | 7 | 3 | – | – | – | – | 1 |
| GARP | 7 (58.3) | 5 (41.7) | 3 | 1 | – | – | – | 1 | – |
| Exp2 | | | | | | | | | |
| SARP | 8 (26.7) | 22 (73.3) | 7 | 4 | – | 1 | 43 | 3 | 3 |
| GARP | 11 (36.7) | 19 (63.3) | 8 | 1 | 2 | 3 | 1 | 1 | 3 |

Sippel's experiment replicated the standard panoply of orthodox consumer choice theory in a set of consumption choices his subjects were given with varying incomes and prices. The subjects were required to make choices between eight different commodities – an apparently restricted range of options – and were actively encouraged to work out the combinations that maximized their utility, by both the subject's participation fee, and the fact that they were required to consume one of their chosen bundles at the end of the experiment.

The results of the experiment constituted a clear refutation of the neoclassical model of consumer behavior. Overall, more than 75 percent of subjects violated SARP – the strong axiom of revealed preference, the formal definition of a utility maximizer, whereby if a consumer prefers bundle A to B and bundle B to C, he/she will never choose C when A is also affordable – and over 50 percent violated the weaker GARP (generalized axiom of revealed preference).

Though Sippel's examination of this experimental contradiction is exemplary, he did not provide an interpretation of why the model failed: Why do consumers, in a well-designed experiment, fail to behave rationally? What is known as the curse of dimensionality provides a simple explanation that is a good starting point for introducing behavioral economics: the consumers were overwhelmed by the range of choice available, even in this simple situation.

Sippel's consumers were allowed to choose any quantity of the nominated goods, but even if we discretize the choices made to just four options for each commodity (so that we group all choices made of video clips into 0, 30, 31–45 and 46–60 minutes), each consumer was confronted with four possible quantities of each of eight commodities – which results in $4^8 = 65,536$ different bundles of commodities to compare with each other. The human brain simply isn't designed to store and rank so many options – let alone as many as consumers confront every day when they enter a supermarket, where 10,000+ items are on display, and the number of distinct bundles blows out to inconceivable numbers.[17]

Instead, true rationality in practice is not considering every option, as neoclassical theory emphasizes, but reducing the bewildering complexity of options available to enable decisions to be made in finite time. Here all the behaviors that neoclassical theory effectively ignores – culture, convention, habit – become truly rational, because they make decision-making possible.

## Elements of a political economy microeconomics

Though many non-traditional schools of thought can contribute to a heterodox microeconomics, my personal preference is to begin with Schumpeter's *Theory of Economic Development* (1934). I present this innovation-focused perspective prior to an exposition of the price formation theories of post-Keynesian or Sraffian economists because there is a danger that a desire to provide a replacement for every aspect of the traditional panoply still lets it set the agenda: orthodoxy has a theory of price formation, political economists need one too. Non-traditional theories still over-emphasize price formation of homogeneous products in isolated markets. Yet a political economy theory of price formation that abstracts from product diversity and innovation may be as flawed as the neoclassical one it attempts to replace.

While Schumpeter focuses on explaining cycles, his explanation of why and how firms compete remains ground-breaking, because it ascribes an evolutionary and far from equilibrium perspective upon firm behavior. Schumpeter's analysis of competition begins, not with the process of price formation, but with the means by which a firm distinguishes itself from competitors, and make a profit via innovation:

> (1) The introduction of a new good (2) The introduction of a new method of production (3) The opening of a new market (4) The conquest of a new source of supply of raw materials or half-manufactured goods (5) The carrying out of the new organization of any industry.
> 
> (Schumpeter 1934: 66)

Schumpeter's modern descendant is Porter's *Competitive Advantage of Nations*, which provides an application of Schumpeter's framework to explain why some countries have developed competitive advantages in some industries – Italy in fast cars, for example. There is much material of interest for political

*A pluralist approach to microeconomics* 139

economists, but for systemic analysis of microeconomics, his conclusion of two sources of competitive advantage is vital:

> It is difficult, though not impossible, to be both lower-cost and differentiated relative to competitors.... Any successful strategy, however, must pay close attention to both types of advantage while maintaining a clear commitment to superiority on one.
>
> (Porter 1998: 38)

After discussing case studies from Porter, I give an exposition of one of the most accessible and compelling models of evolutionary competition available – Paul Ormerod's model of competition in a newly deregulated industry (Ormerod *et al.* 2002).[18] The model simulates competition in both price and quality, and considers what happens to a once-monopolized industry opened to competition.

Traditional economics measures the degree of competition based on the number of firms and the dispersal of market share. Ormerod instead defines the degree of competition on the basis of the degree to which price *and quality* improve over time. Traditional economics predicts – spuriously, as shown above – that a high degree of market concentration will be correlated with a high price, but Ormerod's model finds no correlation (see Figure 9.9).

An important aspect of Ormerod's model is that, with a spectrum of firms competing on both price and quality, there is no single price for the hypothetical commodity in this simulated market. This fits the real-world phenomenon whereby there is no such thing as the price of, for example, a car. Instead, there are a multitude of products that all fit the generic classification of a car, but which have vastly differing qualitative features and widely dispersed prices. This

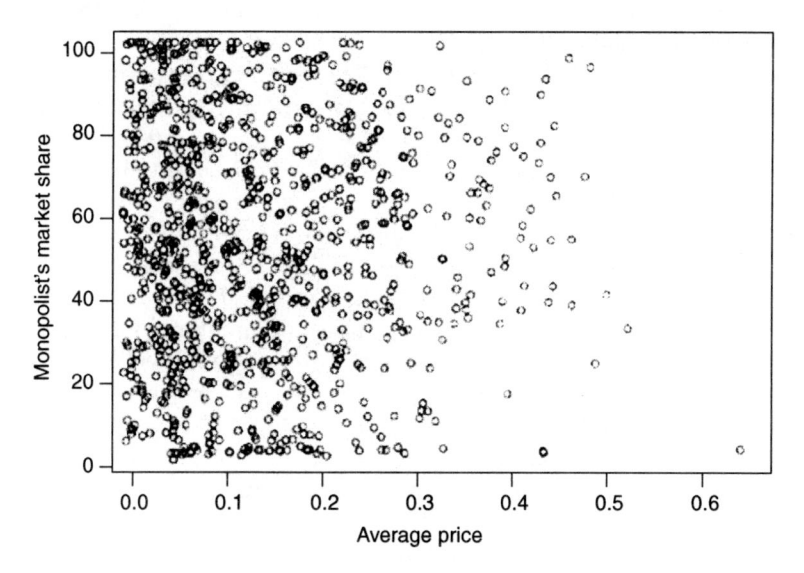

*Figure 9.9* No correlation between monopolist's share of output and average price.

was first treated analytically in Farjoun and Machover (1983), using concepts from statistical physics long before the modern school of econophysics developed. Though its primary objective was to dispute the concept of a uniform rate of profit, this now freely available work underscores that the emphasis on a price of a homogenous commodity is misplaced.

That, nonetheless, is the primary manner in which Kalecki's degree of monopoly price-setting model developed, as well as Sraffa's model of price-setting in an input-output framework. Both deserve coverage in a political economy microeconomics course, and there is an extensive literature on both. As well as using two of Kalecki's original expositions (Kalecki 1940, 1942) and Lee's masterful survey (Lee 1998), I juxtapose a modern exposition of Kalecki (Kriesler 1988), a Sraffian critique of markup pricing (Steedman 1998), and my argument, from a dynamic modeling perspective, that Kaleckian markup pricing and Sraffian input-output pricing are compatible in a dynamic, non-equilibrium context (Keen 1998).

This achieves three results: it covers the major political economy theories of price formation; introduces dynamics; and shows students that economics remains open to debate. Orthodox pedagogy has done an enormous disservice to education by pretending that economics is a done deal, with no outstanding areas of disagreement. I find that students respond positively to the realization that economics is a contested discipline.

## Game theory

One manifestation of the dumbing down of economics tuition is that conventional intermediate microeconomics texts treat Cournot–Nash game theoretic analysis as an advanced topic, but only at an introductory level (Varian 2006: chs. 27–29). Nonetheless, game theory is the refuge of choice when orthodox economists are confronted with my critique of Marshallian economics – somehow it seems excusable to teach bad mathematics if it reaches the same result as a sound but more complicated analysis. Game theory will also be confronted by students who move on to postgraduate economics courses – so its applicability as an analysis of microeconomic behavior must be considered in a course on heterodox microeconomics.

I commence by acknowledging that Cournot–Nash analysis does not rely upon the fallacy that afflicts Marshallian analysis: if firms behave strategically as outlined by Cournot, then as the number of firms in an industry increases, price will converge to marginal cost – not because firms are profit-maximizing, as Marshallian analysis erroneously asserts, but because strategic interactions with other firms force them to produce a greater than profit-maximizing quantity.

However there are at least two major problems with Cournot–Nash analysis – one of which is well known. Although the defect strategy is a Nash equilibrium in a single-shot Prisoners' Dilemma game, the cooperate strategy is dominant in repeated games – and real-world competition. If the analysis is to be modeled as a strategic game, it is clearly better modeled by repeated games than a single shot. Cournot–Nash analysis, though a fertile ground for academic papers, is thus an

*A pluralist approach to microeconomics* 141

unsatisfactory pedagogic device from the traditional perspective; this probably explains its reluctance to abandon the tired (and fallacious) Marshallian argument.

The second major flaw in the game theoretic analysis of competition is that, while the defect strategy is a global Nash equilibrium *if* firms have perfect knowledge of each other's possible strategies, it can be shown to be locally unstable; and while the cooperate strategy is not a Nash equilibrium, it is locally stable if firms lack perfect knowledge of their rivals' strategies. I illustrate this using the same numerical example as above for a duopoly.

The first step in the illustration shows that the defect strategy actually amounts to firms following the orthodox quantity-setting rule of equating marginal cost to marginal revenue, while the cooperate strategy results from firms being profit-maximizers: orthodoxy here is, in effect, criticizing firms for being self-interested! Using the algebraic example on p. 121, each firm in a duopoly will produce $(a - c)/(4b + 2d)$ units of output if both firms profit-maximize, and $(a - c)/(3b + 2d)$ if both set marginal revenue equal to marginal cost. These output levels provide the diagonal elements in the Prisoners' Dilemma table; the off-diagonal amounts occur when one firm follows an equilibrium profit-maximizing strategy while the other sets $MR = MC$: the firm following the neoclassical strategy will produce a larger amount while the output of the other firm will fall. The full pattern of outputs is shown in Table 9.6.

The profit numbers derived from this table in Table 9.7 ostensibly tell a convincing argument in favour of the Cournot strategy as a Nash equilibrium. Taking the Keen strategy pair as a reference point, each firm will gain (and the other lose) if it changes to the Cournot strategy *while the other firm maintains the Keen strategy*. Therefore, the Cournot strategy pair is a Nash equilibrium.

But what if one firm doesn't know what the other firm's costs or strategies might be, and its strategy instead amounts to varying output to see what happens? And what if the firm reacts to the impact of a change in the other firm's strategy on its profits? Then a very different picture emerges – because for a pair of strategies to be maintained, it must be true that both firms benefit from that pair.

Table 9.8 shows what happens if both firms are at the Keen equilibrium, and each firm experiments with changing its output by +/–1 unit. For a pair of strategies to be maintained, a positive change in profit must occur in the corresponding cells for *both* firms – otherwise the firm that saw its profit fall because

*Table 9.6* Quantity strategy combinations for duopoly

| Quantities Firm | Firm strategies | Firm 1 outputs | Cournot | Firm 1 outputs | Keen |
|---|---|---|---|---|---|
| 2 | Cournot | 1 | $\frac{a-c}{3 \cdot b + 2 \cdot d}$ | 1 | $\frac{a \cdot b + 2 \cdot a \cdot d - b \cdot c - 2 \cdot c \cdot d}{5 \cdot b^2 + 10 \cdot b \cdot d + 4 \cdot d^2}$ |
| 2 | Cournot | 2 | $\frac{a-c}{3 \cdot b + 2 \cdot d}$ | 1 | $\frac{2 \cdot (a \cdot (b+d) - c \cdot (b-d))}{5 \cdot b^2 + 10 \cdot b \cdot d + 4 \cdot d^2}$ |
| 2 | Keen | 1 | $\frac{2 \cdot (a \cdot (b-d) - c \cdot (b-d))}{5 \cdot b^2 + 10 \cdot b \cdot d + 4 \cdot d^2}$ | 1 | $\frac{a-c}{4 \cdot b + 2 \cdot d}$ |
| 2 | Keen | 2 | $\frac{a \cdot b + 2 \cdot a \cdot d - b \cdot c - 2 \cdot c \cdot d}{5 \cdot b^2 + 10 \cdot b \cdot d + 4 \cdot d^2}$ | 2 | $\frac{a-c}{4 \cdot b + 2 \cdot d}$ |

*Table 9.7* Profit outcomes from quantity strategies

| Profit relative to Keen Equilibrium | Firm 1 ⇒ | | | | |
|---|---|---|---|---|---|
| Firm 2 ⇓ | Strategies | Firm profits | Cournot | Firm profits | Keen |
| | Cournot | 1 | $-5.7 \cdot 10^{10}$ | 1 | $-1.8 \cdot 10^{11}$ |
| | Cournot | 2 | $-5.7 \cdot 10^{10}$ | 2 | $1.3 \cdot 10^{11}$ |
| | Keen | 1 | $1.3 \cdot 10^{11}$ | 1 | 0 |
| | Keen | 2 | $-1.8 \cdot 10^{11}$ | 2 | 0 |

*Table 9.8* Profit outcomes from varying output at Keen equilibrium

| Output changes from Keen Equilibrium | Profit results for Firm 1 | | |
|---|---|---|---|
| | Firm 1 ⇒ | | |
| Firm 2 ⇓ | $-1$ | 0 | $+1$ |
| $-1$ | $-2.1 \times 10^{-7}$ | $-166.7$ | $-333.3$ |
| 0 | 166.7 | 0 | $-166.7$ |
| $+1$ | 333.3 | 166.7 | $-2.1 \times 10^{-7}$ |

| Output changes from Keen Equilibrium | Profits results for Firm 2 | | |
|---|---|---|---|
| | Firm 1 ⇒ | | |
| Firm 2 ⇓ | $-1$ | 0 | $+1$ |
| $-1$ | $-2.1 \times 10^{-7}$ | 166.7 | 333.3 |
| 0 | $-166.7$ | 0 | 166.7 |
| $+1$ | $-333.3$ | $-166.7$ | $-2.1 \times 10^{-7}$ |

of the strategy pair will change its strategy. It shows that there is no pair of strategies which is self-reinforcing: if Firm 1 chooses a strategy that initially will cause its profit to rise, Firm 2 will adopt a strategy that turns Firm 1's originally successful strategy into a losing one. Therefore the Keen equilibrium is locally *meta-stable* – any deviation from it by one firm will cause responses by the other firm that push its competitor back to the Keen equilibrium.

Table 9.9 shows the corresponding situation for the Cournot equilibrium. Here there *are* stable strategy pairs: if both firms reduce their output by one unit, then both will gain profits. A second try of the strategy by both firms (reduce output by two units from the Cournot level) will add even more profit, and so on. The Cournot equilibrium is thus locally *meta-unstable* in the direction of reductions in output by both firms.

Thus profit-maximizing behavior will destabilize the Cournot equilibrium while reinforcing the Keen one. The game theoretic defence of the proposition that competition will force firms to produce where marginal revenue equals marginal cost is thus at best fragile. Even with traditional assumptions on the nature of costs and demand, profit-maximizing firms will tend to produce where their marginal revenue greatly exceeds marginal cost, and market price will exceed marginal cost.

*Table 9.9* Profit outcomes from varying output at Cournot equilibrium

| *Output changes from Cournot Equilibrium* | *Profit results for Firm 1* | | |
|---|---|---|---|
| | *Firm 1* ⇒ | | |
| Firm 2 ⇓ | –1 | 0 | +1 |
| –1 | 218.7 | $-1.1 \cdot 10^{-7}$ | –218.8 |
| 0 | 218.7 | 0 | –218.7 |
| +1 | 218.7 | $-1.1 \cdot 10^{-7}$ | –218.8 |
| *Output changes from Cournot Equilibrium* | *Profit results for Firm 2* | | |
| | *Firm 1* ⇒ | | |
| Firm 2 ⇓ | –1 | 0 | +1 |
| –1 | 218.7 | 218.7 | 218.7 |
| 0 | $-1.1 \cdot 10^{-7}$ | 0 | $-1.1 \cdot 10^{-7}$ |
| +1 | –218.7 | –218.7 | –218.8 |

## Conclusion

This is a demanding course, but one I find students respond well to.[19] At its end, students have a very deep and critical understanding of neoclassical microeconomics, and the beginning of a vision of what a heterodox alternative might be. Hopefully, some of them will be encouraged to help us develop such a richly needed alternative.

## Appendix A: market simulation program

This program is written in Mathcad and uses arrays rather than agents, but has the same effect. It could easily be implemented in any number of programming

```
Firms(i) :=  Q_0 ← | round(runif(i, q_K(i), q_C(i)))   if i > 1
                   | q_C(i)   otherwise
             P_0 ← | P(ΣQ_0)   if i > 1
                   | P(q_C(i))   otherwise
             dq ← | round(rnorm(i, 0, q_C(i)/100))   if i > 1
                  | q_C(i)/100   otherwise
             for j ∈ 0.. runs − 1
                 Q_{j+1} ← Q_j + dq
                 P_{j+1} ← | P(ΣQ_{j+1})   if i > 1
                           | P(Q_{j+1})   otherwise
                 dq ← vectorize[sign[(P_{j+1}·Q_{j+1} − P_j·Q_j) − (tc(Q_{j+1}, i) − tc(Q_j, i))]·dq]
                 F_j ← Q_j
             F
```

*Figure 9A.1* Mathcad implementation of a multi-agent simulation.

environments – from NetLogo to C# – but I prefer Mathcad because its code is so compact and readable.

Line by line:

1  The program assigns each of the $i$ firms in the simulation a starting amount which is uniformly randomly distributed between my equilibrium prediction $q_K = \frac{a-c}{n \cdot (2 \cdot b + d)}$ and the neoclassical prediction $q_C = \frac{a-c}{b \cdot (n+1) - n \cdot d}$.[20] This is a vector operation, so for the 10,000 firm simulation, 10,000 different initial amounts are set; the subscript 0 in $Q_0$ refers to the first time step in the 1000 iterations of the model.
2  This covers the case when a monopoly is simulated.
3  The initial market price is determined from the sum of the initial outputs of all firms – this is a classic price-taker simulation where producers simply determine an output level and then receive the price set by the market demand curve.
4  This covers the case of a monopoly.
5  Each firm is assigned an amount $dq$ to change its output by each time step, following a Normal distribution with a mean of zero and a standard deviation equivalent to 1 percent of the neoclassical prediction of the equilibrium output for a firm.
6  This covers the case of a monopoly.
7  A loop is set up to run over *runs* instances (in the simulations shown here $runs = 1000$).
8  A new output level for each firm is set by adding its change amount $dq$ to its initial output level $Q_0$ (this is a vector operation, so with 10,000 firms, 10,000 different $dq$s are added to 10,000 different initial amounts $Q_0$).
9  A new price $P_{j+1}$ is established based on the new aggregate industry output level $\Sigma Q_{j+1}$.
10  This covers the case of a monopoly.
11  Each firm calculates the change in profit between the $i^{th}$ and $i+1^{th}$ iteration. If profit rose, then the firm changes output in the same direction; if profit fell, then the firm reverses direction.
12  The array $F$ then stores the results of the output of each firm at the $j^{th}$ iteration.
13  The program returns $F$, which is a matrix where the rows contain the output of each firm and each column is a time step in the simulation.

## Appendix B: true profit-maximizing behavior

If market demand and the cost function of the firm can be expressed mathematically, then the output level that maximizes the firm's profits $\pi_i$ can be objectively defined. *Whether or not a given market structure – or a given type of strategic interaction between firms – actually results in the profit-maximizing level being the equilibrium level is irrelevant to the question of what the profit-maximizing level actually is.*

Orthodox pedagogy asserts that this maximum is given by the quantity at which the firm's marginal revenue equals its marginal cost:

$$\pi_{iMax}(\text{Marshall}) : MR_i(q_i) = MC_i(q_i) \tag{9.11}$$

Given the definition of marginal revenue and the substitution that $\frac{d}{dq_i}P = \frac{d}{dQ}P$, this expands to:

$$P(Q) + q_i \cdot \frac{d}{dQ}P = MC_i(q_i) \tag{9.12}$$

However, the profit-maximizing output level for the $i^{th}$ firm is a function not merely of its output, but also of the output of all other firms in the industry – regardless of whether or not the $i^{th}$ firm can influence their behavior, or knows what that behavior is. The true profit maximum is therefore given by the zero, not of the *partial* differential of the $i^{th}$ firm's profits $\pi_i$ with respect to its output $q_i$, but by the *total differential* of its profits with respect to industry output $Q$: not by the value of $q_i$ for which $\frac{\partial}{\partial q_i}(\pi_i) = 0$ – which economists normally erroneously write as $\frac{d}{dq_i}(\pi_i) = 0$ – but by the value of $Q$ for which $\frac{d}{dQ}(\pi_i) = 0$. Though the individual competitive firm can't ensure that the market produces this amount, it can work out what its own output level should be, given a specified market inverse demand function $P(Q)$ and firm cost function $TC_i(q_i)$. We start by expanding $\frac{d}{dQ}(\pi_i) = 0$ in terms of $P$, $Q$, $q_i$ and $TC_i$:

$$\frac{d}{dQ}\pi_i = \frac{d}{dQ}(P(Q)q_i - TC_i(q_i)) = 0 \tag{9.13}$$

This total derivative is the sum of $n$ partial derivatives in an $n$-firm industry:

$$\frac{d}{dQ}(P(Q)q_i - TC_i(q_i)) = \sum_{j=1}^{n}\left[\left(\frac{\partial}{\partial q_j}(P(Q) \cdot q_i - TC_i(q_i))\right) \cdot \frac{d}{dQ}q_i\right] \tag{9.14}$$

In the Marshallian case, atomism lets us set $\frac{d}{dQ}q_j = 1 \; \forall \; j$. Expanding the RHS of (9.15) yields:

$$\sum_{j=1}^{n}\left(P(Q) \cdot \frac{\partial}{\partial q_j}q_i + q_i \cdot \frac{\partial}{\partial q_j}P(Q) - \frac{\partial}{\partial q_j}TC_i(q_i)\right) = 0 \tag{9.15}$$

Under the Marshallian assumption of atomism, the first term in the summation in (9.16), $P(Q) \cdot \frac{\partial}{\partial q_j}q_i$, is zero where $j \neq i$, and $P(Q)$ where $j = i$. The second term is equal to $q_i \cdot \frac{\partial}{\partial q_j}P(Q) \forall j$, and $\frac{\partial}{\partial q_j}P(Q) = \frac{d}{dQ}P$, so that this yields $n$ copies of $q_i \cdot \frac{d}{dQ}P$; the third term $\frac{\partial}{\partial q_j}TC_i(q_i)$ is zero where $j \neq i$, and equal to marginal cost $MC_i(q_i)$ where $j = i$. Equation (9.16) thus reduces to

$$P(Q) + n \cdot q_i \cdot \frac{d}{dQ}P = MC_i(q_i) \tag{9.16}$$

This is the true profit-maximization formula, and it coincides with the neoclassical formula only in the case of a monopoly, when $n = 1$. It is easily shown that the rule in (9.17), which I call the Keen formula, results in a substantially higher profit than the standard Marshallian formula. This formula, which is more accurate for individual firms than the representative firm derivation given in the body of this chapter, may explain the variation in individual firm behavior displayed in the multi-agent simulation.

## Appendix C: differing cost structures

The standard orthodox diagram comparing a monopoly to a competitive industry blithely assumes that exactly the same line can be drawn to represent the marginal cost curve for the monopoly and the aggregate marginal cost curve (a.k.a. the supply curve) for the competitive industry. In fact, the identity of these two cost curves can be shown to occur only when either (a) marginal costs are identical and constant or (b) a quirk applies so that the sum of the marginal cost curves of the competitive firms happen to overlap with the marginal cost curve for the monopoly (this requires that the number of firms in the industry is an argument into the marginal cost function of the firm, which is of course bizarre).

If we treat labor as the variable input, then marginal cost is the wage rate $w$ times $\frac{dL_i}{dq_i}$, where $L_i$ is the labor input of the $i^{th}$ firm. $\frac{dL_i}{dq_i}$ is the inverse of marginal product for the firm $\frac{dL_i}{dq_i}$, so the identity of marginal costs for many competitive firms and a monopoly also requires the identity of marginal products – and this lets us transfer the problem from the realm of costs to output. For marginal products to be identical, total products can only differ by a constant (since marginal product is the derivative of total product). If output with zero labor input is zero, then this constant of integration is also zero. So the identity of marginal cost functions requires that the output of the monopoly with its labor input is identical to the output of the competitive industry with its labor input at all scales of output. If we consider an $n$-firm competitive industry where each firm employs $x$ workers and has a production function $q_i = f(x)$, and a monopoly with $m$ plants each employing $y$ workers with production function $q_j = g(y)$, then for the respective marginal cost curves to be identical, the following condition must apply:

$$n \cdot f(x) = m \cdot g(y)$$

$$\text{where } y = \frac{n \cdot x}{m} \tag{9.17}$$

It is then easily shown using a straightforward application of Euler's theorem that this is only possible if marginal costs are identical and constant (Keen 2004: 121). Another happenstance possibility – that the number of firms in an industry is an argument in an individual firm's marginal cost function, so that in the aggregate marginal costs are identical and rising for all industry scales – was used in the multi-agent program above. Thus while marginal cost at the industry was as defined above, marginal cost for an individual firm in an $n$-firm industry was defined as $MC_i(q_i) = c + d \cdot n \cdot q$. Aggregation then ensures that $MC(Q)$ is independent of the number of firms in the industry. Of course, in real life, it is highly likely that an industry's marginal costs will be lower when it is dominated by large (non-competitive) firms than when it is dominated by smaller competitive ones. Rosput gives an excellent example of this with respect to the natural gas industry (Rosput 1993).

# Notes

1. The identical fixed cost figure for vastly differing industry sizes can be replaced by one that depends on the scale of output, with no effect on the simulation results.
2. The program is shown in Appendix A.
3. In contrast to the Cournot–Nash game theoretic model, which I discuss later.
4. Even in the minds of political economists!
5. A fourth offered by Stigler himself in his paper (Stigler 1957: 8) is that marginal revenue for the $i^{th}$ firm converges to market price as the number of firms in the industry increases. This is true, and understood by a minority of neoclassical economists – but it is also irrelevant, as shown below (p. 127).
6. A fifth defense, that if price exceeds marginal cost, other firms will enter from other industries, is also fallacious since all other industries will likewise have price greater than marginal cost, if the firms in them are profit maximizers.
7. Using a modified version of this program, it can be shown that the neoclassical result applies if about 25–50 percent of firms behave *irrationally* – by increasing output when this decreases profits, and vice versa (Keen and Standish 2005).
8. Although this is difficult, I find that intermediate micro students can understand it. Orthodox economists might object to this proof, given that it requires firms to know the aggregate industry output. More advanced proofs without this ostensible flaw are given in Keen and Standish (2006, 2008). One is shown in Appendix B.
9. The marginal cost of aggregate industry output $Q$ is the same as the marginal cost for the $i^{th}$ firm in that industry of producing $q_i$.
10. Appendix C shows that this is the exception rather than the rule.
11. Strictly speaking, the market inverse demand curve $D(P)$ can have any shape that can be described by any polynomial equation. Orthodox economists prefer that, like an individual Hicks-compensated demand curve, it necessarily slopes down – implying restrictions on the coefficients of the polynomial so that $D(P + \Delta P) < D(P)$.
12. See Keen (2001) for a non-mathematical overview of these flaws.
13. The number of firms of a given size (measured here in terms of employees per firm) is a function of the number of firms raised to a negative power. See also Axtell (2001).
14. As I have demonstrated above, neoclassical theory's predictions are erroneous, even when the (simulated) empirical data conform to the theory's assumptions.
15. Downward and Lee (2001) review this work from a post-Keynesian perspective.
16. For why this is a parable, see Keen 2001: ch. 6.
17. Even if we classify commodities into 100 bundles and discretize decisions to either buy or not buy a single item of each, $2^{100} = 1,267,650,600,228,229,401,496,703,205, 376$ distinct bundles result! A neoclassical shopper would need a brain the size of a galaxy to store its preference map.
18. Many other attempts have been made to effectualize Schumpeter's vision – see for example, Andersen (www.business.aau.dk/evolution/esa/) – but I find this model the most tractable and easiest to reproduce.
19. This can also be taught with additional content on macroeconomics and finance, under the guise of managerial economics.
20. See Appendix C for an explanation of these predictions.

# References

Axtell, R.L. (2001) "Size Distribution of U.S. Firm Sizes," *Science*, 293: 1818–1820.
Blatt, J.M. (1983) *Dynamic Economic Systems*, Armonk, NY: M.E. Sharpe.
Blinder, A.S., Canetti, E., Lebow, D., and Rudd, J. (1998) *Asking About Prices: A New Approach to Understanding Price Stickiness*, New York: Russell Sage Foundation.
Downward, P. and Lee, F. (2001) "Post Keynesian Pricing Theory Reconfirmed? A critical Review of Asking About Prices," *Journal of Post Keynesian Economics*, 23: 465–483.
Eiteman, W.J. (1947) "Factors Determining the Location of the Least Cost Point," *American Economic Review*, 37: 910–918.
Farjoun, E. and Machover, M. (1983*)* "Laws of Chaos: A Probabilistic Approach to Political Economy. Verso: Farjoun and Machover," http://iwright.googlepages.com/lawsofchaos. See also www.probabilisticpoliticaleconomy.net/.
Friedman, M. (1953) *Essays in Positive Economics*, Chicago: University of Chicago Press.
Gorman, W.M. (1953). "Community Preference Fields," *Econometrica*, 21: 63–80.
Kalecki, M. (1940) "The Supply Curve of an Industry Under Imperfect Competition," *Review of Economic Studies*, 7: 91–112.
—— (1942) "Mr Whitman on the Concept of Degree of Monopoly – A Comment," *Economic Journal*, 52: 121–127.
Keen, S. (1998) "Answers (and Questions) for Sraffians (and Kaleckians)," *Review of Political Economy*, 10: 73–87.
—— (2001) *Debunking Economics: The Naked Emperor of the Social Sciences*, London: Zed Books.
—— (2004) "Deregulator: Judgment Day for Microeconomics," *Utilities Policy*, 12: 109–125.——
Keen, S. and Standish, R. (2005) "Irrationality in the Neoclassical Definition of Rationality," *American Journal of Applied Sciences* (special issue): 61–68.
—— (2006) "Profit Maximization, Industry Structure, and Competition: A Critique of Neoclassical Theory," *Physica A*, 370: 81–85.
—— (2008 forthcoming) "Debunking the Theory of the Firm – A Chronology," *American Review of Political Economy.*
Kirman, A. (1989) "The Intrinsic Limits of Modern Economic Theory: The Emperor Has No Clothes," *Economic Journal*, 99: s126–s139.
Kriesler, P. (1988) "Kalecki's Pricing Theory Revisited," *Journal of Post Keynesian Economics*, 11: 108–130.
Lee, F. (1998) *Post Keynesian Price Theory*, Cambridge: Cambridge University Press.
Mankiw, G. (2001) *Principles of Microeconomics*, Orlando, Fla.: Harcourt College Publishers.
Marshall, A. (1920) *Principles of Economics* (8th edn) London: Macmillan.
Ormerod, P., Rosewell, B., and Smith, L. (2002) "An Agent-Based Model of the Evolution of Market Structure and Competition," www.paulormerod.com/documents/paper23Sept2002.pdf.
Porter, M.E. (1998) *The Competitive Advantage of Nations*, New York: Free Press.
Rosput, P.G. (1993) "The Limits to Deregulation of Entry and Expansion of the US Gas Pipeline Industry," *Utilities Policy*, 3: 287–294.
Schumpeter, J.A. (1934) *Theory of Economic Development*, New Brunswick, NJ: Transaction Publishers.
Shafer, W. and Sonnenschein, H. (1982) "Market Demand and Excess Demand Func-

tions," in Arrow, K.J., and Intriligator, M.D. (eds.), *Handbook of Mathematical Economics* Vol. 2, Amsterdam: North Holland Press.

Sippel, R. (1997) "Experiment on the Pure Theory of Consumer's Behaviour," *Economic Journal*, 107: 1431–1444.

Sraffa, P. (1960) *The Production of Commodities by Means of Commodities*, Cambridge: Cambridge University Press.

Steedman, I. (1992) "Questions for Kaleckians," *Review of Political Economy*, 4: 125–151.

Stigler, G. (1957) "Perfect Competition, Historically Contemplated," *Journal of Political Economy*, 65: 1–17.

U.S. Census Bureau (2008) www.census.gov/csd/susb/susb.htm.

U.S. Small Business Administration Office of Advocacy (2008) www.sba.gov/advo/research/data.html.

Varian, H. R. (2006) *Intermediate Microeconomics: A Modern Approach* (7th edn) New York: W.W. Norton.

# 10 Mathematics for pluralist economics

*Steve Keen*

Most traditional economics departments have one educational objective in mind: to produce believers in, and academic practitioners of, traditional economics. This "Darwinian" desire to reproduce blinds traditional academics to the reality that the vast majority of their students will never be academic economists. It also explains the relentless emphasis upon forever expanding teaching of technical quantitative subjects (and core subjects like microeconomics) that has contributed to the political economy backlash against mathematics in general.

If, as many of us have, you spend your time fighting against the encroachment of quantitative subjects on teaching slots once allocated to courses in economic history and the history of economic thought, you become reflexively opposed to mathematics whenever more of it is suggested. However, I hope that political economists can be less obsessed with self-reproduction and, perhaps ironically, more responsive to the job market for which most of our students need to be prepared. The vast majority of economics graduates are not going to become academic economists – or even private-sector or government economists – but will use some economic thinking while working in much more broadly defined roles in business, government, and the community sector.

For these students, *and also the minority who go on to actually practice as economists*, the fundamentals of a political economy education should be courses in economic history, the history of economic thought, and political economy – the study of the key literature in political economic thought. These subjects could be reintroduced to the many courses in linear quantitative methods. For the minority departments where they are no longer compulsory by eliminating the current who actually want to practice as economists (academic or otherwise), I argue that mathematics and computing courses are necessary. But this sets me against a significant perspective in political economy today, which is to eschew mathematics on the grounds that the use of mathematical methods is the major reason why traditional economics has failed. Tony Lawson, the founder of the influential "Critical Realism" movement within political economy, provides the most eloquent expression of this anti-mathematical view.[1]

## Should political economists use mathematics?

Lawson argues against mathematics in economics, on the grounds that "the disarray of modern economics follows because methods of mathematical-deductive modelling are regularly applied in conditions for which they are not appropriate" (Lawson 2005: 428).

I concur with Lawson's critique of the deductive mathematical method as it has been practiced in economics. But Lawson applies this critique too widely. Though traditional economics in particular has used inappropriate mathematical methods, mathematics (and computing) can and should play a role in the development of political economy – albeit a role that is cognizant of the limitations of the mathematical method. It is precisely because traditional economics is undertaken largely in denial of – and sometimes in flagrant breach of – these limitations, that it is in disarray. The flaws in traditional economics arise partially from the use of mathematics, but predominantly from its abuse.

I have detailed the abuses extensively in *Debunking Economics* (Keen 2001). Here, I wish to identify the key ways in which I believe Lawson "doth protest too much" at mathematics, as well as to properly characterize the aspects of the traditional (ab)use of mathematics that Lawson rightly critiques.

Lawson notes that "the mainstream methods presuppose a closed atomistic reality, whereas heterodox conceptions can be shown to be based on a vision of social reality as open, structured, processual, highly internally related, among much else" (Lawson 2005: 435–436). Here we are in complete agreement about both the nature of reality and the inappropriateness of the mathematical methods the mainstream has chosen to use.

However, he later conflates the concept of *equilibrium* – and the traditional insistence on its relevance, versus the predominant opposition to it by political economists – with the mathematical method itself:

> It is equally possible to explain our remaining puzzle, the polarization of attitudes over the relevance of an equilibrium notion. I have already noted that attitudes have tended to divide along mainstream/heterodox lines, with the mainstream, unlike heterodoxy, insisting the equilibrium notion is essential, and with the heterodox opposition becoming increasingly marked over time. We now have before us the resources to understand why. Consider first the mainstream insistence that the notion be retained. The reason for this must now be clear. This mainstream project is defined by its insistence that mathematical methods be everywhere and always employed, despite the dearth of explanatory successes to date.
> 
> (Lawson 2005: 435–436)

Lawson thus asserts that the dispute over "the relevance of an equilibrium notion" is the product of the mainstream insistence on mathematical methods, versus a heterodox opposition to them. This implies that mathematical methods and equilibrium are inseparable – but this is not the case.

Lawson's conflation of "equilibrium" with "mathematical methods" is thus, in general, mistaken. However, the initial conflation of "a closed world of isolated atoms" with "insisting the equilibrium notion is essential" is correct: if the former assumption is made, then the equilibrium concept *is* an essential aspect of mathematical reasoning.

But the second conflation of "insisting the equilibrium notion is essential" with the identification of the mainstream project "by its insistence that mathematical methods be everywhere and always employed" is false, if "mathematical methods" may be taken to mean "mathematics in general," rather than "mathematics as traditional economists employ it."

The former indeed appears to be what Lawson implies, since, when conceding that the traditional paradigm is still evolving, he notes as an instance of this evolution the use of complexity theory. He then states that "complexity theory is providing a new way to conceptualise equilibrium states" (Lawson 2006).

This may describe how some misguided traditional economists have attempted to employ complexity theory, but it is easily shown that complexity theory itself is effectively antithetical to the "equilibrium notion" as it is applied in traditional economics. Truly complex systems exhibit far from equilibrium behavior, and therefore cannot be analyzed in terms of their behavior in equilibrium – *because they will never be in equilibrium*.

The first complex systems model, the Lorenz model of convection currents in the atmosphere, provides a simple illustration of this.

The model itself is incredibly simple, with only three variables and three parameters,[2] but can generate very complex behavior – because it has multiple equilibria, all of which are unstable for some parameter values. Additionally, it is possible to alter some quantitative aspect of the model and drastically alter the system's tie path, without changing the system's equilibria at all.

Figure 10.1 shows two plots of the convection intensity variable ($x$) in the model for two different values of its relevant parameter $\rho$. The value of $\rho$ does not determine any of the equilibria, but changes in $\rho$ drastically alter the time path of the weather. An "equilibrium analysis" of the Lorenz model of the weather would then assert that convection intensity has no impact – which is manifestly false.

Figure 10.1 also illustrates one of the key reasons why standard statistical methods fail with complex systems – because of, amongst many other factors, the phenomenon of "sensitivity to initial conditions." Two initial conditions that differ infinitesimally result in time paths that, after a finite time, diverge completely. The possibilities for quantitative prediction are thus extremely limited for complex systems – though there are nonlinear techniques that provide a limited capacity to forecast – and modelers tend to focus on reproducing the qualitative aspects of empirical data rather than the tight fit to the empirical record that is the unattainable Holy Grail of conventional econometrics.

Finally, though the equilibria of the model can be helpful in analytically characterizing the model's *qualitative* behavior,[3] the system itself will never be in any of its equilibria – and neither the historic time average, nor any of the

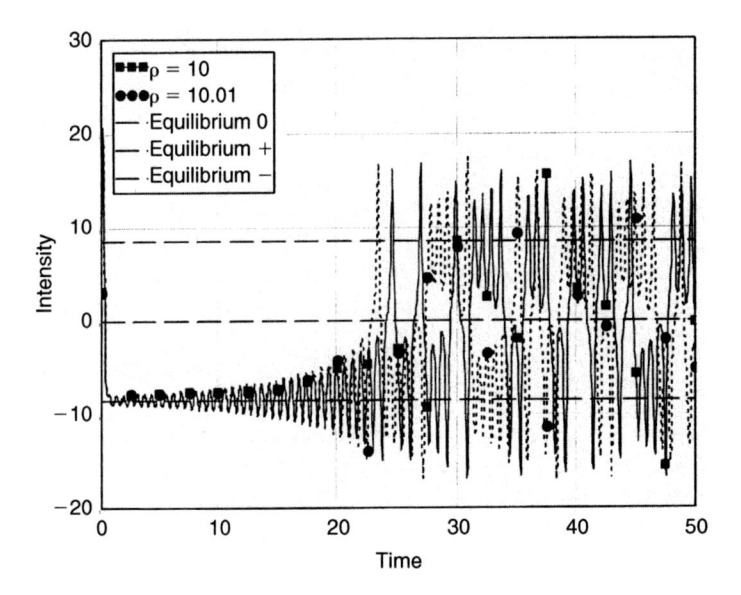

*Figure 10.1* The irrelevance of equilibrium for complex systems.

equilibria, will have any capacity to predict the system's future path. These characteristics of this specific example are found in many mathematical models of complex systems.

It can also be shown that another of Lawson's conflations, of mathematical reasoning with atomism,[4] is not a characterization of mathematical methods in general, but of the traditional economics usage of inappropriate mathematics. Lawson notes that,

> The social realm is also highly interconnected and organic. Fundamental here is the prevalence of internal social relations. Relations are said to be internal when the relata are what they are and/or can do what they do, just in virtue of the relation to each other in which they stand. Obvious examples are relations holding between employer and employee ... you cannot have the one without the other; each is constituted through its relation to the other. In fact, in the social realm it is found that it is social positions that are significantly internally related.
>
> (Lawson 2006: 495–496)

This is true, but it does not preclude appropriate nonlinear dynamic mathematical modeling – and that modeling can provide insights into such relations that cannot be gained by verbal logic alone. A classic instance of an organic social relation between employers and employees in economic literature is Marx's description of a cycle in employment and income distribution in Section 1 of Chapter 25 of *Capital*:

accumulation slackens in consequence of the rise in the price of labor, because the stimulus of gain is blunted. The rate of accumulation lessens; but with its lessening, the primary cause of that lessening vanishes, i.e., the disproportion between capital and exploitable labor-power. The mechanism of the process of capitalist production removes the very obstacles that it temporarily creates. The price of labor falls again to a level corresponding with the needs of the self-expansion of capital, whether the level be below, the same as, or above the one which was normal before the rise of wages took place.... To put it mathematically: the rate of accumulation is the independent, not the dependent, variable; the rate of wages, the dependent, not the independent, variable.

(Marx 1867: 580)

Richard Goodwin realized that this argument was akin to the predator–prey population dynamic models developed by the biologist Alfred Lotka and mathematician Vito Volterra in the 1920s, and in 1967 he rendered it as a pair of coupled ordinary differential equations (ODEs) (Goodwin 1967). The model generates the same perpetual cycle Marx describes, because of precisely the kind of internal social relations emphasized by Lawson: workers' share of output depends on the investment decisions of capitalists, and the investment decisions of capitalists depend on the wage demands of workers.

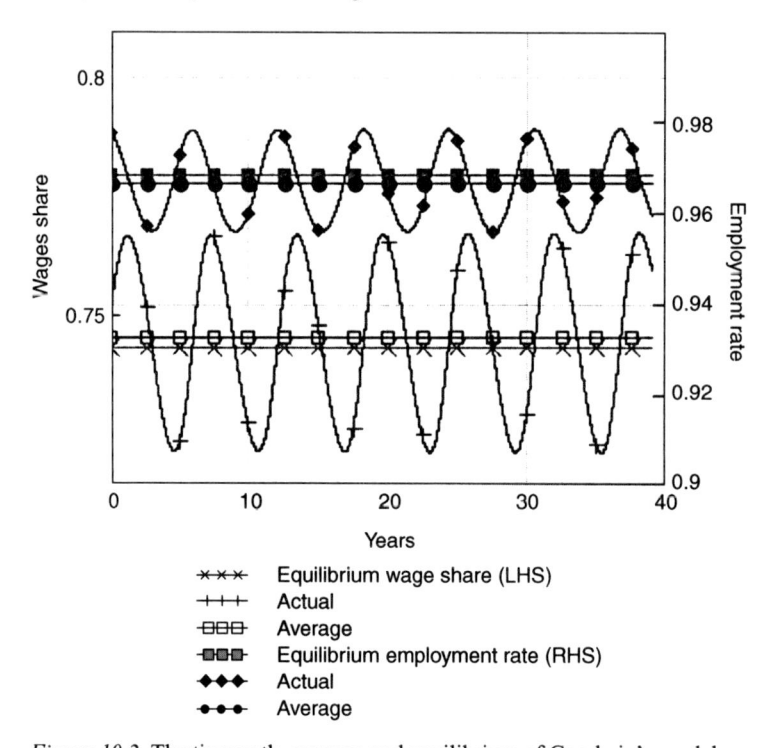

*Figure 10.2* The time path, average and equilibrium of Goodwin's model.

With the nonlinear investment and wage demand functions used here, the model also illustrates another feature common to nonlinear dynamic systems: *the equilibrium and the average of the system do not coincide*. The equilibrium of the model could not therefore be used to predict even the system's average value over time, let alone its time path, which keeps it continually in *dis*equilibrium. With an extension to include finance, the model can, given suitable initial conditions, have neither an equilibrium, nor an average – but it remains a valid mathematical model (Keen 1995).[5]

The Lorenz and Goodwin models are just two examples of a whole class of mathematical models that are non-atomistic, non-ergodic,[6] non-equilibrium, structured, and internally related.

The one aspect of economic reality that mathematical methods cannot capture, according to Lawson, is openness. Mathematical models as such cannot capture the phenomenon of truly new entities appearing in a system, such as the development of new commodities or technologies in a productive system, or the development of new economic institutions over time. A model of production that explicitly includes all existing products, for example, can't suddenly sprout a new equation to cope with the development of a new industry.

Computer-based methods of modeling can cope with this to some extent – see, for example, Standish's Ecolab modeling environment, which models evolution as an open-dimensional process (so that new species and new phenotypic characteristics can appear over time) (Standish 2000), but this type of work is still tentative and likely to remain so for a substantial period.

There are, however, circumstances in which closure is appropriate. Modeling capitalism as if it always consists of only "*n*" commodities – a common technique in neo-Ricardian as well as traditional economics neoclassical practice – can be a denial of the open nature of capitalism (and be atomistic to boot, when linear equilibrium techniques are used to analyze the model). However, working at a level of aggregation at which there are a fixed number of sectors – such as worker consumption, investment, capitalist consumption – or a fixed classification of social classes – worker, capitalist, rentier – may be valid for some models of economic reality. Closure in this sense results from functional classification rather than a denial of the innate nature of social reality – and even verbal methods frequently force us to classify open processes into closed categories.

There is a final reason why heterodox economics needs mathematical methods: sometimes verbal logic alone fails us. The long-running controversy in Circuitist literature about whether capitalists in the aggregate can make profits is a classic instance of this.

## The Circuit School and the need for mathematics

The Circuit School is a largely European group of heterodox economists, inspired by both Keynes and Marx, whose ambition was to provide a truly monetary model of a production economy. They developed a compelling explanation of why a monetary economy is fundamentally different to the barter model of traditional economics, but then struggled to turn this explanation into a viable model of an economy.

Working from first principles, Graziani argued that a monetary economy must be using a token for money, and that the only way this could happen without seignorage was if "any monetary payment must therefore be a triangular transaction, involving at least three agents, the payer, the payee, and the bank" (Graziani 1989: 3). He and subsequent authors then tried to model the monetary circuit verbally – and occasionally mathematically, using the inappropriate tool of simultaneous equations – by tracing the process from the initial creation of credit (where Graziani assumed that initial credit requirements were equal to the wage bill [Graziani 1989: 4] to the alleged eventual destruction of money when the debt was repaid [Graziani 1989: 5]).

Several conundrums arose. Circuitist economists concluded that firms were unable even to pay interest on debt, let alone make a profit – "Money will never be available for the payment of interest" (Graziani 1989: 17). Savings by workers implies that firms could not even repay the principal of loans in full, so that workers' savings forced firms to take on ever-higher debt – if wage-earners save, "the money stock and debt of firms becomes increasingly higher and higher" (Graziani 1989: 19).

Gallingly, though their ambition was to build a purely monetary model of the economy, it also appeared that barter could not be avoided, since it seemed that was how interest was paid – "In substance, what has taken place is a barter, firms having paid interest in kind" (Graziani 1989: 18).

All this arose from an attempt to, amongst other things, provide a monetary expression of Marx's circuits analysis of capitalism, when his logic was predicated on the concept that production generated a surplus. How could there be a physical surplus, but no monetary profits? Yet this seemed to be the conclusions of the Circuit approach. This implicit conflict between the Circuitist School's inspiration and its results led to the following lament,

> The existence of monetary profits at the macroeconomic level has always been a conundrum for theoreticians of the monetary circuit: not only are firms unable to create profits, they also cannot raise sufficient funds to cover the payment of interest. In other words, how can $M$ become $M^+$.
> (Rochon 2005: 125)

In fact, all these conclusions from verbal argument are wrong: firms *can* pay interest and make a profit, savings by workers *do not* compromise firms' solvency, rising debt is *not* necessary to sustain constant economic activity, and interest *is* repaid, as it should be, in money rather than in kind. The Circuitist School is thus consistent with Marx, and does explain how a physical surplus is monetized – but reaching these correct results requires the application of the correct mathematical logic. As the conundrums of the Circuit make abundantly clear, verbal intuition frequently gets lost in the complexities of flows in a verbal model of a market process.

*Mathematics for pluralist economics* 157

However, these are easily kept track of using the correct mathematical tool to analyze the dynamics of monetary flows: ordinary differential equations.[7] If we consider the simplest possible case of a stationary pure credit economy, financed by an initial loan from the banking sector to the firm sector of $L, then the following operations apply:

1. The bank pays the firm interest at the rate $r_D$ on the deposit account $F$ that is created simultaneously with the loan and therefore starts with $L in it.
2. The firm pays the bank the interest charged on its debt at the rate $r_L$, making a transfer from its deposit account $F$ to the bank's account $B$.[8]
3. The firm then hires workers, making a transfer from its deposit account $F$ to the workers' deposit account $W$ at some rate ($w$) proportional to the current balance in the $F$ account.
4. The banking sector pays the workers interest on their savings, making a transfer from its account $B$ to the workers account $W$.
5. Bankers and workers then buy the products produced by the firm sector, making transfers from their accounts to the firm sector's deposit account at a rate proportional to the current balances in their accounts (respectively β and ω).

The equations of this system are easily derived by placing the above flows in a table akin to the double-entry book-keeping of accountancy (see Table 10.1).

The three equations of the system can then be written by simply adding up the entries in each column:

$$\frac{d}{dt} F = r_D \cdot F - r_L \cdot L - w \cdot F + \beta \cdot B + \omega \cdot W$$
$$\frac{d}{dt} B = -r_D \cdot F + r_L \cdot L - r_D \cdot W - \beta \cdot B \quad (10.1)$$
$$\frac{d}{dt} W = +w \cdot F + r_D \cdot W - \omega \cdot W$$

With realistic values for its parameters, this model generates positive profits that are well in excess of interest payments, as well as wages and interest income for the two other classes (see the Appendix for the derivation of profits). Constant output and income levels can be sustained indefinitely without additional

*Table 10.1* Account flow dynamics in the simplest Circuitist model

| Accounts activity | Firm (F) | Bank (B) | Workers (W) |
|---|---|---|---|
| Interest payment on deposit | $+r_D \cdot F$ | $-r_D \cdot F$ | |
| Interest repayment on loan | $-r_L \cdot L$ | $-r_L \cdot L$ | |
| Wages | $-w \cdot F$ | | $+w \cdot F$ |
| Interest payment on workers' account | | $-r_D \cdot W$ | $+r_D \cdot W$ |
| Consumption by banks and workers | $+\beta \cdot B + \omega \cdot W$ | $-\beta \cdot B$ | $+ -\omega \cdot W$ |

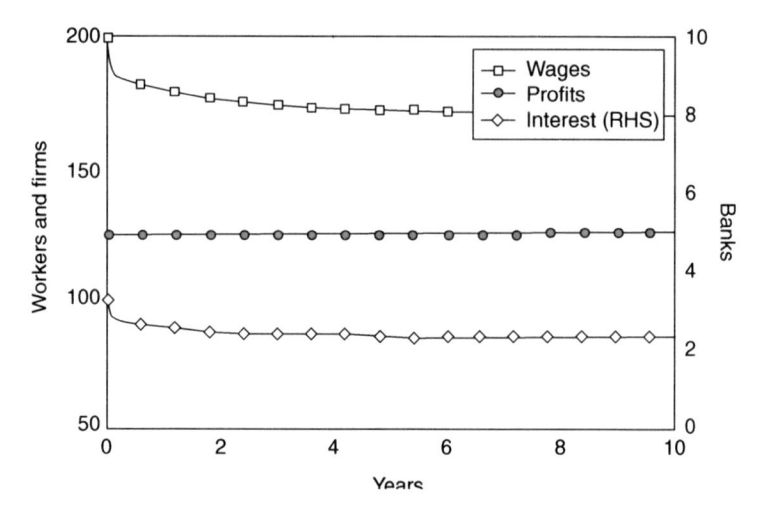

*Figure 10.3* Incomes in the simple circuit model.

injections, and positive bank balances for workers don't force losses on capitalists.

All the conundrums of the Circuitist debate were therefore simply the result of verbal logic making it difficult to differentiate between stocks and flows. Perhaps also the mental difficulties of keeping verbal track of a dollar's circulation caused Circuit authors to forget Marx's fundamental insights about a turnover period between investing and receiving (and also the generation of a surplus).

There are thus good reasons why a heterodox education in economics should include mathematics in its curriculum – but as noted, this should be limited for the general cohort of students who do not plan to become professional economists. For these students, I would require only one mathematically oriented course in analytic methods – a subject that introduces modern approaches to dynamic modeling, and also, as an addendum, provides a warts-and-all critique of the equilibrium methodology that dominates neoclassical model building.

## Analytic methods for heterodox economics

Far, far away from the obsession with equilibrium that dominates mathematical methods in economics, mathematicians, computer programmers, and engineers have developed a range of software programs that simplify the processes of developing and exploring models of complex physical, social, and biological processes. They fall into three main classes.

*Mathematics for pluralist economics* 159

### *Direct entry and numerical simulation of dynamic models*

Programs like *Mathcad* (www.ptc.com/products/mathcad/), *Mathematica* (www.wolfram.com/), and *Scientific Workplace* (www.mackichan.com/) give a user-friendly interface to these equations, which can be entered and run using standard mathematical notation (other mathematical programming environments like *Matlab*, *Scilab*, etc., have routines for the numerical simulation of systems of differential equations, but provide only awkward text-only interfaces for writing the equations).

### *Flowchart models of system dynamics*

There is a plethora of commercial programs now, including *Simulink* (a component of *Matlab* – www.mathworks.com/), *Vensim* (www.vensim.com/), *Vissim* (www.vissol.com/), *Stella*, and *iThink* (www.iseesystems.com/), as well as free software implementations such as the system dynamics component of *NetLogo*, and *Scicos* (www.scicos.org/), a component of *Scilab* (www.scilab.org/), that lets you model dynamic processes using causal flowcharts. These models can often be built by tracing out a causal chain as one does in a standard flowchart diagram, and then filling in the mathematical links later.

### *Multi-agent simulations of complex interactions between heterogeneous populations*

The most accessible of these – meaning the one that involves the smallest computer-programming learning curve – is *NetLogo* (http://ccl.northwestern.edu/netlogo/). It is also free, and contains a systems dynamics subset as well as a multi-agent environment.

This subject would illustrate dynamic modeling in economics using all these methodologies, with examples of their application to the economic literature and data encountered in the foundation subjects of heterodox economics. Here I will indicate what each of these look like using a Lotka-Volterra predator–prey model which, as noted above, is the class of model to which the Marx–Goodwin growth cycle model belongs.

As a pair of differential equations, the model is:

$$\frac{d}{dt}S = a \cdot S - b \cdot S \cdot W$$
$$\frac{d}{dt}W = -c \cdot W + d \cdot S \cdot W \qquad (10.2)$$

where $S$ is the number of prey (sheep) and $W$ the number of predators (wolves), and $a$, $b$, $c$, $d$ are positive constants. Implemented in *Mathcad* – one of the direct entry class of programs – the model is as shown in Figure 10.4. The equations are written exactly as they would be on paper, and simulated by the Odesolve function for different parameter values and initial conditions ($S_0$ and $W_0$ respectively).

160  S. Keen

Given $\dfrac{d}{dt} S(t) = a \cdot S(t) - b \cdot S(t) \cdot W(t)$  $\qquad S(0) = S_0$

$\dfrac{d}{dt} W(t) = -c \cdot W(t) + d \cdot S(t) \cdot W(t)$  $\qquad W(0) = W_0$

PredPrey $(a, b, c, d, S_0, W_0) := \text{Odesolve}\left[\begin{pmatrix}S\\W\end{pmatrix}, t, 100\right]$

$\begin{pmatrix}S_e\\W_e\end{pmatrix} := \text{PredPrey}\left(2, \dfrac{1}{10}, 1, \dfrac{1}{300}, 300, 20\right)$

$\begin{pmatrix}S\\W\end{pmatrix} := \text{PredPrey}\left(2, \dfrac{1}{10}, 1, \dfrac{1}{300}, 290, 25\right)$

A flowchart representation of exactly the same system is shown in Figure 10.4, using the simulation program *Vissim*. The mathematical operators are now shown graphically, and in most instances of this class of software, the model is simulated dynamically on screen

Finally, a multi-agent Netlogo version of the model is shown in Figure 10.5. Here, as opposed to equations, the system is built by defining the behavior of the entities that comprise it – sheep, wolves, and, in this version, the grass that the

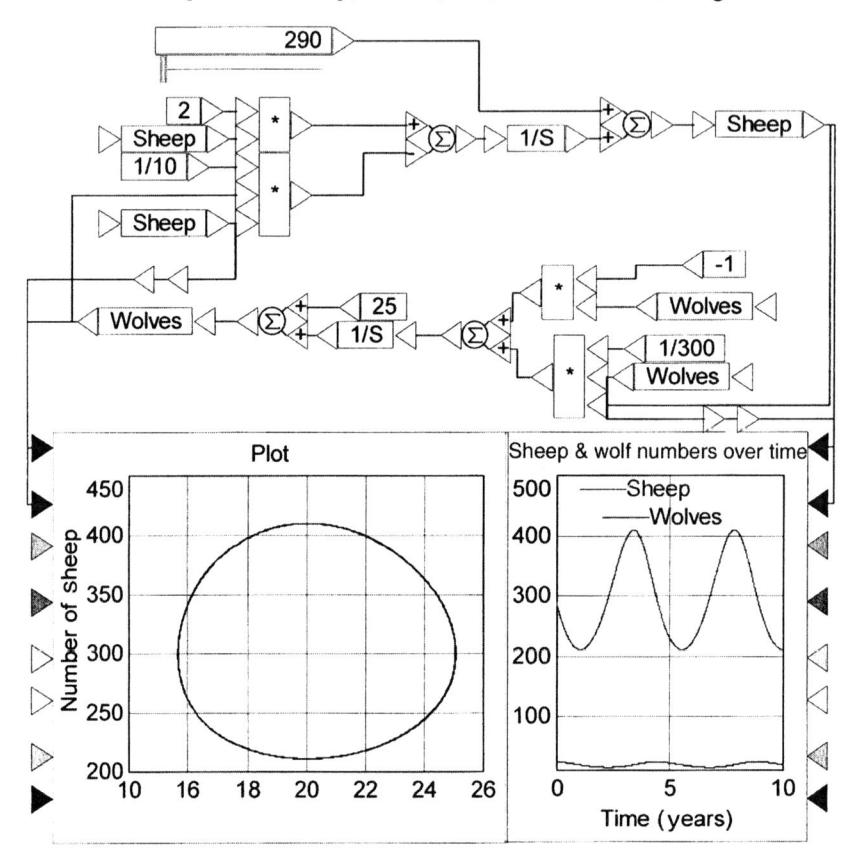

*Figure 10.4* The predator–prey model implemented as a dynamic flowchart.

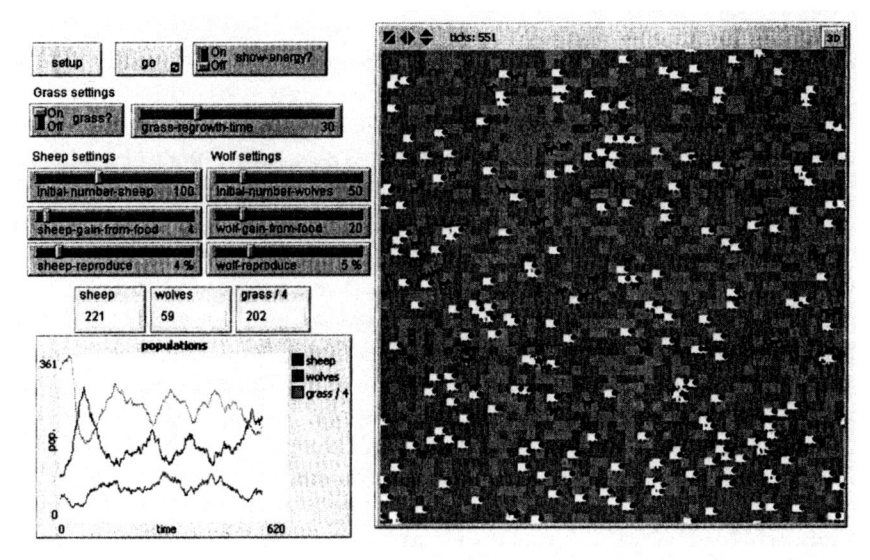

*Figure 10.5* NetLogo multi-agent simulation of predator–prey interactions.

sheep themselves eat. Rather than modeling an entire population from the top down, the multi-agent approach works from the bottom up, and requires computer programming to instruct individual agents how to behave. A simulation is then run, in which large numbers of agents interact.

An overhead of learning how to program is unavoidable, but NetLogo drastically reduces this overhead when compared to any other programming environment. For example, the code that specifies wolf behavior in the above model is:

```
ask wolves [
move
set energy energy – 1; wolves lose energy as they move
catch-sheep
reproduce-wolves
death
]
```

The module catch-sheep is:

```
to catch-sheep;; wolf procedure
let prey one-of sheep-here;; grab a random sheep
if prey != nobody;; did we get one? if so,
[ ask prey [ die ];; kill it
set energy energy + wolf-gain-from-food ];; get energy from eating
end
```

This is extremely minimal – and intelligible – computer code, with operations like working out whether a wolf is on the same patch as a sheep (and can therefore catch one) simplified by the keywords "one of" and "here," that are built-in functions in NetLogo.

The question arises of who would teach such a course. Ideally, political economists themselves would already be equipped to do so but, with few exceptions, we are currently trapped between the bad training in inappropriate mathematical methods we received as students on the one hand, and a lack of exposure to modern mathematical and computer methods on the other. The initial solution would therefore be to recruit graduates from systems engineering schools – and there are many of these around the world, because modeling unstable dynamic processes is a bread-and-butter exercise in engineering these days. A list of institutions teaching systems engineering is maintained by the International Council on Systems Engineering.[9] This subject would also be undertaken by students intending to become professional economists, who therefore choose to do an economics degree with a larger mathematical component.

## Mathematics for heterodox economics

The objective of the common modeling subject would be to enable those who do not intend to work as economists (whether in academia or industry) to understand dynamic economic models and how they are constructed, and to enable those who do plan to be professional economists to know how to design – and understand the limitations of – such models. This second professional cohort must have the deeper understanding of these methods that comes from doing specialized mathematics.

The essential topic here is differential equations – the study of processes of change which are described by equations of the form:

$$\frac{d}{dt} y = f(y) \tag{10.3}$$

This is not the simple calculus of optimization that forms the basis of the math courses traditional economists inflict on their students, which are based on equations of the form:

$$\frac{d}{dx} y = f(x) \tag{10.4}$$

For those who are not familiar with differential equations, the key differences between equations (10.3) and (10.4) are:

1 In (10.4), the rate of change of the dependent variable $y$ is a function simply of the independent variable $x$; in (10.3), it is a function both of the independent variable $t$, *and its own value.*
2 The independent variable $x$ in (10.4) is normally some other economic variable ($L$ in a production function relating output $Y$ as a function of labor input

*L*, for example); in (10.3), the ultimate independent variable is time itself, and therefore signified by *t*.

These two superficially minor differences make a world of difference to the practice of mathematics. First, whereas almost all equations like (10.4) can be solved, almost none like (10.3) can be. Second, and most important, these equations are designed to analyze processes when equilibrium does *not* apply. Conceptually, these equations are easily extended to include multiple variables (see the examples in the Appendices), and when systems have more than two variables and nonlinear relations, sustained far-from-equilibrium behavior becomes the norm. Prediction – especially by econometric techniques that assume linearity – then becomes impossible. The objective of modeling then switches from prediction to qualitative description of the model's behavior.[10]

In order to properly comprehend differential equations, foundation courses in calculus and linear algebra are necessary.

*All three subjects should be taught by mathematics departments, and not by economists.*

Economists, even mathematically savvy heterodox economists, lack the capacity to deliver these topics properly to students – in part simply because they are economists, not mathematicians, and are therefore isolated from the mainstream of developments in mathematics and modeling in the sciences and engineering. Many of the travesties in the use of mathematics in economics have resulted from precisely this isolation, and the self-referential way in which mathematical economics has evolved. We need to delegate the task of teaching fundamental mathematics to professional mathematicians, so that mathematics in economics can become what it is in other sciences and engineering – a good servant, rather than the poor master it has been in economics to date.

Practicing political economists may also need an introduction to differential equations – if only to realize that there are other ways to practice mathematical analysis than the econometrics they suffered as undergraduates. Here the most readable text I have encountered is Martin Braun's *Differential Equations and Their Applications: An Introduction to Applied Mathematics* (1992). A description given of it by a customer on Amazon.com captures its appeal very well:

> I have used this to teach DE's in a one to one tutoring context for a couple of years now, since I first picked it off a library shelf and felt literally like jumping for joy over how good it was. Not that I dislike Boyce/DiPrima, but suddenly I had a text that was really fun! Now, this is definitely a "what DE's are good for" kind of text, so if you feel that your students should suffer teething pains on a dry theoretical tome, this is NOT the book for you. Nevertheless, having had students chew up all their available time on this book, because they loved it, makes me recommend it highly. (Check www.amazon.com/Differential-Equations-Their-Applications-Introduction/dp/0387978941/ref=sr_1_1?ie=UTF8&qid=1226288501&sr=1–1 for more details.)

## Conclusion: of babies and bathwater

There is no doubt that mathematical economics as it has been practiced by neoclassical economics is a large part of why the neoclassical method has failed. But to eschew mathematical analysis in the development of heterodox economics as a result would be a classic case of throwing the baby out with the bathwater. Mathematics and computing will play important roles in the evolution of heterodox approaches to economics into a realism-based economics of the future.

## Appendix I: Lorenz's model

The equations of Lorenz's model are:

$$\frac{d}{dt}x = \rho \cdot (y - x)$$
$$\frac{d}{dt}y = x \cdot (\tau - z) - y \quad (10.5)$$
$$\frac{d}{dt}z = x \cdot y - \beta \cdot y$$

$x$, $y$, and $z$ are variables (respectively the convection intensity, the temperature difference between rising and falling currents, and the degree to which the vertical temperature profile of the air cell differs from linearity) while $\rho$, $\tau$, and $\beta$ are parameters. The equilibria of the model, all of which are unstable for the parameter values used in this chapter, are:

$$\begin{matrix} x_e \\ y_e \\ z_e \end{matrix} = \begin{bmatrix} 0 \\ 0 \\ 0 \end{bmatrix}, \begin{bmatrix} \sqrt{\beta \cdot (\tau-1)} \\ \sqrt{\beta \cdot (\tau-1)} \\ (\tau-1) \end{bmatrix}, \begin{bmatrix} -\sqrt{\beta \cdot (\tau-1)} \\ -\sqrt{\beta \cdot (\tau-1)} \\ (\tau-1) \end{bmatrix} \quad (10.6)$$

Notice that none of the equilibria depend on the value of the parameter $\rho$ – and therefore they do not change when $\rho$ changes. Yet changing $\rho$ has a dramatic effect upon the time path of the system.

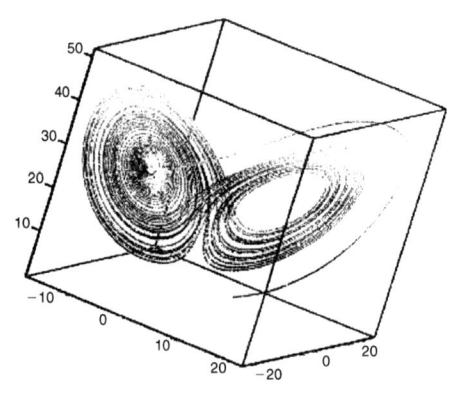

*Figure 10A.1* 3D map of the Lorenz position.

## Goodwin's model

The equations of Goodwin's model are:

$$\frac{d}{dt}\omega = \omega \cdot (P[\lambda] - a)$$
$$\frac{d}{dt}\lambda = \lambda \cdot \left(\frac{\Pi[\frac{1-\omega}{v}]}{v} - \gamma - \alpha - \beta\right) \quad (10.7)$$

where $\omega$ is the workers' share of output, $\lambda$ is the employment rate, $P[\lambda]$ is a relationship between the rate of change of wages and the employment rate, $\Pi[\ ]$ is an investment function, $v$ is the accelerator, $\alpha$ is the rate of productivity growth, $\beta$ the rate of population growth, and $\gamma$ is depreciation.

The empirical fit of the Goodwin model was somewhat criticized in Harvie (2000). In fact there was a simple schoolboy error in the econometrics (Harvie's words in personal correspondence) of not converting percentages into decimal points. With this error corrected, the empirical fit of the model to OECD data was quite good – and it improves further with a nonlinear Phillips curve and investment function, as used in the simulation shown in Figure 10.2.

### *Circuitist model*

The differential equations of the Circuitist model are the sum of the columns of Table 10.1. $F$, $B$, and $W$ are the deposit accounts for firms, banks, and workers respectively, while $L$ is the initial loan; $r_D$ is the rate of interest on deposits, $r_L$ the rate on loans; $w$ is a parameter indicating the rate at which wages are paid to workers (this can be shown to be equivalent to the share of surplus from production that goes to workers as wages (1–5), divided by the time delay $\tau$ measured in years between the outlay of $M$ to finance production, and the receipt of $n^+$ – Marx's concept of a turnover period); $\beta$ and $\omega$ are consumption rate parameters for bankers and workers respectively.

With parameter values of L=\$100, $r_L$=5%, $r_D$=1%, $S_S$=1/3, $\tau_S$=1/3, $\beta$=1/2 and $\omega$=26, the model generates the dynamics for wages, profits and gross interest income shown in Figure 10.3.

## Notes

1 For those unfamiliar with Tony Lawson and Critical Realism, the latter philosophy argues that while there is an independent, objective reality, our sensory perceptions of it includes components that do not necessarily represent objective entities. Lawson and others apply this to economics, in particular to the constructs of econometrics and mathematical deductivism. The Critical Realist movement has become influential amongst political economists, though it is far from universally accepted.
2 The variables are the intensity of convection in a weather cell, the temperature difference between ascending and descending currents, and the degree of curvature of the temperature gradient across the cell.
3 The stability properties of the equilibria can be characterized using eigenvalue analysis, and the probable qualitative nature of orbits can be implied for different parameter combinations.

4 Reliance on methods of mathematical deductive modeling more or less necessitates a focus on conceptions of atomistic individuals and closure (Lawson 2004: 334).
5 This is an instance of the inverse tangent route to chaos (Schuster and Just 2006: 69–88). Such systems have no equilibrium for some initial conditions, but equilibria for others. In general, they have to be analyzed using non-equilibrium methods.
6 There has been considerable confusion over the term ergodic in the political economy literature. An intelligible, accurate definition of ergodicity is given in Wikipedia: all accessible microstates are equally probable over a long period of time (WikiErgodicHypothesis). On this definition, the Lorenz system and comparable systems are *non-ergodic* – since there is probability zero that the system will enter the area around the equilibria (and other regions in the feasible phase space). See Figure 10.A1 on p. 164.
7 This is why the attempts by several Circuitist writers, including Graziani, to apply mathematical logic to the monetary circuit failed: they used the inappropriate method of solving simultaneous equations – the comparative static method that infests economics – rather than the more appropriate method of differential equations illustrated in this chapter. Comparative static methods failed because they abstract from flows, when income is all about flows: GDP is a flow of output over time, for instance, as is the demand that is used to purchase output – even when it is financed by borrowed money.
8 I have omitted the loan account here, since I am not considering debt repayment.
9 See www.incose.org/educationcareers/academicprogramdirectory.aspx. One omission from that list is the Norwegian Institute of Technology (www.itk.ntnu.no).
10 There are techniques, such as the Levenberg-Marquardt algorithm, that can estimate parameters that enable a nonlinear model to empirically fit a dataset, but even here the emphasis is upon description rather than prediction.

## References

Barnett, W., Chiarella, C., Keen, S., Marks, R., and Schnabl, H. (eds.) (2000) *Commerce, Complexity and Evolution*, New York: Cambridge University Press.
Braun, Martin (1992) *Differential Equations and Their Applications: An Introduction to Applied Mathematics*, 4th edn, New York: Springer Verlag.
Fontana, G, and Realfonzo. R. (eds.) (2005) *The Monetary Theory of Production*, New York: Palgrave.
Goodwin, R. M. (1967) "A Growth Cycle," in Feinstein, C.H. (ed.) *Socialism, Capitalism and Economic Growth*, Cambridge: Cambridge University Press.
Graziani, A. (1989) "The Theory of the Monetary Circuit," *Thames Papers in Political Economy* 4: 1–26.
Harvie, D. (2000) "Testing Goodwin: Growth Cycles in Ten OECD Countries," *Cambridge Journal of Economics* 24: 349–376.
Keen, S. (1995) "Finance and Economic Breakdown: Modeling Minsky's Financial Instability Hypothesis," *Journal of Post Keynesian Economics* 17: 607–635.
——. (2001) *Debunking Economics: The Naked Emperor of the Social Sciences*, London: Zed Books.
Lawson, T. (2004) "Reorienting Economics: On Heterodox Economics, Themata and the Use of Mathematics in Economics," *Journal of Economic Methodology* 11: 329–340.
——. Lawson, T. (2005) "The (Confused) State of Equilibrium Analysis in Modern Economics: an Explanation," *Journal of Post Keynesian Economics* 27: 423–444.
——. (2006) "The Nature of Heterodox Economics," *Cambridge Journal of Economics* 30: 483–505.
Marx, K. (1867) *Capital Vol. I*, Moscow: Progress Publishers, www.marx.org/archive/marx/works/1867-c1/ch25.htm.

Musella, M. and Panico, C. (eds.) (1995) *The Money Supply in the Economic Process*, Aldershot: Elgar.
Rochon, L. P. (2005) *The Monetary Theory of Production*, New York: Palgrave.
Schuster, H. G. and Just, W. (2006) *Deterministic Chaos*, New York: Wiley-VCH.
Standish, R. (2000) "The Role of Innovation within Economics," in W. Barnett, C. Chiarella, S. Keen, R. Marks, and H. Schnabl (eds.) *Commerce, Complexity and Evolution*, Cambridge: Cambridge University Press.
Wikipedia "Ergodic Hypothesis," http://en.wikipedia.org/wiki/Ergodic_hypothesis.

# Part IV
# Advanced courses/electives

# 11 Pluralism in labor economics

*Dell Champlin and Barbara A. Wiens-Tuers*

Introducing pluralism into labor economics should be relatively easy; after all, labor economics has historically been a very pluralistic field. For the first half of the twentieth century, courses in labor were dominated by Institutional economists and were often called "labor problems," because they dealt with actual labor markets rather than with abstract models. Major contributions to the field have also been made, and are still being made, by Marxist radical economists and feminist scholars. However, in recent years these alternative approaches have been almost completely eliminated from the study of labor economics at the undergraduate level and even in many graduate programs. As a result, the task of reintroducing pluralism into the undergraduate labor economics course means that instructors will have few resources to draw upon.[1] Moreover, the "core" orthodoxy now expected in a standard course leaves little room for adding more material. Thus, while introducing pluralism into labor economics is a worthy goal, it may seem like a daunting task.

There are two ways to incorporate the wide diversity of approaches into a labor economics course. One, introduce alternative schools of thought: and two, introduce the idea of economic pluralism. Each of these two approaches has distinct advantages and disadvantages. The choice of which approach will be most appropriate and most successful depends on the teaching environment and on the interests and capabilities of the students. Julie Nelson, Chapter 6 above, "The principles course," distinguishes between a paradigmatic framework that "focuses on argumentation between (or among) different schools" and a pluralistic one, that "while not being uncritical or seeking false unity, involves a less adversarial effort to examine reality from different perspectives."

As voiced by other contributors to this volume, several problems exist with the paradigmatic approach. In many colleges and universities, the economics curriculum provides students with very little background on alternative approaches to orthodoxy. In fact, students may have little exposure even to relatively recent contributions to traditional economics that deviate from the conventional orthodoxy.[2] Thus, it might be unreasonable to expect students with little knowledge of history of thought (other than orthodoxy) to tackle additional schools of thought as part of their labor economics course. Students have just spent an entire course learning the basics of traditional orthodox microeconomics, often required as a prerequisite for labor economics; it is unrealistic then to expect them to reach the same level of familiarity with other schools of thought in just a few weeks.

The second approach to introducing economic pluralism establishes a more modest and realistic goal of introducing students to the existence of pluralism in labor economics without overloading the course with new material. The organizing principle is to introduce key labor topics along with alternative views or perspectives for each topic as appropriate. The primary objective is to teach labor economics; learning about alternative economic doctrines is a secondary objective. A weakness of the traditional approach to labor economics is that the course is more about orthodox microeconomics than labor economics, which as Chapter 6 above demonstrated is fraught with its own internal contradictions. Putting the primary emphasis on schools of thought and then choosing sides would only compound this problem.

## When you "assume"...

The second approach does not mean that students master the different models or paradigms, but instead that they understand the assumptions behind the different approaches to thinking about key labor topics. The traditional model for understanding how labor markets work is part of the overall orthodox model for understanding how markets work. Its philosophical foundations are libertarianism and utilitarianism, visible in the assumptions of the model. The traditional model is deductive: it starts from several simplifying assumptions and builds an elegant explanation of how, given the assumptions of consumer and producer behavior, an efficient and socially optimal outcome will be attained. The focus of traditional economics orthodoxy is the individual driven by *rational self-interest* to make choices, given scarce resources. Those choices become the basis of supply and demand curves supposedly illustrating market interactions. The analysis takes place outside of space (geographical or physical location) and time (history).

The first exposure most undergraduate students have to the labor market occurs early in their economics education. After learning the basics of supply and demand in principles courses, students are introduced to price ceilings and price floors. The minimum wage is routinely presented as a "real-world" example of a price floor (Mankiw 2007). Even before entering labor economics, many students have already learned the basic tenets of traditional economics, which is assumed a necessary and sufficient prerequisite. First, labor economics is microeconomic analysis; thus, labor markets can be analyzed with the perfect competition model. Second, regulation or government policy in the labor market is undesirable. While the better labor textbooks include topical chapters outside this narrow framework, the microeconomic model along with its policy implications still forms the foundation for the course. Issues such as inequality, discrimination, immigration, and unemployment are treated as deviations from the perfectly competitive norm; they are simply "frictions" in the labor market (Enhrenberg and Smith 2006).

For political economists, the basic unit of analysis is groups based on social categories of individuals and group relationships. Individual decisions and behaviors are based on and informed by group membership and associations – religion, family, race, gender. In other words, the institutional context of individual decisions matters. (Of course, it is the collective decisions of individuals that form groups: a chicken and egg problem.) The relationships between groups and the definitions of groups change over time. An analysis of group relationships in one period may be much different in another time period. Thus, history matters and there is path dependence: we are the sum total of all that has gone before.

Conflict and issues of power are the norm: groups with power seek to keep it; groups without power seek it. Political economy emphasizes the unequal distribution of political and economic power, oppression, and exploitation. Labor wants higher wages, and businesses want lower costs. Instability and change are created by conflict. There is relatively broad agreement that lack of group or class analysis plays an ideological role in maintaining the system. Some mobility exists and plays an ideological role in maintaining the current economic and political system. The political system is responsive to the interests of the wealthy. The method of theory building tends to be inductive: observation of events and building explanations and models tend to be more qualitative than quantitative in general. See Figure 11.1 for a visual map illustrating the differences between and the overlaps of the various models.

**Neoclassical analysis**
*Methodological individualism*
  *Economics as a science of exchange*
*Consensual relationships (voluntary transactions)*
  Marginal analysis
  Utility and profit maximization
  Human capital theory

**Microeconomic aspects:**
  Wage and income determination, suppy
  and demand for labor
**Macroeconomic aspects:**
  Unemployment, distribution of earnings,
  productivity

**Market institutions and contracts**
  Private property rights
  Competitive market theories
    External labor markets
  Non-competitive market theories
    Monopoly, monopsony
    Internal labor markets

  Industrial organization

**Institutional/political analysis**
*Methodological collectivism*
  *Economics as a study of relations of production*
*Conflict in relationships (power)*

**Capital/labor**
  Relations of production
  Surplus product/exploitation
  Reserve army of
  the unemployed

**Non-market institutions**
  Historical context, cultural and
  social context, ideology
  Unions, government

  Industrial relations

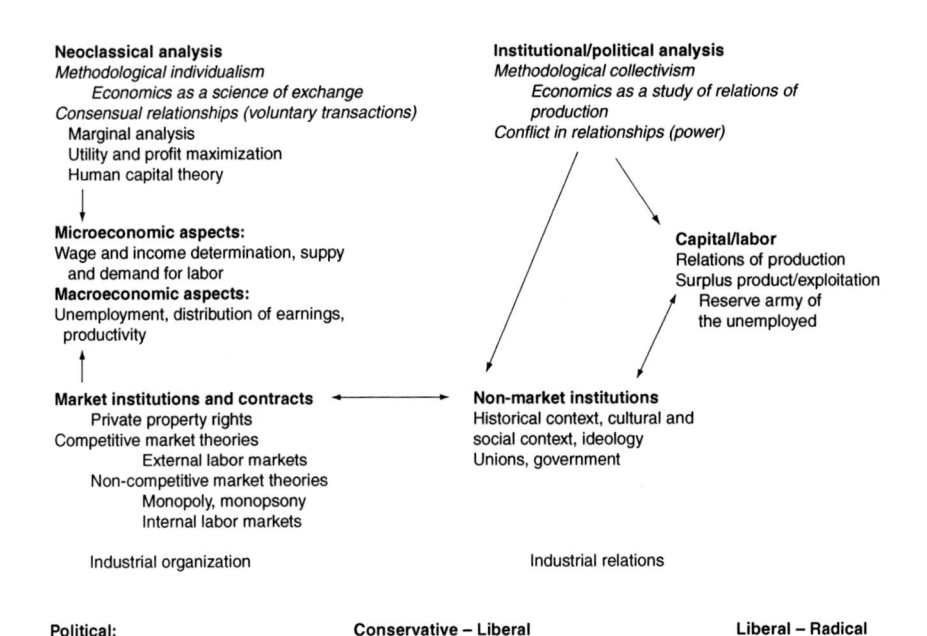

**Political:**  Conservative – Liberal    Liberal – Radical

*Figure 11.1* Approaches to labor market analysis.

## Key labor topics and pluralism

### What is labor?

The purpose of this section is to examine important topics in labor economics and how they can be incorporated into a pluralist pedagogy. The starting point is to ask, "Just what is 'Labor'?" In classical economics, labor was a social class, separate from capitalists. The interaction between labor and capitalists involved vast differentials in power and social status. In traditional economics, labor became a commodity divorced from any social context. Capitalists and workers became employers and employees, or more simply, buyers and sellers interacting on a level playing field and reaching a mutually beneficial agreement on labor exchange. Institutional Economists view the labor transaction as vastly more complicated, and Marxists/radicals/feminists assume a fundamental degree of exploitation.

Thus, the purpose of this first question is to provoke discussion and thinking about the quintessence of labor; how a labor market differs from a simple commodity market, and to provide a brief introduction into several schools of thought – classical, institutional, neoclassical, and feminist. Classical readings should include the following brief selections:

1 Adam Smith, *The Wealth of Nations* (1976) "Of the Wages of Labor" (Chapter 8, Book I, pp. 72–97), "Of Wages and Profit in the Different Employments of Labor and Stock" (Chapter 10, Book I, pp. 111–160).
2 Karl Marx. *Capital* (1967) "The Buying and Selling of Labor-Power" (Chapter 6, Vol. I, pp. 167–176) and "The Labor Process and The Process of Producing Surplus-Value" (Chapter 7, Vol. I, pp. 177–198).
3 John R. Commons (1909) "American Shoemakers: 1648–1895: A Sketch of Industrial Evolution," *Quarterly Journal of Economics* 24: 39–84.

Adam Smith had a multi-faceted understanding of labor, discussing concepts such as wage differentials, non-competing groups, and collusion among employers. Thus, Smith is a superb example of a pluralistic approach to labor. Marx's view of class conflict contrasts nicely with orthodoxy's assumption of harmony of interests. In the real world, of course, lack of power in bargaining over jobs and working conditions, exploitation, and constraints on exit and voice are commonplace. And Commons reminds us that economic transactions take place within a legal and social environment and that not all transactions take place between persons of equal legal status and power.[3]

### Wage determination

In the traditional model the wage is simply a market price. This conventional wisdom, mastered by students in earlier courses, is very powerful. The goal of this section is to broaden students' view of the wage from the one-dimensional view of "price." The key is to recognize the link between wage and income. A useful technique is to build on the analysis of the minimum wage already familiar to students. In traditional economics, the minimum wage is simply a price floor: the minimum price that most employers will pay, not the minimum wage required for subsistence. The contrast between a subsistence wage and minimum wage is instructive. The subsistence wage is the minimum amount needed to maintain a worker. What is today's subsistence wage? How is such a wage calculated? Most municipal and county living wages in the U.S. are linked to federal poverty levels, which could not sufficiently reproduce the labor force. J.M. Clark's (1923) concept of overhead costs touches on this idea by noting that employers do not pay the full cost of maintaining their workforce.

Another aspect is to introduce the customary or fair wage. While traditional economics ostensibly avoids normative judgments, marginal productivity theory implies that workers in perfectly competitive markets are paid what they contribute. However, other notions of fairness surface in alternative schools of thought. Marxists clearly regard the capitalist system as unfair to workers. Institutionalists also see the system as unfair due to the imbalance of power and inherent conflict of interest between employers and workers. Institutional economists were reformers rather than revolutionaries and generally argued for policy reform and collective bargaining as remedies rather than discarding the economic system. Feminist economics can be introduced by discussing sexual discrimination in the workplace and the differences between what is considered fair for the primary "breadwinner" and the so-called "secondary" wage earner. In addition, selected chapters from Glickman (1997) provide a useful historical context on the development of wage labor as well as the link between wages and consumption.

## *Wage differentials*

Introducing pluralism into the topic of wage differentials is not difficult, since the very existence of wage differentials represents a departure from the perfect competition model. Indeed, Borjas refers to Adam Smith's observation of differences among jobs and workers and acknowledges that the stringent assumptions of perfect competition must be significantly relaxed:

> The nature of labor market equilibrium in the presence of compensating wage differentials differs radically from the equilibrium typified by the traditional supply–demand framework. In the traditional model, the wage guides the allocation of workers across firms so as to achieve an efficient allocation of resources. Workers and firms move to whichever market offers them the best opportunities, equating wages and the value of the marginal product across markets in the process. In a real sense, workers and firms are anonymous and it does not matter who works where.
>
> (Borjas 2005: 207)

The explanation for wage differentials can be expanded by discussing labor markets in a broader context. For example, in the traditional approach, differences in jobs addressed by compensating wage theory consist of rather narrowly defined job characteristics such as risk. The idea is that employers must pay a wage premium in order to attract workers to dangerous jobs. Since risky jobs do not, in fact, always pay higher wages, what is the explanation? Orthodoxy offers hedonic wage theory which assumes some workers prefer dangerous jobs: "If the marginal worker happens to like being employed in risky jobs or being told what to do on the job, the market wage differential will be in the wrong direction" (Borjas 2005: 224).

A pluralistic approach places the problem of dangerous jobs in context by looking at particular jobs such as meatpackers, coal miners, or commercial crab fishermen. Who are these workers? To what extent did they choose their jobs due to their higher preference for risk? A prominent traditional explanation of wage differentials from a supply perspective is human capital theory. It is deficient in assuming that the responsibility for skill acquisition is an individual investment decision.

A recommended strategy is to reverse the overall premise. Instead of beginning with the individual choice framework of human capital and trying to fit education and skill training into this framework, begin with a broader consideration of education and training. For example, whose responsibility is it to pay for education? Who benefits from education? These questions enable us to examine the roles and responsibilities of employers and the government rather than assuming education and training are an individual investment decision. For example, for many years there has been a shortage of nurses in the United States. Training nurses and other medical personnel is very expensive since classes are small and experiential. Whose responsibility is it to pay for training nurses and medical support personnel? How expensive is it? How is it currently done? A human capital approach to this question would look only at one individual's decision of whether or not to attend nursing school with no broader context at all.

Wage differentials also include the topic of discrimination. Traditional theories of discrimination have been criticized even by orthodox economists, so the instructor will find no shortage of critical resources. The problem is that orthodoxy tries to constrict discrimination into an individual choice framework. For example, Becker's (1971) taste for discrimination model conceives of discrimination as a personal preference or "taste," and statistical discrimination is a choice made under conditions of imperfect information.

The contrast between this and alternative views could not be more stark. Alternative views begin from the social context (Albelda *et al.* 1996). Discrimination is a social construct derived from historical, legal, social, and economic power. This is ignored by traditional economics which distills discrimination to the expression of a personal preference while making an economic choice. In this case, rather than simply limited in its approach, it is actually harmful. Viewing discrimination as a "preference" places it in the category of other preferences. The result is that discrimination is minimized and viewed as something we all have a "right" to, just as we have a right to other preferences. More serious is the fact that discrimination is viewed as an economic decision. Since all economic decisions are rational, it follows that discrimination is also a rational choice. Teaching students that discrimination is a rational or reasonable expression of individual preferences is not something that any economics professor would want to do. Thus, a pluralistic approach to discrimination is vital.

## Labor market structure

Labor market structure used to be integral in labor economics courses. In the past few years, however, its importance has been minimized. For example, Borjas (2008) does not address the topic at all. In his chapter "Wage structure" only income distribution is discussed; there is no discussion of labor market structure. McConnell *et al.* acknowledge that labor courses used to emphasize actual labor market structures, but now they disparage this topic as "old" labor economics, while the "new" labor economics is called the "economic perspective" (2007: 4).

A great deal of research on labor market structure occurred over the course of the twentieth century and still continues. Although much has been done by economists, interesting and innovative research has also been done by scholars in related fields such as industrial relations or human resources, investigating important questions such as job opportunity, job security, contingent working arrangements, employee benefits, and pay structures within firms. In addition, scholars in industrial relations and employment law have examined workers' rights, health and safety laws, and immigration policy.

Labor market structure includes most of the topics of interest to students. The key issue to emphasize here is the concept of opportunity (Champlin 1995), assumed away by traditional economics since under the guise of human capital all jobs are available to all workers. No discussion exists of the many structures in actual labor markets that limit access to job opportunity.

Important for most workers is the opportunity to move to a better job. Traditional economics ignores job quality except tangentially in the theory of compensating wage differentials. In the traditional model, a worker moves from one job to another by moving from one market to another – presumably from one employer to another. By ignoring career paths, internal job structures, or the fact that the same job can have very different characteristics in different institutional settings, orthodoxy omits a fundamental aspect of employment. For example, a computer programmer may be employed full time at a high salary with access to benefits and a degree of job security. Another computer programmer may be employed as a temporary or subcontractor at a much lower salary with no benefits and no job security. The concept of structure is necessary to analyze this situation, which thanks to globalization is increasingly common in U.S. and international labor markets, and an increasing fear among students.

*Topics of interest*

The final part of the course discusses topics of interest to the students. A good approach is to choose topics that have been in the news such as executive compensation, pensions, globalization, and immigration. Pertaining to immigration, traditional economics, typified by Borjas who has written extensively on the issue, utilizes human capital theory to analyze immigration as a cost/benefit calculation. A pluralistic approach, however, analyzes the context rather than just the individual calculus. Analyzing the supply of immigrants is incomplete without considering the demand for immigrants. A recent article in the *Los Angeles Times*, for example, reported that the Colorado Department of Corrections planned to use prisoners as farm workers to replace immigrant workers who have become increasingly scarce in response to tougher laws and political rhetoric (Riccardi 2007). This outrageous idea would no doubt spark a lively class discussion, which could address immigration law and policy, as well as demand and supply of immigrant workers. The traditional focus on individual investment in human capital only includes legal status as a possible increased cost factor, without explaining why some workers are illegal and what is necessary to become fully documented.

Other topics of interest should be approached in the same manner by considering the issue in its social and historical context and then demonstrating how the traditional and political economy approaches may lead to very different conclusions.

## Final thoughts

In closing, we want to address a significant challenge confronting any instructor considering a pluralistic approach to labor economics. In addition to developing course content, instructors must also cope with the academic culture in economics. Unfortunately, the goal of the economics curricula in most colleges and universities is to teach students about economic theory, not about actual economies (except in economic history courses). In fact, the more theoretical a course, the more esteemed it is. Courses with a higher amount of theory are considered "rigorous," while courses focusing on current economic issues and policies suffer a lower status. Courses should include both theory and real-world information, of course, but the status attached to theory tends to produce a certain bias toward abstract technique and away from applications. Thus, instructors who choose to introduce pluralism into labor economics by reducing orthodox content may be criticized for lowering the academic "rigor" of the course. Nothing could be further from the truth, however, since introducing pluralism will actually achieve the opposite effect. Students will have understood not just one theory, but several. In addition, instructors will have the satisfaction of knowing that they have achieved a better balance between pure theory and real-world analysis.

Over the past quarter century, labor economics has suffered from the prejudice in favor of abstract theory and the tendency to dismiss real-world applications as "descriptive economics." All of the controversies in labor economics, as in other fields such as economic development or environmental economics, occur in applied analysis. There is relatively little controversy within the world of traditional microeconomics; thus in making a course such as labor economics more "rigorous" by expanding the orthodox content, we produce a course with few disagreements, debates, or nuances. Not only does this "conflict-free" approach make for a very dry and boring course, it is also fundamentally misleading. Many of the crucial issues of our time – education, immigration, health care, discrimination, and poverty, to name just a few – have their basis in the labor market. While a labor economics course cannot address all of these issues in depth, it should, at the very least, acknowledge their existence and provide students with some useful background. After all, these students must confront these problems in their own lives and attempt to find answers.

## Notes

1 Approximately a dozen undergraduate labor economics textbooks have been published in the last 20 years. In the United States, however, only a few have survived on the market long enough to go into second editions. As a result, the labor economics textbook market is dominated by a few bestsellers including *Modern Labor Economics* by Ronald Ehrenberg and Robert Smith (2008), *Labor Economics* by George Borjas (2008), *Contemporary Labor Economics* by Campbell McConnell, Stanley Brue, and David Macpherson (2007), and *The Economics of Labor Markets* by Bruce Kaufman and Julie Hotchkiss (2006). With the exception of the Kaufman and Hotchkiss text, none of the bestsellers offer a pluralistic approach. A somewhat greater degree of pluralism can be found in textbooks prepared for courses in the economics of race and gender, industrial and labor relations, or personnel economics. Professors of undergraduate labor economics with an interest in pluralism will find themselves not only preparing lectures but preparing their own reading lists and course materials as well.
2 Many schools no longer offer a history of economic thought course, and even when they do, orthodoxy is the main topic, with alternative approaches confined to a single chapter or less (Bethune 1992).
3 Kaufman and Hotchkiss (2006) nicely contrasts twentieth-century neoclassical and institutional approaches. Prasch (2004) examines the question: What is labor?

## References

Albelda, R. Drago, R., and Shulman, S. (1996) *Unlevel Playing Fields*. Sommerville, Mass.: Dollars and Sense.
Becker, G. (1971) *The Economics of Discrimination*. Chicago: University of Chicago Press.
Bethune, J. (1992) "The History of Economic Thought: A Survey of Undergraduate Textbooks," *The Journal of Economic Education* 23: 153–161.
Borjas, George J. (2008) *Labor Economics*. New York: McGraw-Hill Irwin.
Champlin, D. (1995) "Understanding Job Quality in an Era of Structural Change: What Can Economics Learn From Industrial Relations?," *Journal of Economic Issues* 29: 829–841.
Clark, J.M. (1923) *Studies in the Economics of Overhead Costs*. Chicago: University of Chicago Press.

Commons, J.R. (1909) "American Shoemakers: 1648–1895: A Sketch of Industrial Evolution," *Quarterly Journal of Economics* 24: 39–84.

Enhrenberg, R. and Smith, R. (2006) *Modern Labor Economics: Theory and Public Policy*, 9th edn. Reading, Mass.: Addison Wesley Longman.

Glickman, Lawrence (1997) *A Living Wage and the Making of Consumer Society*. Ithaca, NY: Cornell University Press.

Kaufman, B. and Hotchkiss, J.L. (2006) *The Economics of Labor Markets*, 7th edn. Mason, OH: South-Western.

McConnell, C.R., Brue, S.L., and Macpherson, D.A. (2007) *Contemporary Labor Economics*, 8th edn, New York: Irwin McGraw Hill.

Mankiw, G. (2004) *Principles of Economics*, 3rd edn. Mason, OH: South-Western.

Marx, K. (1967) *Capital, Vol. I.* New York: International Publishers.

Prasch, R.E. (2004). "How Is Labor Distinct from Broccoli?," in D.P. Champlin and J.T. Knoedler (eds.), *The Institutionalist Tradition in Labor Economics*. Armonk, NY: M.E. Sharpe.

Riccardi, Nicholas (2007) "Going Behind Bars for Laborers," *Los Angeles Times*, March 1, print edition, p. A-1.

Smith, A. (1976) *The Wealth of Nations*. Chicago: University of Chicago Press.

Waltman, J. (2000) *The Politics of the Minimum Wage*. Urbana, Ill.: University of Illinois Press.

# 12 Sustainability economics

*Peter Söderbaum*

When university scholars are unhappy with the current state of affairs in some particular field, they tend to look for similarly inclined colleagues and arrange workshops or conferences. In 1982, two respected ecologists at Stockholm University arranged a symposium on the relationship between ecology and economics. The two were concerned about environmental issues and invited ten well-known ecologists and other natural scientists and an equal number of economists, most of them traditional. Each presented his or her view of environmental problems along with proposed solutions. The result is presented in Jansson (1984).

Traditional environmental economists already had their journals and research associations and were not particularly impressed by the arguments proffered by ecologists. A minority of economists, notably Herman Daly (and some of us not present at the symposium but informed afterwards in a meeting with journalists), advocated something new. In 1989, the International Society for Ecological Economics (ISEE) was formed and its first international conference was held in 1990 under the auspices of the World Bank.

In addition to scientists demanding new thinking, students have opinions, as exemplified in other parts of this book, and even politicians may voice concerns. In 2003, for example, the German Ministry for Education and Research turned to a respected traditional economics research institute in Berlin, Deutsches Institut für Wirtschaftsforschung (DIW), expressing demand for 'sustainability economics' while at the same time highlighting the inadequacy of traditional economics. Partly in response, the DIW leadership initiated workshops to solicit more useful alternatives for sustainability issues. Ecological economists like me were among the participants in these workshops (www.sustainableconomics.de).

Given the monopoly of traditional economics across the globe, the initiative of the German government is extremely important and other governments should follow this example. But for present purposes, the main issue is not the usefulness of traditional economics in relation to a particular category of problems but rather to open the door for competing approaches. Among ecological economists, some have argued vigorously for pluralism (Norgaard 1989; Sneddon *et al.* 2006), since an open, rather than dogmatic, attitude to different schools of thought will increase the chances of successful research. Limiting university research and education to traditional economics, or any one approach for that matter, is incompatible with democracy. A university department should not become a political propaganda centre; rather, it should to some extent reflect society's different ideological orientations (Söderbaum 1999, 2004a, 2008a).

## Interpretations of sustainable development

Traditional ideas of good science suggest that each concept should be clearly defined. In social science, however, there are several 'contested concepts', that are understood (and defined) in multiple ways (Connolly 1993). This is not necessarily a disadvantage and is often a precondition for new thinking. Conversely, exclusive reliance on one definition may limit the possibilities for successful research activities. 'Democracy', 'power', 'governance' are contested concepts, as is 'sustainable development' (SD). Different interpretations are possible and each is specific not only scientifically but also ideologically.

Actually, a power game is ongoing between different actors about how to understand sustainable development. Consider the following interpretations of SD:

1 *Business-as-usual* – SD is understood as 'sustained high-rate economic growth' in GDP terms at the national level and 'sustained monetary profits' in a business context. This dominated during the 1960s and is still valid for many actors even today.
2 *Social and ecological modernization* (Hajer 1995) – Here environmental problems and social problems related to human rights, poverty, equality, etc. are taken seriously and it is assumed that they can be handled through modification of the present political economic system. Environmental labeling, environmental management systems (such as ISO 14 001), codes of conduct such as corporate social responsibility (CSR), environmental taxes as substitutes for income taxes, and establishing markets for pollution permits are among the measures to handle perceived problems.
3 *Radical change in the current system* – While acknowledging the importance of #2, as a good start, more is needed. Radical changes in the political-economic system should be considered. Judgments that 'more is needed' may be vague, suggesting a direction of change only. It is important to encourage debate in such a field with many social barriers to dialogue.

Of these three, 1 is a conservative option, while 3 is more radical, and 2 is intermediary. Present environmental and development policies in Sweden and the European Union include most measures listed under 2.

Development should be understood and measured multidimensionally. Monetary indicators, such as GDP and profits in business, are not enough. Some advocate a 'triple bottom line' where social and ecological indicators are used in addition to monetary ones (Zadek 2001). Indicators related to health and culture should be included. Non-monetary indicators should be understood and measured in their own terms and attempts to reduce all impacts to one dimension avoided. Ethical and ideological issues need to be articulated and made transparent in the development dialogue. There is no one 'correct' ethics or ideology; rather the horizons of all actors should be extended in time and space. The Brundtland report (World Commission on Environment and Development 1987 (WCD)) refers explicitly to future generations and its title *Our Common Future* suggests that no region can solve the sustainability problem on its own; therefore cooperation in many different forms is needed, along with ethical consideration of non-human life.

Humanity is facing a number of risks. A policy of prevention and security is recommended based on the precautionary principle, best defined and understood in a negative sense by reference to cases where the principle has not been respected (Harremoës *et al.* 2002). To get closer to sustainable development, a strengthening of democracy is recommended. There are limits to the knowledge of experts. All kinds of actors should participate in an interactive learning process where transparency, responsibility, and accountability are important.

## Traditional economics is incompatible with sustainable development

Traditional economics may be useful for some purposes but it is built on assumptions far from the essence of SD. Traditional economics is essentially an analysis of markets and prices. GDP measurement as well as profit/loss accounts exemplify monetary reductionism, and are far from the multidimensional analysis recommended above. Traditional economics assumes self-interest as the ethical and guiding principle of economic actors, an assumption which contravenes recommendations to consider alternative ethical/ideological standpoints and to extend horizons. Traditional economics oversimplifies risk and uncertainty. New approaches are needed (Funtowicz and Ravetz 1991; Frame and Brown 2008). Issues of risk must be considered in multidimensional terms and cannot be reduced to probabilities and one-dimensional pay-offs. Traditional economics is limited to market considerations and sheds little light on power relationships, governance, and democracy.

Our challenge is to suggest something that outperforms traditional economics. This is not difficult and there are many schools of thought that can contribute to a sustainability economics.

## Economics is always political economics

Gunnar Myrdal (1975, 1978) argued that values are unavoidable in economics. Thus, in any research project or educational program, one should explicitly state how values and ethics enter. In focusing on problems of one kind rather than another; in referring to specific concepts and theories; in choosing a method of inquiry, values are involved – there is no value-free economics.

There are many reasons to consider both individuals and organizations as political actors. While national governments play a key role in influencing development paths, reference to 'governance' (Pierre and Peters 2000) suggests that many kinds of actors are influential in politically shaping the future. Governance includes but is not limited to national government and representative democracy. National government still plays a leading role in policy making and institutional change. Politicians influence policy dialogue and shape the development process. Individuals as actors, guided by their ideological orientation, may influence the development process through their roles, relationships and activities and different kinds of organizations. The same is true of organizations as actors, guided by their mission statements or business concepts.

Governance also refers to the existence of multiple levels of actors from local through regional, national and international. Development of a single geographical entity is always to some extent influenced by outside factors, suggesting that actors within an entity should be concerned with outside events, participate in a dialogue about geographically broader issues and develop a policy for this interactive learning process. Actors may strengthen their power positions not only by cooperation and network building within one group but also through coalitions or partnerships across categories. Corporations, for example, may work together with environmental organizations for specific purposes. The result of the combined activities of policy-makers need not be limited to compromise or average outcome. Specific aggregates of actors may shape their own communities in order to reduce the influence of external factors. Democracy is how different actors should relate to each other. Whether governance in some particular region is 'good' or 'bad' depends on how the imperatives of democracy are understood and the observer's ideological orientation.

This meaning of governance will be elaborated below by further articulating the ideas of individuals and organizations as political actors. A way of understanding institutional change processes will also be presented.

## Political economic person and political economic organization assumptions

Actors in a democratic society should be understood in political terms. I suggest a political economic person (PEP) as an alternative to the economic man of traditional economics (Söderbaum 2000). In addition to market relationships, roles as professional, parent, citizen, etc. are pertinent for the PEP. The PEP is guided by an ideological orientation, which is understood as a means–ends relationship. The individual knows something about her present situation, about future desired positions and about the means of getting there. We rely on habits of thought, habitual behavior, while curious about new possibilities. This is very different from the traditional economics starting point of complete information, given preferences, etc. Ideas about how we progress and develop, along with ideological orientation, should be problematized and investigated.

In understanding the behavior of the PEP, a large part of the conceptual framework of social psychology is useful along with contributions from early institutional economists such as Thorstein Veblen, who conceptualized 'conspicuous consumption' (Veblen 1899) and the importance of habits in human behavior. Rather than search for the best alternative in every situation – which may be costly – we look for 'satisfactory' ways of behaving which often means relying on experience from similar situations.

PEP decision-making differs from that of the Economic Man. While not excluding mathematical optimization, the main idea is to think in terms of a 'matching' process and 'appropriateness'. An individual's ideological orientation as decision-maker is 'matched' against the expected (multidimensional) impact profile of each considered alternative (Figure 12.1). Sometimes the alternative fits the ideological orientation of a particular decision-maker and is thus appropriate; in other cases, a mismatch might exist.

Likewise, organizations can be understood in multiple ways. Traditional economics narrowly assumes firms maximize monetary profits. In discussing sustainability, however, broader ideas of the organization are needed. One option is understanding an organization in terms of stakeholder theory (Freeman 1984), suggesting that many interests, both monetary and nonmonetary, with attendant tensions, are relevant.

The political economic organization (PEO) model assumes a 'mission statement' for the organization that is more or less shared by members, but each stakeholder also has an ideological orientation. Thus the PEO model is polycentric. The organization as actor at the collective level is visible, but the individual also acts and has a specific role within the organization. When organizations change, it is not dissimilar to social change in general. While the organization's leader has an important role, other actors may initiate important change processes. An organization becomes certified according to ISO 14 001 often as the result of initiatives by single persons and professionals with a 'green' ideological orientation. Ideas that initiatives always come from above or that all members of an organization change their minds at the same time are not realistic.

## Overview of orthodox and institutional economics

In Table 12.1, elements of orthodoxy are compared with institutional ecological economics. To understand individuals in the economy, PEP is offered as an alternative to economic man, along with PEO as an alternative to the profit-maximizing firm.

Orthodox understanding of the economy in terms of markets and the forces of supply and demand is interesting but not sufficient. Ecological economists argue for considering non-monetary factors, such as the 'source' aspect (ecosystem services etc.) and the 'sink' capacity of ecosystems (Daly and Cobb 1989;

{ Ideological orientation of actor or decision-maker } ⟷ { Expected impact profile of alternative }

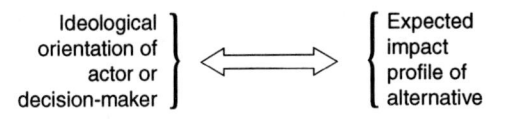

*Figure 12.1* Decision-making as a matching process or matter of appropriateness.

186   P. Söderbaum

*Table 12.1* A comparison of traditional and institutional economics

| View of: | Traditional economics | Institutional economics |
|---|---|---|
| Individual | Economic man | Political economic person (PEP) as actor |
| Organization | Firm maximizing profits | Political economic organization (PEO) as actor |
| Economy | Market relationships (in terms of supply and demand) between households and firms | Market and non-market relationships between PEPs and PEOs. The market is embedded in a social and ecological context |
| Progress in society | Maximum growth of GDP | Multidimensional indicators and profiles as part of sustainability assessment |
| Market | Supply and demand of single commodities | PEP and PEO as market actors where ethics may matter (e.g. 'fair trade') |
| Decision-making | Optimization | Appropriateness, matching process |
| Method to illuminate policy options and decision situation | Cost-benefit analysis (CBA) | Positional Analysis (PA) as Sustainability Assessment Model (SAM), Other approaches such as Environmental Impact Assessment (EIA) |
| Social and institutional change | Market change, public choice theory, governmental regulation | Governance, Actor-initiated institutional change processes |

Costanza *et al.* 1997). Limits exist to the absorptive capacity of ecosystems and the atmosphere, as exemplified by the ozone layer and climate change issues. The management of water resources, fish stocks, land resources, and other resources have to be carefully considered.

Three items in Table 12.1 will now be further discussed: traditional and institutional ideas of social and institutional change processes; competing interpretations of markets; and different approaches to sustainability assessment.

Our main interest is to discuss possible origins of institutional change processes outside government, which may in turn affect government regulation. The PEP may interpret phenomena cognitively while also relating to them emotionally. The PEP can to some extent choose between different interpretations, which in turn become instruments influencing other actors. The following citation is relevant: 'By deliberately changing the internal image of reality, people can change the world' (Korten 2001: 233).

The traditional theory of the firm suggests a profit-maximizing entity, whereas the 'stakeholder model' is less simplistic, suggesting tensions between competing interests. The 'triple bottom line' idea implies that the performance of a firm can and should be separately described and measured in social and ecological terms. Consider, for example, the Environmental Management Systems (EMS), such as ISO 14 001. Monetary performance has been the accepted measurement of business; in addition, the legal context of a corporation also points in the direction of measuring profits, and shareholder value. Some actors, however, recognize that environmental performance matters. Environmental impacts are part of an organization's performance and must be scrutinized; a promise is made that environmental performance will be improved on a yearly basis; and to become certified and retain certification, an audit must verify any improvements. As illustrated by this example, given environmental concern by some stakeholders, initiatives to improve environmental performance become legitimate. The following aspects of the process of institutional change are key: interpretation of a phenomenon; manifestation of the phenomenon; naming of the phenomenon; and acceptance and legitimacy of the phenomenon as an institution.

In the case of EMS, the idea of measuring and improving an organization's environmental performance was developed into an 'institution', manifested in different ways with environmental coordinators or controllers, auditing organizations, etc. The name of the new institution, 'ISO 14 001', is one subcategory of EMS. The number of organizations and actors supporting this institution increased over time, although with substantial differences between countries and cultures. While it spread quickly in Sweden and Northern Europe, the American business culture has been less receptive. The EMS is an innovation; thus theories about diffusion and adoption of innovations discussed in marketing literature (Kotler 2000: 354–357) may be useful to understand the process of institutional change.

To the extent that EMS becomes legitimized, it may influence our understanding of organizations and businesses. The exclusive monetary interpretation of the corporation becomes less legitimate. Thus, the addition of a new institution, EMS, influences how some actors understand a previously existing institution – the business corporation. This dynamic between institutions will continue in the future: EMS may fade away and perhaps be replaced by more ambitious institutional arrangements. Interpretations with their cognitive and emotional aspects play a key role. This underscores the importance of education and the suggested interpretations or models used in education and in public dialogue.

The market is the crux of traditional economics and therefore deserves special attention. In Table 12.2, the traditional approach is on the left, and an alternative interpretation of markets – institutional economics – is on the right. Although the orthodox approach is useful for some purposes, our understanding improves if we learn alternative ways of interpreting markets. In some cases one interpretation is clearly more useful: in others, different interpretations increase our understanding. It is important to remember that an actor's preference for a particular conceptual framework, model or interpretation is a function of science and ideology.

In traditional economics, history is not relevant, whereas institutional economists emphasize evolutionary elements, such as path dependence and inertia: an institution's present position is a function of previous decisions, habits and events, and likewise today's options are more or less constricted by historical development. Traditional economics, like Newtonian physics, has a preference

Table 12.2 Competing interpretations of markets

| View of: | Traditional economics | Institutional economics |
| --- | --- | --- |
| Time | History not important | History important, path dependence |
| Explanatory model | Mechanistic | Evolutionary, social, administrative |
| Ethics/ideology | Closed | Open |
| Economics | Impacts reducible to money | Multidimensional impacts related to different actors and stakeholders |
| Trading parties | Consumers and firms | PEPs and PEOs as market actors |
| Interaction between seller and buyer | Supply and demand | Multi-faceted relationship between potentially responsible market actors |
| Goods and services | Homogeneity, one commodity at a time | Heterogeneity, multiple transactions, multi-functionality |
| Motives for transactions | Maximum utility or profits (optimization) | Ideological considerations, 'monetary price and beyond' (matching) social responsibility of market actors |
| Features of relationship | Contract based on self-interest of the trading partners | Inclusive ('I and we paradigm,' 'person in community') |
| Third parties | Externalities should be internalized through government intervention (at least in principle) | All kinds of impacts of trade and no trade alternatives should be illuminated and related to stakeholders; government intervention based on fairness |

for mechanistic models. Institutional economics on the other hand is similar to other social sciences and humanities; social psychology is more relevant for understanding the PEP and PEO. Prices are not necessarily the result of impersonal factors but may be 'administered' (Galbraith 1963: 180–182). And trust is regarded as an important characteristic of many business relations (Ford 1990).

Traditional economics argues that global commodity prices result from impersonal market forces. But some actors on the purchasing side may argue that current market prices are too low, that they reflect 'exploitation' and are unfair. This ethical judgement may be shared by some consumers. Fair trade with connected certification schemes has become an institution that can be understood in terms of our previous analysis of institutional change.

Table 12.2 suggests that specific ethical/ideological assumptions (self-interest, utility and profit maximization, etc.) are built into traditional economics, with no openings for alternatives. But why adhere dogmatically to one set of assumptions? One possible explanation is that traditional economics is so committed to certain modes of presentation – mathematics, graphical presentation – that it only permits ethical assumptions that are amenable to such presentation.

Traditional economics also assumes that environmental impacts can be monetarized by reference to scientifically 'correct' prices. Even impacts on third parties, so called externalities, can be 'internalized', i.e. valued correctly according to monetary terms. Such monetary reductionism is opposed by institutional economists in favor of a multidimensional analysis. Environmental concern becomes a matter of fairness and ethics rather than orthodox correctness.

In Table 12.2, the term 'multi-functionality' on the right needs further clarification. In any trade relation at least two parties are directly involved. But other actors are often affected by the decisions. In addition to interpreting the transaction in terms of impacts, both monetary and non-monetary, one can identify the kinds of 'functions' that will be affected and for whom. Consider, for example, rice production and marketing in Japan. According to traditional economics, it is clear that rice can be produced cheaper outside Japan where labor costs are significantly lower. Low prices benefit domestic consumers. Japan may import rice in exchange for exporting high-tech commodities. But rice is not homogenous: many species exist, each with specific qualities, and trade may threaten some with extinction. More importantly, rice production in Japan serves specific cultural functions. In addition, landscapes will be affected, both in Japan and in the new producer country; ecosystems will be affected depending on how and where rice is cultivated. Some individuals will lose and others will gain in terms of employment.

Reasoning in terms of 'multi-functionality' does not deny the potential advantages of trade; rather, it suggests a more ambitious approach to illuminating its impacts and a more open attitude to the ethical and ideological issues involved. In a democracy, competing ideologies must be respected. Is it fair for the Japanese government to financially support farmers producing rice to protect a cultural heritage? Will the monetary cost advantage of a foreign producer be temporary or permanent? The preference for absolute/comparative advantage to unequivocally declare what is 'best for society' is limited and out of date.

In addition, the term 'I & we paradigm' needs clarification. It was developed by Etzioni (1988), who questioned an exclusive reliance on self-interest, arguing instead that each individual is part of many 'we-contexts', some extremely important for the individual, like the family, local village, nation, political party, environmental organization, etc. Healthy individuals focus both on self-interest and responsibilities connected with various we-groups. Daly and Cobb similarly refer to 'person-in-community' (1989: 169), arguing that we are individuals and, at the same time, part of a larger social context.

## Democracy, sustainability assessment and decision-making

Traditional economics is about choice and decision-making. Reference is often made to opportunity cost, implying that alternatives should be systematically compared and assessed. But more than one method exists for systematically comparing alternatives, suggesting that opportunity cost can be applied at the level of methods. We distinguish between four categories of methods (see Table 12.3).

Table 12.3 Categories of approaches to decision processes and sustainability assessment

|                  | Closed ethics | Open-ended ethics |
|------------------|---------------|-------------------|
| One-dimensional  | I             | II                |
| Multi-dimensional| III           | IV                |

Traditional cost-benefit analysis (CBA) is one-dimensional since a high degree of aggregation is recommended with monetarized impacts. CBA represents a case of 'closed ethics' since impacts are evaluated in present (actual or hypothetical) prices (see category I in Table 12.3). A discount rate is used to estimate a 'present value' of future costs and benefits for each alternative. This ostensibly informs all parties about the best alternative from a societal point of view, i.e. the alternative with the highest present value or benefit-cost ratio. Needless to say, the idea of correct prices represents a specific ideology.

In the opposite corner of Table 12.3 (category IV), Positional Analysis (PA) exemplifies a multidimensional, ethically more open method, which is more relevant for Sustainability Assessment than CBA. The role of the PA analyst is to facilitate a dialogue and interactive learning process and to illuminate a number of aspects including how the problem or issue is perceived by the parties; ideological orientations among the decision-makers to identify relevant alternatives; alternative choices to be considered; expected impacts of each alternative in different dimensions; the total impact profile of one alternative compared with the other alternatives; conditional conclusions, i.e. compatibility between ideological orientations (that appear relevant) and impact profiles of alternatives.

Ideally each actor will participate and contribute to the problem-solving process at each stage of the PA debate. Participation should be documented so that each actor is responsible and accountable for his proposals. When the final report is presented to decision-makers, each actor should feel that her arguments and opinions have been accounted for. Among the preconditions for acceptance is that a project is assessed ex post through monitoring programmes which will contribute to a continued learning process.

Such dialogue involves gradual or more radical changes in the positions of actors with respect to knowledge and ideological orientations. Sometimes a broad consensus is reached. But it is illusory to assume dialogue will eliminate all differences of opinion, for aggravated conflict is equally possible. While some will observe the principles of democracy, other actors may try to manipulate it. To strengthen democracy, dialogue should ideally take place in different arenas. It is advantageous if complementary studies are conducted by actors starting from alternative ideological viewpoints. Universities play a crucial role here, since they are less dependent on different pressure groups and decision-makers.

It is possible to think of multidimensional approaches with a threshold level in each dimension that has to be reached, category III, for example, in Table 12.3. One can also think of a one-dimensional approach in monetary terms for instance, where prices of specific impacts are adapted to the ideological orientation of each decision-maker (category II). This approach differs from CBA with correct prices and thus a closed ethics. While being ethically open in some sense, this approach also suffers from the problems connected with one-dimensional thinking and analysis.

## Thinking in non-monetary and positional terms

In Table 12.4, a distinction is made between monetary and non-monetary terms of impact. A second distinction is between a period of time (flow) and a position in time. The two distinctions leave us with four impact categories: monetary flows (A); monetary positions (B); non-monetary flows (C); and non-monetary positions (D). Nationally, Gross Domestic Product is a monetary flow (category A); the financial debts of the national treasury at the end of a year, a monetary position (B); annual pollution of $CO_2$ a non-monetary flow (C); and country's annual land-use for urban purposes a non-monetary position (D).

For the business firm, the annual turnover in monetary terms is a monetary flow; the market value of the company's assets at year-end, a monetary position; pollution of mercury in a nearby lake, a non-monetary flow; and mercury in fish caught in the same lake a non-monetary position. For the individual, monthly salary is a monetary flow and individual debts at a point in time are a monetary position. The monthly petrol used is a non-monetary flow, while knowledge at a point in time is a non-monetary position. Obviously interaction occurs over time between monetary flows and monetary positions and between non-monetary flows and non-monetary positions in specific dimensions.

Why are non-monetary impacts so important and why is it not enough to focus on the monetary aspect? The answer is trivial, involving common sense, but since traditional economics assumes that resource management is best handled in monetary terms, the issue has to be approached in a step-by-step manner. In the mid-1960s, I was asked to participate with business actors involved in the management of R&D activities. They represented companies in the pharmaceutical, steel and machine-tool industries and were confronted with choices among R&D projects. With a large degree of uncertainty, it was recognized that the usual procedure of direct monetary calculation did not work. I suggested abandoning total monetary calculation in favor of a two-dimensional multiple-step reasoning. Monetary costs of specific R&D projects for the next year are relatively easy to estimate: the knowledge situation at present and at

*Table 12.4* Categories of impacts in economic analysis

|   | *Flow (referring to a period of time)* | *Position (referring to a point in time)* |
|---|---|---|
| Monetary | A | B |
| Non-monetary | C | D |

192  P. Söderbaum

specific future points is a second dimension. Choosing among R&D project alternatives is then a choice among different future expected stocks of knowledge and their implications in terms of needed time and the monetary costs of increasing the knowledge stock.

More generally one may refer to a decision tree (Figure 12.2). Different points in time are indicated on the time axis, with $P_0$ representing a position of some object of description (in our case, technologies useful for production purposes) at time $t_0$ and $P_{1a}$ for position at $t_1$ provided that alternative Aa was chosen at $t_0$. Choosing alternative Aa in time period $t_0$–$t_1$, will lead to a qualitatively different knowledge position at $t_1$ when compared with a choice of Ab at time $t_0$. And each knowledge position at $t_1$ will in turn lead to specific R&D options at $t_1$ in terms of R&D projects and monetary costs for their implementation. The choice of Aa rather than Ab or vice versa also reflects approximate judgments of monetary potentials on the benefit side in the two cases.

It is important for each actor to have a multiple-step strategy much like that of a chess player. Inertia or path dependence is involved and the actor may regret a move, which unfortunately cannot be undone. A chess game, however, has a specific end, while the choice of strategies in organizations or private life is a never-ending process.

Knowledge and information constitute just one non-monetary dimension where positional thinking is useful. Land-use change is another. In the European Union it is estimated that 'more than 800,000 additional hectares of naturally productive land were converted into artificial surfaces for homes, offices, shops, factories, and roads, adding 6% to the continent's urban areas between

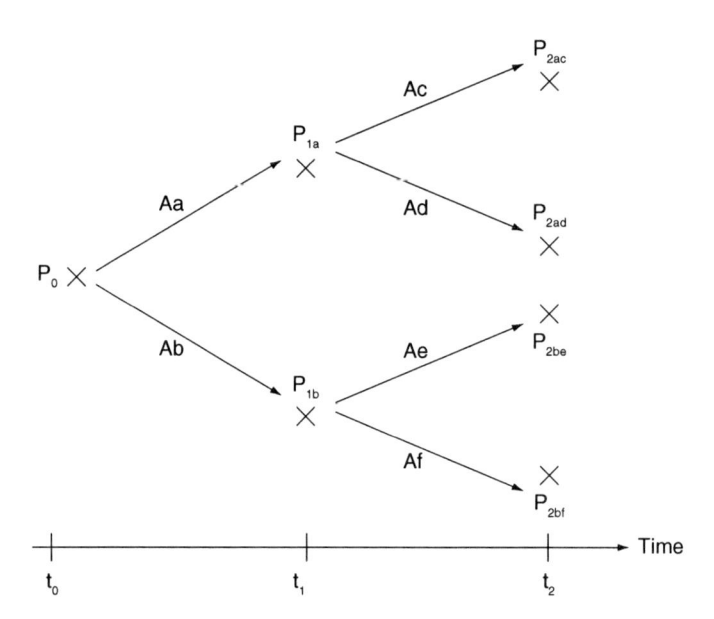

*Figure 12.2* Decision-making in multiple-stage, positional terms.

1990 and 2000' (European Environmental Agency 2005: 17). Such land-use changes are largely irreversible. The same is true for reduced biological diversity and reduced fish stocks. Oil used for transportation purposes is lost for ever, while contributing to climate change. These processes certainly influence markets and the prices of land, fish or oil but it is a mistake to believe that market or monetary reasoning by itself will automatically solve the problems. We need an economics where non-monetary flows and positions are at the heart of the analysis.

Decision-trees are often used in game theory (Hargreaves *et al.* 1995). The results of choosing one path are usually presented as one-dimensional pay-offs, suggesting a clear conceptual ranking of outcomes from the point of view of each party. The positions discussed here, however, are multidimensional rather than one-dimensional. Each position has an immediate value (for the actors and interested parties, each with a specific ideological orientation) and an 'instrumental value' as a starting point (or position) for further moves. There is no simplistic idea about how $P_{2ac}$ compares one-dimensionally with $P_{2ad}$ or any other position at $t_2$. Rather, this tool improves with a degree of complexity:

> we live in a world that is becoming increasingly complex. Unfortunately our styles of thinking rarely match this complexity. We often end up persuading ourselves that everything is more simple than it actually is, dealing with complexity by presuming that it does not really exist.
> 
> (Morgan 1986: 16)

Oskar Morgenstern, considered the father of game theory, commented on my Ph.D. thesis on Positional Analysis:

> your book is another illustration of the fact of how difficult it is to analyze what correct decisions are. That was once thought to be a very simple matter, but as so often happens in scientific development, things turned out to be far more complicated than one ever imagined.
> 
> (Morgenstern 1975)

This letter can be dismissed as a polite comment by an experienced scholar to a young person. But it also underscores the weakness of rationality. Orthodoxy sometimes assumes dogmatically that each problem should have a clear-cut solution, with the implication that only a subset of all problems are relevant for study. I argue, however, that we must improve methodology in systematically dealing with complex problems in terms of limited availability of information and knowledge, multidimensionality and conflicting values among decision-makers. There are multiple solutions rather than a single solution, and any single solution is conditional rather than unanimous. In fact, choosing among (and discussing) ideological options is often the first 'decision' to be approached. For sustainable development to have a chance, business-as-usual strategies have to be challenged.

## Key features of positional analysis

The debate about different approaches to decision-making at the societal level will continue. Many scholars have vested interests in CBA and will not easily abandon it. Scholars and politicians alike have internalized the ideology of CBA and embrace its notion of expertness. But CBA is not unchallenged. While some vigorously defend CBA (Sunstein 2002), others have criticized it (Ackerman and Heinzerling 2004). And attempts have been made to systematically compare different approaches (Söderbaum 2004b).

The Corner House, a British public interest organization, invited scholars and activists opposing CBA to Yale University in October 1999 (Corner House 1999; 'The Cost Benefit Analysis Dilemma' 2001). Interdisciplinary-oriented natural scientists at Roskilde University, Denmark, organized a conference in June 2004 as a dialogue between CBA defenders, pragmatists (i.e. those ready to use CBA if it convinces others about threats to the environment, for instance) and advocates of alternative methods. The contributions were published in a special section of *Integrated Environmental Assessment and Management* (Forbes and Calow 2006). A more elaborate treatment of PA is available in Söderbaum (2000) (see also Hall 2006; Bebbington *et al.* 2007; Söderbaum 2007). Environmental Impact Assessment (EIA) shares some of the features of PA (multidimensional thinking, focus on irreversibility, etc.).

CBA has traditionally been used to increase the legitimacy of large dam construction, as it ostensibly balances costs and benefits correctly in order to reveal to all interested persons the 'best' alternative. But the World Commission on Dams (2000) questions such simplistic calculation and points to resettlement of indigenous people as an example of ethical issues that must be addressed in ways other than CBA. The WCD proposed a specific kind of multi-criteria approach.

The (biased) judgment of this author is that PA can be generalized and applied at all levels, while CBA is more limited to the societal level, if applicable at all. In fact, some of the early applied PA studies referred to the levels of organizations and individuals. For example, a student's options among programs and courses can be approached in positional terms.

## From orthodox monism to pluralism

Orthodox environmental economics (Pearce *et al.* 1989; Pearce and Turner 1990; Pearce and Barbier 2000) is an extension of the mainstream paradigm and thus suffers from its intrinsic problems, such as ideologically specific ideas about human beings as utility-maximizing consumers, of organizations as profit-maximizing firms, and of markets in terms of supply and demand. The analysis is monetary, with a preference for market solutions. Negative externalities, for example, should be 'internalized' through the polluter-pays principle (PPP).

Environmental charges and taxes can in principle correct market failures. Where such monetary instruments have been used, they have to some extent counteracted environmental deterioration. Since environmental impacts are ubiquitous rather than exceptional, however, consistently applying the PPP would lead to a planned economy where almost all prices are corrected through state intervention, which contravenes the fundamental belief held by traditional economics of the efficacy of the market mechanism.

There are good reasons to learn traditional economics and its offshoot environmental economics, but only as part of a pluralistic study. Traditional economics obviously remains influential in addressing society's environmental trends. The Stern report, for example, which estimated the monetary costs of counteracting climate change (Stern 2008), underscores many of our criticisms of traditional economics; nevertheless, to the extent that politicians and other actors change their attitudes as a result, its effect is positive. As part of an ongoing power game between traditional and ecological economists, the Stern report is a tactical response from traditional economists to protect their paradigm.

Students of economics should make their own interpretations and judgments. We should all be cognizant of failure beyond the ballyhooed market failure of traditional economics. Paradigms may fail and the same is true of too limited ideas about science, specific ideologies and institutional arrangements. In order to be 'free to choose', economics students need some basic knowledge about alternatives to traditional economics. Only by applying the opportunity cost principle at the level of theoretical perspective or paradigm will they learn economics in a meaningful manner. The fact that each paradigm is specific not only in scientific but also in ideological terms makes the present tendency to protect orthodoxy in university economics departments untenable. Imposing a specific ideology upon students in the name of value-free science is intellectually dishonest.

It is unrealistic to expect one paradigm to be useful enough for all purposes. As has been suggested in this chapter, meeting the challenge of sustainable development requires new thinking. Pluralism, then, is not only a matter of ideology and democracy; it is desirable from a scientific point of view. When faced with competing theoretical perspectives, the chances that creativity will flourish increases compared to a strategy of one-paradigm indoctrination.

## Education for sustainable development

Sustainability is a challenge not only for individuals, business and government, but also for universities, where many disciplines as well as trans-disciplines should flourish. Alternatives to traditional economics have a 'comparative advantage' in relation to sustainability issues. At my own school, Mälardalen University, Västerås, an undergraduate program in ecological economics was started in 1995. This program was renamed 'Economics for sustainable development'. It started as a cooperative effort between the Department of Energy Technology (where courses in environmental science are given) and the Department of Economics (later School of Business). Another social science department was also involved for courses in methodology. Key requirements in the ecological economics part are:

- a background in the history of economic ideas, underscoring the historical tension between different schools of thought;
- systematic comparison of orthodox and institutional economics with respect to individuals, business companies, markets, etc.;
- awareness of the value and ideological aspect of economics and business theory;
- incorporation of traditional business courses such as financial management, accounting, marketing and organization theory, which are more pluralistic than traditional economics courses;
- compared to other places where ecological economics is taught, a stronger focus on sustainability issues in business such as CSR and EMS;
- examination largely in terms of short papers and longer essays where theory is applied to empirical cases. Third year students organize a conference with presentations by invited persons and the students themselves.

Today, sustainable development is part of the profile of Mälardalen University and the previous School of Business has become part of a School of Sustainable Development of Society and Technology. This change means a strengthened role for developed programs but all students at the university now take an interdisciplinary course in sustainable development. Among the textbooks in economics for sustainable development used, Costanza *et al.* (1997) and Söderbaum (2000, 2008b) are recommended.

The undergraduate program has been successful, given that our students are now employed in municipalities, county administration, governmental agencies and business companies as environmental coordinators and in other professional roles. A criticism raised by some students is that we have questioned orthodoxy at an early stage while not requiring courses in traditional economics, which have been voluntary. Our rationale is that starting with a required course in orthodoxy loses something. I feel that more than one paradigm has to be present in economics pedagogy, that instructors should be encouraged to compare their preferred theoretical perspective with competing perspectives and that instructors with different paradigmatic preferences should be recruited as part of each program.

## References

Ackerman, F. and Heinzerling, L. (2004) *Priceless. On Knowing the Price of Everything and the Value of Nothing.* New York: New Press.

Bebbington, J., Brown, J., and Frame, B. (2007) 'Accounting Technologies and Sustainability Assessment Models', *Ecological Economics*, 61: 224–236.

Connolly, W. (1974; 3rd edn 1993) *The Terms of Political Discourse.* Oxford, UK: Blackwell.

Corner House (1999) 'The Cost-Benefit Analysis Dilemma, Strategies and Alternatives'. Accessed September 18, 2008 from www.thecornerhouse.org.uk/item.shtml?x=52026.

Costanza, R., Cumberland, J., Daly, H., Goodland, R., and Norgaard, R. (1997) *An Introduction to Ecological Economics.* Boca Raton, Fla.: St. Lucie Press.

The Cost Benefit Analysis Dilemma (2001) *Economic and Political Weekly*, 36 (21): 1824–1837.
Daly, H. and Cobb, J.B. (1989). *For the Common Good. Redirecting the Economy Toward Community, the Environment, and a Sustainable Future*. Boston: Beacon Press.
Etzioni, A. (1988) *The Moral Dimension: Toward a New Economics*. New York: Free Press.
European Environmental Agency (2005) *The European Environment. State and Outlook*. Copenhagen.
Forbes, V. and Calow, P. (eds) (2006) 'Ecology in a Cost-Benefit Society: The Issues', *Integrated Environmental Assessment and Management*, 2: 154–199.
Ford, D. (ed.) (1990) *Understanding Business Markets. Interaction, Relationships, Networks*. London: Academic Press.
Frame, B. and Brown, J. (2008) 'Developing Post-Normal Technologies for Sustainability', *Ecological Economics*, 65: 225–241.
Freeman, E. (1984) *Strategic Management. A Stakeholder Approach*, London: Pitman.
Funtowicz, S. and Ravetz, J. (1991) 'A New Scientific Methodology for Global Environmental Issues', in R. Costanza, *Ecological Economics. The Science and Management of Sustainability*. New York: Columbia University Press.
Fusfeld, D. (1995) *The Age of the Economist*. New York: Harper Collins.
Galbraith, J.K. (1963) [1958] *The Affluent Society*. Harmondsworth: Penguin Books.
Hajer, M. (1995) *The Politics of Environmental Discourse. Ecological Modernization and the Policy Process*. London: Clarendon Press.
Hall, R. (2006) 'Understanding and Applying the Concept of Sustainable Development to Transportation Planning and Decision-Making in the U.S.' (Ph.D. thesis) Massachusetts Institute of Technology, Cambridge, Mass.
Hargreaves, H., Heap, S., and Varoufakis, Y (1995) *Game Theory. A Critical Introduction*. London: Routledge.
Harremoës, P., Gee, D., MacGarvin, M., Stirling, J., Wynne, B. and Sofia, G. (eds) (2002) *The Precautionary Principle in the 20th Century. Late Lessons from Early Warnings*. London: Earthscan.
Jansson, Ann-Mari (ed.) (1984) *Integration of Economy and Ecology. An Outlook for the Eighties. Proceedings of the Wallenberg Symposia*. Stockholm: Askö Laboratory, University of Stockholm.
Korten, D. (2001) *When Corporations Rule the World*. Bloomfield, Conn.: Kumarian Press.
Kotler, P. (2000) *Marketing Management*. London: Prentice Hall.
Morgan, G. (1986) *Images of Organization*. London: Sage.
Morgenstern, Oskar (1975) 'Letter of July 17, 1975 to P. Söderbaum'.
Myrdal, G. (1975) *Against the Stream. Critical Essays on Economics*. New York: Vintage Books/Random House.
—— (1978) 'Institutional Economics', *Journal of Economic Issues*, 4: 771–783.
Norgaard, R. (1989) 'The Case for Methodological Pluralism', *Ecological Economics*, 1: 37–57.
Pearce, D. and Turner, R. (1990) *Economics of Natural Resources and the Environment*. New York: Harvester Wheatsheaf.
Pearce, D. and Barbier, E. (2000) *Blueprint for a Sustainable Economy*. London: Earthscan.
Pearce, D., Markandya, A., and Barbier, E. (1989) *Blueprint for a Green Economy*. London: Earthscan.

Pierre, J. and Peters, B.G. (2000) *Governance, Politics and the State*. New York: St. Martin's Press, New York.
Sneddon, C. Howarth, R., and Norgaard, R. (2006) 'Sustainable Development in a Post-Brundtland World', *Ecological Economics*, 57: 253–268.
Söderbaum, P. (1999) 'Values, Ideology and Politics in Ecological Economics', *Ecological Economics*, 28: 161–170.
—— (2000) *Ecological Economics. A Political Economics Approach to Environment and Development*. London: Earthscan.
—— (2004a) 'Politics and Ideology in Ecological Economics', ISEE homepage, Encyclopaedia: www.ecoeco.org/publica/encyc_entries/PoliticsIdeology.pdf.
—— (2004b) 'Decision Processes and Decision-making in Relation to Sustainable Development and Democracy – Where Do We Stand?', *Journal of Interdisciplinary Economics*, 14: 41–60.
—— (2006) 'Democracy and Sustainable Development – What Is the Alternative to Cost-Benefit Analysis?', *Integrated Environmental Assessment and Management*, 2: 182–190.
—— (2007) 'Issues of Paradigm, Ideology and Democracy in Sustainability Assessment', *Ecological Economics*, 60: 613–626.
—— (2008a) 'Only Pluralism in Economics Research and Education Is Compatible with a Democratic Society', *International Journal of Green Economics*, 2: 45–64.
—— (2008b) *Understanding Sustainability Economics: Towards Pluralism in Economics*. London: Earthscan.
Stern, N. (2008) *The Economics of Climate Change*. Cambridge, UK: Cambridge University Press.
Sunstein, C. (2002) *Risk and Reason. Safety, Law and the Environment*. Cambridge, UK: Cambridge University Press.
Veblen, T. (1899) *The Theory of the Leisure Class*. New York: Macmillan.
World Commission on Environment and Development (1987) *Our Common Future*. Oxford, UK: Oxford University Press.
World Commission on Dams (WCD) (2000). *Dams and Development. A New Framework for Decision-Making*. London: Earthscan.
Zadek, S. (2001) *The Civil Corporation. The New Economy of Corporate Citizenship*. London: Earthscan.

# 13 International economics

*Maria Alejandra Caporale Madi and
José Ricardo Barbosa Gonçalves*

Recurrent global crises show that self-regulated markets do not generate market equilibrium and economic growth; rather, they increase instability and structural poverty, and lessen the possibility of achieving sustainable economic development. As Gilpin states,

> the Herculean task of raising the great mass of humanity from poverty to acceptable levels of economic welfare is one of the most difficult tasks facing the world economy. There is intense disagreement among economists, public officials, and other experts over the best way to achieve this goal. Indeed, there is not even a generally accepted commitment to accord priority to economic development.
>
> (2001: 305)

A pluralist approach to international political economy is based on the configuration of the international system and the existing relations of power, interdependence, hierarchies, asymmetries, and poverty. The organization of economic and social institutions within this framework shapes policy goals and results. The global political economy is thus defined as the interaction among powerful actors – states, multinationals, and international organizations (Gilpin 2001: 17). Given the importance of capital reproduction, investment and capital movements within this framework become crucial. The following pedagogical questions are fundamental to our purpose:

1. What are the historical international institutional scenarios and how have they enabled/restricted development?
2. What are the features of homogeneity and heterogeneity among national economies in the international system? How are the national and the international levels intertwined in development possibilities?
3. How are the global dynamics of capital accumulation linked to different institutional configurations?
4. What are the benefits of international trade? What are the effects of regional blocs?

5 How does the international monetary system work? What are the relations between its dynamics and conditions for development?
6 What are the connections between the hierarchy and interdependency relationships among nations in the international order and what are the challenges for defining national economic policies?

Part I of this chapter will discuss the evolution of the international economy from the nineteenth century to today, in order to highlight changes in the configuration of the international system. Part II will analyze the conflict centered on the contemporary process of financialization and the disequilibria in the global order.

## Part I: Evolution of the global economy

The current international system and its possible future perspectives cannot be adequately understood outside the context of its historical evolution (Eichengreen 1996).

Analyzing the historical development of capitalism underscores increasing economic and social disparities rather than universal prosperity (Wallerstein 1976: 233). Arrighi and Silver (1999) reminds us that the current state of development has been shaped by processes during the last 400 years, particularly the transition from Dutch to British world hegemony in the eighteenth century and from British to U.S. world hegemony in the early twentieth century.

The theory of international trade privileges the relation between relative prices in order to understand the organization of the international exchange system. According to this approach, given free trade, relative prices express productivity and factor conditions. We, however, argue that the structure and dynamic of the international exchange system necessitates incorporating economic, political, and social conditions. Thus, international hegemony is based on the ability of a nation to integrate global domestic markets. In the nineteenth century, the Pax Britannica observed a classic division between an industrialized "center" and a periphery producing raw materials. The British economy was central in the development of the nineteenth-century world economy.

> **In-class activity**
>
> Depending on the time of your class, bring in a palatable snack – enough for every student. Experiment with different initial distributions whereby, for example, one person has all, two students have most, three people have some but not all, etc. Ask students how desired goods, equitable terms of exchange, and an equitable final distribution can be obtained.

Before World War I, capital controls on international financial transactions did not exist, enabling capital mobility to reach high levels, which in turn did not hinder the successful operation of the fixed exchange rate system (Eichengreen

1996). Stable currency values constituted a major national policy concern. Countries operating on the gold standard linked domestic policy to their share of international gold reserves. Economic growth was contingent on obtaining surpluses via trade and by attracting capital flows in the form of loans, flows of foreign direct investment, or other financial investments.

---

**Box 1 Exchange rate and balance of payments**

*Main definitions*

1. The nominal exchange rate is the rate at which one currency trades against another on the foreign exchange market.
2. The real exchange rate is the exchange rate after adjusting for inflation; it therefore more accurately reflects purchasing power.
3. A floating exchange rate regime occurs without intervention: market forces determine the level of a currency.
4. A fixed exchange rate regime occurs when the central bank fixes the value of one currency against another.

*Balance of payments: overview of accounts*

1. Transaction in goods and services accounts and international transfers: current account balance.
2. Net lending and borrowing and other changes in financial assets and liabilities: financial/capital account balance.
3. The annual net variation of foreign reserves is the result of the annual performance of the current and the financial/capital account.

Source: www.imf.org/external/np/sta/bop/pdf/chap2.pdf

*Website references*

www.imf.org   The International Monetary Fund (IMF) home page offers links to news, Fund Rates, IMF Publications, Standards and Codes, Country Information, and featured topics.

www.worldbank.org   The home page of the World Bank provides information on country profiles. The website also offers advice and an array of customized resources to more than 100 developing countries.

---

**Key concept: gold standard**

A monetary standard where the basic unit of currency of a country is a fixed quantity of gold and the currency is freely convertible at home and abroad into the fixed amount of gold per unit of currency.

Source: Greenwald (1973)

Economic expansion via expansionist monetary policy without gold reserves leads to inflation and an unstable rate of exchange. The stability of the nominal exchange rate and demand deflationary policies were privileged, particularly in the periphery of the system. In fact, to preserve international integration under the gold standard, stability of domestic prices and its effects on exchange rates necessitated expansion of the domestic and foreign markets.

After the Second Industrial Revolution, Britain's international role eroded, even though it still remained important as an international trader and banker. Financial capital expanded as capital markets evolved, speeding up monopolization of industry and magnifying international expansion. Indeed, enlargement of markets is linked to the development of financial capital and the foreign direct investment. Rosa Luxemburg (1913) argued the need to expand markets abroad as a crucial aspect of the historical process of expanded capital reproduction and imperialism. International trade relations reveal the interchange between capitalist and non-capitalist production.

> **Classical readings: David Ricardo.** *On the principles of political economy and taxation*
>
> - Under a system of perfectly free commerce, each country naturally devotes its capital and labour to such employments as are most beneficial to each. This pursuit of individual advantage is admirably connected with the universal good of the whole. By stimulating industry, by regarding ingenuity, and by using most efficaciously the peculiar powers bestowed by nature, it distributes labour most effectively and most economically: while, by increasing the general mass of productions, it diffuses general benefit, and binds together by one common tie of interest and intercourse, the universal society of nations throughout the civilized world. It is this principle which determines that wine shall be made in France and Portugal, that corn shall be grown in America and Poland, and that hardware and other goods shall be manufactured in England.
> - If Portugal had no commercial connection with other countries, instead of employing a great part of her capital and industry in the production of wines, with which she purchases for her own use the cloth and hardware of other countries, she would be obliged to devote a part of that capital to the manufacture of those commodities, which she would thus obtain probably inferior in quality as well as quantity.
> - The quantity of wine which she shall give in exchange for the cloth of England, is not determined by the respective quantities of labour devoted to the production of each, as it would be, if both commodities were manufactured in England, or both in Portugal.
> - England may be so circumstanced, that to produce the cloth may require the labour of 100 men for one year; and if she attempted to make the wine, it might require the labour of 120 men for the same time. England would therefore find it in her interest to import wine, and to purchase it by the exportation of cloth.
> - To produce the wine in Portugal, might require only the labour of 80 men for

one year, and to produce the cloth in the same country, might require the labour of 90 men for the same time. It would therefore be advantageous for her to export wine in exchange for cloth. This exchange might even take place, notwithstanding that the commodity imported by Portugal could be produced there with less labour than in England. Though she could make the cloth with the labour of 90 men, she would import it from a country where it required the labour of 100 men to produce it, because it would be advantageous to her rather to employ her capital in the production of wine, for which she would obtain more cloth from England, than she could produce by diverting a portion of her capital from the cultivation of vines to the manufacture of cloth.

- Thus England would give the produce of the labour of 100 men, for the produce of the labour of 80. Such an exchange could not take place between the individuals of the same country. The labour of 100 Englishmen cannot be given for that of 80 Englishmen, but the produce of the labour of 100 Englishmen may be given for the produce of the labour of 80 Portuguese, 60 Russians, or 120 East Indians. The difference in this respect, between a single country and many, is easily accounted for, by considering the difficulty with which capital moves from one country to another, to seek a more profitable employment, and the activity with which it invariably passes from one province to another in the same country.

Source: Ricardo (1821); www.econlib.org/library/Ricardo/ricP2a.html, p. 10

Until the end of the nineteenth century, control over the circulation of goods restricted the possibilities of production and consumption, with control over markets redefined at the system level. In this new period of national rivalries, neocolonialism expressed tensions emerging from the organization of the international economic system. Contrary to the orthodox faith, relative prices were not the axis of the organization of the international exchange system of goods.

**Pause for Thought 1: Does the Ricardian model of international trade explain the internationalization of economies?**

Most theories of international trade address the effect of exchange rates on national specialization. The Ricardian model and the Hecksher–Ohlin–Samuelson models emphasize comparative advantages and a country's endowment of primary factors

David Ricardo's (1821) simplified model emphasized differences in factor costs of production as the basis for trade. Each country produces according to its comparative advantage with exchange explained by comparative costs. Ricardo offered the example of wine and fabric: since the labor cost of producing wine was lower in Portugal than England, Portugal possessed a comparative advantage for wine, while England for fabric. The normative aspect of free trade allows the market to guide specialization. The Ricardian principles of differentiation, and specialization of the national functions of production, given the assumption of perfect competition, leads to a global market where the flows and composition of international trade are defined by equilibrium relative prices. Thus, relative prices are integral in understanding price equilibrium, since they express comparative advantages among nations.

The neoclassical theory of international trade, initiated by Hecksher and Ohlin, adapted Ricardian ideas to a model of multiple factors of production within a production function subject to constant returns and perfect competition. The dynamic of international trade, that is to say, the flows of goods, centers on the movement of relative prices toward equilibrium in atomized international markets. Production cost differences and factor endowments are relevant: countries with a more favorable labor endowment have a lower labor cost; thus, they will specialize in labor-intensive activities. Factors of production explain specialization in international trade.

The Hecksher–Ohlin–Samuelson model predicts a strong relationship between the country's abundant factor and relative prices of the goods produced. Consider: two goods: good X, capital intensive and, good Y, labor intensive; two countries and their abundant factors, A – capital, and B – labor. If relative prices of the goods within both countries follow this trend:

$$\frac{PXA}{PYA} < \frac{PXB}{PYB}$$

Country A has a comparative advantage in the production of good X. Country B would produce Y and import X on behalf of its abundant factor, labor, regardless of the evolution of conditions of demand.

However, in the 1940s, when analyzing Latin American development, Prebish (1949) argued that productivity differences between developed and developing regions could adversely affect trade relations. Gains in productivity observed in the industrialized countries did not result in falling prices of industrialized goods. At the same time, benefits from the developing countries' technical progress in agriculture were usually appropriated by the center, which was explained by cyclical movement of the prices in the international economy.

During ascending phases of global economic cycles, prices of agricultural products increase more quickly than industrialized products. However, with a cyclical crisis, the value of exports falls, due to either a reduction of the unitary price of the products exported or a decrease in the total quantity of exports; the fall in the prices of manufactured goods, however, is usually slower and less intense. As a result, the cyclical price movement favors the center via deterioration of trade exchange relations, i.e. the price index of exports divided by the price index of imports.

Thus, even when international prices express relations of equivalence, important differences exist in the composition of goods traded – manufactured vis-à-vis primary goods – with long-run effects on the evolution of the exchange relations. The relations of exchange express differences to which the investment process could create differentials of productivity and aggregate value. Thus, another dimension is a nation's technological content and the aggregate value of its exports, as well as the productive linkages that the exporting activities create in the domestic economy. After the 1970s, the "new international economy" (Krugman and Obstfeld 2003) incorporated imperfect competition to analyze how global oligopolies and intra-firm trade affects international commercial flows.

*Website reference*

www.wto.org  The World Trade Organization home page provides information on the agreements and rules of trade between nations. This website contains statistics, cases, discussions, and regulations useful for negotiations and disputes.

After World War I, the main focus of international agreements was defending national interests, overwhelmed by fragmentation. During the interwar period the international monetary system collapsed and the international movement of capital declined, abetted by the imposition of capital controls. How nations join the global picture affects transmission of fluctuations and interdependence. In the 1920s, interdependence among the national economies was heightened by capital mobility flows and expressed in the sensitivity of the European economies to American conjunctures. An example is Europe's vulnerability in the interwar period to the fluctuations in the U.S. economy and the dependence on U.S. external financing. In fact, competition between international financial spaces reinforced the instability of the period (Kindleberger 1996).

> **Key concept: terms of trade**
>
> The relationship, frequently analyzed in international trade, between the prices a producer must pay and those received for its products. An improvement in terms of trade means that the producer's selling price has increased to a greater extent (or fallen to a lesser extent) than prices of items needed, leaving the producer better off.
>
> Source: Greenwald (1973)

The 1929 crisis intermixed two elements of cyclical transmission: one, retraction of American capital flows due to increased interest rates and credit rationing; and two, decrease in American imports due to the contraction of business activities. After the 1929 crisis, countries of the periphery felt the impact of reduced exports and constricted capital outflows.

> **In-class activity**
>
> Present the class with data relative to main macroeconomic international problems at the beginning of the twenty-first century. Break the class into groups and ask each group to compare the current situation to the 1930s and the 1970s. Have the groups present their results to the whole class.

In the mid-twentieth century, global expansion of capitalism under American hegemony changed the international labor division and the center–periphery axis. After World War II, trade agreements favored a gradual liberalization of trade flows. American hegemony was exerted via corporate expansion, which in turn enhanced inter-country trade flows. It is crucial in analyzing capital circulation to focus on multinational investment, which can be analyzed through interrelations among production, investment flows, and international trade. Localization strategies combine the logic of costs and competition, in which the role of technology and innovation has a decisive impact, abetted by the exercise of power.

### Classical readings: Joseph Schumpeter. *The Sociology of Imperialism*

The character of capitalism leads to large-scale production, but with few exceptions large-scale production does not lead to the kind of unlimited concentration that would leave but one or only a few firms in each industry. On the contrary, any plant runs up against limits to its growth in a given location; and the growth of combinations, which would make sense under a system of free trade, encounters limits of organizational efficiency. Beyond these limits there is no tendency toward combination inherent in the competitive system. In particular, the rise of trusts and cartels – a phenomenon quite different from the trend to large-scale production with which it is often confused – can never be explained by the automatism of the competitive system. This follows from the very fact that trusts and cartels can attain their primary purpose – to pursue a monopoly policy – only behind protective tariffs, without which they would lose their essential significance. But protective tariffs do not automatically grow from the competitive system. They are the fruit of political action – a type of action that by no means reflects the objective interests of all those concerned but that, on the contrary, becomes impossible as soon as the majority of those whose consent is necessary realize their true interests. To some extent it is obvious, and for the rest it will be presently shown, that the interests of the minority, quite appropriately expressed in support of a protective tariff, do not stem from capitalism as such. It follows that it is a basic fallacy to describe imperialism as a necessary phase of capitalism, or even to speak of the development of capitalism into imperialism. We have seen before that the mode of life of the capitalist world does not favour imperialist attitudes. We now see that the alignment of interests in a capitalist economy – even the interests of its upper strata – by no means points unequivocally in the direction of imperialism. We now come to the final step in our line of reasoning.

Since we cannot derive even export monopolism from any tendencies of the competitive system toward big enterprise, we must find some other explanation. A glance at the original purpose of tariffs provides what we need. Tariffs sprang from the financial interests of the monarchy. They were a method of exploiting the trader which differed from the method of the robber baron in the same way that the royal chase differed from the method of the poacher. They were in line with the royal prerogatives of safe conduct, of protection for the Jews, of the granting of market rights, and so forth. From the thirteenth century onward this method was progressively refined in the autocratic state, less and less emphasis being placed on the direct monetary yield of customs revenues, and more and more on their indirect effect in creating productive taxable objects. In other words, while the protective value of a tariff counted, it counted only from the viewpoint of the ultimate monetary advantage of the sovereign. It does not matter, for our purposes, that occasionally this policy, under the influence of lay notions of economics, blundered badly in the choice of its methods. (From the viewpoint of autocratic interest, incidentally, such measures were not nearly so self-defeating as they were from the viewpoint of the national economy.) Every custom house, every privilege conferring the right to produce, market, or store, thus created a new economic situation which deflected trade and industry into "unnatural" channels. All tariffs, rights, and the like became the seed bed for economic growth that could have neither sprung up nor maintained itself without them. Further, all such economic institutions dictated

> by autocratic interest were surrounded by manifold interests of people who were dependent on them and now began to demand their continuance – a wholly paradoxical though at the same time quite understandable situation.
> Source: Schumpeter (1966); www.mises.org/books/imperialism.pdf, pp. 88–90

During the Cold War, Soviet-bloc trade also grew enormously. However, commercial opportunities did not enhance profits as in the capitalist world, since they did not access countries that had advanced technology or competitive efficiency (Madisson 1992: 100).

The history of the global economy since the mid-1940s cannot be apprehended without understanding the evolution of the dollar in the monetary and financial international system (Belluzzo 2008). In the immediate postwar period, under Bretton Woods, the power of the convertible dollar supported not only Europe and Japan's industrial reconstruction, but also the industrialization of many peripheral countries. The Marshall Plan resulted from the Truman doctrine – founded on American supremacy in the postwar period. Its objectives were to rebuild and create a stronger foundation for the allied European countries, along with parrying communism. Between 1948 and 1952, the Plan involved US$13 billion in economic and technical assistance, mostly to the UK, France, Germany, and Italy.

Nevertheless, expanding the dollar liquidity helped create the crisis of the monetary standard since the only convertible currency in gold was the dollar. The United States did not have enough gold to convert dollars. The Triffin dilemma expressed the fundamental imbalances in the Bretton Woods system (Triffin 1964).

Thus, the post-World War II period was characterized by the gradual relaxation of capital controls and the gradual recovery of capital flows. Bretton Woods allowed policy makers to define domestic objectives without destabilizing exchange rates. National politics focused on aggregate demand and job creation, resulting in expansionist monetary and fiscal policies, while preserving the stability of the fixed exchange rate regime in a context of capital controls. The state guaranteed macroeconomic policy in order to achieve employment goals. Specific and historical market mechanisms shape economic policy and its capacity to stabilize the economy, affecting the results of decentralized market processes on employment and income distribution.

> **Key concept: trade barriers**
>
> An artificial restraint on the free exchange of goods and services between nations. The most common types are tariffs, quotas and exchange controls.
> Source: Greenwald (1973)

Between 1950 and 1973, national development was linked to state intervention, which guaranteed the sustainability of this process. This, in turn, enabled long-run investments as corporations defined their investment strategies conditioned by the monetary, fiscal, and exchange rate policies in an international context that favored the implementation of "Keynesian policies."

> **Key concept: Keynesian economics**
>
> The body of economic thought developed by John Maynard Keynes and his followers. The central objective is to analyze the causes and results of variations in aggregate spending and income. To prevent mass unemployment in the business cycle downturn, Keynes argued that the central government should compensate aggregate demand deficiency with deficit financing to stimulate spending and to create investment which would raise income to the full-employment level, aided by the investment multiplier.
>
> Source: Greenwald (1973)

The dynamics of industrialism and urbanization incorporated workers into the formal market by means of economic growth. Production and reproduction of material life, as well as the conditions of citizenship and inclusion into industrial society, became a constitutive aspect of national development involving job patterns and social benefits that guaranteed universal conditions of social inclusion. Table 13.1 summarizes the performance of the international economy between 1900 and 1987.

The increasing disequilibria of the American balance of payments ended the Bretton Woods convertibility system and fixed exchange rates when President Nixon closed the "gold window" in 1971 and the adopted the floating exchange rate regime in 1973. The growth of international financial markets, characterized by increased liquidity and scales of transactions much above the level of international reserves, made it nearly impossible to adjust to the fixed exchange system. The prolonged period of U.S. dollar depreciation in the 1970s was followed by intense speculative and flight movements of capital.

> **Key concept: speculation**
>
> Assuming above-average risks in order to gain above-average returns on a business or financial transaction. Speculation is usually applied to the buying and selling of securities, commodities, or foreign exchange, hoping for profits due to price changes.
>
> Source: Greenwald (1973)

Transformations in international institutions help us understand the crisis of the postwar Keynesian system. The dollar was once again the universal standard thanks to an unprecedented increase in U.S. interest rates after 1979. The strengthened dollar as reserve currency and as a key unit in commercial and

*Table 13.1* The international economy, 1900–1987 (% change)

| Growth rates* | OECD countries (16) | Asian countries (9) | Latin American countries (6) | USSR | Total (32 countries) |
|---|---|---|---|---|---|
| GDP | | | | | |
| 1980–1987 | 3.0 | 2.7 | 4.1 | 3.3 | 3.0 |
| Population | | | | | |
| 1900–1950 | 1.3 | 0.8 | 1.9 | 0.8 | 1.0 |
| 1950–1987 | 0.5 | 2.1 | 2.6 | 1.2 | 1.7 |
| 1900–1987 | 0.9 | 1.3 | 2.2 | 1.0 | 1.3 |
| Per capita GDP | | | | | |
| 1900–1950 | 1.1 | −0.2 | 1.5 | 2.1 | 1.1 |
| 1950–1987 | 3.3 | 3.5 | 2.2 | 2.6 | 2.5 |
| 1900–1987 | 2.0 | 1.4 | 1.8 | 2.3 | 1.7 |
| Exports volume | | | | | |
| 1900–1950 | 1.5 | 1.6 | 1.5 | 1.2 | 1.5 |
| 1950–1987 | 6.5 | 6.6 | 4.9 | 7.8 | 6.5 |
| 1900–1987 | 3.6 | 3.6 | 3.0 | 3.9 | 3.5 |
| Imports volume | | | | | |
| 1900–1950 | 0.7 | 0.8 | −0.4 | 0.4 | 0.5 |
| 1950–1987 | 6.0 | 4.5 | 2.3 | 6.6 | 4.7 |
| 1900–1987 | 2.8 | 2.3 | 0.7 | 2.9 | 2.3 |

Source: Madisson (1992: 13, 30).

Notes
*annual composite average rate.
OECD countries: Germany, Austria, Australia, Belgium, Canada, Denmark, the United States, Finland, France, the Netherlands, Italy, Japan, Norway, the United Kingdom, Switzerland, Sweden. Asian countries: Bangladesh, South Korea, China, the Philippines, Taiwan, India, Indonesia, Pakistan, Thailand. Latin America countries: Argentina, Brazil, Colombia, Chile, Mexico, Peru.

financial transactions deeply altered the structure and dynamics of the global economy. After the 1970s, international trade became increasingly associated with high capital mobility and capital internationalization. Intra-firm trade and firm networks became more important. During the 1980s, the dollar valuation stimulated the redistribution of global productive capacity, mainly in manufacturing, which fostered not only disequilibria in the balance of payments among the U.S., Asia, and Europe, but also the advance of financial globalization.

**Pause for Thought 2: Was the Bretton Woods crisis only monetary?**

The central question for policy makers was how to devaluate the dollar while retaining its international currency role. In the monetarist regime a flexible regime would allow the economy to achieve general equilibrium. Free markets ostensibly express rational choice and free exchange rates permit adjustment of domestic prices to international costs. Each country would take care of its monetary policy, ascribing to exchange markets the determination of currencies' relative prices. In the long run, the domestic price level and the stock of money supply would be compatible with internal and external equilibrium, resulting from rational choices of economic agents without restrictions to price adjustments.

Exchange rate flexibility enables achievement of the monetary rules because it equilibrates the gap between prices and costs among countries. The defense of exchange rate flexibility by Friedman (1962) is based on the possibility of rescuing the autonomy of monetary policy, while surmounting the "impossible trinity" in a changing international order towards liberalization of capital flows.

As a matter of fact strong speculation in the international exchange market and the depreciation of the dollar fueled the expansion of the Euromarket, which offered ample liquidity to the international system. This period is marked by increased capital mobility and greater importance of the capital account in relation to the current account.

The economic crisis of the postwar period reveals the inner contradictions of capital movements, while its solution required reorganizing economic and social relations. High liquidity preference, rather than a cause, was a manifestation. The centralization of capital, through waves of mergers and acquisitions, besides expanding subcontracting schemes, regrouped social capital and through transfers of ownership created new structural forms (Aglietta 1979: 220). The centralization process fueled financial circulation and fed speculation and inflation, because uncommitted cash flows to production are now channeled toward financial markets. Investment dynamics is based on the existence of a monetary economy whose foundations are credit relations, organized markets of financial assets, speculation, and uncertainty. In this economy, interrelated balance sheets and cash flows among the income-producing system and the financial structure are crucial for the valuation of capital assets and the pace of investment.

*Website references*

www.federalreserve.gov   The Federal Reserve System home page provides useful information about its organization, policies, and practices.

www.bundesbank.de/index.en.php   The Central Bank of Germany home page provides information about its organization and services, besides publications, archives, and statistical findings published under topic areas.

www.boj.or.jp/en   The Bank of Japan home page contains information relative to its organization, policies and operations, and links to further research on monetary and economic studies.

Neoliberalism was a response to the crisis in post-World War II capitalism (Minsky 1986). After deregulation, the institutional structure was inadequate to "stabilize instability." The adjustment process of the 1990s was conditioned by the national dimension of the institutions, historically constructed and consolidated in the postwar period. The current market flexibilization is connected to eliminating restrictions in order to enlarge market integration by a new pattern of interactions between formal and informal circuits of expenses and revenues.

> **Key concept: stability**
>
> Most economists would consider three aspects of economic activity relevant to the measurement of stability: production, employment and prices.
>
> Source: Greenwald (1973)

Adjustment of domestic policies to the requirements of the global economy occurred by expanding self-regulated markets to achieve economic development. Besides liberalization of the capital account, privatization and flexibilization of the labor market, the commercial, financial, and tax reforms resuscitated economic growth with the role of the state defining property rights, and establishing an efficient legal and judicial system. A key objective of reform was commercial and financial integration. Economic liberalization was adopted to take advantage of the long-term benefits advocated by multilateral institutions. Financial deepening advanced due to profitability differences between the finance and production spheres. As a result, the evolution of effective demand turned unemployment into a permanent and cumulative process.

Global growth since the 1990s has been fueled by Asia, particularly China and India. According to Hobsbawm,

> Clearly this has not yet greatly changed the relative weight of Asia and the old North Atlantic – the US, the European Union and Japan between them continue to account for 70 per cent of the global GDP – but the sheer size of Asia is already making itself felt. In terms of purchasing power, south, south-east and east Asia already represent about two thirds larger than the US.
>
> (Hobsbawm 2007: 39)

Industrial production advanced in Asia, impacting raw material and food imports, abetted by cheap labor, devaluated currencies, and huge amounts of direct foreign investments. Initially, China's economy depressed prices of manufactured goods, which in turned depressed global inflation until the second half of the decade 2000–2010 (Belluzzo 2008). Table 13.2 shows the most dynamic importers over 1991–2000. The countries benefiting most from the evolution of trade between 1985 and 2000 are illustrated in Table 13.3.

An increasing degree of export specialization has occurred in Latin America (CEPAL 2003) thanks to cheap labor and abundant natural resources.

*Table 13.2* Most dynamic global importers, 1991–2000

|    | Country         | % Share in global import market |
|----|-----------------|---------------------------------|
| 1  | United States   | 24.3 |
| 2  | Belgium         | 5.7  |
| 3  | China           | 5.2  |
| 4  | Japan           | 4.6  |
| 5  | UK              | 4.3  |
| 6  | Mexico          | 4.2  |
| 7  | Canada          | 3.9  |
| 8  | Hong Kong, China| 3.6  |
| 9  | Germany         | 3.5  |
| 10 | France          | 3.5  |
| 11 | Holland         | 3.0  |
| 12 | Korea           | 2.6  |
| 13 | Taiwan          | 2.5  |
| 14 | Singapore       | 2.2  |
| 15 | Spain           | 2.0  |
| 16 | Italy           | 1.8  |
| 17 | Malaysia        | 1.5  |
| 18 | Russia          | 1.4  |
| 19 | Brazil          | 1.2  |
| 20 | Turkey          | 1.1  |
| 21 | Czech Republic  | 1.0  |
| 22 | India           | 1.0  |
| 23 | Poland          | 1.0  |
| 24 | Ireland         | 1.0  |
| 25 | Australia       | 1.0  |

Source: COMTRADE at www.eco.unicamp.br/pesquisa/CECON/index.php.

*Table 13.3* Countries that contributed most to global trade growth, 1985–2000

| Country | Growth rate relative to share in global trade growth (%) |
|---|---|
| China | 240.0 |
| Thailand, Malaysia, the Philippines and Indonesia | 56.0 |
| Mexico | 45.0 |
| Chile | 40.0 |
| South Korea, Hong Kong, Taiwan and Singapore | 34.0 |

Source: WTO (2001).

Specifically, three Latin American export patterns can be distinguished: one, integration of vertical flows in the trade of manufactured goods, basically parts and components, to the U.S. market; two, integration of South American countries into horizontal trade flows, i.e. flows of homogeneous products into international trade chains; and three, a Caribbean pattern of increased service exports, mainly tourism, but also finance and transport services.

> **Pause for Thought 3: Are multinationals global players?**
>
> Gilpin (2001) defines a multinational corporation as a firm of one nationality with partially or wholly owned subsidiaries in at least one other national economy. Their expansion is primarily by foreign direct investment, which entails either purchasing an existing firm or building a facility.
>
> Rugman and Verbeke (2006) support the regional nature of world business. They argue that most international business is semi-global, that is, between firms expanding via strategies to benefit from scale, scope and exploitation of national differences; and between firms with strategies centered on their home nation and operating in each individual host country with quasi-autonomy.
>
> Nevertheless, the scope of the globalization has been overstated: evidence suggests growing difficulties in managing internal networks beyond a single region due to cultural, administrative, geographic, and economic factors. The unfortunate reality of international business is that only a handful of firms (nine of 500 firms), namely IBM, Sony, Philips, Nokia, Intel, Canon, Coca-Cola, Flextronics, and Moët Hennessy–Louis Vuitton, have been able to achieve a balanced distribution of their sales in North America, Europe, and Asia (Rugman and Verbeke 2006: 2).
>
> *Website reference*
>
> www.unctad.org   The United Nations Conference on Trade and Development home page provides information on trade, investment and development opportunities of developing countries while helping them face the challenges of globalization. The website includes sections with information concerning international trade and commodities, investment in enterprises and transnational corporations.

Trade liberalization during the 1990s increased the participation of emergent countries in international trade, without a corresponding increase in their share of global income (UNCTAD 2002). This happened because the value added to exports was relatively low when compared to capital-intensive products exported by developed countries. Among the emerging economies, the only exception was the eastern Asian countries. A virtuous relationship between trade and growth does not happen automatically; rather, it depends on the composition of exports and the participation of developing countries in international productive networks and flows of foreign direct investment.

> **Key concept: value-added by manufacture**
>
> The difference between the value of a good and the cost of materials used to produce it. Value added is derived by subtracting the cost of raw materials, parts, supplies, fuel, goods purchase for resale, and electricity from the value of shipments. It is the best money gauge of the relative economic importance of a manufacturing industry because it measures its contribution to the economy rather its gross sales.
>
> Source: Greenwald (1973)

During this period two trends are palpable: One, increased primary and labor-intensive products and natural resources in global commerce; and two, the thirty most important sectors in international trade account for over 50 percent of global exports. Tables 13.4 and 13.5 illustrate the technological structure of exports in developed and developing countries.

This period also witnessed an intensification of trade-related conflicts. The latest round of negotiations, the Doha Development Round under the WTO's Fourth Ministerial Conference, started in November 2001 and broke down in July of 2008. It was the first round of multilateral negotiations of the WTO and the ninth since the creation of the GATT. On July 21, 2008 the WTO expansion negotiations started again only to collapse eight days later. The Doha Agenda addressed a broad range of topics of interest for all countries, including agriculture, services, access to markets for non-agricultural products, intellectual property, trade and investment relations, trade facilitation, electronic commerce, the relation between trade and the environment, etc. The failure of the Doha Round underscores the difficulties in pro-liberalization rounds of negotiations.

Table 13.4 Evolution of the technological structure of exports in developed countries (average annual rates, %)

|  | 1985–1990 | 1990–1995 | 1995–2000 | 2000–2005 | 1991–2000 | 2001–2005 |
|---|---|---|---|---|---|---|
| Natural resources and labor intensive | 11.0 | 11.0 | 0.8 | 11.1 | 3.7 | 14.7 |
| Low technological intensity | 15.0 | 12.7 | 3.7 | 8.0 | 5.6 | 10.9 |
| Medium technological intensity | 15.6 | 13.3 | 6.4 | 6.9 | 8.2 | 10.1 |
| High technological intensity | 19.5 | 12.9 | 3.5 | 9.9 | 7.5 | 14.5 |

Source: COMTRADE at www.eco.unicamp.br/pesquisa/CECON/index.php.

Table 13.5 Evolution of the technological structure of exports in developing countries (average annual rates, %)

|  | 1985–1990 | 1990–1995 | 1995–2000 | 2000–2005 | 1991–2000 | 2001–2005 |
|---|---|---|---|---|---|---|
| Natural resources and labor intensive | 24.5 | 13.0 | 5.2 | 7.3 | 8.4 | 9.5 |
| Low technological intensity | 12.3 | 15.9 | 5.4 | 17.5 | 10.2 | 22.9 |
| Medium technological intensity | 26.1 | 24.0 | 10.4 | 14.3 | 16.6 | 18.5 |
| High technological intensity | 28.2 | 22.8 | 11.2 | 13.5 | 17.1 | 19.1 |

Source: COMTRADE at www.eco.unicamp.br/pesquisa/CECON/index.php.

*International economics* 215

# Part II  Financialization and global unbalances in the twenty-first century

## *Challenges to development*

A striking new unbalance in the early twenty-first century is the rapid shift of the gravity centre of the global economy to Asia (Hobsbawm 2007: 39). Among other issues, this poses macroeconomic adjustments centered on the efficacy of monetary policy to assure balance-of-payments equilibrium.

---

**Pause for Thought 4: Can the current unbalance be solved with macroeconomic adjustments centered on monetary policies?**

Traditional economics assumes money demand as a stable function of income. Without state intervention, markets are believed to be inherently stable; so that expanding the money supply directly affects aggregate demand and domestic price levels, causing a balance of payments deficit and loss of international reserves. External disequilibrium is caused by economic policy.

The monetarist approach assumes the incompatibility of free capital mobility, a fixed exchange rate regime and autonomous monetary policy. If currency stability is prioritized over domestic macroeconomic targets, it affects the money supply and interest rates, thereby setting limits to the autonomy of monetary policy. The defense of exchange rate flexibility is based on the possibility of rescuing the autonomy of monetary policy and surmounting the "impossible trinity," while exchange rate variations equilibrate the inter-country gap between prices and costs. Since the 1990s, the credibility of central bank actions has been based on new monetary rules centered on interest rules compelling fiscal surplus in order to finance government expenditure.

The canonic discussion between fixed and flexible exchange rate regimes is related to the choices between rules or discretionary actions to conduct monetary policy (Rojas-Soarez 2004). More recently, some countries have anchored their currencies to the dollar, signaling that a fixed exchange regime is more amenable for macroeconomic stability. Unfortunately, the result is reduction of investment.

Beyond the balance-of-payment adjustment (saving–investment adjustment) there is a redefinition of the investment process in the international economy.

*Website reference*

www.bis.org   The Bank of International Settlements home page provides information regarding coordination of regulations among the world's central banks. Publications and statistics cover topics including global macroeconomics and monetary, banking, and financial issues.

---

## *Global unbalances*

Since the 1990s, a critical factor in the U.S. economy has been the evolution of disequilibrium, as observed in Table 13.6. After the 1997 Asian crisis, the combination of high domestic consumption and decreased exports exacerbated the

Table 13.6 U.S. current account, 1992–1997 ($ billion)

|  | 1992 | 1993 | 1994 | 1995 | 1996 | 1997 |
|---|---|---|---|---|---|---|
| Current account | −51.81 | −85.94 | −123.21 | −115.22 | −135.44 | −155.38 |
| Goods: exports | 442.13 | 458.73 | 504.45 | 577.69 | 613.89 | 681.27 |
| Goods: imports | −536.45 | −589.44 | −668.59 | −749.57 | −803.32 | −877.28 |
| Services: credit | 175.04 | 184.35 | 199.25 | 217.80 | 236.71 | 256.16 |
| Services: debt | −116.49 | −122.41 | −132.50 | −141.98 | −152.00 | −166.19 |
| Incomes: credit | 125.15 | 126.85 | 157.89 | 204.00 | 213.36 | 241.95 |
| Incomes: debt | −105.53 | −106.07 | −144.98 | −188.42 | −202.98 | −251.43 |
| Transfers: credit | 6.39 | 4.70 | 5.21 | 5.900 | 6.22 | 6.34 |
| Transfers: debt | −42.05 | −42.64 | −44.00 | −40.64 | −47.31 | −46.19 |

Source: IMF (1998: 852).

Table 13.7 U.S. Net International Investment Position (NIIP), 1991–1997 ($ billion)

|  | 1991 | 1992 | 1993 | 1994 | 1995 | 1996 | 1997 |
|---|---|---|---|---|---|---|---|
| NIIP | −263.10 | −454.64 | −180.38 | −232.96 | −537.05 | −743.65 | −1,322.47 |

Source: IMF (1998: 858)

trade disequilibrium. The volatility of international investors' behavior, as well as huge short-term liabilities, contributed to the economic crisis (Gilpin 2001). The trade deficit, on the other hand, reflects the continuous growth of the American economy, which created an enormous demand for imports. In 1999 the U.S. accounted for one-eighth of global exports, while Germany accounted for one-tenth. The current account is the most effective measure of a nation's international position, since its balance indicates the status of net international assets. An increasing deficit implies a greater need for external financing, i.e. a greater demand for American assets on the part of foreigners. As long as foreign investors keep financing U.S. current account deficits, pressure on the dollar is reduced. However, given that the capital account requires foreign loans, it can reduce future U.S. saving rates. Table 13.7 presents aggregate data on the net international investment position of the U.S. during the 1990s.

Vis-à-vis the structural asymmetries of the global economy, the desired corrections of disequilibria by means of the realignment of currencies become problematic.

> **Pause for Thought 5: Is the Euro a reply to the globalization of the international economy?**
>
> The Eurozone today is comprised of: Austria, Belgium, Finland, France, Germany, Greece, Ireland, Italy, Luxembourg, Holland, Portugal, Slovenia, Spain, the Vatican City, the Republic of San Marino, Cyprus, and Malta. The transition to the Euro (introduced in January 1999) was a major step toward consolidating monetary policies and a higher level of convergence in national economic policies. The United States and the European Union produce about half of the world's goods and services, accounting for over half of global trade. The European Union is the main commercial partner of United States. After the full introduction of the Euro in 2002, focus on interest rates became paramount for the European Central Bank and became decisive for the future of the Euro for unemployment in Europe.
>
> *Website references*
>
> www.europa.eu   This home page provides press releases, legislation, and factsheets published by the European Union and its institutions.
>
> http://ec.europa.eu/index_en.htm   The European Commission home page contains information on EU policies in agriculture, fisheries, and food; business; culture, education, and youth; citizens' rights; external relations and foreign affairs; science and technology; and many other issues of interest.
>
> www.ecb.int/home/html/index.en.html   The European Central Bank and Eurosystem home page provides a detailed overview of the economic and monetary developments in the Eurozone, and the structure and organization of the Central Banks within the Eurosystem.

A pressing question in international macroeconomics today is whether the U.S. current account deficit will force some type of macroeconomic adjustment. In the 1990s, the U.S. was able to attract capital while keeping interest rates low due to increased reserves of the Asian countries – the mirror image of the U.S. current account deficit – and expansion of credit and foreign assets in the U.S. Such expansion, however, culminated in the mortgage crisis of late 2007, as explained in Pause for Thought 6.

> **Pause for Thought 6: Fundamentals of the recent crisis from an orthodox and pluralist perspective**
>
> Mortgage rates started falling in 1981 and reached a record low in 2003 while housing prices steadily increased from 1991 to 2005. Thus the cost of financing decreased while the price of capital assets increased. Burgeoning profits in the real estate market encouraged more investment. Due to the growing needs of the financial industry, lending requirements were eased. The industry encouraged speculation relying on future housing prices, the future price of securitized assets, and the renewal of lending. This persisted until housing prices began dropping and the previously risky lending led to a flood of foreclosures. Housing prices decreased, profits fell, and marginal home buyers who invested in speculative mortgages and

could not pay were subject to foreclosure. The term "subprime" refers to mortgagees unable to qualify for prime mortgage rates, usually due to high value ratios and poor credit histories.

Mainstream economists assume financial markets efficaciously transfer funds and that deregulation will increase efficiency and the supply of loanable funds. Yes, some consumers acted irrationally by borrowing beyond their means, and some banks unscrupulously lent money but the financial crisis is the result of wrong policy. Financial crises are a monetary phenomenon: central banks actively maintain a stock of money supply incompatible with the conditions of domestic and external equilibrium. Variation in domestic money supply greater than the growth rate of real income is key to understanding imbalances between the real and monetary sides of the economy. The ex-ante saving–investment disequilibrium stimulated by the credit expansion caused the global financial imbalance. Thus, the crisis is caused by keeping the domestic income level too high vis-à-vis its non-inflationary level.

Traditional economics assumes monetary and credit restrictions will end the crisis. Credit restraints and reduction of aggregate spending will dampen the effects of the crisis. A key assumption is the exogenous money supply and the duality "real versus monetary." An active role for money, financial institutions and their speculative and destabilizing behaviors is denied. Financial market imperfections might be avoided and, eventually corrected, since adequate monetary policies would be implemented.

A political economy approach emphasizes the endogenous fragility of capitalist economies: their dependence on favorable access to financial markets; the random behavior of investors and cash flows; and the narrow interconnection among the exchange, credit, and the bond markets. Not only did the increased clout of the industry result in favorable legislation but it systematically influenced consumer preferences.

Given the importance of global debt, any central bank is inefficacious in finding solutions, which must be done as Keynes argued during the 1940s, via coherent and democratic international cooperation. As Minsky warned, "finance cannot be left to the free markets" (Minsky 1986: 292). Interdependence among domestic macroeconomic policies impugns autonomy in the management of monetary policy. The central bank does not have control over the complexity of global, innovative, and speculative financial markets. Thus, it is not possible to think about central bank action independent of private and public pressure. In a pluralist approach, the endogenous character of finance, the relevance of the financial institutional set-up and the private and public pressures on the central bank are key to thinking about efficacious solutions.

*Website references*

www.treas.gov/   The U.S. Department of Treasury home page has topics such as Accounting and Budget; Currency and Coins; Financial Markets; Bonds and Treasury Securities.

www.nyse.com   The New York Stock Exchange website provides news to traders and investors as well as current data relative to listed companies, bonds and equities.

www.londonstockexchange.com/en-gb/   The London Stock Exchange home page offers world indicators and current news on international trading.

Under the rubric of "good" global governance, the canonic discussion about exchange rate regimes ignores the specifics of integration in financial globalization and the international currency hierarchy. The option of strengthening credibility might reinforce deflationary adjustment, because the sustainability of currencies ultimately depends on the dynamic of capital flows in foreign currency so as to adjust the balance of payments (Winkler *et al.* 2004). Productivity, value added and exchange rates are subordinated to the financial dynamics.

Liberalized financial markets are unstable and inefficient from the allocative and productive perspective; in other words, international capital flows could not finance the necessary investment to encourage development. Another consequence is that the costs of finance are relatively high: volatile capital flows and price assets increase the risks of banking systems, pushing domestic interest rates higher (Akyüz 1993). Financial crises underscore the fragility of exchange rate regimes and balance of payments vulnerability.

The decade starting in 1990 was marked by high global liquidity, along with a rapid expansion of private capital flows, abetted by American monetary policy and the deregulation of financial markets. In Latin America, debate focused on the sustainability of capital flows to finance deficits in current accounts. The main objective of economic policy was to support stable debt and capital flows, instead of preserving competitiveness or employment.

IMF recommendations to increase capital formation by attracting external saving flows, as a result of fiscal austerity and high real interest rates, are the antithesis of a post-Keynesian approach, which states that savings do not lead to development. Under the post-Keynesian perspective, excess savings do not lead to development, and investment is limited not by previous saving, but by lack of credit and high real interest rates. The precedence of investment over saving must be understood in the context of the circuit investment– finance–saving–funding.

### Classical readings: John Maynard Keynes. Proposals for an international clearing union

About the primary objects of an improved system of International Currency there is, today, a wide measure of agreement:

- (a) We need an instrument of international currency having general acceptability between nations, so that blocked balances and bilateral clearings are unnecessary; that is to say, an instrument of currency used by each nation in its transactions with other nations, operating through whatever national organ, such as a Treasury or a central bank, is most appropriate, private individuals, businesses and banks other central banks, each continuing to use their own national currency as heretofore.
- (b) We need an orderly and agreed method of determining the relative exchange values of national currency units, so that unilateral action and competitive exchange depreciations are prevented.
- (c) We need a quantum of international currency, which is neither determined in an unpredictable and irrelevant manner as, for example, by the technical

> progress of the gold industry, nor subject to large variations depending on the gold reserve policies of individual countries; but is governed by the actual requirements of the world commerce, and is also capable of deliberate expansion and contraction to offset deflationary and inflationary tendencies in effective world demand.
> - (d) We need a system possessed of an internal stabilizing mechanism, by which pressure is exercised on any country whose balance of payments with the rest of the world is departing from equilibrium in either direction, so as to prevent movements which must create for its neighbors an equal but opposite want of balance.
> - (e) We need an agreed plan for starting off every country after the war with a stock of reserves appropriate to its importance in world commerce, so that without due anxiety it can set its house in order during the transitional period to full-peace conditions.
> - (f) We need a method by which the surplus credit balances arising from international trade, which the recipient country does not wish to employ for the time being, can be set to work in the interests of international planning and relief and economic health, without detriment to the liquidity of these balances and to their holder's faculty to employ them himself when he desires to do so.
> - (g) We need a central institution, of a purely technical and non-political character, to aid and support other international institutions concerning with the planning and regulation of the world's economic life.
> - (h) More generally, we need a means of reassurance to a troubled world, by which any country whose own affairs are conducted with due prudence is relieved of anxiety, for causes which are not of its own making, concerning its ability to meet its international liabilities; and which will, therefore, make unnecessary those methods of restriction and discrimination which countries have adopted hitherto, not on their merits, but as measures of self-protection from disruptive outside forces.
>
> Source: Keynes (1980: 168–169)

Financial instability means price instability in financial asset markets (Brunhoff 1998). The instability of exchange rates is a related question, since domestic currencies assume the character of financial assets competing among themselves. Currently, exchange rate determination depends on the hierarchy among monetary policies and the arbitrage/speculation in financial markets (Tavares and Melin 1998). Deregulated finance is associated with monetarist deflation domestic policies where the level of domestic interest rates depends not only on the management of domestic currency in the exchange market but also on the new international financial pattern – high returns and low inflation (Chesnais 1998: 51).

The Monterrey Consensus of 2005 provides an agreement for international cooperation for development; however, it neglects the crucial international trade problem of price and wage inflexibility and the need to preserve competitiveness. The short-term approach focusing on financing current account deficits neither considers different institutional arrangements in labor markets, nor different rates of growth experienced by countries after commercial and financial openness.

> **Key concept: currency convertibility**
>
> The privilege extended to a holder of a nation's currency to exchange his holdings, at a rate of exchange, for the currency of another nation for any purpose. Under a condition of full currency convertibility, any holder of any national currency is guaranteed unrestricted currency exchange privilege even in times of balance of payments difficulties.
>
> Source: Greenwald (1973)

Do domestic governments have much discretion, given capital account openness and currency convertibility? Traditional economics assumes that exchange rate fluctuations equilibrate the gap between prices and costs among countries, enabling central banks to rescue the autonomy of monetary policy. In spite of the chosen exchange rate regime, the autonomy of monetary policy is limited by the demands of globalized financial markets. Correcting international disequilibria involves redistributing deficits and surplus between regions, demanding a coordination of policies to reactivate the sources of growth in Europe and Japan beyond moderating the mercantilist strategies of the Asian countries. Today's challenges suggest supranational solutions to supranational problems. Nevertheless, there is no global authority – not the World Bank, the IMF, or the WTO (Hobsbawm 2007: 53). As Keynes foresaw in his preparatory writings for the Bretton Woods discussions, any attempt to conduct an international coordination of policies is not easy.

> **In-class activity**
>
> Divide the class into groups. Have each group devise a general plan of economic reform pertaining to the open domestic and international challenges of the 2008 world-wide financial crisis. After the discussion bring the groups together to present the ten major elements of the plans.

Good global governance does not eliminate financial risk. Many factors have contributed to the consolidation of the financial system since the 1980s: capital adequacy requirements, technological development, elimination of geographic restrictions, securitization, and changes in the composition of institutional investors (Table 13.8). The universal nature of financial institutions is not compatible with the segmentation of the process of supervision and inspection in many agencies, as revealed in the American subprime crisis. The transformation of more concentrated and internationalized financial structures crystallizes thinking about central banks as an agency that arbitrages competitive conditions (Campilongo *et al.* 2000).

Table 13.8 Rate of growth of the institutional investors:* selected countries, 1980–1990 (%)

|  | 1980 | 1985 | 1990 |
|---|---|---|---|
| United States | 20.0 | 26.0 | 31.2 |
| Japan | 15.6 | 20.2 | 26.4 |
| Germany | 22.6 | 29.0 | 35.1 |
| France | 10.6 | 23.6 | 36.3 |
| United Kingdom | 41.5 | 53.1 | 58.6 |
| Canada | 20.4 | 24.9 | 29.7 |

Source: OECD (1993: 2).

Note
*Collective financial assets as a percentage of household's assets.

---

**Pause for Thought 7: Is it possible to solve the current global unbalance with just the Washington Consensus?**

Macroeconomic stability and international integration synthesize the debate about global governance. According to traditional economics, market imperfections may be corrected, if adequate policies are implemented. Needless to say, this approach ignores the active role of finance and its destabilizing effects.

The multilateral institutions defending financial liberalization, such as the IMF, assumed that long-term benefits would include a better allocation of global saving (Fischer 1997). In addition, other purported benefits include: (a) lower cost of domestic credit as domestic saving is complemented with foreign savings; (b) diversifying risk by acquiring assets not available domestically; (c) supplementing domestic investment with foreign investments, through access to new technologies and new markets; (d) offering more efficient and complete financial services in a new environment characterized by competition between domestic and foreign players.

Under financial liberalization, investors punish the "wrong" economic policy, an idea associated with the concept of credibility (Grabel 2000). In other words, capital deregulation can potentially succeed as long as governments adopt the right macroeconomic policies and regulation of financial systems.

A challenge to good international governance is the absence of a common project involving many countries to achieve an adequate provision of liquidity, the recognition of stable financial flows to developing countries, and novel forms of debt negotiation (Griffith-Jones 2002). The lack of representation of developing countries in multilateral agencies such as the IMF, World Bank, and Bank of International Settlements, make the challenges even greater and the possibilities of change more difficult.

*Website reference*

www.g20.org/G20/ The Group of Twenty (G20) home page is an important forum promoting dialogue between advanced and emerging countries on key issues regarding economic growth and stability of the international system. This website provides case studies and useful links for further research.

Global financial integration has increased exposure of countries, thereby increasing the possibilities of transmission mechanisms becoming destabilizing and decreasing the potential of financial regulation. First, there is a delay between regulation patterns and banking practices. Second, the banking structure is vulnerable to changes in macroeconomic conditions. Financial regulation can induce better practices but cannot eliminate the possibility of crisis. The 2008 global financial crisis until September 2008 when the manuscript went to press (Box 2) reveals that global action is required, with coordination in the actions of international agencies, and perhaps new institutions.

---

**Box 2  Chronology of the 2008 global financial crisis**

*June 2007* – Two hedge funds belonging to New York investment bank Bear Stearns collapse as a result of the subprime mortgage crisis. The failure of the funds cause investor losses of some $1.8 billion.

*July 2007* – German banks – including IKB, Sachsen LB, WestLB, and BayernLB – are caught in the crisis. Multi-billion Euro bailouts are needed to stabilize the banks' balance sheets.

*September 2007* – Worried customers queue outside branches of the British Northern Rock to withdraw savings.

*October 2007* – U.S. financial services company Citigroup's profits collapse. Henceforth, one financial group after another announce billions of dollars of writedowns and high losses.

*January 2008* – Swiss bank UBS announces writedowns of more than $18 billion for 2007 due to turbulence in U.S. property markets. In April, the bank announces an additional $19 billion in writedowns.

*February 2008* – U.S. Congress approves an economic stimulus package of about $150 billion.

*March 2008* – Bear Stearns stands on the brink of collapse, leading to JP Morgan Chase acquiring the investment bank under pressure from the US Federal Reserve. The Fed assumes the risk on $30 billion in Bear Stearns investments.

*April 2008* – Deutsche Bank announces a loss of £141 billion ($203 billion) for the first quarter – the bank's first quarterly loss in five years.

*July 2008* – Californian mortgage bank IndyMac collapses. U.S. mortgage giants Fannie Mae and Freddie Mac fall into increasing difficulties. In Spain, real estate and construction group Martinsa-Fadesa is forced to declare bankruptcy.

*September 2008* – The U.S. government takes over Fannie Mae and Freddie Mac. The crisis at Lehman Brothers, a US investment bank, becomes acute. Other financial institutions such as Merrill Lynch, AIG, and Washington Mutual – the biggest U.S. savings bank – are all affected.

*September 15, 2008* – Black Monday. Lehman Brothers declares bankruptcy, Merrill Lynch is purchased by Bank of America, and AIG announces it needs billions in stop-gap loans. Bank writedowns from around the world total nearly $500 billion.

*September 16, 2008* – News that AIG, the world's largest insurer, is threatened with insolvency creates massive instability in financial markets. The Federal Reserve announces it will provide AIG with an $85 billion loan in exchange for a nearly 80 percent stake in the troubled giant.

> *September 17, 2008* – Scottish mortgage bank Halifax Bank of Scotland (HBOS) captures worldwide attention with more bad news. Bank of Scotland enters talks with Lloyd's, according to the BBC. The state-owned German development bank KFW transferred €300 million ($426 million) to Lehman Brothers in New York just prior to the investment bank's collapse. More than half of the sum is lost.
>
> *September 21, 2008* – US Treasury Secretary Henry Paulson announces the planned creation of a $700 billion rescue package to buy bad credit from failing banks. After a weekend of negotiations in Washington, the fate of the bill is to be decided within a week.
>
> *September 22, 2008* – News of the possible $700 billion bailout calms the financial markets but only temporarily. The price of oil rises more than $25 per barrel in just a few hours – the highest daily increase since monitoring of oil prices began. Experts see this as a reason for skepticism. The dollar also loses considerable value.
>
> *September 23, 2008* – The price of crude oil eases during trading on the Asian markets. Traders attribute the price decrease to investors cashing in on profits.
>
> *September 24, 2008* – US investor Warren Buffett makes headlines with a hefty investment in Goldman Sachs. Analysts hail the legendary financial strategist as a savior.
>
> *September 25, 2008* – A summit in the White House to discuss the rescue package falters. A few hours later, bank supervisors announce that U.S. savings bank Washington Mutual is broke.
>
> *September 28, 2008* – It looks as though both Democrats and Republicans in the U.S. Congress will support the $700 billion bailout plan.
>
> *September 29, 2008* – The financial crisis reached new heights in Europe. German mortgage bank Hypo Real Estate is bailed out with €35 billion ($50 billion). British mortgage lender Bradford & Bingley and Belgian-Dutch Hypo Real Estate Holding AG are rescued for billions of Euros. U.S. representatives reject the $700 billion bailout package, and stock markets collapse around the world.
>
> Source: www.spiegel.de/international/

## *Social and cultural inequalities*

Traditional economics does not analyze the economic process in historical and social terms and, consequently, has not been able to apprehend the forces and tensions beyond macroeconomic price stability. Historical changes in social relations, modifying the conditions of social reproduction, particularly in periods of crisis and transition, are related to qualitative transformations in the accumulation and competitive processes. In fact, the emphasis on macroeconomic stabilization has precluded more fruitful perspectives in analyzing contemporary capitalism.

> **In-class activity**
>
> Begin the class with a ten-minute presentation on the evolution of socioeconomic data since the 1990s. Split students into the following groups: U.S., Latin America, European Union, China, India.

Financialization has reshaped social organization and has intensely transformed labor relations. Investment decisions are analyzed within the context of capitalist speculative finance in which liquidity shortens the length of decision periods and broadens the possibilities of valorization. Finance regulates the pace of investment, while the pace of investment determines income and employment. Thus, the dynamics of investment and employment are discussed primarily in financial terms. Managers and firm owners view their organizations in terms of short-term financial performance. Assets, debts, current stock market evaluation, and mergers and acquisitions predominate in investment decisions (Minsky 1986). The firm is viewed as a set of assets to be financed, whose divisions and product lines may be bought/sold to increase short-term profits. The labor force is subordinated to profit targets (Fligstein 2001).

The logic of short-term decisions increases interest rate volatility and shortens the forecast horizon of economic agents while provoking stop-and-go movements in the dynamics of economic growth. At the same time, economic openness redefines investment options. While the importance of exporting integration increases, the performance of domestic product depends on the dynamics of the international economy. As a result, economic expansion by industrial integration is redefined, while working conditions are transformed to comport with the demands of financialization.

Financial capital has redefined the operation of the economy, inducing macroeconomic policies and regulation of markets under new parameters. This process was abetted by multilateral institutions defending free markets. As a result, responsibility for economic and social development devolved to individuals. The deflationary macroeconomic policies have displaced the focus from demand generation to the supply side and increased tensions between macroeconomic deflationary trends and the microeconomic agenda. The World Bank microeconomic agenda, for example, emphasizes entrepreneurship, social responsibility, and corporate governance. Citizens must redefine their skills or become informal entrepreneurs. The conditions of social exclusion have been redefined and enlarged because of the lack of social adequacy to the new behavior parameters.

The relationship between corporate social responsibility and the valorization of the asset portfolio of institutional investors reinforces the submission and reorganization of economic and social life to financial markets. New forms of enterprise organization based on capital markets have increased the potential conflicts between short-run and long-run decisions to meet expectations of global investors. Corporate governance principles configure a legal framework in order to democratize access to capital markets. The multilateral institutions approach is based on the New Keynesian perspective: good corporate governance surmounts asymmetric information, thus structuring efficient financial leverage systems with greater investor transparency (Fligstein 2001).

Micro-entrepreneurship, corporate governance and social responsibility are self-protection mechanisms of capitalism as it adjusts to new forms of accumulation and valorization under the aegis of globalized financial markets. Unfortunately, unemployment rates increase while real incomes decrease. Thus, the impacts of deregulation on the labor market must be understood in the context of the new international financial order: high returns and low inflation. Current macroeconomic policies are structured to preserve price stability rather than employment. The pace of investment tends to decrease since liquidity preference hinders production and employment.

---

**Pause for Thought 8: Could liberalization policies guarantee sustainable conditions to eradicate poverty and inequality in Latin America?**

Neoliberalism has increased economic and social inequalities not only within states but also between states, despite decreases in extreme poverty (Hobsbawm 2007: 3). In the last few decades the World Bank has stimulated the structural transformation of the Latin American economy, based on the systemic incorporation of technical progress, in order to integrate the region in the global economy.

The adjustment of domestic policies to the requirements of the global economy occurs by expanding self-regulated markets to achieve economic development. In relation to market imperfections, the World Bank recognizes three areas for state intervention: infrastructure, essential services, and financial services for the poor. It was thought that liberalization of financial markets would create an environment in which the financial intermediaries would offer better financial services to the poor. Competitive forces would produce attractive financial products while reducing transaction costs. Nevertheless, the liberalization of the financial market is not a pro-poor strategy. Despite poverty rate reduction in some countries, the unemployment rate and the Gini coefficient continue to show a wide income gap.

Source: www.eclac.org/

*Website references*

www.eclac.org   The Economic Commission for Latin American and the Caribbean (ECLAC) home page provides useful statistics and research studies on challenges to Latin American and Caribbean social and economic development.

www.iadb.org   The Inter-American Development Bank Group home page offers information about its activities, organization, members and partners, loans approved, and research tools.

www.un.org/   The United Nations home page contains information relative to the global association of governments in order to facilitate cooperation in international law, security, economic development, and social equity.

---

The increasing liquidity of capital and the velocity of investment, expressed in the short-run investment yield horizon, are incompatible with societal claims of citizenship, employment, and income. As a result, labor markets are affected by the global financial structure, nurtured by speculative behavior. Increasing employment after World War II was enhanced by the advance of industrialism and urbanization, whose growth dynamics economically enfranchised workers.

Nevertheless, current flexibilization and informality are connecting increasing numbers of insecurely employed and low-skilled workers. The growing heterogeneity of labor markets underscores the dismantling of the social inclusion that characterized the postwar pattern of accumulation. The new growth conditions, framed by the financial dynamic, create and reinforce social heterogeneity, where, at the same time, access to societal benefits are restricted.

Employment is held hostage to private portfolio investment decisions since the state has transferred responsibility of economic growth to private agents. Investment decisions are also conditioned by labor risks, including the level of monetary wages, labor qualification, diversity of labor contracts, and collective organization. Consequently, private strategies to achieve cost reductions and innovations involve new labor relations and impacts on social organization, since labor flexibility must be compatible with capital mobility. Investment velocity has increased globally, influenced by the volatility in financial markets. In this context, the liquidity of capital assets explicitly determines investment. The development of financial markets increases the liquidity of capital assets, i.e. the ability to generate cash flows by selling a capital asset without large price concessions. This has further increased mergers and acquisitions since the 1990s. Investment and consumption are socially and historically conditioned activities. The financial markets have imposed a decision-making horizon incompatible with productive investment and employment. As a result, social vulnerability is dependent on the global financial architecture.

---

**In-class activity**

Divide the class into four groups – industrial capitalists, financial capitalists, government, unions – and ask them to organize a presentation regarding the impacts of the 2008 international crisis on employment conditions of developing countries. Have the groups return to the whole class in order to enhance discussion and criticism. Alternatively, specify the countries to be analyzed.

---

## References

Aglietta, M. (1979) *A Theory of Capitalist Regulation*. London: NLB.
Akyüz, Y. (1993) "Financial Liberalization: The Key Issues," Unctad Discussion Papers.
Arrighi, G. and Silver, B. (1999) *Chaos and Governance in the Modern World System*. Minneapolis: University of Minnesota Press.
Basel Committee on Banking Supervision (2001) *Overview of the New Basel Capital Accord*. Basel: BIS.
Belluzzo, L. G. M. (2008) *Dinamismo e crise na economia global*. São Paulo: Valor.
Brunhoff, S. (1998) "A instabilidade financeira internacional," in F. Chesnais (ed.) *A mundialização financeira – gênese, custos e riscos*. São Paulo: Ed. Xamã.
Campilongo, C., Veiga da Rocha, J. P., and Mattos, P. T. L. (eds.) (2002) *Concorrência e regulação no sistema financeiro*. São Paulo: Max Limonad Editora.
Chesnais, F. (1998) "Mundialização financeira e vulnerabilidade sistêmica," in F. Chesnais (ed.) *A mundialização financeira – gênese, custos e riscos*. São Paulo: Ed. Xamã.

Comissão Econômica para a América Latina e o Caribe (CEPAL) (2003) *Panorama de la inserción internacional de América Latina e Caribe*. Santiago, Chile: Nações Unidas.

Eichengreen, B. (1996) *Globalizing Capital. A History of the International Monetary System*. Princeton, NJ: Princeton University Press.

Fischer, S. (1997) *Capital Account Liberalization and the Role of the IMF*. Washington, DC: IMF.

Fligstein, N. (2001) *The Architecture of Markets*. Princeton, NJ: Princeton University Press.

Friedman, M. (1962) *Capitalism and Freedom*. Chicago: University of Chicago Press.

Gilpin, R. (2001) *Global Political Economy*. Princeton, NJ: Princeton University Press.

Grabel, I. (2000) "The Political Economy of 'Policy Credibility': The New-Classical Macroeconomics and the Remaking of Emerging Economies," *Cambridge Journal of Economics* 24: 1–9.

Greenwald, Douglas (1973) *The McGraw-Hill Dictionary of Modern Economics: A Handbook of Terms and Organizations*, 2nd edn. New York: McGraw-Hill.

Griffith-Jones, S. (2002) "Uma nova arquitetura financeira internacional como bem público global," in R. Fendt and M. Tedesco Lins (eds.) *Arquitetura assimétrica. RJ, Fundação Konrad Adenauer*. Série Debates.

Hilferding, R. (1957) *El capital financeiro*. Mexico City: Fundo de Cultura Econômica.

Hobsbawm, E. (2007) *Globalisation, Democracy and Terrorism*. London: Abacus.

International Monetary Fund (IMF) (1998) *Balance of Payments Statistics Yearbook*. www.imf.org/external/pubs/cat/longres.cfm?sk=17593.0.

Keynes, J. M. (1980) *The Collected Works of John Maynard Keynes*, vol. XXV. Cambridge, UK: Cambridge University Press.

Kindleberger, C. (1996) *Manias, Panics, and Crashes: A History of Financial Crises*, 3rd edn. New York: John Wiley & Sons.

Krugman, P. and Obstfeld, M. (2003) *International Economics: Theory and Policy*, 6th edn. Reading, Mass.: Pearson Education – Addison-Wesley.

Lenin, V. (1968) *Imperialism*. Moscow: Progress Publishers.

Luxemburg, R. (1953) *The Accumulation of Capital*. London: Routledge.

Madisson, A. (1992) *La economía mundial en el siglo XX*. Mexico City: Fundo de Cultura.

Marx, K. (1973) *El capital: Crítica de la economía política*. Mexico City: Fundo de Cultura.

Minsky, H, (1986) *Stabilizing an Unstable Economy*. New Haven, Conn: Yale University Press.

Organization of Economic Cooperation and Development (OECD) (1993) *Financial Market Trends* 55.

Prebisch, R. (1949) "El desarrollo económico de la América Latina y algunos de sus principales problemas," in CEPAL, *Boletín Económico de América Latina* 16: 347–432.

Ricardo, D. (1821) *On the Principles of Political Economy and Taxation*. London: John Murray.

Rojas-Soarez, L. (2004) "Política monetária e taxas de câmbio: diretrizes para um regime sustentável," in P. Kuczynski and J. Williamson (eds.) *Depois do Consenso de Washington*. São Paulo: Saraiva.

Rugman, A. and Verbeke, A. (2006) "Liabilities of Regional Foreignness and the Use of Firm Level and Country Level Data: A Response to Dunning et al.," http://ideas.repec.org/a/pal/jintbs/v38y2007i1p200–205.html (accessed August 1, 2008).

Schumpeter, Joseph (1971) "The Sociology of Imperialism," in J. Schumpeter (ed.) *Imperialism/Social Classes*. New York: World Publishing.

Stiglitz, J. (2003) *Os exuberantes anos 90*. São Paulo: Cias das Letras.
Tavares, M. C. and Melin, L. E. (1998) "Pós-escrito 1997: a reafirmação da hegemonia norte-americana," in M. Tavares and J. L. Fiori (eds.) *Uma economia política da Globalização*. Petrópolis, RJ: Ed. Vozes.
Triffin, R. (1964) *The Evolution of the International Monetary System: Historical Appraisal and Future Perspectives*. Princeton, NJ: Princeton University Press.
United Nations Conference on Trade and Development (UNCTAD) (2002) *Trade and Development Report 2002*. Geneva: UNCTAD.
Wallerstein, I. (1976) *The Modern World-System: Capitalist Agriculture and the Origins of the European World-Economy in the Sixteenth Century*. New York: Academic Press.
Winkler, A., Mazzaferro, F., Nerlich, C. and Thimann, C. (2004) "Official Dollarization/ Euroisation: Motives, Features and Policy Implications of Current Cases," European Central Bank, Occasional Paper series, no. 11.
World Bank (1992) *Report on International Development*. Washington, DC: World Bank.
World Trade Organization (WTO). (2001) *Annual Report*. Geneva: WTO.

# 14 Money, credit, and finance in political economy
## National, regional, and global dimensions

*Phillip Anthony O'Hara*

An understanding of modern capitalism requires comprehension of money, credit, and finance since they represent its defining features. This is especially true in a relatively deregulated environment when money and credit take on a life of their own. Historically, businesses, the rich, and governments were the principal agents of finance capital. But more recently, the lower-middle class and even some working-class households have become more involved with financial assets and portfolios. When speculative bubbles dominate the economy more people join the circus, and when they crash many people lose, so fewer households become involved in this risky business.

Political economy perspectives of money and credit are distinctive from traditional economics in that the former seek to be realistic, institutional, historical, and systemic in their methodology. They are realistic since they develop a Wall Street perspective on the financial system, where cash flow and net worth are a critical part of the edifice (Dillard 1987). Successive institutional changes are embedded into the theory, so knowledge becomes relevant to changes in the real economy. The analysis is historical as different phases of evolution are delineated through time as hysteresis and path dependence impact the economy. Central to the political economy perspective is to link the financial system to the workings of the capitalist system, where capitalism represents complex, long-term investments in productive structures of factories, warehouses, machinery, organizations, and human capital.

Several schools of thought contribute to the political economy view of money, including neo-Marxian, Schumpeterian, institutional, and post-Keynesian. Neo-Marxian contributions emphasize the circuit of money capital, fictitious capital, and the break-up of surplus value into profit, interest, and rent. Schumpeterian perspectives emphasize the role of credit-money in financing innovation or its use for general accumulation or speculation. Institutional themes include the financial instability hypothesis and social structures of accumulation. And post-Keynesian approaches recognize the role of uncertainty in complex capital investments plus the role of endogenous finance. The political economy approaches complement each other while acknowledging the core contradiction of industry versus finance and the need for a dynamic, circuitous vision of finance capitalism (Lavoie 1992).

## Dynamic circuit of money capital

Traditional perspectives of money and credit are based on money as a stock, a static process where money is part of an equilibrium, final-phase analysis. Money is in a state of rest where nothing changes, information is well disseminated, and the economy undergoes no persistent tendencies through time. In this equilibrium framework, money performs the tasks of buying and selling commodities. Money is a veil, in the sense that it has no long-term impact on output and employment, except under special circumstances that are unlikely to occur. Accordingly, money should not grow much faster than the rate of change of productivity, for if it does, there will be inflation. Hence the main objective of government policy is to control the money supply to ensure against inflation.

Recent advances in political economy have resulted in deviations from orthodoxy, due to two factors. First, recognition of asymmetric information has led to the development of a non-neoclassical theory of money and credit, especially under the impact of Joseph Stiglitz and Frederick Mishkin. Asymmetrical information improves our understanding of the dynamics of capitalism, especially vis-à-vis creditors and debtors, the state and banking system, households and business, and capitalists and workers. Imperfect information means we can never return to the perfect information situation where nothing changes and everyone is happy. As a result, capitalism is continuously threatened by financial crisis, instability, and recession as moral hazard and adverse selection play a critical role.

Second, this non-Walrasian system undergoes motion and instability due to entrepreneurs interested in generating profit. Post-Keynesians, Schumpeterians and neo-Marxists are especially interested in the impact of entrepreneurs on money and credit. According to Schumpeterians, entrepreneurs introduce dynamics into the system through innovation, which requires credit for long-term projects. For post-Keynesians, entrepreneurs finance their innovations partly through credit, which enhances instability as decisions are made about the future, of which we have little knowledge. Neo-Marxists extend these views to recognizing that such credit is required for the production and realization of surplus-value, the basis of profit and capital accumulation. Schumpeterians, post-Keynesians, neo-Marxists and indeed many institutionalists link money and credit into the circuit of capital to understand how the system changes through time. This circuit is illustrated in Figure 14.1.

The circuit of money capital, also called the Monetary Theory of Production, illustrates the phases and stages involved in the general motion of social capital in the national and global political economy (Palloix 1975; O'Hara 2006). All of the four phases of the circuit – finance, sourcing, production, and sale – are institutionally linked in a complex cybernetic of motion through corporate, financial and governance structures and processes.[1] Money and credit (M) are required to initiate the process, via corporate revenue, financial institutions and central banks. These largely endogenous funds, propelled by the demand for finance, activate local, national, regional, and global sources of labor power (LP) and the

```
                    Global and national
                    Money and credit
                  ╱                    ╲
                 ↓                      ↑
M↔C{LP, MOP}  →  ......P......  →   [C+c]↔[M+m]
     ↑               ↑                   ↑
 ┌────────┐     ┌──────────┐         ┌───────┐
 │Sourcing│     │Production│         │ Trade │
 └────────┘     └──────────┘         └───────┘
```

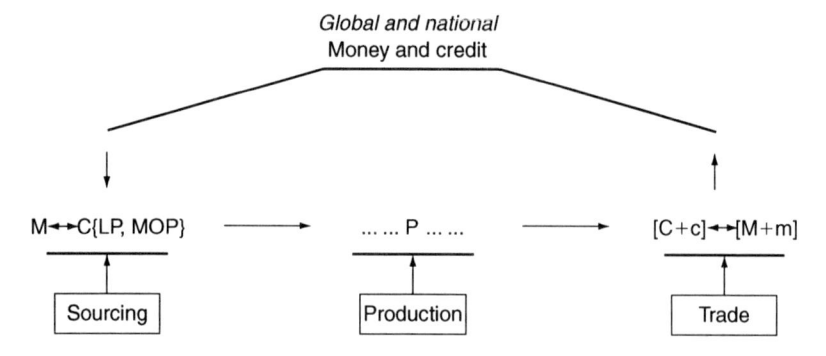

*Figure 14.1* The circuit of money capital.

means of production (MOP). This enables regional and global production value chains to be formed (......P......), thereby enhancing the process of valorization, resulting in the production of surplus product. Commodity value (C) and surplus product (c) must be sold on the market for value (M) and surplus value (m) to be realized via trade.

The regulation and social structure of accumulation schools argue that this circuit of money capital cannot operate through purely market arrangements, and that networks of institutions provide the organizational, network, and social capital upon which long-term economic performance is based (Jessop 2001). The global economy, especially, must be embedded in a series of institutional organizations, agreements, bodies, and dynamic structures of finance, sourcing, production, and trade in order to enhance the workings of the complex circuit. Periodically these institutional structures are rebuilt and break down, impacting on socio-economic performance. When they are not performing well, they do not constitute a suitable social structure or mode of regulation underlying accumulation. The three critical functions of a viable financial social structure of accumulation include: (a) financial stability; (b) historical relative resolution of the conflict between industry and finance and; (c) promotion of industrial-financial productivity and performance.[2]

Hence, the conditions necessary for a new (viable) social structure of accumulation or mode of regulation within the circuit are multifarious, ranging from a suitable level, quality, and price for the inputs of labour power and means of production; the effective mobilization of labor and machines within the production process; a requisite level of global demand and trade; an efficient and relatively stable and sustainable level of money and credit to finance industry; a minimum level of innovation and business enterprise; plus a sufficient supply of support structures and processes to keep the elements of the circuit in motion.

This approach recognizes that money and credit under capitalism constitute a dynamic force, linked to investment, production, trade, and demand. Money is not a "veil" since it finances much of the investment and consumption needed for growth and development. Any theory of money and credit, therefore, must be linked inextricably to the forces of enterprise, innovation, accumulation, and speculation. As Marx, Veblen, Keynes, and Schumpeter realized, capitalism could not exist without markets and credit. The ability of businesses to realize a profit depends partly on their ability to finance investments so the circuit can increase capital stock over time. Anything that upsets this circuit, including disruptions to financial flows, insufficient demand, bottlenecks, and conflict at the point of production (e.g. credit crunches) will ultimately inhibit profit and capital. But if the flow continues unabated, value added is possible through the creation of surplus value (Marx, Schumpeter), intangible value (Veblen), and prospective yield (Keynes).[3]

## Endogenous versus exogenous money and credit

Traditional economics assumes that the money supply is exogenous; thus, the government can control and effectively manage it through the Reserve Bank and Treasury. By influencing the monetary base – cash and coin – governments can (at least theoretically) control the level of economic activity and demand, and therefore the rate of inflation, which is done mainly via open market operations – buying and selling of government securities in the open market. Discretionary control is facilitated if the central bank is independent of elected officials in order to more effectively control inflation. Any problems in controlling inflation are thus the fault of government, either not effectively undertaking its monetary duties or not allowing the central bank enough independence.

Orthodox alternatives to exogenous money and credit have developed over the past few decades. One particularly influential trend is a new-Keynesian theory of broad money transmission mechanisms. The idea is that governments cannot control a narrowly defined money supply; that they can influence broad measures of economic activity through the credit process. This is a pragmatic perspective recognizing that economic activity is impacted by the financial system. Money and credit are thus not veils since they promote lending and borrowing through the financial system, which propels production and broad economic performance. This view thus realizes that money and credit have a critical element of endogeneity; that is, they are influenced by and in turn promote economic activity.

Post-Keynesian, institutionalist, and neo-Marxist perspectives of money and credit are similar, although they extend the new Keynesian theory in several directions (Arestis 1988). The central hypothesis is that money demand stimulates money supply and credit, which in turn propels economic activity. Business cycle upswings generate their own momentum as the demand for finance stimulates supply. This is the essence of endogenous money and credit: capitalist economies thus undergo endogenous business cycles, where the upswings and downswings have a central element of self-reinforcing dynamics.[4]

During the recovery phase of the business cycle, businesses seek funds, and if they are not forthcoming from government, substitutes will emerge. This is the idea of structural or innovative endogenous money and credit. In the absence of government accommodation, banks/firms will generate new forms of finance or expand existing means of finance not controlled by the central bank. This may take the form of bank bills, trade credit, negotiable certificates of deposit, overseas finance, and exotic options or swaps. This finance enables business cycle upswings to emerge through the normal workings of business. It is likely that this will overextend the system beyond fundamental variables and that speculative bubbles will eventually emerge as the expansion continues. Structural endogeneity is perhaps the most important element of endogenous money and credit.

A second form of endogenous finance is the government accommodating the demand for money through additional liquidity. If the government actualizes the greater demand for money by expanding money and finance, then this is another form of endogenous finance. Some have argued that it is normal for the government to legitimize the greater demand through enhancing system-wide liquidity. One such way is through open-market operations or reduced reserve ratios. In the contemporary environment this normally means reducing interest rates or not increasing them. Indeed, to the extent that the government can either control interest rates or money, and generally targets interest rates, endogenous government finance has become institutionalized into the system.[5]

The operation of endogenous–exogenous money and credit depends upon the shape of the money supply curve, and whether money-finance demand is satisfied through supply. Figure 14.2 illustrates some possibilities.

Ms1 indicates that money and credit are entirely endogenous as the higher demand for finance expands the supply. Ms2 illustrates the exogenous situation where higher credit demand has no impact on supply. And Ms3 is the middle of the road where finance is sometimes endogenous, sometimes exogenous, and sometimes in between. Ms3 indicates that the degree of endogeneity/exogeneity depends on the reality of the institutional situation of the time. Endogenous finance analysts support a combination of Ms1 and Ms3, stressing that the current institutional environment, where finance is mostly deregulated, supports

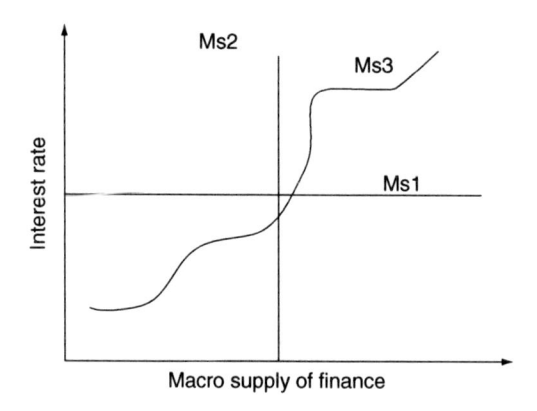

*Figure 14.2* Endogenous–exogenous finance.

structural endogeneity, while a system of interest rate targeting supports accommodative endogenous credit.

Analysis of structural endogenous money and credit involves a game about the behavior of economic agents and organizations over time. This involves conflict between systemic and individual interests of business and government: business requires funds as an expansion begins, with the government usually providing liquidity to stimulate profit and investment, and businesses (including banks) often generating liabilities to enhance credit. This is the essence of endogenous funds: they are stimulated by both government and business.

But as the apogee of the expansion approaches, risk increases as inflation, speculative bubbles, and recession loom. In this environment, the reserve bank may decide that the boom has gone on for too long and will try and moderate it. Thus, accommodative money and credit are not forthcoming and these funds become exogenous in the sense that they do not flow with the highs of the cycle. Instead, business may depend upon their own endogenous sources of funds, such as bank bills, overseas finance, or certain exotic "innovations" such as mortgage-backed bonds. The central bank may, however, try to limit the extent of these structural sources of endogenous finance by placing (higher) reserve requirements upon them (Rochon and Vernengo 2001).

However, the reserve bank may not successfully prevent the creation of structural endogenous finance as financial institutions and other businesses create ongoing alternative sources of funds. This cat-and-mouse game can continue through several runs, especially over successive business cycles, as Figure 14.3 illustrates.

This shows that if the reserve bank decides not to accommodate private finance during the apogee of the business cycle, then private banks and other businesses will likely create their own instruments of finance. This will heighten the business cycle, although the government may intervene and introduce or increase reserve requirements on these forms of liability management. In response, the private sector generates further innovative finance (or modifies existing ones) to stimulate financial capabilities. It thus demonstrates that endogenous and exogenous money, credit, and finance are variously impacting the system, depending on the changes occurring in the institutions. Realistically, some combination of accommodative and structural finance generates higher booms in the cycle which can lead to deeper recessions. This is because the apogee of the booms, especially during long-wave downswings, indicate the extent of unproductive finance, bubbles, and overextended accumulation.

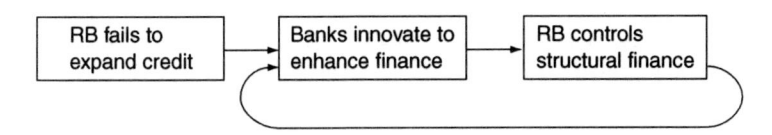

*Figure 14.3* Interactive game between reserve bank and banks.

## Industry–finance contradiction

According to orthodoxy, given free and open markets, resources will be distributed across the economy according to relative marginal productivities. Both industry and finance are equally productive given optimal market conditions. The government is likely to misallocate resources if they distort prices and quantities between industry and finance. Long movements and unstable dynamics in finance are likely to be short-lived as the free market adjusts rapidly to potential instability.

However, the combined insights of Marx, Veblen, Schumpeter, and Keynes provide a different understanding of the relationship between industry and finance (O'Hara 2002a). Industry is the productive activity of increasing value added in the leading sectors of the economy, providing the foundation for surplus value, intangible value, or prospective yield. Finance is the necessary but less productive activity of providing the financial backing for business activities, whether through credit, equity, or other means. There is a potential conflict between industry and finance, in the sense that the interests of industrial capital and financial capital can be disharmonious.

However, if either industry or finance is significantly out of balance, problems emerge (Cypher 1998). For instance, when industry is much more powerful than finance, overproduction generally results since competition is too strong and markets too thin. The period of the 1870s–1890s exemplifies this in many economies of the world. During that time, output expanded rapidly through economies of scale and larger corporations, but without sufficient development of finance and business. Before and after the turn of the century, the development of investment banks, mergers, imperial expansion, and international corporative accounting techniques helped to temporarily solve this problem.

When the power relationship between industry and finance is in balance or slightly in favor of industry, the economy is likely to be on a sustainable growth path. During the years of the Keynesian welfare state (1950s–early 1970s), a strong link existed between the returns to industry and finance. Both promoted economic growth and development through advanced economies. This great boom was a classic period of relative buoyancy when optimism pervaded the dominant institutions.

When finance is too strong this will likely generate speculative bubbles and a misallocation of resources toward equity, banking, financial, real estate, and foreign exchange, as happened during the 1920s–1930s and 1980s–2000s. The financial system was largely deregulated, Treasury views dominated government actions, and speculative bubbles were regular occurrences that crashed periodically. The Great Depression and the recent global subprime crisis are classic examples of this. During the era of neoliberalism (1980s–2000s), evidence exists that there was little correlation between the returns to industry and finance, as finance came to dominate the economy, leading to bubbles and deeper recessions in the major economies. Investment in finance was too strong relative to industry, thereby resulting in reduced growth and accumulation. Shareholder value was strong while the dominant industries had inadequate profit (Aglietta 2000; Boyer 2000; Binswanger 2000; Stockhammer 2004).[6] This culminated in the internet equity crash and corporate crisis of the early 2000s plus the global subprime crisis of the late 2000s. Institutional changes resulting from these financial anomalies will quite likely result in the emergence of a more progressive form of governance where industry and finance are in relative balance (O'Hara 2009).

## Financial instability hypothesis

According to traditional economics, financial stability is the normal state of a free market. If markets are deregulated and industry productive, then the credit system will operate efficiently since value will be determined by fundamental variables such as long-term dividends. The financial system will be efficient since well-developed markets enable resources to be distributed to those areas as required. In the extreme orthodox version of free banking, it is necessary to have free markets in money and currency as well. There thus should be no state monopoly of central banking as this promotes instability and disarray in the markets. Nevertheless, the dominant view amongst orthodoxy is that central banks are needed to promote currency and inflation control, while deposit insurance may help to instill confidence and hence stability into the system.

Political economy perspectives generally support the financial instability hypothesis (FIH), whereby financial instability is endogenous to the free market system of production, distribution, and exchange. The FIH has three key elements: uncertainly; endogenous money and credit; and the relationship between prospective yield and supply price. Hyman Minsky's FIH is an application of the industry–finance contradiction. Uncertainty is critical because entrepreneurs contemplate the viability of projects over long time frames when specific knowledge is lacking. Investment in capital projects with a future life of ten or twenty years is based on a time frame which corporate planners know little of. They calculate prospective yield and supply price in an uncertain environment when proper calculation is not possible. Future events cannot be known with any degree of certainty; thus the weight of confidence about future probabilities is very low. Needless to say, making decisions about financing such projects in this world of uncertainty is fraught with problems.

For this reason, as Minsky argues, business decisions are made via the prevailing business climate, accounting rules, and financial models. Without such conventions little action would be taken on critical business projects with a long gestation period. Instability is endogenous to the capitalist system since large credit-based projects run a high risk of failure as the business cycle moves from recovery to boom to financial crisis and recession. This is supported by evidence that most businesses fail in the formative stages of their development, with few firms incorporating such cycle dynamics into accounting systems.

Minsky (1986) developed a model explaining the endogenous nature of this instability, based on cash flow (income and contractual commitments) and capitalized values (of expected income and contractual commitments) plus degrees of safety. The model has two time periods, short and long, and a profit and loss account as well as a balance sheet. For the short run, cash flow is related to the difference between current income (Y) and current contractual commitments (CC), which is related to debt. For the long term, net worth is linked to capitalized income (or prospective yield) through many periods (K(Y)) compared with capitalized contractual commitments, or supply price, over the long term (K(CC)). For business cycle phases, with high profit levels and low risk, "Hedge Finance" prevails:

Hedge Finance
$Y = \delta CC$ or $Y > CC$
$K(Y) = \beta K(CC)$ or $K(Y) > K(CC)$

where $\delta$ and $\beta$ represent margins of financial safety that are above unity (>1); in other words, income, on average, is greater than contractual commitments by a certain margin of safety in every period. The recovery and moderate boom in the cycle are generally good for business since the profit rate is relatively high while risk is low. Minsky (1982, 1986) and Wolfson (1994b, 1994a, 2000) argue that endogenous financial factors lead from this safe type of finance (hedge finance) to less secure types, i.e. Speculative and Ponzi Finance.[7]

The generation of endogenous finance during the boom in the cycle typically overextends economic activity beyond fundamentals, since uncertainty about the future forces firms to depend on current business activity to guide investment. Firms thus generate massive investment during a euphoric, prolonged expansion. Income increases to extraordinary highs relative to supply price or contract commitments, even as interest rates increase due to either higher demand (Minsky) or monetary policy (modern parlance). The increased interest rates do not attenuate the expansion just yet, though, since exuberant conditions still sustain prospective yield despite moderate increases in capitalized supply price. We thus have a slight deterioration in financial safety since, on average, cash flows become negative where income is often less than contractual commitments (short term) while capitalized income is still greater than capitalized contractual commitments (long term). This is called "Speculative Finance," where long-term conditions are still buoyant and credit demand high:

Speculative Finance:
$Y < CC$
$K(Y) < K(CC)$

Lastly, buoyant conditions gradually stimulate instability and crisis (especially during long-wave downswing) as a number of environmental conditions deteriorate, costs increase and bubbles crash. Because exuberant conditions push investment and stock prices beyond long-term fundamentals, decline is highly likely (Raines and Leathers 2000). In the age of neoliberalism (with a concomitant increase in shareholder value) during the 1980s–2000s in the US, UK, and many other advanced nations, the stock market gained relative autonomy from the real sector. A far greater proportion of credit went to finance equity expansion, while a lesser degree financed real investment (hence declining inflation). Thus the crash in the stock market prior to and during recession was far greater than the historical average. Such periodic crashes might be stimulated by higher raw material prices, increased interest rates as monetary authorities moderate demand, corporate excesses and crises, as profits are inflated and subsequently diminish as corporate bankruptcies escalate. All these factors lead to a deterioration in the business climate, lower than expected profits, declining investment, stock market crash and recession (especially during the mid-1970s, early 1980s, early 1990s, and 2000s in most western nations). This leads to a further decline in financial safety as more firms move from Speculative to "Ponzi Finance," where cash flows are often negative with income lower than contractual commitments and capitalized cash flows (prospective yield) being often smaller than capitalized contractual costs (supply price):

Ponzi Finance:
$Y < CC$
$K(Y) < K(CC)$

Ponzi Finance is thus the worst form of financial condition for the economy as many firms undergo bankruptcy, the stock market is crashing, corporate excesses are unsustainable, and deep recession emerges during long-wave downswings (Dymski and Pollin 1994; Fazzari and Papadimitriou 1992). Due to intersectoral linkages these crises are typically regionally and internationally synchronized, although somewhat uneven.

A higher prospective yield is the endogenous force stimulating the movement from Hedge to Speculative Finance, as uncertainty ostensibly declines, in addition to a higher interest rate. On balance this is a positive environment. The endogenous force moving the system from Speculative to Ponzi Finance is a crash in prospective yield, where also input prices often rise considerably. On balance this is a periodic systemic crisis of finance. Speculative bubbles tend to crash during these times of Ponzi Finance, corporate accounting crises are highly likely, and chains of bankruptcy are probable. They are endogenously linked to the system dynamics of state capitalism throughout most advanced nations of the world.

## Financial and social structures of accumulation

The extent of financial instability and fragility, however, depends on the nature of the institutions. Post-Keynesian, institutionalist, and neo-Marxist perspectives of money and credit are based on the principle that the economy should be minimally dislocated (Bush 2001), meaning that a degree of institutionalized stability is required, especially for a dynamic economy such as capitalism. This is similar to Polanyi's (1944) argument that free market economies cannot exist in the long run because they increase instability due to inadequate public goods. Deregulated monetary systems increase the volatility of the business cycle as endogenous finance escalates during expansions while diminishing rapidly during recession. Corporations suffer inadequate governance leading to periodic over-reporting of profitability and other accounting irregularities during expansion booms along with concentrations of economic power leading to higher levels of white collar crime, fraud, and insider trading.

Political economy recognizes that financial excesses vary over short business cycles and long waves. Long waves are especially important; these are long movements of the economy, typically characterized by twenty or thirty years of relatively high economic activity along with minimum financial instability and crises, followed by twenty or thirty years of greater instability characterized by periodic deep recessions and financial crises. A schematic view of these long waves for the advanced capitalist economies is presented in Table 14.1.

Long-wave upswings characterized the 1780s–1810s, 1850s–1870s, 1890s–1910s, and 1940s–1970s and will possibly characterize the 2010s–2040s in the advanced nations. Minor recessions, minimal financial instability, and development characterize these periods. The main reason for prevailing financial stability is that long-term rates of profit are high and the prevailing business climate is positive. Industry profit rates, therefore, are critical for financial stability.

Long-wave downswings characterized the periods 1815–1849, 1873–1895, 1915/1925–1944, and 1973–2010s. During these periods financial instability was (and is) high as periodic financial crises and deep recessions were (are) common. Average industry profit rates are low and/or highly volatile, financial risk

*Table 14.1* Long waves and financial dynamics

|  | Long wave | Upswing | Downswing | Financial developments |
|---|---|---|---|---|
| 1780s–1840s | Competitive capitalism | 1780s–1810s | 1810s–1840s | Predominant money and commodity economy |
| 1850s–1890s | Industrial Revolution | 1850s–1870s | 1870s–1890s | Equity capital and money capital in firms |
| 1890s–1940s | Imperialism–finance capital | 1870s–1910s | 1910s–1940s | Investment banks and Credit-money for finance capital |
| 1940s–2000s | Fordism–Welfare State | 1940s–1970s | 1970s–2010s | Industry-finance balance → shareholder value economy |
| 2010s–2040s? | Electronics and biotechnology | 2010s–2030s? | 2030s–2050s? | Predominant electronic credit and finance economy |

excessive, and investment subdued. In addition, debt crises in the Third World typically emerge as credit is excessive in the face of low profit and investment.

The basis of these long waves is the shape and character of institutions. With sustaining institutions, demand and productivity increase, and long upswings are typical. With inhibiting institutions, demand and productivity decreases, and long downswings are typical. Successive waves see major evolutionary developments in all institutions, including finance. For instance, the transformation of capitalism over numerous waves witnessed the emergence of the original predominant money and commodity economy (1780s–1840s); followed by the evolution of equity business finance (1850s–1890s); the credit-money and investment banks (1890s–1940s); then regulation followed by deregulation (1940s–2000s).

During the long-wave upswing of 1945–1973, well-developed financial social structures of accumulation operated through central banking, credit creation, financial intermediaries and business–household savings and investment institutions (Wolfson 1994b; O'Hara 2000; Guttman 2001). These financial structures helped develop a viable system of industry and technology along with a favorable profit rate. However, long-wave downswing emerged in the 1970s–2000s in the advanced economies as contradictions developed in the institutions of production–distribution, finance, the state, the world economy, and the family. Finance came to dominate industry as the rate of industrial profit declined and financial assets ruled business decisions.

The tendency for fictitious capitals to periodically dominate industry occurs when there is substantial misallocation of resources between the real and the financial sector. In advanced nations this has persistently occurred during the 1970s–2000s, generating financial crises and deep recessions. During the 1980s, corporate finance led to excesses as debt financed unproductive speculative activity, leading to the major stock market crash of 1987, soon followed by the recession of the early 1990s. The 1990s led to excesses, especially in the internet and high-tech sectors, leading to a series of speculative bubble crashes and accounting crises. The 2000s led to excesses especially in the subprime mortgage market, which spilled over into the general and global economies. Critical to these instabilities are financial and other "innovations" (e.g. mortgage-backed bonds) that take time to develop and which involve overproduction and overinvestment in certain sectors such as the share market and residential housing.

## Global money, payments, and prices

Political economy assumes that capitalism is by its very nature a global system, with centre–periphery uneven relations affecting global growth and development; and that economic power is central to its functioning, with money power a critical aspect. Market relations are imbued with power differentials because of certain centripetal and centralizing tendencies of business. Money tends to be dispersed to those who are able to gain monopoly rents, be they individuals, organizations, firms, sectors, areas, nations, or commodity chains. By and large, most rents accrue to those able to commodify the dominant technological, social, and informational resources. In particular, those able to organize global and regional networks of business will gain the most profit and money (Grou 1985).

Power is linked to hegemonic processes, especially nations and areas that lead the world in production, commerce, finance, and international relations. Global power shifted from the Dutch in the seventeenth century, to the British in the nineteenth century, and to the United States in the twentieth century. Debate continues about US hegemony and dominance, with many arguing that the US has moved from absolute hegemony in the late twentieth century to relative hegemony in the early twenty-first century.

The money-currency of the hegemonic power tends to be the world currency. At present the US dollar is the dominant global currency, although it is slowly losing power relative to the Euro, the Yen, and the Chinese Yuan (Renminbi). A potential problem is that asymmetric power leading to the dominant role of the US dollar may inhibit global performance if the hegemon underplays critical system functions or global public goods. There is thus a contradiction between the US dollar performing the dual role of national and global currency. The efforts of US monetary authorities to safeguard national objectives are often in conflict with the smooth workings of the international financial system. For instance, during the early 1980s when the US authorities doubled interest rates from 5 to 10 percent to attenuate domestic inflation, this initiated debt crises in Latin America, with debt denominated in US dollars. This pushed development back for many nations by a decade or more. Also, during the Asian crisis of the late 1990s, most contracts were denominated in US dollars and often with US banks. When US authorities began increasing interest rates in the light of the emerging speculative bubble of the late 1990s this had a major negative impact on Asian debt, leading to massive hot capital outflows and recession (Schulmeister 2000).

Post-Keynesians argue for a truly "global currency," one that transcends national power relations and currencies. Such a currency would eschew the hegemon's preferences and policies when they abrogate global public goods. A truly global currency will make world monetary relations fairer and increase global stability. Post-Keynesians also argue that balance of payments equilibria is better obtained through a new rule: nations experiencing persistent current account surpluses are obliged to increase demand for goods and services of nations with current account deficits. Currently the opposite prevails, especially for developing or underdeveloped nations: balance-of-payment-deficit developing nations are "forced" by the IMF to reduce government spending, increase interest rates, and reduce demand in the domestic economy to supposedly equilibrate payments imbalances. The opposite, however, will rectify the current trend toward inadequate global effective demand and periodic financial instability.[8] This global view of capital explains why political economy advocates a Monetary Theory of Production in a system of circular and cumulative causation, summarized in Figure 14.4,

It is critical to enhance effective demand in the global economy and to ultimately expand investment, both private and public. When uncertainty is

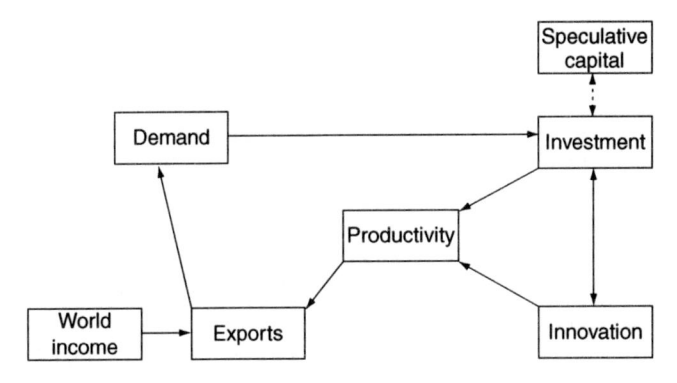

*Figure 14.4* Kaldorian dynamics of circular and cumulative causation.

relatively low, private investment tends to be high, but when uncertainty is high, public investment can help through crowding in private investment in education, health, communications, and infrastructure. Demand is in fact interdependent with supply, since increased consumer demand manifests in greater demand for capital, through economies of scale; in addition, embodied innovative investment may stimulate productivity. Relatively high global income– especially when governments do not impose austerity measures – translates into higher demand for global exports. This in turn propels greater demand, and so on, as the system works this through in multiple rounds of circular and cumulative action. If demand can be sustained, productivity and profitability increase, thus moderating financial crises and recessions.

It is necessary, though, to moderate levels of speculative and hot capital when they crowd out investment, both private and public (Wincoop and Yi. 2000; O'Hara 2003). If speculative bubbles rise to great heights, finance dominates industry with resources transferred to relatively unproductive areas. Rules need to be devised to moderate this dominance, so that real investment is enhanced. Although to some extent the generating force of the bubble tends to be cultural and historical, policy can help. For example, introducing asset-based reserve requirements can moderate bubbles. If the authorities, for instance, believe that bubbles are rising rapidly in the stock market and property and/or foreign currency markets, increasing reserve requirements on these specific bubble assets can redirect finance to more productive areas. This may eliminate the need for increasing interest rates, which can be a very blunt tool, not discriminating between productive and unproductive areas (Mishkin 2001).

The global financial instabilities of the 1990s and early 2000s taught many financial analysts about the problems of hot capitals, i.e. borrowing funds from international banks for short maturity periods. Most countries linked to the Asian crisis, for instance, experienced escalating incoming loans before the crisis, followed by massive outflows during the crisis. It is not simply a problem of developing a sound financial system prior to deregulation, since the US experienced similar unstable finance in the early 2000s. Deregulating finance completely is the major problem (Coggins 1998).

Apart from the need for transparency, accountability, prudential regulation, and speculative asset controls, it is incumbent to moderate hot capitals. This can be accomplished through the introduction of a Tobin Tax, with, say, a small 0.2 percent tax on international loans of less than twelve months' duration. This may not only "put grains of sand into the wheels of international finance" but also help finance development projects in poor nations.

Political Economy recognizes the generally negative financial impact of the terms of trade on developing and underdeveloped nations. Probably the most important financial constraint on development is the inability of poor nations to produce and export goods and services with a high price reflective of income elasticity of demand, and the monopoly rents associated with the leading commodities and services. Empirical research indicates two major problems. First, there have been two periods of declining terms of trade for poor nations, the 1920s and the 1970s; and second, poor nations tend to produce goods – usually commodities – with volatile prices. Both problems have constricted development, creating a financial limit to productive investment and government spending (O'Hara 2006).

The IMF and World Bank have extolled the theory of comparative advantage, i.e. countries should produce commodities and low value-added manufactures in which they possess a relative advantage. To exhort poor nations to produce more such commodities that are already in over-abundance is problematic, since it will further depress low prices. Poor nations must develop a long-term strategy of enhancing human, social, and specialist capitals to create the finance needed for development. This will necessitate judicious industrial policy to create high value-added goods and services, along with protecting infant industries, and generating human, social, and network capitals for development.

## Finance and socio-economic development

Political Economy seeks to enhance community living standards and promotion of a reasonably efficient and equitable society. It promotes conventional rights where the rules of society generate less division on the basis of class, ethnicity, gender, and nation. Political economy emphasizes a participatory social economy, where people not only have the right to a decent job (or alternative compensation) but also the inclusive right to decision making in the dominant institutions of business, state, community, and family. Political economy agrees that CEOs and business vested interests gain too much remuneration compared with the underlings who often work harder and longer, or lack the resources for adequate inclusion in the social economy.[9]

Political economy macro dynamics posits an investment-led growth program for social development. Traditional economics assumes that savings stimulate investment by providing funds for productive projects and encouraging the growth of savers; hence the concern about recent trends toward lower savings rates in advanced capitalist economies. Political economy has no such concern, since investment is the core variable for sustainable growth. The creation of an institutional apparatus for reducing uncertainty will encourage higher levels of private investment, thus stimulating national income and savings. Once effective demand is forthcoming, long-term progress is more likely.

One way to encourage inclusion and justice is to expand productive government investment in education, health, communications, and infrastructure. Extensive global research supports the case for public investment crowding in private investment. Such productive investment is generally better for business and individuals than subsidies, which tend to crowd out private investment. Providing productive state spending and an environment for greater private investment is the core method of providing jobs and enhancing conventional rights to employment. The best way to improve the conditions of working people and the financially disadvantaged is to encourage them to gain the skills and creative arts of a modern technological society.[10]

Recently a new theory of money and credit –Taxes-Drive-Money (TDM) – has emerged to support employment, inclusion, and justice. This theory follows the Chartalist view that the core role of government is to sustain proper levels of aggregate demand, and that functional rules of public finance should prevail over rigid ideology. The major tenets of TDM are summarized in Table 14.2 below.

TDM believes that budget deficits are required by government to enhance private investment, especially during recession. In the long run, productive government spending will enhance aggregate demand and thus produce balanced budgets, or even government surplus (in the old-fashioned vocabulary). Balanced and surplus budgets tend to be generated during high points in the business cycle, but the government should spend adequately to attenuate recessions. Taxes do not finance central government spending; rather, taxes increase the demand for government money. Government spending is financed instead by money, since the Treasury writes a check to finance state spending, and does not need preexisting taxes to do so.

The right to employment can only be achieved when pragmatic rules of finance are undertaken by the government. It should spend more when demand is low and spend less when inflation looms. The role of government borrowing,

*Table 14.2* Core elements of the taxes-drive-money approach v. orthodoxy

|  | TDM function | TDM government finance | TDM purpose for government | Orthodox government accounting |
|---|---|---|---|---|
| Taxes | Drives demand for money | Does not finance government | Modifies demand | Balances budget |
| Money | Provides reserves for the system | Finances government spending | Government financing | Finances budget deficit |
| Bonds | Interest rate targeting | Does not finance government | Modifies demand | Finances budget deficit |

on the other hand, is to activate monetary policy through open market operations. Government borrowing from the public is done purely for interest rate targeting purposes. TDM thus believes that financing spending via deficits to prevent recession does not crowd out private investment via higher interest rates. Although higher spending may increase rates, financing from money reduces rates, the net effect likely being neutral. But if the spending is productive this has the added advantage of crowding in private investment, as argued earlier.[11]

Social justice may thus prevail as Taxes-Drive-Money encourages governments to stimulate social and regional development, especially if they can moderate the tendency to waste resources on major wars and military expansion. Political economy recognizes that money and credit matter and it is unlikely that productive finance acts as a veil, or fails to impact production in the short, medium, and long runs. Political economy takes the quantity theory of money and its modern variants as a point of critical departure for governance. Social inclusion and justice require a humanistic and realistic view of economic agents, who exhibit bounded rationality. Economic agents are affected by the institutional environment in which they are brought up and coexist with others. As a general rule, it is thus unlikely that agents anticipate adequately the actions of monetary authorities and, even less, the impact of such actions on economic activity. The "rational agent" model and "policy ineffectiveness proposition" are extreme, without empirical basis: people are subject to habit, social influences and instincts that impact behavior. Finance thus affects real social variables through technological and institutional innovations, large-scale production, economies of scale, and productive government investment into infrastructure, education, health, and communications. Demand thus affects social inclusion and justice by directly impacting employment and income.

The financial environment is especially critical for people with less income, wealth, and power. They tend to have low levels of collateral, finance, and material assets, thus making it difficult to get sizeable loans from banks and other formal institutions. Thus community reinvestment programs, microfinance, and government financial priorities must assume an important role. Those with low collateral tend to congregate among society's lower classes. Government programs can influence this through public productive capital such as education, communications, health, transportation, and infrastructure. Microfinance can help if the borrower uses it for capital purposes rather than for consumption items that can be quickly exhausted.

The institutional environment requires a critical level of dynamic stability. Being able to provide such conditions reduces the level of liquidity preference through lower levels of uncertainty. Both the speculative and precautionary demands decline as the institutional environment stimulates business and consumer confidence. While the finance demand for money may increase along with investment confidence, overall there is a more intense turnover of the circuit of capital through purchase, production, sale, and reinvestment of the surplus. It is not just the speed of the circuit but also the stability of the speed through time that determine socio-economic prosperity.

## Conclusion

This chapter presents the main contours of a political economy approach to money. Its essence is that the money circuit is a dynamic process operating through time, subject in turn to hysteresis and path dependence. History matters in political economy; therefore a dynamic view of credit and finance is central to its core theory and policy. Credit and finance are mostly endogenous, as the liquidity requirements of business tend to be satisfied through innovations and changes. Business and government together try to stimulate investment when business desires funds for expansion. However, when finance dominates industry, institutional changes are needed to activate productive spending and investment.

There is a tendency for capitalism to create instability since it depends upon prospective yield, knowledge of which is lacking because of the long-term nature of expected profit. Since the future is unknowable, conventions are introduced to deal with investment in the face of such radical uncertainty. Business thus tends to finance such projects partly with credit, but during exuberant conditions finance becomes overextended. This leads to periodic crises and recessions as speculative bubbles crash and real values assert themselves. Fictitious capital often rules business decisions when fundamental variables are difficult to ascertain (O'Hara 2000). Financial conditions thus evolve variously through hedge, speculative, and Ponzi positions as business lacks the required knowledge for stability.

Meanwhile, the dominant theories of finance tend to sustain the myths either of stability and certainty under business conditions or of the systemic need for periodic major insolvency to regenerate the spirit of innovation and motion. Political economy maintains that uncertainty is rampant and also that major insolvency is undesirable. Aggregate demand is thus the critical interdependent variable when finance funds productive investment and sustains industrial profit. The role of government is essentially to encourage and stimulate private spending through institutions and innovations that propel the circuit of money. It should stimulate industry, moderate speculative bubbles and aid the process of recreating financial social structures underlying accumulation. The government needs to be proactive rather than just reactive or neutral in its approach to business.

Political economy also recognizes that power and the asymmetric distribution of information and knowledge affects finance capital. Relying on interest rate mechanisms to moderate spending may fail as high rates create risk and instability in the system. They also function as a blunt instrument while not distinguishing between real and speculative values. Thus an asset-based reserve requirement may assist in moderating bubbles and instability. Policy should stimulate the power of industry over finance. It should also ensure that hegemonic-inspired nations do not rule international money, creating contradictions with their own national policy. A truly global currency will provide major public goods while current account surplus nations are encouraged to spend to stabilize international finance.

Political economy embeds financial theory in a pragmatic and realistic edifice based on endogenous processes. The institutions of business and government are in symbiotic unity if the principles of circuit, instability, endogeneity, and power are serviced to sustain demand and reduce liquidity preference. But in doing so the state needs to consider the system as a whole rather than its sectional interests, while business is required to create some degree of balance between industry and finance. Such are the lessons of the political economy of money, credit and finance.

## Appendix 1: questions and discussion points

1 Discuss the following assumptions of traditional economics. Why are they usually or often problem-assumptions for political economy?
    a    Exogenous money, credit and finance
    b    Rational agents
    c    Policy ineffectiveness proposition
2 Discuss and illustrate the workings of the following principles or empirical regularities:
    a    Circuit of social capital
    b    Endogenous money, credit and finance (structural and accommodative)
    c    The endogenous cyclical movement of hedge to speculative and then to Ponzi Finance
    d    The importance of financial innovations and institutional changes
    e    The role of speculative bubbles, prospective yield relative to supply price, and recession
3 Examine the following historical and empirical aspects of modern finance-capitalism long waves of evolution and metamorphosis:
    a    Financial social structure of accumulation
    b    Global money and credit; US hegemony; changing hegemonies
    c    Skills and creative arts; bounded rationality; circular and cumulative causation

## Appendix 2: useful journals to aid study and research in political economy money, credit, and finance

*Cambridge Journal of Economics*
*Capital and Class*
*Ecological Economics*
*Economy and Society*
*Feminist Economics*
*Forum for Social Economics*
*International Journal of Pluralism and Economics Education*
*International Journal of Political Economy*
*International Review of Applied Economics*
*Journal of Economic Issues*

*Journal of Evolutionary Economics*
*Journal of Human Development*
*Journal of Institutional Economics*
*Journal of Post Keynesian Economics*
*New Political Economy*
*Rethinking Marxism*
*Review* (from Fernand Braudel Centre)
*Review of International Political Economy*
*Review of Political Economy*
*Review of Radical Political Economics*
*Review of Social Economics*
*Structural Change and Economic Dynamics*
*Studies in Political Economy*
*World Development*

## Appendix 3: useful references for political economy approaches to money, credit, and finance

### Historical and general material

Douglas, V. (1959) *Studies in the Theory of Money, 1690–1776.* New York: Chilton.

Godley, W. and M. Lavoie (2006) *Monetary Economics: An Integrated Approach to Credit, Money, Income, Production and Wealth.* London: Palgrave/Macmillan.

O'Hara, P.A. (2007) "Circuit of Social Capital," in Phillip Anthony O'Hara (ed.), *Encyclopedia of Political Economy.* New York: Routledge.

Rochon, L.P. and Rossi, S. (2003) *Modern Theories of Money: The Nature and Role of Money in Capitalist Economies.* Cheltenham, UK: Edward Elgar.

Seccareccia, M. (2001) "Money, Credit and Finance: History," in Phillip Anthony O'Hara (ed.), *Encyclopedia of Political Economy*, Vol. I. New York: Routledge.

Wray, L.R. (2001) "Money, Credit and Finance: Major Contemporary Themes," in Phillip Anthony O'Hara (ed.), *Encyclopedia of Political Economy.* New York: Routledge.

### Endogenous v. exogenous money

Palley, T. (2002) "Endogenous Money: What It Is and Why It Matters," *Metroeconomica* 53: 152–180.

Rochon, L.P. (1999) *Credit, Money and Production: An Alternative Post-Keynesian Approach.* Cheltenham, UK: Edward Elgar.

Rossi, S. (2008) "Endogenous and Exogenous Money or Credit," in Phillip Anthony O'Hara (ed.), *International Encyclopedia of Public Policy – Governance in a Global Age.* Perth, Australia: GPERU, pp. 188–198. http://pohara.homestead.com/encyclopedia/volume-2.pdf.

Wray, L.R. (1990) *Money and Credit in Capitalist Economies: The Endogenous Money Approach.* Aldershot, UK: Edward Elgar.

### Financial instability hypothesis

Davidson, P. (2008) "Is the Current Financial Distress Caused by the Sub Prime Mortgage Crisis a Minsky Moment? Or Is It the Result of Attempting to Securitize Illiquid Non Commercial Mortgage Loans?," *Journal of Post Keynesian Economics* 30: 669–679.

Dymski, G. and Pollin, R. (eds) (1994) *New Perspectives in Monetary Macroeconomics: Exploration in the Tradition of Hyman P. Minsky*. Ann Arbor: University of Michigan Press.

Fazzari, S. and Papadimitriou, D. (eds) (1992) *Financial Conditions and Macroeconomic Performance: Essays in Honor of Hyman P. Minsky*. Armonk, NY: M.E. Sharpe.

Minsky, H.P. (1986) *Stabilizing an Unstable Economy*. New Haven, Conn.: Yale University Press.

Wray, L. Randall (2002) "What Happened to Goldilocks? A Minskian Framework," *Journal of Economic Issues* 26: 383–391.

### Financial social structure of accumulation

Boyer, R. (2000) "Is a Finance-Led Growth Regime a Viable Alternative to Fordism? A Preliminary Analysis," *Economy and Society* 29: 111–145.

Guttman, R. (1994) *How Credit-Money Shapes the Economy: The United States in a Global System*. Armonk, NY: M.E. Sharpe.

—— (2001) "Social Structure of Accumulation," in Phillip O'Hara (ed.), *Encyclopedia of Political Economy*, Vol. 2, London: Routledge.

O'Hara, P.A. (2002) "A New Financial Social Structure of Accumulation in the United States?," *Review of Radical Political Economics* 34: 295–301.

Wolfson, M.H. (1994) "The Financial System and the Social Structure of Accumulation," in D.M. Kotz, T. McDonough, and M. Reich (eds.), *Social Structures of Accumulation: The Political Economy of Growth and Crisis*. Cambridge: Cambridge University Press.

### Industry–finance contradiction and financial crises

Binswanger, M. (2000) "Stock Returns and Real Activity: Is There Still a Connection?," *Applied Financial Economics* 10: 379–388.

Raines, J.P. and Leathers, C. (2000) *Economists and the Stock Market: Speculative Theories of Stock Market Fluctuations*. Cheltenham, UK: Edward Elgar.

Stockhammer, E. (2004) "Financialisation and the Slowdown of Accumulation," *Cambridge Journal of Economics* 28: 719–741.

Wolfson, M. (1994) *Financial Crises: Understanding the Postwar U.S. Experience*, Second Edition. Armonk, NY: M.E. Sharpe.

Wolfson, M. (2000) "Neoliberalism and International Financial Instability," *Review of Radical Political Economics* 32: 369–378.

### Government finance and Taxes-Drive-Money

Arestis, P. and Sawyer, S. (2004) "On the Effectiveness of Monetary Policy and of Fiscal Policy," *Review of Social Economy* 62: 441–464.

Bell, S., Henry, J.F., and Wray, L.W. (2004) "A Chartalist Critique of John Locke's Theory of Property, Accumulation, and Money: Or, Is It Moral to Trade Your Nuts for Gold?," *Review of Social Economy* 62: 51–66.

Kadmos, G.A and O'Hara, P.A. (2000) "Taxes-Drive-Money and Employer of Last Resort Approach to Government Policy," *Journal of Economic and Social Policy* 5: 1–22.
Lavoie, M. Seccareccia, M. (eds.) (2004) *Central Banking in the Modern World: Alternative Perspectives*. Cheltenham, UK: Edward Elgar.
Wray, L. Randall. (1998) *Understanding Modern Money: The Key to Full Employment and Price Stability*. Cheltenham, UK: Edward Elgar.

### Global money and finance

Arestis, P., Basu, S., and Mallick, S. (2005) "Financial Globalisation, the Need for a Single Currency and a Global Central Bank," *Journal of Post Keynesian Economics* 27: 507–532.
Harvey, J. (2007) "Teaching Post Keynesian Exchange Rate Theory," *Journal of Post Keynesian Economics* 30: 147–168.
O'Hara, P.A. (2006) *Growth and Development in the Global Political Economy*. London: Routledge.
Rochon, L.P. and Vernengo, M. (2001) *Credit, Interest Rates and the Open Economy: Essays on Horizontalism*. Cheltenham, UK: Edward Elgar.

### Finance efficiency and equity

Nugroho, A. and O'Hara, P.A. (2008) *Microfinance and Social Capital in Indonesia*. Perth, Australia: Global Political Economy Research Unit. Working Research Paper No. 2008/1. http://pohara.homestead.com/GPERU/WRP2008-1.pdf.
Rochon, L.P. and Setterfield, M. (2007) "Interest Rates, Income Distribution and Money Policy Dominance: Post Keynesians and the 'Fair Rate of Interest'," *Journal of Post Keynesian Economics* 30: 13–42.
Zaleweski, D. (2005) "Economic Security and the Myth of the Efficiency/Equity Trade-off," *Journal of Economic Issues* 39: 383–390.
Zezza, G. (2008) "US Growth, the Housing Market and the Distribution of Income," *Journal of Post Keynesian Economics* 30: 375–401.

## Notes

1 Considerable work has been done lately on the financial circuit of money and credit, especially by the French–Italian circuitists (Rochon 1999); on the link between the circuit and endogenous finance (Parguez 2001); and on linkages to the Marxian circuit of capital (Campbell 1998). In addition, see the classic works of Levine (1978, 1982l).
2 These conditions are linked to the financial system by Wolfson (1994b, 1994a) and O'Hara (2002, 2006).
3 Surplus value is the value added in production created by labor, given the conditions of circulation, manifesting in profit. The break-up of surplus value into profit, interest and rent reveals the money-finance aspects of surplus in a multi-capital model (Marx 1894). Intangible value was used by Veblen (1923) to describe the financial generation of value, enabling finance capital to generate profit and hence surplus. Prospective yield is the expected valuation of productive investment by entrepreneurs and capitalists that posits a return on their capital in the long-term horizon (Keynes 1936).
4 Sherman (2003) applies endogenous business cycles to all institutions of contemporary

capitalism, including financial capital; while Matutinovic (2005) analyses the endogenous nature of cycles along the lines of Marx, Keynes, Schumpeter, and Mitchell but with a more microeconomic foundation.

5  For classic contemporary studies on structural and accommodative endogenous money, credit, and finance, see Moore (1988), supporting accommodative approaches; Wray (1990), who analyses the institutional complexities of endogenous money and credit; and Pollin (1991), who empirically supports structural credit and finance.

6  See Zhu et al. (2004) on anomalous stock market liquidity; Stockhammer (2004) on the destabilizing influence of US/UK style financial dominance via equity markets; and Binswanger (2000) on the problems of financial dominance of industry.

7  Recent studies on Minsky's hypothesis and related topics cover the destabilizing influence of interest rate adjustments on investment (Hannsgen 2005); the more selective policy developed by Thomas Palley (2004) of asset-based reserve requirements; and the relevance of the FIH to Asia (Sau 2003).

8  For recent work on post-Keynesian perspectives on global money and credit, and the link to global growth and development, see Moore (2004). On the need for a global currency see Davidson (2004). On failures and policy potential in the international economy, see Kregal (2006). For international financial innovations for developing nations; and on the need for a single global reserve currency and global reserve bank Arestis et al. (2005).

9  Recent studies that examine standard of living and governance on the basis of divisions of class, ethnicity, and gender include Brennan (2005) on pension reform, Zalewski (2005) on the equity–efficiency tradeoff, and Drydyk (2005) on democratic participation.

10 Recent studies on productive government spending underscore the importance of education, health, infrastructure, and communications (O'Hara 2004); Arestis and Sawyer (2004) on fiscal policy as an important source of demand; and Weber (2000) on the lack of productive government spending in the US causing recent recessions.

11 Modern studies reveal considerable evidence supporting the Chartal Taxes-Drive-Money theory. See Bell et al. (2004) on a debt-based theory of money; and Kadmos and O'Hara (2000) on recent empirical material supporting money finance and budget deficits.

## References

Aglietta, M. (2000) "Shareholder Value and Corporate Governance: Some Tricky Questions," *Economy and Society* 29: 146–159.

Arestis, P. (1988) *Contemporary Issues in Money and Banking: Essays in Honour of Stephen Frowen*. London: Macmillan.

Arestis, P. and Eichner, A. (1988) "The Post-Keynesian and Institutionalist Theory of Money and Credit," *Journal of Economic Issues* 22: 1003–1033.

Arestis, P. and Luintel, K. (2001) "Financial Development and Economic Growth: The Role of Stock Markets," *Journal of Money, Credit, and Banking* 107: 16–41.

Arestis, P. and Sawyer, M. (2004) "On the Effectiveness of Monetary Policy and of Fiscal Policy," *Review of Social Economy* 62: 441–464.

Arestis, P., Basu, S., and Mallick, S. (2005) "Financial Globalization, the Need for a Single Currency and a Global Central Bank," *Journal of Post Keynesian Economics* 27: 507–532.

Bell, S.; Henry, J.F., and Wray, L.R. (2004) "A Chartalist Critique of John Locke's Theory of Property, Accumulation, and Money: Or, Is It Moral to Trade Your Nuts for Gold?," *Review of Social Economy* 62: 51–66.

Binswanger, M. (1999) "Stock Markets, Speculative Bubbles and Economic Growth," *New Dimensions in the Co-evolution of Real and Financial Markets*. Cheltenham, UK: Edward Elgar.
—— (2000) "Stock Returns and Real Activity: Is There Still a Connection?," *Applied Financial Economics* 10: 379–388.
Boyer, R. (2000) "Is a Finance-Led Growth Regime a Viable Alternative to Fordism? A Preliminary Analysis," *Economy and Society* 29: 111–145.
Brennan, D. (2005) "Fiduciary Capitalism," *Review of Radical Political Economics* 37: 39–62.
Bush, P. (2001) "Minimal Disallocation," in P.A. O'Hara (ed.), *Encyclopedia of Political Economy*. London and New York: Routledge, pp. 845–847.
Campbell, M. (1998) "Money in the Circulation of Capital," in C.J. Arthur and G. Reuten (eds.), *The Circulation of Capital: Essays on Volume Two of Marx's Capital*. London: Macmillan.
Coggins, B. (1998) *Does Financial Deregulation Work? A Critique of Free Market Approaches*. Cheltenham, UK: Edward Elgar.
Cypher, J. (1998) "Financial Dominance in the US Economy: The Increased Relevance of Veblen's Analysis in a Post-Keynesian Structure," in S. Fayazmanech and M.R. Tool (eds.), *Institutionalist Theory and Applications: Essays in Honor of Paul Dale Bush*, Vol. 2. Cheltenham, UK: Edward Elgar.
Davidson, P. (2004) "The Future of the International Financial System," *Journal of Post Keynesian Economics* 26: 591–606.
Dillard. D. (1987) "Money as an Institution of Capitalism," *Journal of Economic Issues* 21: 1623–1647.
Drydyk, J. (2005) "When Is Development More Democratic?," *Journal of Human Development* 6: 247–268.
Dymski, G. and Pollin, R. (eds.) (1994) *New Perspectives in Monetary Macroeconomics: Exploration in the Tradition of Hyman P. Minsky*. Ann Arbor: University of Michigan Press.
Fazzari, S. and Papadimitriou, D. (eds.) (1992) *Financial Conditions and Macroeconomic Performance: Essays in Honor of Hyman P. Minsky*. Armonk, NY: M.E. Sharpe.
Grou, P. (1985) *The Financial Structure of International Capitalism*. Heidelberg: Berg Publishers.
Guttman, R. (1994) *How Credit-Money Shapes the Economy: The United States in a Global System*. Armonk, NY: M.E. Sharpe.
—— (2001) "Social Structure of Accumulation: Financial," in P. O'Hara (ed.), *Encyclopedia of Political Economy*, Vol. 2. London: Routledge.
Hannsen, G. (2005) "Minsky's Acceleration Channel and the Role of Money," *Journal of Post Keynesian Economics* 27: 471–487.
Haugen, R.A. (1999) *The New Finance: The Case Against Efficient Markets*. Englewood Cliffs, NJ: Prentice-Hall.
Jessop, B. (ed.) (2001) *Regulation Theory and the Crises of Capitalism*. Cheltenham, UK: Edward Elgar.
Kadmos, G. and O'Hara, P. (2000) "The Taxes-Drive-Money and Employer of Last Resort Approach to Government Policy," *Journal of Economic and Social Policy* 5: 1–22.
Keynes, J.M. (1936) *The General Theory of Employment, Interest and Money*. London: Macmillan.
Kregal, J. (2006) "Can We Create a Stable International Financial Environment that Ensures Net Resource Transfers to Developing Countries?," *Journal of Post Keynesian Economics* 26: 573–590.

Lavoie, M. (1992) *Foundations of Post-Keynesian Economic Analysis*. Aldershot, UK: Edward Elgar.
Levine, D. (1978) *Economic Theory, Volume One: The Elementary Relations of Economic Life*. London: Routledge.
—— (1982) *Economic Theory, Volume Two: The System of Economic Relations as a Whole*. London: Routledge.
Marx, K. (1981) *Capital*, Vol. 3. Harmondsworth: Penguin.
Matutinovic, I. (2005) "The Microeconomics of Business Cycles: From Institutions to Autocatalytic Networks," *Journal of Economic Issues* 39: 867–898.
Minsky, H.P. (1982) *Can "It" Happen Again? Essays on Instability and Finance*. Armonk, NY: M.E. Sharpe.
—— (1986) *Stabilising an Unstable Economy*. New Haven, Conn.: Yale University Press.
Mishkin, F.S. (2001) "The Transmission Mechanism and the Role of Asset Prices in Monetary Policy." NBER Working Paper 8617. New York, National Bureau of Economic Research.
Moore, B. (1988) *Horizontalists and Verticalists: The Macroeconomics of Credit Money*. Cambridge: Cambridge University Press.
Moore, B.J. (2004) "A Global Currency for a Global Economy," *Journal of Post Keynesian Economics* 26: 631–654.
O'Hara, P. (2000) "Money and Credit in Marx's Political Economy and Contemporary Capitalism," *History of Economics Review* 32: 83–95.
—— (2002) "A New Financial Social Structure of Accumulation for Long Wave Upswing in the United States?," *Review of Radical Political Economics* 34: 342–348.
—— (2002a) "The Contemporary Relevance of the Critical Economic Systems Approach to Political Economy in the Tradition of Marx, Veblen, Keynes," *International Journal of Applied Economics and Econometrics* 10: 126–150.
—— (2003) "Recent Changes to the IMF, WTO and FSP: An Emerging Global Money-Trade-Production Social Structure of Accumulation for Long Wave Upswing?," *Review of International Political Economy* 10: 481–519.
—— (2004) "Viability of National Government Policies in a Global Political Economy," in P.A. O'Hara (ed.), *Global Political Economy and the Wealth of Nations: Performance, Institutions, Problems and Policies*. London: Routledge.
—— (2006) *Growth and Development in the Global Political Economy: Social Structures of Accumulation and Modes of Regulation*. London: Routledge.
—— (2008) "Political Economy of the Global Subprime Mortgage Market Crisis." Global Political Economy Research Unit. Working Paper. December.
Palley, T.I. (2004) "Asset-Based Reserve Requirements: Reasserting Domestic Monetary Control in an Era of Financial Innovation and Instability," *Review of Political Economy* 16: 43–58.
Palloix, C. (1975) "The Internationalization of Capital and the Circuit of Social Capital," in H. Radice (ed.), *International Firms and Modern Imperialism*, Harmondsworth: Penguin.
Parguez, A. (2001) "Money without Scarcity: From the Horizontalist Revolution to the Theory of the Monetary Circuit," in L.P. Rochen and Matias Vernengo (eds.), *Credit, Interest Rates and the Open Economy: Essays on Horizontalism*. Cheltenham, UK: Edward Elgar.
Polanyi, K. (1944) *The Great Transformation*. Boston: Beacon Press.
Pollin, R. (1991) "Two Theories of Money Supply Endogeneity: Some Empirical Evidence," *Journal of Post Keynesian Economics* 13: 366–396.

Raines, J.P. and Leathers, C.G. (2000) *Economics and the Stock Market: Speculative Theories of Stock Market Fluctuations.* Cheltenham, UK: Edward Elgar.

Rochon, L.P. (1999) *Credit, Money and Production: An Alternative Post-Keynesian Approach.* Cheltenham, UK: Edward Elgar.

Rochon, L.P. and Vernengo, M. (2001) *Credit, Interest Rates and the Open Economy: Essays on Horizontalism.* Cheltenham, UK: Edward Elgar.

Sau, L. (2003) "Banking, Information and Financial Instability in Asia," *Journal of Post Keynesian Economics* 25: 493–513.

Schulmeister, S. (2000) "Globalization Without Global Money: The Double Role of the Dollar as National Currency and World Currency," *Journal of Post Keynesian Economics* 22: 365–395.

Sherman, H. (2003) "Institutions and the Business Cycle," *Journal of Economic Issues* 37: 621–642.

Stockhammer, E. (2004) "Financialisation and the Slowdown of Accumulation," *Cambridge Journal of Economics* 28: 719–741.

Veblen, T. (1923) *Absentee Ownership and Business Enterprise in Recent Times: The Case of America.* New York: Augustus M. Kelley.

Weber, C.E. (2000) "Government Purchases, Government Transfers, and the Post-1970 Slowdown in U.S. Economic Growth," *Contemporary Economic Policy* 18: 107–123.

Wincoop, E. van and Yi, K.M. (2000) "Asia Crisis Postmortem: Where Did the Money Go and Did the United States Benefit?," *Economic Policy Review* 6: 51–70.

Wolfson, M. (1994a) *Financial Crises: Understanding the Postwar U.S. Experience*, 2nd edn. Armonk, NY: M.E. Sharpe.

—— (1994b) "The Financial System and the Social Structure of Accumulation," in D.M. Kotz, T. McDonough, and M. Reich, *Social Structures of Accumulation: The Political Economy of Growth and Crisis*, Cambridge: Cambridge University Press.

—— (2000) "Neoliberalism and International Financial Instability," *Review of Radical Political Economics* 32: 369–378.

Wray, L.R. (1990) *Money and Credit in Capitalist Economies: The Endogenous Money Approach.* Aldershot, UK: Edward Elgar.

—— (1998) *Understanding Modern Money: The Key to Full Employment and Price Stability.* Cheltenham, UK: Edward Elgar.

—— (2002) "What Happened to Goldilocks? A Minskian Framework," *Journal of Economic Issues* 26: 383–391.

Zalewiski, D. (2005) "Economic Security and the Myth of the Efficiency/Equity Trade-off," *Journal of Economic Issues* 39: 383–390.

Zhu, A., Ash, M., and Pollin, R. (2004) "Stock Market Liquidity and Economic Growth: A Critical Appraisal of the Levine/Zervos Model," *International Review of Applied Economics* 18: 63–71.

# 15 Green economics
## Emerging pedagogy in an emerging discipline

*Miriam Kennet*

Green economics is fast emerging as *the* economics story. The European Business Summit in February 2008 told industry leaders, including leaders of Shell and Lufthansa, that the only hope for the European economy is to go green. In October 2008, green economics made the front cover of *Newsweek*. In the UK, government officials were told that mainstream economics is so fragile that it should be considered radical – and that the only way forward from now on was to use green economics, the only robust methodology. Ban Ki-moon, leader of the United Nations, declared "*we are in an age of global transformation – an age of green economics*" (Dickey and McNicoll 2008).

More and more people are cognizant that human kind is at a crossroads: we can either save or destroy ourselves and the planet. Either way, the choice is ours. Unfortunately, economics has long been out of balance with the environment, and the hegemony of orthodox economics remains a formidable stumbling block: the two are on a collision course (Anderson 1999). If disaster is to be avoided, they have to become mutually compatible – the voice of the earth has to be heard.

Voice comes through diversity, but at present we only have, thanks again to the hegemony of orthodoxy, "monocultures of the mind" which alienate people by precluding other voices from being heard, in turn depleting the strength of the whole. Green economics, on the other hand, has a strong subjective element and is more concerned with life narratives and outcomes than theoretical prescriptions, monoculture or grand narratives. It respects and empowers diversity and other voices. Green economics combines earth voices, green issues, and a practical, real approach characterized by fairness and respect for the environment; it is economics with access for all.

Green economics is by its nature multi-, inter-, and trans-disciplinary:

> We build on ideas of ecologism, conservation, socialism, feminism, political economy, civil society and counter hegemony, as well as all aspects and limits of natural science. These areas are indivisible – not one of them can be simply a social or positivist science. They are an indivisible unit, which must now be explored in a holistic manner.
>
> (Kennet and Heinemann 2006a: 3)

This chapter is the first attempt to discuss the challenges of teaching green economics. Green economics is interactive – it is economics by doing. The *means* are as important as the *ends* and the ends are as important as the means, so, for example, achieving an equitable distribution of resources without including women or minorities in the decision-making process contravenes the modus operandi of green economics, which includes diversity of methodology and of practitioners within its core. Green economics does not impose one system on the world; we work and create the spaces to allow diversity to flourish.

This chapter will first discuss the core concepts and principles of green economics. The principles of green economics, including the all-important dictum that the means are inseparable from the ends, provides a recipe for teaching: trans-disciplinary, providing access for all. Teaching pluralistically is intrinsic to green economics and completely congruent and intertwined with its main principles.

## The core principles of green economics

The core challenge for green economics is that rather than imposing a grand narrative we must ensure economic systems meet minimum requirements for social and environmental justice while also incorporating local needs. Unlike traditional economics, which filters out awkward elements as externalities, green economics recognizes the ultimate interdependence of economic justice and the environment.

Three main objectives of green economics are:

1 to create economic conditions where social and environmental justice thrives, benefiting all people everywhere, along with non-human species, nature and the planet;
2 to re-examine new and broader versions of reality, beyond vested interests, to listen to different voices. Green economics jettisons ceteris paribus as a limitation of scope and rejects "rational economic man" as a benchmark; instead listening and incorporating the voices of all;
3 to establish new thinking in order to provide the means for all people everywhere to participate in the economy with equal power, equal rights, and equal access to decision making. Green economics provides "out of the box" thinking while combining trans- and inter-disciplinary studies to counteract the myopic thinking of orthodoxy. "The world needs a new economics more than it needs a new anything else" (Anderson 1999: 6). Green economics requires that economic models reflect the complexity of the real world; it does not tolerate simplistic economics, which factors out the facts.

The key to uniting the three objectives is factoring nature and people back into economic theory. Just when people assumed they had completely tamed nature, climate change has forced rethinking of our position in the universe and our role as stewards of the earth. Rather than use science to control nature, we need to use our knowledge to live within nature and respect it. Green economics argues that nature has its own intrinsic value, which it extends to animals (Singer 1985). Green economics extends this to all life forms. Arne Naess (1973) argued for the preservation of the biosphere, geological and biological systems, and all life forms for their own sake, not only for human benefit. Green economics is highly critical of anthropocentric ethics and the "shallow anthropocentric technocratic environmental movement," concerned primarily with pollution, resource depletion, and the health and affluence of people in developed countries (Sessions 1995: xii).

Since its inception, orthodoxy has assumed nature as an expendable and plentiful given resource, while only valuing scarce resources. It is, however, palpable that nature and the economy are mutually dependent, with the former becoming more fragile and scarce. Georgescu-Roegen (1966) highlighted the continuous mutual influence between economic processes and the natural world, long ignored by orthodoxy. In addition, White (1967) criticized Western attitudes to nature and attributed them to the influence of Christianity on the development of technology and assumption of human mastery through the taming of the natural world. He argued that Christianity has desacralized nature, encouraged its exploitation, and promoted a world view in which humans are superior to the rest of nature.

In order to address these topics and revisions, new and critical ways of thinking are needed that include questioning the scope and meanings of economics, facts, evidence, and reality in positivist economics, as well as so-called rational and reasonable choices. Green economics welcomes the insights from sister social sciences (Kennet and Heinemann 2006b) as well as Eastern spiritual traditions of questioning the assumed virtues of competition rather than cooperation, and exploitation rather than engagement and reciprocity.

Kennet (2007) argues that reciprocity arose from sharing of meat and is strongest in capuchin monkeys, chimpanzees, and people. Confucius, asked if there was a single word to sum one's life, responded, "reciprocity: don't do to others what you would not want yourself" (Kennet 2007 and Guenter-Wagner 2007). Aristotle argued that reciprocity may not be adequate to account for corrective and distributive justice; thus we need to introduce an exchange bond and exchange justice which provides and governs reciprocity (Meikle 1995: 10).

Thus, in reconceptualizing "value," we need further to consider how each individual decision based on value would be assessed in the light of absolute boundaries to consumption that might be imposed by ecological restrictions to human activity.

Despite and probably because of the popularity of green economics, our message has been usurped and distorted for myriads of reasons. Sometimes, what passes for green is more greenwashing – passed off as green but without merit, existing for contrarian purposes. It is easier to comprehend the confusing array of policy outcomes when they are viewed as a continuum.

Central is the ambivalent relationship between green economics and the multi-faceted and multi-layered term "sustainable development," defined by Brundtland (1987) as meeting "the needs of the present without sacrificing the ability of the future to meet its standards." The approach argues for a more enlightened globalization to reach these standards and to resolve environmental degradation. Sustainable development has been eagerly adopted by such groups as the World Business Council of Sustainable Development and it nicely comports with Corporate Social Responsibility and stakeholder theory. Acknowledging that many nation states are weaker than global corporations, sustainable development argues for the corporation to be the agent of change.

In contrast, many green economists regard corporations as agents of hegemony; and as undemocratic, unelected, lacking in transparency, and the fundamental cause of the problem. Green economics seriously questions how it can be in a corporation's short-term interest to implement equity and environmental justice through the managerial "environmentalist" approach of sustainable development. Dobson (2000) and Springett and Foster (2005) criticize short-term techno fixes which on the one hand remain within the confines of traditional economics and, on the other, hijack environmentalism and the language of "sustainability" (Welford and Gouldson 1993).

Sustainable development is regarded by green economists as an oxymoron, often in reality counteracting existing community economic patterns. Greens instead seek to reverse the trends of neo-colonialism and corporate destruction of local assets, replacing them with new subsistence, local self-determination and community control (Norberge-Hodge 1991; Mies and Shiva 1993). In addition, gigantism, monopoly, and oligopoly contravene green economics arguments for "small, appropriate and diverse production" developed by Schumacher (1976), Hines (2000), Woodin and Lucas (2004).

Nevertheless, given the inexorable complexity of the environmental crisis, there is a growing realization within the business world that business as usual is no longer a choice An ongoing task among green economists is to analyze the growing, complex, and multi-faceted role of the corporation (Reardon 2007b). Needless to say, the nineteenth-century orthodox firm, assumed to maximize profits and externalize any environmental concerns, must be replaced by a more realistic humane and benevolent model.

Pertaining to policy, the UN version of greening the economy focuses on the three Fs: fuel, food, and the financial crisis. Just as Roosevelt's New Deal set the stage for the biggest economic growth the world has seen, green economics argues today for a similar vision except that new growth must be structured to benefit all people, nature and the planet. Rather than jump-start consumption to aid an ailing economy, however, green economics seeks conversion to greener technologies to enable greener lifestyles so we can live within our means and that of the planet. Accelerating this transition is at the core of the green economy initiative and is the best bet for global sustainable wealth and employment generation for the world's 1.5 billion poor.

A formidable barrier to this transition is the myopic vision of traditional economics, which has been instrumental in the commodification of nature and perpetuation of poverty. Central to green economics is the incorporation of knowledge from other disciplines, particularly the sciences, which helps to circumscribe the forms and extent of economic activity within realistic environmental parameters.

Postmodern ideas are absent from traditional economics and from a green perspective this misses important developments in human thought. In particular, the prevalence of the Western-dominated, white, middle-class, "homo economicus" ignores the experience of most of the world's people. Derrida (1978) rejects single narratives and investigates whether reality is fact, truth, myth, interpretation, or one person's view of events. Derrida analyzes binary oppositions and dualisms such as West and East, feminine and masculine, light and dark, civilized and primitive, them and us, to criticize the power structures in which they are embedded.

## Green economics and pedagogy

I tend to think of green economics as a slippery eel – if you catch it and think you have understood its imperatives, something else arises and you need to conceptualize more deeply or in another dimension in order to capture its meaning. Green economics continues to evolve, provoke, and question. So how to teach this evolving slippery eel? Perhaps it is best to reflect on what it is trying to achieve, which is interaction, responsibility, and accessibility. This suggests that its classroom and lecture hall are very different places from the usual conventional lecture as solution provider. Green economics looks for a new mode of enablement and empowerment as well as a two-way process.

The ambitious aims of green economics to start a new discipline and to change the paradigm of economics to one which creates social and environmental equity means taking the practice of economics beyond the classroom, i.e. making it economics by doing. This means more instruction on site, which differentiates green economics from its sister social sciences. Green economics is holistic, pluralist, and progressive; thus its pedagogy has to reflect its nature. This is one discipline which cannot be amended to the usual macro/micro stuff with a small portion of the lesson looking at the costs of energy. Green economics is different and its foundational concepts are different and this must be reflected in the entire approach of teachers, trainers, and lecturers.

A rewarding aspect of green economics is that because it supports diversity and means/ends approaches, it is not country specific. Thus, teaching green economics has to appeal to all kinds of cultures.

Should we equip a new generation of students to learn only the reformed version of greener economics or should we teach our students enough about the mainstream to enable them to cogently critique it? I feel it is important to map previous developments in economics, especially those concerned with nature and social equity, and to provide students with enough knowledge to enable them to understand and respect differences between schools of thought and their foundations, development and modus operandi. This is especially necessary in order to provide students with the tools to begin investigation of newly evolving issue for themselves.

Green economics is equally relevant to the very young and the very old, so the Green Economics Institute has been experimenting with teaching the very young and very old together, as the enforced separation of one group has been a disabling factor, similar to segregating different racial groups.

In summation, based on the discussion of the core principles of green economics, the following are central elements in the pedagogy of green economics:

1  Incorporate scientific evidence on the environment and how it adapts and changes. This can easily be incorporated into the circular flow diagram usually given on opening day (Reardon 2007a). Throughout the course, additional scientific data can be incorporated, particularly regarding interest rates, externalities, economies of scale, public goods, and the role of government. This will teach students that no one discipline has a unique solution to global problems, and the necessity for pluralist, integrated thinking. Not to do so is to proselytize, which contravenes not only the principles of green economics, but the objective of this book.
2  Continuously discuss the value-laden concepts of economics, such as freedom, the market, externalities, etc. Is, for example, reliance on the continuous, competitive pressure of the market to force people to behave in a certain way antithetical to the classical economists' demand for more freedom from an obtrusive state? Whether markets enable or disengage and whether markets are congruent with the environmental demands is fundamental to green economics.
3  Understand the historical evolution of economics, particularly the visions of classical economics and how they sharply differ from traditional economics, which jettisoned political and social concerns in favor of an ostensibly neutral, scientific and value-free economics (Dowd 2004). I place economic theories and concepts in their intellectual and historical background, discussing all available information about the economists – their backgrounds, their looks and hairstyles, etc. This provides a vivid, lively, personal account, previously discouraged as hearsay, but which nevertheless elucidates how and why a theory/concept was developed.
4  Emphasize students as the greatest ambassadors for our ideas. As teachers, we should regard each learning experience as a moment in the learning chain which extends into the past and hopefully well into the future, to be handed down like the verbal stories of the ancient world.
5  Teachers must engage in outreach – speaking/lecturing in nonacademic settings – as well as in inreach – inviting others to participate in class. If you are passionate about your subject (especially given a rapidly dwindling window of opportunity), in addition to lecturing to traditional students it is incumbent to lecture and teach to potential students, idea makers, policy makers, and activists. My most successful courses are those where former students continue their presence in my life and teaching, where former student and teacher continuously learn from each other. Teaching green economics breaks past assumptions and conceptions of the world. The next generation is witnessing real climate change, species extinction, and festering poverty and inequality. We can no longer assume all problems will be

solved by technology and economic growth; but we need a more realistic assessment of human capabilities and the mutual dependency between humans and the environment. And we can no longer assume that the teacher has all the answers; any solutions will be forged in a continuous and ongoing dialogue.
6   We must listen to other voices, from the South, from special needs, voices of older people, younger people, voices of women, and the economically disenfranchised, and engage with them in both outreach and inreach. We need to provision in a more precarious world. We as teachers have to pave (rather than lead) the way forward.

## Conclusion

These ideas describe the learning landscape possible within the new paradigm of green economics. They set the scene for the development of a new way of doing economics. While the roots of green economics are extremely eclectic and diverse, its scope is truly global, its methods innovative and its context long term and holistic. It aims to reestablish true "planetary equilibrium" between individuals, peoples, communities, nations, genders, and nonhuman species and the planet. As civilization enters a new phase, the need for innovation in economics education and the requirement for innovative and engaging teaching is paramount. Teaching green economics goes beyond the classroom and into the real economy and into the real world. This might be the muddy field the impromptu gathering, the protest camp, the government, or the UN.

## References

Anderson, V. (1999) "Can There Be a Sensible Economics?," in S. Cato and M. Kennet (eds) *Green Economics – Beyond Supply and Demand to Meeting People's Needs*. Aberystwyth, UK: Green Audit Press.

Brundtland, G.H. (1987) *Our Common Future: World Commission on Environment and Development*. Available online at http://www.un-documents.net/wced-ocf.htm.

Derrida, J. (1978) *Writing and Difference*. Chicago: University of Chicago Press.

Dickey, C and McNicoll, T. (2008) "The Green Rescue," *Newsweek*, November 3, www.newsweek.com.

Dobson, A. (2000) *Green Political Thought*. Abingdon, UK: Routledge.

Dowd, Douglas (2004) *Capitalism and Its Economics – A Critical History*. London: Pluto Press.

Georgescu-Roegen, N. (1966) "The Entropy Law and the Economic Problem," in H.E. Daly and K. Townsend (eds) *Valuing the Earth: Economics, Ecology, Ethics*. Cambridge, Mass.: MIT Press.

Goldsmith, E. (2005) *Rewriting Economics*, www. greeneconomics.org.uk (accessed January 17, 2006).

Guenter, W.H. (2007) "Buddhist Economics – Ancient Teachings Revisted," *International Journal of Green Economics* 1: 326–340.

Kennet, M. and Heinemann, V. (2006a) "Foreword," *International Journal of Green Economics* 1: 1–10.
—— (2006b) "Green Economics: Setting the Scene," *International Journal of Green Economics* 1: 68–102.
Meikle, Scott (1995) *Aristotle's Economic Thought*. New York: Oxford University Press.
Mies, M. and Shiva, V. (1993) *Ecofeminism*. London: Zed Books.
Naess, A. (1973) "The Shallow and the Deep, Long-Range Ecology Movement," *Inquiry* 16: 95–100.
Norberge-Hodge, H. (1991) *Ancient Futures Learning from Ladakh*. San Francisco: Sierra Club Books.
Reardon, J. (2007a) "How Green Are Principles Texts? An Investigation Into How Mainstream Economics Educates Students Pertaining to Energy, the Environment and Green Economics," *International Journal of Green Economics* 1: 381–393.
—— (2007b) "Comments on Green Economics Setting the Scene," *International Journal of Green Economics* 1: 532–538.
Sessions, G. (1995) *Deep Ecology for the 21st Century*. Boston: Shambhala.
Schumacher, E.F. (1976) *Small is Beautiful*. London: Sphere Press.
Singer, Peter (1985) The Animal Liberation Movement: Its Philosophy, Achievements, and Its Future. Abingdon, UK: Routledge.
Springett, D. and Foster, B. (2005) "Whom Is Sustainable Development for? Deliberative Democracy and the Role of Unions," *Sustainable Development* 13: 271–281.
Wall, D. (2005) *Babylon and Beyond*. London: Pluto Press.
Welford, R. and Gouldson, A. (1993) *Environmental Management and Business Strategy*. London: Pitman.
White, L. (1967) "The Historical Roots of our Ecological Crisis," *Science* 155: 1203–1207.

# Part V
# Conclusion

# 16 Conclusion

*Jack Reardon*

Education is our most important function as human beings: it is an investment in ourselves, future generations, and the planet. The ultimate objective of this book is to improve economic education by fostering and creating pluralism.

The increased interdependencies of today's problems has changed the responsibility and goals of education, as Weehuizen explains:

> The main responsibility of education is no longer the mere transmission of some existing stock of knowledge, but rather training students in dealing with new knowledge in a meaningful way. Since we neither know what kind of knowledge will be available in the future, nor what kind of problems students will face ... transmission of knowledge has been reduced from being the main function of education to merely being a part of it. Students have to learn how to learn.
>
> (Weehuizen 2007: 178)

The chapters in this volume represent a well-articulated and enthusiastic agenda to incorporate pluralism into the classroom. Several themes emerge. One, pluralism enables students to understand that other views have a legitimate right to exist. Each view has its strengths and weaknesses. No view is completely efficacious or without limitation. Some views, however, are more efficacious in certain situations, such as post-Keynesian for macro and international economics, ecological and institutional for environmental economics, and institutional for labor economics.

Second, pluralism, by teaching respect for different views, educates and enables. Pluralism instills empathy, dialogue, humility, and understanding. Monism, by filtering out different views, prevents one from knowing which view is better in certain situations. Monism is antithetical to pluralism and antithetical to education. It proselytizes rather than educates. If monism discusses alternatives, it is usually to show the superiority of its own approach. Public policy benefits from a healthy pluralist debate. Pluralism enables student choice, monism constrains and disables.

Third, pluralism endorses the study of the history of thought as a repository of ideas and instructive advice. Rather than dismiss history as antiquarian, pluralism embraces the richness of economic thought. Pluralism is not teleological; rather, theory informs practice, which generates debate, which in turn influences theory. The repository of pluralism thus mirrors the history of economic thought – a wealth of fruitful ideas to be mined, if one knows how to look.

Fourth, pluralism elucidates the existence and effects of power in market systems. Role playing games are especially useful. Pluralism easily lends itself to active learning, and active learning, in turn, is intrinsic to pluralism.

Finally, pluralism is intrinsically more interesting. Students are more engaged and energized by pluralism, which itself leads to discussion, questioning and thinking – the essence of education.

Hopefully this book will recharge economic education so that economics can solve our more pressing problems. As pluralism gains currency, there is a continuing need to identify and discuss its theoretical elements. A central problem, for example, is the trade-off between specialization and generalized knowledge. A true pluralist would argue for a judicious mix of specialists and generalists able to work together.

Economics is exciting and, like a good novel, economic education should "hook the student [and] captivate and compel with arresting interest that fosters lifetime learning" (Reardon 2004: 841). We hope the pluralist methods outlined in this book will help "bring life back into economics" (Groenewegen 2007: 13). To paraphrase C.P. Snow, "there is no excuse for letting another generation be as vastly ignorant" (1998: 61).

## References

Groenewegen, J. (2007) "On Pluralism and Interdisciplinarity in Economics," in J. Groenewegen (ed.) *Teaching Pluralism in Economics*, Cheltenham, UK: Edward Elgar.

Reardon, Jack (2004) "Suggestions to Effectuate a Multi-paradigmatic Approach to the Teaching of Principles of Economics," *Journal of Economic Issues* 38: 839–841.

Snow, C.P. (1998) *The Two Cultures*, Cambridge: Cambridge University Press.

Weehuizen, Rifka (2007) "Interdisciplinarity and Problem-based Learning in Economics Education: The Case of Infonomics," in J. Groenewegen (ed.) *Teaching Pluralism in Economics*, Cheltenham, UK: Edward Elgar.

# Author index

Ackerman, F. 60, 61, 65n3
Aglietta, M. 210, 237
Akyuz, Y. 219
Albelda R. 176
Allen, B. 44
Anderson, V. 256, 257
Arestis, P. 231, 252n10
Aristotle 258
Arrighi, G. 200
Arrow, K. 34
Ash, M. 252n6
Axtell, R. 147n13

Bacon, F. 3
Barbier, E. 194
Basu, S. 252n8
Bebbington, J. 194
Becker, G. 32, 176
Bell, S. 252n11
Belluzzo, L. 211
Bénicourt, E. 34, 36
Berlinski, D. 12
Bethune, J. 179n2
Binswager, M. 237, 252n6
Blinder, A. 81, 134
Bober, S. 59
Boland, L. 71
Borjas, G. 175, 176, 177, 178, 179n1
Bouchaud, J. 22
Bowles S. 6, 8, 12, 13, 59
Boyer, R. 237
Braun, M. 163
Brennan, D. 252n9
Brown, J. 183, 194
Brue, S. 177, 179n1
Bush, P. 239

Caldwell, B. 44
Campbell, M. 251n1
Campilongo, C. 221

Carlton, D. 36
Carson, R. 65n1
Case, K. 10
Champlin, D. 13, 177
Chesnais, F. 220
Chick, V. 45, 50, 52n6
Chua, A. 13
Clark, J. 175
Coats, J. 47
Cobb, J. 185, 189
Coggins, B. 244
Cohn, E. 71
Colander, D. 71
Commons, J. 40n2, 174
Confucius 258
Connolly, W. 182
Costanza, R. 196
Cournot, A. 41
Coyle, B. 6, 34, 44, 52n4
Cumberland, J. 196
Cypher, J. 236

Daly, H. 96, 181, 185, 189
Davidson, P. 252n8
Davis, J. 15n4, 44, 47, 49
Debreu, G. 44
DeMartino, G. 105
Derrida, J. 260
Dewey, J. 21
Dobson, A. 259
Dow, S. 5, 10, 44, 45
Dowd, D. 10, 12
Downward, P. 50, 147n15
Drago, R. 176
Drydyk, J. 252n9
Dubner, S. 26
Dymski, G. 239

Edwards, M. 6, 8, 12, 13, 59
Eichengreen, B. 200–1

Eiteman, W. 136
Enhrenberg, R. 172, 179n1
Etzioni, A. 189

Fair, R. 10
Farjoun, E. 140
Fazzari, S. 239
Ferber, M. 64
Fireside, D. 65n1
Fischer, S. 222
Fligstein, N. 225
Ford, D. 188
Forrester, J. 71
Forrester, N. 71
Frame, B. 183, 194
Frank, R. 65
Freeman, E. 185
Frey, B. 96
Friedman, M. 30, 70, 121, 122, 125, 134, 210
Friedman, T. 14
Fullbrook, E. 8, 9, 60
Funtowicz, S. 183

Galbraith, J. 17, 52n4, 188
Garnett, R. 5, 60
Gee, D. 183
Georgescu-Roegen, N. 258
Gilovich, T. 65n3
Gilpin, R. 199, 213, 216
Gingras, Y. 21
Glickman, L. 175
Goncalves, J. 14
Goodland, R. 196
Goodwin, N. 60, 61, 65n2
Goodwin, R. 154
Gorman, W. 120, 128
Gouldson, A. 259
Grabel, I. 222
Graziania, A. 156, 166n7
Green, J. 37
Greenwald, D. 201, 205, 207, 211, 213, 221
Griffith-Jones, S. 222
Groenewegen, J. 8, 46, 60, 268
Grou, P. 242
Guenter, W. 258
Guerrien, B. 9, 34, 36
Guttman, R. 241

Hahnel, R. 59
Hajer, M. 182
Hall, R. 194
Hampden-Turner, C. 70

Hargreaves, H. 193
Harremoes, P. 183
Harvie, D. 165
Hayden, F. 70
Heap, S. 193
Hecht, J. 65n1
Henry, J. 252n11
Hermann, A. 6, 7
Hobsbawm, E. 211, 215, 221, 226
Hodgson, G. 5
Hogben, L. 21
Holcombe, R. 6, 14n4
Hong, H. 51n3
Hotchkiss, J. 179n3
Howarth, R. 181
Hume, D. 49
Hurwicz, L. 41n15

Jallais, S. 9
Jansson, A. 181
Jessop, B. 232
Jevons, S. 21
Just, W. 166n5

Kadmos, G. 252n11
Kahneman, D. 51n3
Kalecki, M. 140
Kaufmann, B. 179n3
Keen, S. 2, 69, 120, 146, 147n7, 147n8, 147n12, 147n16, 151, 155
Kennet, M. 15, 256
Keynes, J. 47, 94, 99, 155, 219–20, 233, 236, 251n3, 252n4
Ki-Moon, B. 256
Kindleberger, C. 205
Kirman, A. 40n4, 129
Klaes, M. 48, 49
Klamer, A. 52n5
Knoedler, J. 59
Korten, D. 186
Kotler, P. 187
Kregal, J. 252n8
Kreps, D. 33, 37, 39, 40
Kriesler, P. 140
Krugman, P. 52n4, 204
Kuhn, T. 45
Kunstler, H. 4

Lavoie, M. 230
Lawson, T. 45, 150–5, 165n1, 166n4
Layard, R. 61
Leathers, C. 238
Leclaire, J. 69
Lee, F. xiv, 134, 140, 147n15

Levine, D. 251
Levitt, S. 26
Lotka, A. 154
Luxemburg, R. 202

McCloskey, D. 46, 47
McConnell, C. 177, 179
MacGarvin, M. 183
McGoldrick, K. 64
Machover, M. 148
Macpherson, D. 177, 179
Madi, M. 14
Madisson, A. 207, 209
Mallick, S. 252n8
Mankiw, G. 9, 17–22, 26, 40n3, 172
Markandya, A. 194
Marshall, A. 4, 10, 70, 121, 132
Marx, K. 94, 153, 154, 155 156, 158, 159, 174, 233, 236, 251n3, 252n4
Mas-Colell, A. 37
Maskin, D. 41n15
Mass, N. 71
Mattos, P. 221
Matutinovic, I. 252n4
Mazzaferro, F. 219
Mearman, A. 15n3, 50, 51, 59
Meis, M. 259
Melin, L. 220
Mill, J. 40, 41n18
Miller, J. 65n1
Minsky, H. 211, 218, 225, 237, 238
Mishkin, F. 231, 243
Mitchell, W. 252n4
Moore, B. 252n5
Morgan, G. 193
Morgan, M. 48
Morgenstern, O. 193
Myerson, R. 41n15
Myrdal, G. 183

Naess, A. 258
Nelson, J. 10, 64, 65n5, 171
Nerlich, C. 219
Norberge-Hodge, H. 263
Norgaard, R. 181, 196

O'Hara, P. 14, 231, 236, 237, 241, 243, 244, 247, 251n2, 252n11
Obstfeld, M. 204
Ormerod, P. 139

Palley, T. 252
Palloix, C. 231
Papadimitriou, D. 239

Parguez, A. 251n1
Pearce, D. 194
Peters, B. 184
Pierre, J. 184
Polanyi, K. 239
Pollin, R. 239, 252n5
Porter, M. 139
Prasch, R. 179
Pringle, D. 69

Radzicki, M. 71
Raines, J. 238
Rao, S. 65n1
Ravetz, J. 183
Reardon, J. 5, 259, 261, 268
Regan, D. 65n3
Ricardo, D. 202, 203
Riccardi, N. 178
Richardson, G. 71
Riddell, T. 59
Robbins, L. 18, 21
Rochon, L. 156, 251n1
Rodrik, D. 105
Rojas-Soarez, L. 215
Roosevelt, F. 6, 8, 12, 13, 59
Rosput, P. 147
Rossini, R. 51n2
Rubinstein, A. 38
Rugman, A. 213
Rutherford, M. 48

Samuelson, P. 26, 48
Sandri, G. 51n2
Sau, L. 252n7
Sawyer, S. 250
Scazzieri, R. 51n2
Schaffernicht, M. 88n13
Schneider, G. 59
Schulmeister, S. 242
Schuster, H. 166n5
Schumpeter, J. 133, 138, 147, 206–7, 233, 236, 252n4
Screpanti, E. 46
Sen, A. 5, 95
Shackelford, J. 59
Shafer, W. 120, 128
Shearman, D. 4
Sherman, H. 251n4
Shiva, V. 259
Shulman, S. 176
Silver, B. 200
Singer, P. 258
Sippel, R. 136
Skinner, Q. 49

Sloman, J. 119
Smith, A. 49, 94, 174
Smith, J. 4
Smith, R. 172, 179
Sneddon, C. 181
Snow, C. 268
Snyder, B. 65n1
Soderbaum, P. 13, 20, 182, 184, 194, 196
Sofia, G. 183
Sonnenschein, H. 120, 128
Sraffa, P. 135
Stamos, S. 59
Standish, M. 120, 147n7, 147n8
Staveren, I. 11
Steedman, I. 140
Stein, J. 51n3
Sterman, J. 88n9
Stern, N. 195
Stigler, G. 124, 147n5
Stiglitz, J. 35, 38, 231
Stirling, J. 183
Stockhammer, E. 237, 252n6
Stretton, H. 20
Stutzer, A. 96
Sunstein, C. 194

Tavares, M. 220
Thomas, W. 65n1
Tinbergen, J. 72
Triffin, R. 207
Trompenaars, A. 70
Turner, R. 194
Underwood, D. 59

Vant, A. 5, 14, 33
Varian, H. 41n17, 128, 129, 130, 136
Varoufakis, Y. xiv, 193
Veblen, T. 40, 185, 233, 236, 251n3
Veiga, J. 221
Verbeke, A. 213
Vernengo, M. 235
Volterra, V. 154
Vromen, J. 5, 10, 15n4, 44

Wallersten, I. 200
Walras, L. 21, 40n5
Walsh, C. 35
Weber, C. 252n10
Weehuizen, R. 6, 268
Weintraub, E. 49
Weisskopf, T. 60, 61, 65n2
Welford, R. 259
Wheat, D. 11, 71, 74, 88n11
Whinston, M. 37
Wiens-Tuers, B. 13
Wincoop, E. 243
Winkler, A. 219
Wolfson, M. 238, 241, 251n2
Wray, R. 252n11
Wynne, B. 183

Yi, K. 243

Zadek, S. 182
Zaleweski, D. 252n9
Zeigert, A. 64
Zhu, A. 252n6

# Subject index

absolute advantage 189
adverse selection 41n14
*Affluent Society* 52n4
Africa 108–9
*An Essay on the Nature and Significance of Economic Science* 18
Asian crisis (1997) 99, 242, 243
astronomy 45
asymmetric information 38, 231
Austrian economics 57

balance of payments 201
Bank of England 50
Bank of Japan 210
behavioral economics 136
biology 46
Brazil 106
Bretton Woods 207, 209, 210
Brundtland Report 183, 259
business cycle 104, 234–5

calculus 12
*Capital* 174
capital controls 200, 207
Central Bank of Germany 210
Chile 102
China 102, 106, 108, 211, *212*, 224
circuit of money capital 231–3
circuit school 155
circuitist model 155–8, 165
closed system 5–6, 47, 50, 100
comparative advantage 189, 244
competing paradigms 59
*Competitive Advantage of Nations* 138
complex models 152
cost benefit analysis: compared to positional analysis 190; weaknesses of 194
Cournot duopoly 36
critical realism 57, 150, 165

currency convertibility 221

demand, law of 34–5
democracy: dialogue 190
Deutsches Insitutue fur Wirtdschasftdforgor 181
development 182
differential equations: example of 157; explained 162–3
diminishing returns 62
discrimination 176
disequilibrium: correction of 221; evolution in U.S. economy 215–17

Easterlin paradox 96
Ecolab 155
Economic Commission for Latin America and the Caribbean 226
economic liberalization 211
*Economics: A New Introduction* 20
economics: definition 30; education 20, 25, 29, 261, 267; methodology 44–7; restructuring 4; time, importance of 69–71
econphysics 140
Edgeworth diagram 41n16
education: importance of trust 18; *see also* pedagogy
effective demand 242–3
efficiency: normative concept 19, 20
endogenous change 100
endogenous growth 104
Engel curve 128–9
environment 100–1
environmental economics 29–30, 194
environmental impact assessment 186, 194
European Central Bank 50
environmental management systems 186
Euro 217

## 274  Subject index

European Central Bank 217
European Monetary Union 108
European Union 98, 103, 106, 108, 217
exchange rate 201
export specialization of Latin America 211

Federal Reserve System 210
feminist economics 57, 96–7, 175
finance and socio-economic development 244–6
financial and social structures of accumulation 239–41
financial crisis (1929) 99
financial crisis (2008): discussion and chronology 17, 223–4, 237, 238; explanation of 217–18
financial instability hypothesis 104, 237–9
financial integration 223
financialization effect on global economy 215–27
*Freakonomics* 26

game theory 37, 41, 140–2, 193
Gender Empowerment Index 96
Gender-Related Human Development Index 96
global currency 242
global debt 218
global importers *212*
global political economy: defined 199; evolution of 200–14; under British hegemony 200–5; under American hegemony 205–14
globalization 105–7
gold standard 201
Goodwin model 155, 159, 165
Great Depression 63
green economics: core principles 257–60; importance of 14–15; Institute of 260–1; pedagogy 260–2; view of corporations 259
Gross Domestic Product (GDP) 26, 93, 95, 166
Group of Twenty 222

*Handbook of Mathematical Economics* 128
Hecksher–Ohlin–Samuelson Model 204
hedge finance 238
herd behavior 98–9, 104
heterodox *see* political economy
human capital theory 176
Human Development Index 95

immigration 178
imperfect competition 36
imperialism 202
India 211, *212*, 224
industry–finance contradiction 236–7
institutional change 186, 187
institutional economics 57, 171, 174, 175, 186, 187, 188, 189, 230, 233, 239, 267
*Institutional Economics and Psychoanalysis* 6
institutions 97–8, 239, 241
Inter-American Development Bank 226
*Intermediate Microeconomics* 128
International Clearing Union 219
International Confederation of Associations for Pluralism in Economics xiv
International Council on Systems Engineering 162
International Monetary Fund 99, 102, 104, 109, 201, 219, 244
International Society for Ecological Economics 181
international trade: Ricardian model 203–4; theory of 200
Ireland 108
*ithink* 159

Kaldorian dynamics of money and credit *243*
Kansas City Proposal 69
Keynesian economics 208
Keynesian macroeconomics 63, 130
knowledge: development of 46

labor economics: textbooks 179n1
labor markets 177
logical positivism 44
London Stock Exchange 218
long wave economic cycles 240–1
Lorenz model 152, 155, 164
Lotka-Volterra predator prey model 159–61

*Macrolab* 73, 87n3
mainstream economics *see* traditional economics
marginal productivity theory 175
Marshall Plan 207
Marxist economics 29, 104, 105, 175
*Mathcad* 159
*Mathematica* 159
*Mathlab* 159
Mercosur 109

Subject index 275

Mexico 212
*Microeconomic Theory* 41n17
monetary flow 190
monetary policy 215
monetary theory of production 231–3
monism 5, 6, 43, 267
Monterrey Consensus 220
moral hazard 41n14, 104
mortgage-backed bonds 241
multinational firms 213

nature 257–9
neo-Marxian perspective on money 230, 231, 233, 239
neoliberalism 211, 224, 226, 236
neoplatonist theory of truth 18
*NetLogo* 159, 160, 161, 162
New Keynesian perspective 225
New York Stock Exchange 218
non-linear dynamic systems 155
non-monetary flow 190, 193
non-monetary positions 190, 193

*On The Principles of Political Economy and Taxation* 202–3
open system of reality 5–6, 50,100
orthodox economics *see* traditional economics

path dependence 34, 41n8, 192
Pax Britannica 200
pedagogy: alternative approaches to teaching principles 59–60; alternatives to the theory of the firm 28–9; case studies 29–30; definition of labor 174; dynamics, teaching of 69; feedback method 69, 71 – 83; globalization 106–7; incorporating green economics 261–2; incorporating Starpower 130–2; incorporating time 74–84; integrating history of economic thought 50–1; international trade 200, 205, 221, 224, 227; market simulation 143–6; macroeconomics 109–16; money, credit and finance 230–48; paradigmatic approach 60, 171; principles of macroeconomics 63–4; principles of microeconomics 62–3; role-playing 110–16, 268; simulation modeling 84–6; use of math 151–8; writing skills 64; *see also Principles of Economics*
perfect competition 33–4
pluralism: approach to knowledge 50; benefits of 4, 267–8; contrast with monism 43; definition 5; feedback method 71–4; history of economic thought 43, 48–50, 150, 267; levels of 6, 45; origins 49; methodology of 47; macroeconomic policy 108–9; need for 7; power, acknowledgement of 268
pluralist: agency 98–9; alternative to GDP 95–7; international political economy 199–227; microeconomics 121–6; monetary policy 49–51, 248; trade 244
political economic organization 185, 186
political economic person 184, 185, 186
political economy: analytical methods 158–62; assumptions 173; definition 8; endogenous money and credit 233–5; goals of 244; global money 241; importance of investment 245; perspectives on money 230; poverty, view of 102; relation to heterodoxy 8; role of mathematics 151–8; role of money in social relations 107–8
Ponzi finance 239
positional analysis 186, 190, 194
Post-Autistic Economics Movement 3, 50
Post-Crash economist: eleven ways to think like 23
Post-Keynesian economics 57, 104–5, 107, 230, 231, 233, 239, 242, 267
*Post-Keynesian Price Theory* 136
poverty 101–3
power 101, 173, 242
precautionary principle 183
*Principles of Economics* (Mankiw) 17, 40n3
*Principles of Economics* (Marshall) 4
principles of economics: classroom materials 67–8; definition of economics 10–11, 61–2; importance of 10; students of 57–8

radical economics *see* marxist
rationality: normative concept 19; weakness of 193
reservation price, fallacy of 39
resource maintenance 61
*Retreat From Reason* 21

Schumpeterian perspective: endogenous growth 105; money 230, 231
*Scicos* 159
*Scientific Workplace* 159
*Scilab* 159
service learning 62
*Seven Cultures of Capitalism* 70
*Simulink* 159

## Subject index

social capital 97–8
social psychology 49, 184
*Sociology of Imperialisms* 206–7
Sonnenschein–Mantel–Debrue Theorem 35
South Africa 106
speculation 208
speculative bubble 63, 241, 247
speculative finance 238
stability 211
stakeholder theory 185, 259
*STELLA* 87n1, 87n6, 159
*Stern Report* 195
subprime crisis *see* financial crisis 2008
supply, law of 34–5
sustainable development 195, 258–9

taxes-drive-money approach 245–6
terms of trade 205
*The Wealth of Nations* 174
*Theory of Economic Development* 138
Tobin Tax 104, 108, 109, 244
trade barriers 208
trade liberalization 213
traditional economics: assumptions 172; definition 8; de-emphasis of time 69–71; exogenous money 233–5; failure to foresee financial crisis of 2008 17, 70; financial stability 237–9; focus on equilibrium 12, 31, 32, 40, 151, 158; hegemony of 29, 32 , 43; ideology 35; individualism 343–34; incompatibility with sustainable development 183; lack of pluralism 28; limitation of laws of supply and demand 85; macroeconomics 93–4; monism 46; nature 257–9; perspective on moncy 230, 231; poverty, view of 102; principles course 57–8; rationality 34; relation to orthodoxy 8; shortcomings 17–22, 26–8, 57–8; shaping economics education 29; static view of 69–71; textbooks 18–22
traditional theory of the firm: empirical contradictions 134–40; fallacies of 120–8; market demand curve 128–38; Sonnenschein–Mantel–Debreu conditions 128–30; violation of strong axiom of revealed preference 136–8
Triffin dilemma 207
triple bottom line 186
trust 97, 188

underdevelopment 103–4
unemployment 101–3
United Nations 226
United Nations Conference on Trade and Development 213
United States: current account deficit 216–17; Department of Treasury 102, 218
University of Notre Dame: Economics Department 24; Open Letter (origin of) 4, 28
unpaid work 99, 101
Utilitarianism 19, 20

value-added 213
values, importance of 183
*Vissim* 160

wages: determination 174; differentials 175–6; fair 155; minimum 175
Washington Consensus 102, 108–9, 222
Women, United Nations Conference 96
World Bank 102, 109, 201, 225, 244
World Commission on Dams 194
*World Made by Hand, The* 4
World Trade Organization 109, 204; Doha Round 214

# eBooks – at www.eBookstore.tandf.co.uk

## A library at your fingertips!

eBooks are electronic versions of printed books. You can store them on your PC/laptop or browse them online.

They have advantages for anyone needing rapid access to a wide variety of published, copyright information.

eBooks can help your research by enabling you to bookmark chapters, annotate text and use instant searches to find specific words or phrases. Several eBook files would fit on even a small laptop or PDA.

**NEW:** Save money by eSubscribing: cheap, online access to any eBook for as long as you need it.

### Annual subscription packages

We now offer special low-cost bulk subscriptions to packages of eBooks in certain subject areas. These are available to libraries or to individuals.

For more information please contact webmaster.ebooks@tandf.co.uk

We're continually developing the eBook concept, so keep up to date by visiting the website.

## www.eBookstore.tandf.co.uk